"When many conservative Christians serve a[
nation goes to war, Nick Megoran makes a persuasive and passionate case
against war and violence with a refreshing reminder of the core message
of peace in the Gospel of Jesus. By engaging with a broad spectrum of
theological claims (e.g., just war theory, liberal pacifism), key biblical texts,
and salient historical examples (e.g., Adolf Hitler), this book presents a
consistent perspective against war, called 'Gospel peacemaking.' Written by
a political geographer conversant with the studies of political conflicts, the
book deserves careful attention and discussion among all Christians who
take the Gospel of Jesus and Christian discipleship seriously."

—HAK JOON LEE, Lewis B. Smedes Professor of Christian Ethics,
Fuller Theological Seminary

*To Wayne,
Wishing you every blessing
love, Nick*

Warlike Christians
in an Age of Violence

Warlike Christians in an Age of
VIOLENCE

The Evangelical Case against War
and for Gospel Peace

Nick Megoran

Foreword by Nick Ladd

CASCADE *Books* · Eugene, Oregon

WARLIKE CHRISTIANS IN AN AGE OF VIOLENCE
The Evangelical Case against War and for Gospel Peace

Cascade Books
An Imprint of Wipf and Stock Publishers
199 W. 8th Ave., Suite 3
Eugene, OR 97401

www.wipfandstock.com

PAPERBACK ISBN: 978-1-4982-1959-4
HARDCOVER ISBN: 978-1-4982-1961-7
EBOOK ISBN: 978-1-4982-1960-0

Cataloguing-in-Publication data:

Names: Megoran, Nick Solly, author. | Ladd, Nick, foreword.

Title: Warlike Christians in an age of violence : the evangelical case against war and for gospel peace / Nick Megoran.

Description: Eugene, OR : Cascade Books, 2017 | Includes bibliographical references and index(es).

Identifiers: ISBN 978-1-4982-1959-4 (paperback) | ISBN 978-1-4982-1961-7 (hardcover) | ISBN 978-1-4982-1960-0 (ebook)

Subjects: LCSH: Evangelicalism. | War—Religious aspects—Christianity. | Peace—Religious aspects—Christianity. | Mission of the church.

Classification: BT736.4 .M39 2017 (print) | BT736.4 .M39 (ebook)

Manufactured in the U.S.A.   SEPTEMBER 27, 2017

This book is dedicated to my son, Jamie Manas,
and to my godchildren,
Elizabeth Merrigan, Rosie Cooper, William Megoran,
Quentin Baker, and Ben Ferguson,
that may they grow up to be peacemakers.

The world wants a peacemaker; oh! how badly it wants it now! I seem as I walk my garden, as I go to my pulpit, as I go to my bed, to hear the distant cries and moans of wounded and dying men. We are so familiarised each day with horrible details of slaughter, that if we give our minds to the thought, I am sure we must feel a nausea, a perpetual sickness creeping over us. The reek and steam of those murderous fields, the smell of the warm blood of men flowing out on the soil, must come to us and vex our spirits. Earth wants a peacemaker, and it is he, Jesus of Nazareth, the King of the Jews, and the friend of Gentiles, the Prince of Peace, who will make war to cease unto the ends of the earth.

—C. H. SPURGEON, 1870

No wars have been so bloody as those which have arisen out of the collision of religious opinions. . . . May we never forget this! The weapons of the Christian warfare are not carnal, but spiritual (2 Cor. X. 4).

—J. C. RYLE, 1856

Contents

Preface and Acknowledgments
Justice, Peace . . . and Christianity?

The Problem

EVERY YEAR, MANY CHURCHES build their advent services around a prophecy in the ninth chapter of the book of Isaiah that calls the coming savior "the Prince of Peace." Yet, for much of its history, Christianity has been if not the cause then at least the excuse for killing and destruction by warring kingdoms, states and resistance movements. As often as not these have been composed of substantial contingents of Christians who believed that their particular war, rebellion, or humanitarian intervention was "just."

Many Christians are troubled by this history, as they know that the Lord Jesus not only taught his followers to love their enemies but also practiced what he preached and commanded his followers to adopt his example. They might have often heard church leaders and fellow Christians argue that war is an unfortunate but necessary evil to protect ourselves and others from the violence and injustice of tyrants like Hitler and terrorists like Islamic State and al-Qaeda. However, they remain uneasy with this conclusion, troubled by the lurking suspicion that it fits uncomfortably with the Bible. As they talk to those outside the church, they are aware that in practice this modern church teaching that war may be acceptable even though Jesus taught that it wasn't has so often brought the church into disrepute. They wonder if this means that either their theology is wrong or their faith itself is unworkable in the "real world."

I have written this book for such Christians, and for any Christian concerned about how the church can respond to violence in our world today. It argues that not only is participation in warfare incompatible with the teaching and example of Christ and the apostles and the whole direction of the biblical testimony, but that it has done inestimable damage to the cause of the gospel. It has led the church into forgetting its unique call to be "salt and light" (Matt 5:13, 14), that is, to play a distinctive and positive role in the world. This has had profound consequences—for those who have directly suffered as a result of violence, for the reputation of the church, and for the honor of the Name of the Savior. Overviewing the wars, torture, racist violence and genocide committed by churches in the name of Christ over the centuries, atheist writer Sam Harris concludes that "the history of Christianity is principally a story of mankind's misery."[1] Alas, these so-called New Atheist writers do not struggle to find material to adduce in support of such claims.

While I take these arguments seriously, this book contends that such violence is an ugly distortion of Christianity. War is sin, and the church is by definition antiwar, just as it is anti every other sin. For centuries after Christ the early church refused to sanction violence and was more true to its calling as a result, spreading like wildfire in a world weary of war. It was only with the political co-option of the church by the Roman Empire that killing was blessed. What is more, throughout Christian history there have always been those who have held the early church's position, and more often than not it is the examples of these men and women we respect the most. Against the distortions of Catholic just war theory and Protestant liberal pacifism, I argue that now is the time to return to this more authentic understanding of the gospel. This means rejecting war and instead being a biblical gospel church. So doing will allow us to practice and proclaim a more authentic, effective, and infectious Christian faith. Across the world followers of Jesus who take seriously his call to love their enemies are having remarkable impacts on the communities in which they live.

The argument of the book can be summarized by a sermon and an essay written by British Christian leaders at the outbreak of World War II. Answering the question of why God allows war, Martyn Lloyd-Jones, pastor of Westminster Chapel, preached that war is "one of the manifestations of sin, one of the consequences of sin."[2] At the same time, Anglican Bishop George Bell penned an essay in response to the question, "What is the church's function in war-time?" Bell wrote simply, "It is the function

---

1. Harris, *End of Faith*, 106.

2. Lloyd-Jones, *Why Does God Allow War?*, 82.

of the Church at all costs to remain the Church," that organization which is the trustee of the gospel of redemption, "the pillar and ground of the truth" (1 Tim 3:15 KJV).[3] Today Christians around the world are faced with questions about how to understand new and frightening wars, and what they should do in the face of them. Echoing Lloyd-Jones and Bell, this book's message is simply this: war is sin—*so be the church! Preach the gospel!* This does not mean avoiding the challenges of violence, but rather addressing them by making peace in the love and power of God. This position is called "gospel peace." To be clear: it allows no place for participation in war. As sixteenth-century church leader Menno Simons put it, "It is in vain that we are called Christians . . . if we do not walk according to His law, counsel, admonition, will and command and are not obedient to His word."[4]

The various chapters present biblical and historical arguments for this position and address the genuine concerns that many have about this understanding of the scriptures. What about all the battles in the Old Testament and all those soldiering metaphors in the New? What do we do about tyrannies and terrorists like Nazi Germany and the Islamic State? Hasn't the church sanctioned warfare throughout its history? And isn't there such a thing as a just war? This book treats these as serious and important points but examines them carefully and exposes their flaws in the light of both scripture and history.

However, this book is not primarily a series of negative statements. Although it deals at length with the arguments made by some Christian theologians in favor of violence, its primary message is not "don't fight." That may sometimes be good advice, but at other times it is cowardice or unloving neglect that allows injustice to continue by not checking it. Here I share Francis Schaeffer's critique of liberal pacifism, that sometimes "it means we desert the people who need our greatest help."[5] The message of this book is, rather, "be the church!" The church is an alternative community to the war-making powers and authorities of this world. At times of war, those rulers and states call on us to give them our allegiance instead. We must not, if it means disobeying the Bible. We must be true to the church of Jesus Christ. The original testimony and practice of the New Testament church is a glorious fulfillment of the hopes and expectations

3. Bell, "Church's Function in War-Time," 23. For more on Jones and Bell, see ch. 8, pages 201–5.

4. Simons, "Foundation of Christian Doctrine," 111.

5. Schaeffer, *Great Evangelical Disaster*, 128.

of Old Testament prophecy. Alas, however, much of the Christian church over time throughout the world has forgotten this biblical perspective and aligned itself with the armies of whichever host nation it happened to find its churches and chapels were built in. Nonetheless the church remains the bearer of what Paul calls "the gospel of peace" (Eph 6:15). This is not merely good news for individual sinners in need of forgiveness and reconciliation to God: it is profoundly good news for a blood-stained world aching for peace. This book calls on the church joyfully to own this gospel and to proclaim it boldly and gladly to a world that is desperately short of alternatives. This we do not by withdrawing from the world but by resisting evil and making peace in the love and power of God. This means working by the power of the Holy Spirit to transform conflicts and violence in our neighborhoods, countries, and world, and I call it "gospel peace." Numerous examples are outlined throughout the book, and especially in the final chapter, to show what this Christian alternative to war looks like in practice.

I believe that the time is right, as never before, to reclaim the fullness of the "gospel of peace." The so-called social gospel of the late nineteenth and early twentieth centuries reduced Christianity to good works of social and political reform, sidelining the historic doctrinal truths about God, creation, sin, and salvation in favor of noble but ill-fated ideas about political transformation for the causes of justice and peace.[6] It emphasized deeds at the expense of faith. It failed to come to grips with the fallenness of the world. It failed to grasp, as Martyn Lloyd-Jones puts it, that war is a manifestation and consequence of sin, not a failure to cultivate good will or sign up to appropriate international treaties and organizations.[7] This distortion of Christianity emptied it of much of its authentic spiritual life. In an understandable reaction against this caricature of the gospel, conservative evangelical Christianity treated with suspicion any claim that Christianity had political as well as personal implications. This in turn led to another distortion of the gospel, which emphasized faith at the expense of putting it into practice, knowing doctrine at the expense of being disciples, and downplaying the Christian duty to seek justice and peace. In truth, salvation is by grace and through faith alone, but is inevitably followed and evidenced by good deeds. And these deeds include making peace in a world of violence.

6. The classic statement of the social gospel is Rauschenbusch, *A Theology for the Social Gospel*. For a fuller discussion, see page 120 of this book.
7. Lloyd-Jones, *Why Does God Allow War?*, 82.

Over the past few decades the influence of the liberal social gospel has waned and the evangelical, Pentecostal, and charismatic churches have been able to recover the first of those commitments, to justice. Churches have engaged imaginatively and faithfully with issues of global poverty, thinking seriously about being "rich Christians in an age of hunger," as the title to Ron Sider's compelling book on the subject has it.[8] The church has shown that it can embrace the biblical injunction to care for the poor without compromising doctrinal truth: indeed, it has recovered the conviction of the Reformers that caring for the poor is thoroughly biblical. As Puritan theologian John Owen wrote, "caring for the poor" is "one of the priorities of Christian communities because it is the main way we show the gospel grace of love."[9] I believe that the next challenge we face is to recover the second of those commitments, to be peacemakers. How can we stop being "warlike Christians in an age of violence"? The purpose of this book is to point the church in that direction.

The Author

This book is written not by an academic theologian or minister but by a political geographer who is also a follower of Jesus. This has certain disadvantages: I am unable to read the scriptures in their original languages, for example. However, being a political geographer means that I also benefit from certain other perspectives. I am trained in the analysis of *territoriality*—how and why humans divide up the world into spaces labeled "ours" and "theirs," "safe" and "dangerous," "civilized" and "backwards," and so forth, and how such divisions enable the perpetration of violence in the global system.[10] This gives me a perspective on the Bible, theological texts, and church history that theologians may lack. No Bible interpretation (this included) can stand outside its own context, but my background in political studies makes me attentive to theologians' cul-

---

8. Sider, *Rich Christians in an Age of Hunger*.

9. Owen, *True Nature of a Gospel Church*, cited in Chester, *Good News to the Poor*, 33. The whole of chapter 1 of Chester's book, titled "The Case for Social Involvement," makes the case from within the Evangelical/Reformed tradition that Christians are called to care for the poor because of the character of God, the reign of God, and the grace of God.

10. The two classic texts are Gottmann, *The Significance of Territory*, and Sack, *Human Territoriality: Its Theory and History*. A more recent development of these is Storey, *Territory: The Claiming of Space*.

tural assumptions about how the world works that they themselves may take for granted and not be aware of. My research has been on conflicts in Central Asia, the Middle East, and Scandinavia; and also on how the US and UK churches have responded to the wars their governments have been involved in since September 11, 2001. These conflicts are usually more complicated and multifaceted than the simplistic and atheoretical Hollywood-style "goodies versus baddies" versions of them that theologians who write on war too often work with.

Furthermore, political geography is a practical, field-based discipline that recognizes that the world looks different dependent upon where you stand in it. That might sound obvious, but much theological writing on war, either by just war advocates or liberal pacifists, is primarily based upon arguments derived from other theological books about war and peace, and is thus detached from actual war zones or the political complexities of conflicts. In contrast, this book is informed by listening to the experiences of Christians in places marked by violent conflict. This is based on interviews and field research in Europe, Asia, and Africa, and extensive biographical writing on Christians who have faced violence and found creative ways to respond. Some of the best contemporary Christian reflection on war comes to us from the parishes and mission fields where violence is an everyday reality, rather than from pulpits in prosperous parts of Western cities or the theological departments of universities.

I grew up being taught to believe that war is a "necessary evil" and was compatible with being a good Christian and a conscientious citizen of my own country and the world. As I embarked upon a vocation that involved the study of nationalism, conflict, and war in various contexts around the world, I increasingly found cause to question this. Indeed, I came to see that religious justifications of violence were part of the problem not the solution. I also became convinced that the historic Christian gospel presented both the most persuasive account of why war occurs and the most compelling and realistic alternative to it that I had encountered in anything I had ever read or experienced. It is that conclusion that compelled me inexorably to Christ, and is the conviction underlying this book.

The Book

Apart from authorship, there are four ways in which this book is different from most Christian reflections on war. First, it takes the scriptures seriously as a way to engage with war. Although it draws on a wide range of material from historians, political scientists, and theologians, it takes the Bible, as the inspired and infallible word of God, as its ultimate authority. Much theological ethical reflection on war starts with a certain theory or tradition derived from elsewhere (for example, pagan "just war" theory or liberal "pacifism") and then finds biblical texts to support this position. That is the wrong way round. In contrast, this book begins from the position that the Bible is, in the words of the 1647 Westminster Larger Catechism, "the only rule of faith and obedience."

Second, it is grounded theologically in the Reformation doctrines of grace. The Reformed tradition insists upon the goodness of original *creation*, the depravity of humankind due to the *fall*, and the radical transformation of fallen humanity possible through God's *redemption*, which is achieved solely through the death and resurrection of his Son, Jesus Christ. And finally it looks to the sure and certain hope of *restoration* when the Lord Jesus returns at the end of time to make an end to pain and death. At the heart of this book's rejection of warfare is the doctrine of justification by faith. War is not an inevitable part of the human condition: like other forms of violence, it was absent at creation and is not God's ultimate will for our race. It entered our history through rebellion against God's good decrees with the fall, and is thus evidence of the depravity of fallen humanity. Men and women everywhere are called to repent of this rebellion, which is redeemable through the saving work of Christ alone. War was permitted as part of the Law given to Moses in order to protect the holiness of God's people by driving out the nations of Canaan whose practices might lead the people of Israel astray. Like other elements of the Law, such as animal sacrifices and dietary regulations, it was fulfilled in the gospel era and is no longer necessary. Here, the holiness of God's visible nation, the church, is protected through the power of the Holy Spirit poured out on his people, who no longer need to live separately from the world.

Third, and unlike almost every Christian book on war I have seen, it assumes that the Holy Spirit is dynamically and miraculously at work in the world's war zones, enabling God's praying people to be peacemakers in a way that is impossible for non-Christians. Most Christian books on warfare owe more to liberal and idealistic political ideas such as "just war theory" or "pacifism," or to conservative ideas about the inevitably of warfare in a lawless world system of "dog eat dog."[11] In contrast, the starting points of this book are scripture, salvation, and the Spirit.

Finally, this book considers "peace" not as a marginal issue for the church but as central to evangelism, the work of the church, and the advance of the Kingdom of God. The world's greatest need is to be reunited with the God who made it, and that can only happen though the cross. The church's function is to obey the instruction of its Lord to "go and make disciples of all nations" (Matt 28:19). A century ago, the supposed claims of science to negate the Christian faith were one of the main obstacles to faith, but that challenge has been adequately answered.[12] Today, the church's implication in violence over the centuries is one of the greatest obstacles that thinking men and women have to coming to faith in Christ. It is certainly among the strongest arguments against faith put by the "New Atheists." Taking apologetics seriously means thinking through this carefully, but it is an area that our leading writers have been weak on. It is the conviction of this book that to answer our critics we need to recover the church's biblical peace tradition, confess where we have failed to live up to the call to be peacemakers, and change our ways. This means acknowledging, repenting over, and jettisoning the church's seduction by violence, and cultivating its peacemaking culture. Only then can we properly present Christ as the Prince of Peace, whose power brings peace between God and people, and between each other.

In May 2013, former Guatemalan dictator Efraín Ríos Montt was convicted of genocide and crimes against humanity. Between entering office with a coup in March 1982 and leaving office by a countercoup in August 1983, Ríos Montt was feted by evangelical Christians in the United States and elsewhere. Because he was involved in a Pentecostal church and had made "a confession for Christ," US evangelicals saw him as an instrument of God against Marxism. Reflecting on evangelical support of this bloody dictator inside and outside Guatemala, M. Daniel Carroll R. concluded that when it comes to the question of endorsing violence, "Ideology largely determines Christian views on the issue, with the Bible sadly serving as a secondary source. Not enough thought is given to

11. The technical term for this approach in international relations theory is "realism."

12. See, for example, Alexander, *Rebuilding the Matrix: Science and Faith in the 21st Century.*

whether armed conflict truly reflects the gospel of the Prince of Peace or how it furthers the mission of his church."[13] This book argues exactly this: that unbiblical ideological beliefs and assumptions have too often been the greatest influences on evangelical (and other) Christian views on war. Instead, we ought to examine war through the lens of scripture and by asking what supporting it does to the mission of the church.

As should be clear from the above, this book is not an academic text on ethics, comparing the views of different theologians and reaching a conclusion. Instead, it is written for the general evangelical Christian reader or minister. It emerges from within the author's evangelical-Reformed tradition and purposely eschews the move to outline and defend a particular "political theology" in relation to an academic field. The stories and examples that illustrate are drawn more broadly, including from charismatic, Pentecostal, Anglican, Catholic, Lutheran, and many other churches—the only criteria being that the theologies espoused are true to the Bible and the examples used authentically demonstrate gospel-honoring peace-making in the world. Although the book is evangelical in its theology, I believe that we learn a great deal from how other Christians have acted as peacemakers, even if we may not fully agree with their theological formulations.

I am very grateful to the following friends for their helpful comments on the first draft of this book: Richard Smith, Director of the Tank Museum, England; Chris Seiple, of the Institute for Global Engagement, Washington, DC; and particularly John Heathershaw, of Exeter University, who went through the text with a fine-tooth comb and who helped me enormously in revising it and sharpening the argument. I would like to acknowledge, with deep gratitude, a small number of key people who indirectly influenced the thinking behind this book. As a child, Dave and Audrey Longstaff, Anne and Keith Addy, and John and Alex Wilson, of The Church of the Resurrection, Scunthorpe, gave me a practical and inspiring grounding in the Christian faith, lovingly encouraged by my parents, Peter and Helen Megoran. Miss Kingan, my English teacher at High Ridge Comprehensive School, first challenged me to think critically about war in her electrifying teaching of World War I poetry, a challenge that eventually took me to Durham, Roskilde, Cambridge, and Osh universities to explore the topic through undergraduate and postgraduate studies. Three subsequent years spent as a postdoctoral fellow at Sidney

13. Carroll, "Putting War on Trial."

Sussex College, Cambridge, provided the space to reflect and read widely. Lynn Green, Cathy Nobles, Alan Kreider, and Christy Risser, through their teaching, writing, and lives, helped me connect these twin strands of Christian faith and the study of war and peace. I am grateful to Kefa Sempangi of Uganda and John Enyinnaya of Nigeria for their willingness to share their experiences of doing church under Idi Amin and in the face of Boko Haram, respectively. I doubt that all of these remarkable people would fully agree with what I have written in this book. That is a reminder that there is room to differ on important issues of how we work out what church looks like in the messiness of the real world. On this note I am particularly grateful to Chris Seiple for discussions over the years that have constantly obliged me to revisit my assumptions and test my arguments and conclusions in the light of scripture, reason, and history. It is a tall order, but I hope that by all these measures the reader will not judge this work lacking.

Foreword

Nick Megoran was a member of the church in Cambridge that I arrived to lead shortly before 9/11. He was profoundly influential in challenging us to think biblically about our responsibility to live as disciples of Jesus in the face of war and about what an appropriate personal and public response might be for a Christian disciple and a church community. I remain hugely grateful for his practical and biblically grounded challenge, which has grown in breadth and maturity into the substance of this book.

Nick's commitment to the gospel of peace is breathtaking in its passion but also in the way it is carefully and biblically argued. He begins with the evangelical conviction that the gospel of peace is the only hope for a sinful world but he challenges effectively the modern notion that this is only applicable to personal and private transformation.

In ethical thinking, we are used to the assumption that we need a big overarching idea—theologically or philosophically—which we then seek to apply on a case-by-case basis. Nick argues that whether this is the liberal optimism of "pacifism" or the nationalistic compromise of "just war," it leads to wrong action because it places a nonbiblical theory between us and the gospel.

Instead, he challenges us with a scriptural vision of the gospel of peace and explores how this has been both embraced and compromised throughout the history of the church. He offers a thoughtful and challenging recontextualization of the one issue that keeps Western Christians from wholeheartedly embracing this gospel—namely, the experience of Hitler.

This book is not a political theology, nor is it a proposal for government action. It is both a heart cry and a biblical case for the church to be the church in living out the gospel of peace. And Nick gives us countless moving examples of what happens when faithful Christians live by this gospel in fearful and challenging situations; this is biblical theology contextualized in real life.

It may be, as Nick suggests, that in a time when the Western church is more marginalized than since Christendom began, we have the chance to "repent and believe the gospel." If so, this book offers a serious and inspiring contribution to that journey.

Nick Ladd

Director of Practical Theology and Director of Ministry and Formation

St. John's School of Mission

Nottingham

1

Jesus, Prince of Peace

Look! Christ in khaki, out in France thrusting his bayonet into the body of a German workman. See! The Son of God with a machine gun, ambushing a column of German infantry, catching them unawares in a lane and mowing them down in their helplessness. Hark! The Man of Sorrows in a cavalry charge, cutting, hacking, thrusting, crushing, cheering. No! No! That picture is an impossible one, and we all know it.

—ALFRED SALTER, 1914[1]

Hand Grenades in Easter Eggs?

In April 2003, soon after the US and UK began an invasion of Iraq, the sale of an Easter basket in a New York Kmart store created something of a furor. The pretty pink-and-yellow baskets with colorful green-and-purple bows contained not chocolate bunnies but camouflaged soldiers with US flags, machine guns, sniper rifles, hand grenades, Bowie knives, ammunition, truncheons, and handcuffs. The toys were withdrawn following an outcry by shoppers and Christian leaders. Bishop George Packard condemned them as being in "bad taste" and questioned the message sent to Muslims by the mixing of a Christian holiday with images of war.[2]

Most people would, I think, recognize the incongruity of such a striking symbol of violence being used to celebrate the resurrection of

---

1. Cited in Barrett, *Subversive Peacemakers*, 37.
2. *Anglican Journal*, "Chaplain Bishop Disturbed by 'Bizarre,' War-Themed Easter Baskets," April 1, 2003.

1

the "Prince of Peace" and the triumph of life over death. However, Bishop Packard seemed to overlook an even greater contradiction. He was the man responsible for spiritual care of Episcopalian members of the armed services. That is to say, he and his church supported Christians taking on in real life the role that he condemned in a make-believe world!

The Iraq War threw up many such ironies. It was led by two world leaders, US President George W. Bush and UK Prime Minister Tony Blair, who were arguably the most devout Christians to have held those offices for many years. One of their chief opponents, Iraqi deputy-president Tariq Aziz, was one of the most well-known Christian politicians in the Middle East. Some of the war's most vocal critics were Christian leaders around the world, from the pope and the archbishop of Canterbury to former archbishop of Cape Town Desmond Tutu. Even Jim Winkler, at the time one of the leaders of George W. Bush's own denomination, the United Methodist Church, opposed the planned invasion, saying that "war is incompatible with the teaching and example of Christ." Having repeatedly been refused an audience with the president himself, Winkler led a delegation of American Christian leaders on a world tour to meet leaders from Tony Blair to Russian president Vladimir Putin in an attempt to persuade them to oppose the planned war.[3]

But such disagreement is by no means confined to recent wars. Every ten years the bishops of the worldwide Anglican church gather for the Lambeth Conference. Various conferences since 1930 have endorsed the statement that "war as a method of settling international disputes is incompatible with the teaching and example of our Lord Jesus Christ." Yet, at the same time, as Herbert McCabe put it, its "cathedrals are stuffed with regimental flags and monuments to colonial wars. The Christian church, with minor exceptions, has been solidly on the side of violence for centuries, but it has normally been only the violence of soldiers."[4] The Christian church's position on war is clearly inconsistent, and this confusion inhibits its ability to speak meaningfully into the pressing issues of our day.

The argument of this book is simple. If we turn to the pages of the New Testament, we find no such inconsistency: in fact, the whole life and teaching of Jesus and the apostles is utterly incompatible with warfare, and we are commanded to follow his example. This chapter will outline

3. Personal communication, January 2003.

4. McCabe, "Class Struggle and Christian Love," 275.

what that was, while subsequent chapters will discuss some of the difficulties that modern Christians have in accepting it. The book follows Martyn Lloyd-Jones in the biblical understanding that war is a consequence and a manifestation of sin,[5] and Bishop George Bell in insisting that the church's function in wartime is "at all costs to remain the Church," the trustee of the gospel of redemption.[6] The Christian (and the Christian's) response to war is not to fight and kill those fighting and trying to kill us—scripture does not permit that—but simply to *be the church! Preach the gospel!* This entails working creatively by the power of the Holy Spirit to make peace in the communities and world in which we live—a position that this book calls "gospel peace."

The importance of this topic of how to deal with war is hard to overstate. As John Keegan said in his 1998 BBC Reith Lectures, war is the chief "enemy of human life, well-being, happiness, and optimism."[7] It is the great scourge of our age: it undoes God's good creation; it destroys and deforms people made in his image; it prevents humans from relating to each other as he intended; it is the source of untold human suffering; it disproportionately affects those already most vulnerable, such as women, children, the elderly and the infirm; it inflicts mental and physical disabilities on combatants and noncombatants alike for decades after actual fighting has ceased; it sometimes produces enormous population displacements, wrenching families and communities apart; it creates poverty and inhibits attempts to develop sustainable livelihoods and a just distribution of wealth.

By some scholarly estimates, there were one billion casualties of war in the twentieth century.[8] Nowadays, casualties are often largely civilians. For example, the respected British medical journal *The Lancet* suggested in 2006 that up to six hundred thousand people had died in Iraq following the US/UK invasion in 2003 as a result of medical facilities being degraded or rendered inadequate because of the war.[9] A belief system that is unable to speak practically to war is irrelevant to this age. Yet in ignoring plain biblical teaching and allowing our thinking to be influenced by culture more than scripture, we have oftentimes done more to excite war

5. Lloyd-Jones, *Why Does God Allow War?*, 82.

6. Bell, "Church's Function in War-Time," 23. For an extended discussion of Lloyd-Jones and Bell, see ch. 7.

7. Keegan, *War and Our World*, 1.

8. Hunt, "Health Consequences of War and Political Violence."

9. Cited in ibid.

than promote peace. As Reverend Martin Luther King, Jr. asked, "What more pathetically reveals the irrelevancy of the church in present-day world affairs than its witness regarding war? In a world gone mad with arms build-ups, chauvinistic passions, and imperialistic exploitation, the church has either endorsed these activities or remained appallingly silent." He concluded, "A weary world, desperately pleading for peace, has often found the church morally sanctioning war."[10] We have become part of the problem rather than the solution.

Violence more generally is broader than war. It includes violence against women in homes and on the streets, bullying in schools, the racism aimed at minorities, and economic systems that keep some people poor and others rich. Nonetheless the focus of this book is on war and forms of state or nonstate action that resemble it, partially because it is the most spectacular and destructive form of violence, and partially because it is the author's area of scholarly expertise.

In a hard-hitting book about economic justice, Tim Chester observes that Christians commonly live with two sets of values: one that they espouse in church and another that they demonstrate by how they actually use their money.[11] We have done exactly the same with relation to war and peace. It is said that during the Crusades, mercenaries held their swords above the water when they were being baptized so that they didn't have to make them subject to God's rule. In professing to worship the Prince of Peace, and on Sunday morning singing "Crown Him the Lord of peace, / whose power a scepter sways / from pole to pole, that wars may cease, / and all be prayer and praise,"[12] yet allowing ourselves to endorse the possibility of Christian participation in, preparation for, and even celebration of war during the week, we have effectively done the same. The old adage that Christians don't tell lies but they sing them could not be more clearly demonstrated. It is time that we took scripture seriously and started to preach and practice "the gospel of peace" (Acts 10:36; Eph 6:15), which, I believe, is the only hope for humankind.

---

10. King, *Strength to Love*, 63.

11. Chester, *Good News to the Poor*, 43.

12. "Crown Him with Many Crowns," lyrics by Matthew Bridges (1851).

The "Roman Problem"

In order to understand what the New Testament teaches about war, it is important to realize just how violent its times were. Jesus was born into a politically turbulent world and grew up with the ever-present threat of violence. Within a short time of his birth, he had become a refugee, as Herod tried to kill him by slaughtering all boys under two years old in the Bethlehem region (Matt 2:16–18). This incident was indicative of the oppression that his people endured. Occupied by a pagan empire that they looked down upon for being unholy, the nation that regarded itself as the chosen people of God had never faced such humiliation.

In modern language, we would say that the Romans had conquered his country in an unprovoked war of aggression; ruled it by a reign of terror that included genocide, mass violations of civil liberties, and gross human rights abuses; systematically looted and exploited the land and people for their own benefit; and set up a corrupt and unaccountable puppet regime to do their dirty work for them.

This humiliating occupation was sustained by a number of methods. The first was brute power. Whole populations were slaughtered or enslaved. For example, thirty thousand people were enslaved in Tarichaeae in 52 BC.[13] Following revolts in 4 BC, the reconquering Roman armies destroyed some cities and enslaved others: "The whole district became a scene of blood and fire," recorded contemporary historian Josephus. On retaking Jerusalem they crucified two thousand people, terrorizing the Jews into submission by reminding them what would happen if they failed to obey their new masters. In the same year there was also a Jewish revolt in Sepphoris, the capital of the province of Galilee, five miles from Nazareth. Josephus describes revenge by Romans: Varus burned the town to the ground, enslaved the population, and sent his army into the surrounding area to round up and crucify sympathizers. Such events must have been seared into memory of the town that Jesus grew up in.[14] Repression of the dissent that inevitably grew with these actions was enabled by a dense network of spies and informants, who helped soldiers arrest and murder those suspected of plotting disloyalty. As we know from the experience of occupations in recent times, this fear of the Romans and suspicion of each other must have exacted a great psychological toll.

13. Historical claims and quotes in this chapter are taken from Horsley, *Jesus and the Spiral of Violence*, ch. 2.

14. Egan, *Peace Be with You*, 9.

The second method of sustaining the occupation was cultural. Herod's massive program of building Roman-style monumental works such as an amphitheater, maintaining a lavish court, and holding games in honor of Caesar not only imposed a heavy tax burden on the people but also served as a stark reminder that their culture was now dominated by Roman ways. When pious Jews pulled down a Roman eagle blasphemously erected above the holy temple, they were burned alive.

The third was bureaucratic. Jesus was born in Bethlehem because his parents had been forced to take part in a census. We tend to think of a census as a benign exercise in statistics collection undertaken by a polite official who respectfully knocks on our door every ten years. But throughout history the census has been a tool of power, the collection of useful facts to assist the political control and economic exploitation of occupied territories. The Romans were rubbing it into their noses that they were a line item on someone else's inventory. Even in modern democracies today it is difficult to get accurate figures for Jewish populations, as some ultra-Orthodox Jews refuse to participate in censuses. We read in 2 Samuel 24 that one of David's greatest sins was his attempt to undertake a census, an action so abhorrent that even the godless Joab resisted it. The Jews regarded themselves as God's people alone, a people whom God had promised that Abraham would be unable to number (Gen 15:5). This census, on the other hand, was about a human ruler numbering and documenting them for control. The Romans were in effect saying, "You do not belong to God; you belong to us."[15]

The fourth Roman technique for keeping its empire in Palestine intact was "divide and conquer." Some people were granted Roman citizenship and social advancement if they toed the line, while others were excluded and impoverished, splitting the unity of the people. The Romans set up puppet governors like Herod to do their dirty work for them. This group of collaborators, which included the hated tax collectors who fleeced the impoverished local population to line their own pockets as well as enriching far-off Rome, were regarded as traitors. The Herodians and some of the priestly class supported the Romans, whose force kept them wealthy and in power. They became as much a target of popular resistance as the Romans themselves were. Jew was set against Jew.

15. For more on the political significance of the census in biblical thought, see Brueggemann, *Prophetic Imagination*, 102–3.

These four methods of control underpinned the overarching violence of economic injustice.[16] The Jewish people were subject to a double taxation burden, paying taxes to Rome (and the lavish local Roman puppet regimes) and to the temple. The priestly temple aristocracy was corrupt and exploitative, using private armies to exact tithes. People frequently had to borrow money to survive, but a poor harvest would mean the loss of their land to their debtors. The people were thus trapped in a vicious cycle of debt, and so a large landless poor was emerging alongside growing landed classes. The examples that the Lord Jesus uses in his parables give us glimpses into the socioeconomic makeup of Jewish society at this time: the very rich alongside the very poor (Luke 16:19–31), innumerable day laborers who have no land of their own to work (Matt 20:1–6), crippling indebtedness (Matt 18:21–35), and so on. The Jubilee redistribution principles of the Law were set aside with legal temple niceties. It is thus small wonder that one of the first acts of rebels in AD 66 when they finally rose up against these wicked leaders was to burn the treasury where records of debt were kept.

Thus, the people who were meant to be God's chosen people and be a holy society ruled by God—the people who were blessed above any other nation with God's revelation of law and prophets—were humiliated and exploited and oppressed, and let down by their leaders. As anti-apartheid leader and theologian Allan Boesak put it, writing from a context that knew what it was like for one race to be oppressed and humiliated by another, "Jesus was born into a colonised people, ruled by strangers, conquered, afraid, bowed down, oppressed. Overrun, over-taxed, over-burdened. Stripped of honor, dignity and hope, they lived their lives between submission and rebellion, their resentment of their oppressors boiling over every now and then into a revolt, only to be ruthlessly crushed by the Romans."[17]

Repression and Revolt

The Roman occupation was a national crisis, and it generated shame, anger, hatred, and resentment, leading to frequent acts of violence against

16. My understanding of violence and poverty in first-century Palestine under Roman rule in this section is particularly informed by Horsley's excellent book *Jesus and the Spiral of Violence*.

17. Boesak, "Loveless Power," 85–86, 89.

the conquerors. Richard Horsley has described this as a "spiral of violence"—injustice leads to protest, protest to repression, and repression eventually provokes open revolt.[18] We should not at all be surprised at the impulse to violence that Jesus encounters and rebukes in his disciples from time to time in the gospel narratives. It is the story of anticolonial uprising down through time to our own age.

No nation wants to be oppressed by another, but for the Jews it was especially bitter. They considered themselves to be the holy people of God and knew that this holiness was polluted by the Romans. In order to preserve their holiness in the face of the crisis of the "Roman problem," radical groups had emerged. The Essenes (who left us the Dead Sea Scrolls) sought to preserve holiness by literally separating themselves off from the polluting Romans, living in caves in Qumran. Another sect, the Pharisees, likewise tried to preserve holiness through separation from the pollution. Unlike the Essenes, they did not physically remove themselves but built invisible walls of rules and regulations around themselves to keep holy. And thirdly, there were violent resistance movements. Most of these were disorganized groups of brigands, dispossessed by the economic injustices or fugitives from pillaging Roman armies. Some were popular prophetic and messianic movements. Some became more organized, agitating for a war of national liberation, and forming groups such as the Zealots and (after the ascension of Christ) the Sicarii.[19] Revolt was in the air.

But this was an anticolonial movement with one great difference. Israel had experienced national crises before and had seen God miraculously intervene to rescue them. Many believed that he would do so again and were awaiting the Messiah to deliver them. The prophets had spoken of the Messiah whom God would send to deliver them from their enemies and found a new kingdom. Daniel foretold that this kingdom would arise under the fourth empire to rule Palestine after Nebuchadnezzar—and this could readily be interpreted as the Romans. The coming of John the Baptist added to the sense of expectation that something was about to happen very soon, when "every valley shall be exalted, and every mountain and hill made low . . . and all mankind will see God's salvation" (Luke 3:5–6). This Lord is coming, warned John, and "His winnowing

18. Horsley, *Jesus and the Spiral of Violence.*

19. See Horsley, *Jesus and the Spiral of Violence,* ch. 3. Wilkinson, "Why Modern Terrorism?," considers the Sicarii, who waged a campaign of terror and assassination against the Romans in AD 66–70 and murdered Jews who cooperated with them, as a prototypal religious terrorist group.

fork is in his hand to clear his threshing-floor and to gather the wheat into his barn, but he will burn up the chaff with unquenchable fire" (Matt 3:12). This was apocalyptic language, and the Jews, who were longing for a divine deliverer and dreaming "in terms of military conquest and political power,"[20] knew what it meant. Resistance was hardening to some six decades of Roman rule, and the two nations seemed to be heading inexorably to war—as happened in AD 66, around thirty years after Christ's death and resurrection. It was into this time of revolutionary unrest and apocalyptic expectation that Christ was born.

Messiah!

Jesus thus began his public ministry in politically highly charged times; people were looking for a military savior to deliver them from the injustice of Roman occupation. Matthew claims boldly that Jesus came to "lead justice to victory," as the prophet Isaiah foretold (Matt 12:20). In his commentary on Matthew's gospel, Tom Wright shows how the early chapters of the book are what he calls "political dynamite."[21] For example, Matthew's labored genealogy of the Lord Jesus, which opens his gospel, demonstrates Jesus' authentically Jewish, kingly lineage. In chapter 2 his portrait of the tyrannical, false King Herod, murdering wildly as he recognizes the threat from Israel's real king, Jesus, could not be more pointed. The Magi brought gifts appropriate for a king. Joseph, Mary, and Jesus' flight to and return from Egypt, suggests Wright, is the announcement of a new exodus and a new salvation surpassing the first one. In fact, whereas Jesus is mentioned only once in chapter 2's account of his early life, Herod is named nine times.[22] Matthew sets his gospel up as a clash between two very different "kings of Israel"—the raging, warring tyrant and the helpless babe. Yet by the end of the chapter, the tyrant is dead, but the child lives. Political dynamite indeed.

This "political dynamite" continues in Matthew's account as John the Baptist announces the coming of a king so great that pathways for his approach should be made where none existed before, even in the harsh desert itself (ch. 3). The temptations offered to Christ in the wilderness (ch. 4) were to use his status as Messiah "to launch some kind of movement

---

20. Barclay, *Gospel of Matthew*, 1:298–99.

21. T. Wright, *Matthew for Everyone, Part I*, 11.

22. Boesak, "When Loveless Power Meets the Power of Love," 88.

that would sweep Him to power, privilege and glory."[23] The biblical texts Jesus used to counter Satan were all taken from Israel's wilderness travels, drawing a clear parallel: the first Israel failed its temptations and did not achieve its true destiny of being a light to the world, but Jesus, as the new Israel, would not fail to bring salvation. Matthew unambiguously sets the stage for Jesus to claim to be the one whom the Jews expected.

Jesus himself made it crystal clear that he was the Messiah, the anointed one (John 1:41), for whom his people had been waiting for deliverance. According to Luke, Jesus the Messiah began his ministry with a sermon on the prophet Isaiah. He read from chapter 61:

> The Spirit of the Lord is on me,
> because he has anointed me
> to preach good news to the poor.
> He has sent me to proclaim freedom for the prisoners
> and recovery of sight for the blind,
> to release the oppressed,
> to proclaim the year of the Lord's favor. (Luke 4:18–19)

"Poor . . . prisoners . . . blind . . . oppressed"—this was as good a description as any of the misery the Jews felt under foreign occupation. When would this liberty begin, when would the anointed one, the Messiah, usher it in? To whom was it referring? Jesus left his listeners in no doubt: "Today this scripture is fulfilled in your hearing" (Luke 4:21).

But what would the Messiah actually *do*?

That the Jews were expecting this Messiah to be a military leader, one who would fight to deliver them from this oppression, can be understood from the Old Testament references to some of the other names and titles that Jesus was identified by. We will consider three of them: "Son of David," "Son of Man," and "good shepherd."

First, Jesus was identified as the "Son of David" (Matt 9:27). David was the warrior-king who had killed thousands of Israel's enemies, restored national pride, and founded a great dynasty that, at its height, had brought unrivaled peace and prosperity to the people. William Barclay describes the title "Son of David" as "the popular conception of the Messiah," the "promised deliverer of David's line . . . who would not only restore their freedom but lead them to power and glory and greatness."[24]

23. T. Wright, *Matthew for Everyone, Part I*, 29.
24. Barclay, *Gospel of Matthew*, 1:349.

Second, Jesus claimed to be the "Son of Man" (Matt 9:6). Daniel had foretold that the Son of Man would appear at a time of violent upheaval in the nations, to pass judgment over the aggressive pagan kingdoms, and establish the people of God as world superpower by being given "authority, glory and sovereign power," so that "all peoples, nations, and men of every language" would worship him (Dan 7:13). By the first century, this was understood by some Jews as a messianic promise, and Jesus used this as what Tom Wright calls a "cryptic self-designation," thereby identifying himself as the Messiah.[25]

Finally, Jesus described himself as the "good shepherd" (John 10:14). In the Jewish Scriptures, "shepherd" was used as a description of kingly and prophetic leadership of Israel, bravely protecting the people against marauding armies just as a shepherd would guard his flock against wolves and bears. The prophet Ezekiel foretold a time when Israel would be in despair and wretchedness without good shepherds to save them, when all their own shepherds would kill and plunder the flock, but when God would send a great shepherd to save them. What would this shepherd do? Ezekiel had foretold that he would "break the bars of their yoke and rescue them from the hands of those who enslaved them. They will no longer be plundered by the nations, nor will wild animals devour them. They will live in safety, and no one will make them afraid . . . they will no longer be victims of famine in the land or bear the scorn of the nations" (Ezek 34:27–29).

All of these names—Messiah, Son of David, Son of Man, good shepherd—were names that unambiguously identified Jesus of Nazareth as *the* savior of Israel whom the prophets had spoken of and for whom God's special people had waited so long. The scriptures were generally interpreted to imply that this would be a military leader. But this interpretation was profoundly wrong.

The Life of Christ

Jesus was indeed the Messiah, the savior, who ushered in God's promised kingdom. But how different that was from what the Jews of his time expected, and how different from what we would expect to see in a savior! He rejected all three of the options being taken by his God-fearing contemporary Jews in regard to the "Roman problem." He did not retreat

25. T. Wright, *Matthew for Everyone, Part II*, 225.

from his enemies into the hills. He did not erect social barriers against them while living in their midst. Still less did he plot to kill them in a violent uprising. No, more radically still, he proclaimed that the kingdom of God would *embrace* them, making peace with them. Again, as Tom Wright puts it, Jesus' call to Israel for "repentance" ("changing direction," "turning around") was that "as a nation they should stop rushing towards the cliff edge of violent revolution, and instead go the other way, towards God's kingdom of light and peace and healing and forgiveness."[26]

In his longest recorded section of teaching, the so-called Sermon on the Mount (Matt 5–7), Jesus addresses head-on the question of how the Jews should regard and treat their enemies. It runs strikingly counter to common-sense morality of how to act in such horrific circumstances. The naturally expected view is to respond to one's enemies in kind, to say, "Eye for eye, and tooth for tooth" (Matt 5:38). Jesus absolutely rejects this: "If someone strikes you on the right cheek, turn to him the other also." Another natural, common-sense human response to being brutalized is to "love your neighbor, but hate your enemy" (Matt 5:43). Jesus, however, teaches the opposite: "But I tell you, love your enemies, pray for those who persecute you." A third natural response Jesus summarizes in 5:46–47, to "love those who love you"—to stand in solidarity with them against your common enemies. Jesus, shockingly, dismisses this as what godless tax collectors and pagans do. No, we are told to *love* our enemies, seek *their* good, ask what *their* interests are, and pray that God would bless *them*. It's that simple.

These were grand words, but not empty words: Jesus demonstrated love to the enemies of his people. He embraced collaborating traitors like tax collectors; he made despised Samaritans the heroes of his stories; he even praised the faith of an occupying Roman centurion as the greatest he had encountered in Israel. As the theologian John Howard Yoder wrote, "Jesus made it clear that the nationalized hopes of Israel had been a misunderstanding, and that God's true purpose was the creation of a new society, unidentifiable with any of the local, national, or ethnic solidarities of any time."[27] This new society was to be found in the church, as modeled in the New Testament communities formed by the Lord Jesus and his apostles. It was a call to locate political allegiances and to invest hope for peace elsewhere.

26. T. Wright, *Matthew for Everyone, Part I*, 30.
27. J. H. Yoder, *Christian Witness to the State*, 10.

It was not that the Lord Jesus did not have the opportunity to use violence or try to seize power by the force of the mob. He was continually tempted with the option of establishing justice and righteousness through the power of violence.[28] That is the temptation Satan offered him in the wilderness (Luke 4). He resisted being crowned king by the crowds. In chapter 6 of his Gospel, John recounts how crowds tried to crown Jesus king after the messianic banquet he gave in miraculously feeding five thousand people. In Luke 13 people rush to him with the news of a terrible atrocity committed by the authorities against worshippers, desecrating their traditional sacred devotion in defiance of God's law. They are excited; this could be the spark for this king to rebel—after all, according to Luke's chronology, just before that he had said, "I have come to bring fire on the earth, and how I wish that it were already kindled" (Luke 12:49). But Jesus shows that they have misunderstood his words, and, rather than take the chance to rise up, he cools them down and warns them to look at their own sin.

On another occasion he calls Peter "Satan" for trying to prevent him from going to his death, which, we must assume, Peter would have seen as a defeat. As he entered Jerusalem he wept that its inhabitants "did not know the things that made for peace" (Luke 19:41–44), prophesying that the Jews would not love their enemies but would hate and fight them. Missing the kingdom of God, they would literally see their city, Jerusalem, destroyed as a result.

When Jesus was finally arrested by his enemies, Peter took out his sword and struck one of the attackers. But Jesus *healed* his enemy, warning his followers that "all who draw the sword will die by the sword" (Matt 26:52). He practiced what he preached, demonstrating that our enemies were to be overcome through love not hatred.

And this took him finally to the cross. Theologian Miroslav Volf, writing from the experience of his native Croatia being overrun by its enemies and engulfed in a war of tit-for-tat massacres, says that with his death Jesus *breaks the cycle of violence*.[29] The only person ever completely justified to strike back did not do so; rather, he hung on the cross, loving his enemies and praying, "Father, forgive them" (Luke 23:34).

Paul writes that Christ "was delivered over to death for our sins and was raised to life for our justification" (Rom 4:25). In dying for his

28. This and the following paragraph draw heavily upon the reading of Luke in J. H. Yoder, *Politics of Jesus*, ch. 2.

29. Volf, *Exclusion and Embrace*.

enemies out of love and in rising again, Jesus Christ opened the way back to knowing God and at the same time the way to love enemies and bring an end to war. Stanley Hauerwas and Sam Wells note that the early church saw the cross as good news because it was the last sacrifice "that finally took away sin and became the death of war."[30] His death was the ultimate example of enemy love. It is hard to see how we can avoid the conclusion that what applied to the Roman enemy applies to all enemies all down the world's history; all tribal, political, and national enemies, who are likewise beneficiaries of God's sun and rain (Matt 5:45).

Why Should We Love Our Enemies?

On August 22, 2005, televangelist and former US presidential candidate Reverend Pat Robertson used his Christian Broadcasting Network to call for the assassination of Venezuelan President Hugo Chávez. He justified this by saying that Venezuela was in "our sphere of influence," that it controlled oil that the United States needed, and that Chávez was a danger to America. Bob Edgar, General Secretary of the US National Council of Churches and a former member of the House Select Committee on Assassinations, condemned this call as an abandonment of Christian teaching. "It defies logic" he said, that a "Christian leader could so blithely abandon the teachings of Jesus to love our enemies."[31] It seemed obvious to Bob Edgar that Robertson had violated Jesus' teaching to love our enemies, and his intervention was widely condemned in the United States as bad politics and bad diplomacy. But why *did* Jesus tell us to love our enemies? Was it because it was better politics to speak well of one's foes? Was it to win them over, to appeal to their good side and persuade them to be our friends? No, the former reason is simply diplomatic nicety, and the latter cheap sentimentality. Rather, the fundamental reason we are to love our enemies is simply because it is in the very nature of God to do so, and Jesus commands us to be like Him: "Be perfect as your heavenly Father is perfect" (Matt 5:48), "that you may be children of your Father in heaven" (v. 45). What does he do? He is good to all, however undeserving: "He causes his sun to rise on the good and the evil, and sends rain on the

---

30. Hauerwas and Wells, "Breaking Bread," 417.

31. "Edgar: Robertson's Call for the Murder of Chavez Is 'Appalling to the Point of Disbelief,'" National Council of Churches News Service, August 23, 2005, http://www.ncccusa.org/news/050823NCCRobertson.html.

righteous and the unrighteous" (v. 45). And that means us! Jesus spent most of his teaching in Matthew chapter 5 up until these verses rejecting the idea that we are good enough for God. We so easily think that we are able to judge others, that because we have not committed heinous crimes we are more deserving of God's favor than infamous criminals, tyrants, or terrorists. But in verses 21–24, Jesus shows us that if we have even secretly been angry with another human being without reason and hated him or her, we are in danger of the very fires of hell, because the root is the same. "Whoever keeps the whole law and yet stumbles at just one point is guilty of breaking all of it," writes James (2:10), and Paul declares that "all have sinned and fall short of the glory of God" (Rom 3:23).

Until we grasp God's view of ourselves as sinners, we have no chance of understanding why Jesus tells us to love our enemies and be peacemakers and why that makes us children of God. We like to think that we are generally good people. But the Bible declares that "all our righteous acts are like filthy rags" before God (Isa 64:6). However, as Paul declares in utter amazement in Romans 5:8, "God demonstrates his own love for us in this: While we were still sinners"—or "enemies," as he says in verse 10—"Christ died for us." We, his enemies, are justified freely by his grace. It is simply God's grace that makes us his children and gives us eternal life—nothing we ever could do or have done. And that is why we are to love our enemies, imitating the boundless love of God for us, who are by nature his enemies. As Jürgen Moltmann emphasizes, "God's children are *enemies who have been overcome*."[32] "Blessed are the peacemakers, for they"—and only they, adds Moltmann—"will be called children of God."

Charles Reed argues that the idea that Christians should not kill other people in war "reflects an ideal of human nature, which fails to take the fall seriously."[33] Nothing could be further from the truth. If we were only partially sinful we could justify fighting our enemies, but the depth of our sin is shown by the extent to which Christ had to go to rescue us when we were his enemies. Christ's teaching alone takes sin completely seriously, and grace just as seriously. The Bible's teaching on nonparticipation in warfare is grounded in the evangelical biblical doctrine of justification.

The Lord Jesus' teachings are not thus an unobtainable ideal—they are our response to God's grace towards us, as sinners redeemed by his

32. Moltmann, *Power of the Powerless*.

33. Reed, *Just War?*, 29.

grace. They are not the lofty goal of otherworldly hermits, to be admired in a chosen few while the rest of us have to aim for lower standards in "the real world." They are not something we try but fail to achieve and must then spend our lives feeling guilty about. Rather, they are a description of what God does, what Glen Stassen calls "the delivering action of God."[34] By following the teaching of Jesus, we are invited to take part in his new reality. We are not instructed to love enemies as an impossible ideal. Rather, argues Stassen, the teachings of Jesus direct us towards practical alternatives to violence. We will see numerous examples of these in detail in chapters 7 and 8. As we dare to step out in faith in the Lord Jesus' countercultural calling to be peacemakers, we find God's Holy Spirit changing us. As Oswald Chambers put it, "The Sermon on the Mount is not an ideal, it is a statement of what will happen in me when Jesus Christ has altered my disposition and put in a disposition like his own. Jesus Christ is the only One Who can fulfil the Sermon on the Mount."[35]

The Apostles

The disciples did not grasp the meaning or significance of their master's teaching during his time on earth. Like so many subsequently, their reflex reaction to violent injustice was to hate the perpetrator and seek to use violence to protect their freedom and to secure justice. Only after Pentecost did they understand. Peter was initially anxious to protect Jesus from what he saw as defeat by his enemies—even to the end, taking up a sword in his defense (John 18:10). After Pentecost, it was Peter who was given the vision from heaven about a tablecloth full of "unclean" animals, and realized God was telling him that the gospel was for all people. Straightaway he was led to the house of Cornelius, a Roman centurion, emblematic of the enemy force oppressing his people. There the Holy Spirit descended on Cornelius and Peter baptized him—this was true enemy love, bringing God's enemy into God's own household! The account of this event in Acts 10 records Peter's amazement, as he declares, "I now realize how true it is that God does not show favoritism but accepts men from every nation who fear Him" (v. 34). No wonder Peter calls his message "the gospel of peace" (v. 36)! The meaning of this political statement would not be lost on anyone there—the nations of Peter and Cornelius

34. Stassen, *Just Peacemaking*, 41.
35. Chambers, *My Utmost for His Highest*, 275.

are heading for bloody war, yet here they stand as brothers in Christ, the nucleus of a new transnational people of peace.[36] Having resisted Jesus' arrest by violence, Peter was later to realize how wrong he had been, writing, "Christ suffered for you, leaving you an example, that you should follow in his steps. . . . When they hurled their insults at him, he did not retaliate; when he suffered, he made no threats" (1 Pet 2:21, 23). "An example to follow"—for Peter, as for all the apostles, the cross is not only a transaction that brought us forgiveness and new life. It is that, gloriously—but it is much more besides: the very model of how we respond to our enemies.

Peter was not unique in this conversion from violence to peacemaking enemy love. John was likewise a fiery follower of Jesus, zealous for the Jewish people. In Luke 9 when the Samaritans reject Jesus, John wants to "call fire down from heaven to destroy them," but Jesus rebukes him. It is supremely ironic that, when the apostles heard that the Samaritans had accepted the word of God, they sent John—of all people—to baptize them (Acts 8:14). John, the one who had wanted to kill his enemies, was made to welcome them into the people of God! John understood his error later, writing, "Whoever claims to live in him must walk as Jesus did" (1 John 2:6)—that is, practicing that costly enemy love that Jesus showed to us. Jesus had nicknamed this devotee of righteous violence a "son of thunder," but he is known to us as the "apostle of love."

And finally, of course, there is Paul. The "apostle to the Gentiles" was so devoted to the kingdom of God in his youth that he expended his energies violently persecuting the Christians. Yet, when he encountered Jesus, his view of the kingdom was utterly transformed. Where before he believed God approved the use of violence to advance his cause, after his conversion he utterly repudiated this, teaching, "The weapons we fight with are *not* the weapons of the world" (2 Cor 10:4). No, from then on Paul preached what he loved to call "the gospel of peace" (Eph 6:15). Paul explains this most clearly in his great letter to the Ephesians. Whereas before Christ God's people were at enmity with everyone else (and defended themselves with violence), Jesus "came and preached peace to you who were far away and peace to those who were near" (2:17). What did he mean? For Paul, "the unsearchable riches of Christ," the "manifold wisdom of God" (3:8, 10), were made known to all earthly and heavenly powers and principalities "through the church" (3:10). The very existence

---

36. Kreider, *Journey towards Holiness*, 181–84.

of this divine body, which brought all nations together in peace and reconciliation through Christ and ended their conflict (2:14, 16), is the supreme demonstration of God's wisdom and power and glory.

In the gospel account, John retells Jesus' commission to the church in the simple but elegant phrase, "Peace be with you! As the father has sent me, so I am sending you" (John 20:21). How did the Father send Jesus? As a peacemaker, in love, to reach out to his enemies. He sent him as a humble servant, a preacher of righteousness who boldly proclaimed the coming kingdom of God, denounced injustice and all other sin, and pointed the way to salvation through the same enemy love that God showed us. What is more, he lived that out and suffered for that difficult and costly love, refusing to do his enemies harm in return but rather seeking their good. In exactly the same way, Jesus sends us. On that point he allowed no room for doubt. He does not ask us to bless those who curse us in a world where nobody curses us in the first place. He does not ask us if, having chosen to follow him, we will then choose whether to love our enemies in the way he loved his, whether we would like to turn the other cheek, or whether we might consider seeking the welfare of those who want to harm us. That is part of the package in being his disciple and is nonnegotiable. He calls us simply to dare to walk in his footsteps and challenges us to trust that if we do the Lord God Almighty will walk with us.

Gospel Peace

Tony Campolo recounts being interviewed by a draft board for military service. Learning that he was a Christian, a US Air Force officer asked him, "If you were in a bomber flying over an enemy city, and you knew there were civilians down there, would you still go ahead and drop the bombs?" Campolo replied, "I'm not sure. I guess I'd have to pray, and ask Jesus what he'd do." The officer was unimpressed: "That's ridiculous! Everyone knows Jesus wouldn't drop bombs!"[37]

Love your enemies, seek their good, do not harm them but show love even as they harm you, act towards them exactly as Christ acted towards his. Because God is sovereign over all of our lives, this applies to all of our enemies: in families, neighborhoods, schools, workplaces, the nation, and internationally in times of war. This is "gospel peace."

37. Cited in Chalke, *He Never Said*.

Gospel peace is not "pacifism." *Pacifism* is a relatively new addition to our dictionaries (apparently being coined only in 1901)[38] and means a refusal to countenance warfare as a means of solving international disputes. It was popularized in the aftermath of the First World War, which saw widespread revulsion against the slaughter of the trenches. Its underlying philosophy is a liberal belief that the world's problems can be resolved by principled, well-intentioned, rational people eschewing violence and building up a mass movement to push for concerted international cooperation to outlaw and end war. It is conveyed most movingly and compellingly in Vera Brittain's acclaimed 1933 autobiography, *Testament of Youth*.[39] Brittain recounts how the Great War killed all those she was closest to, ruining a generation by robbing it of its promise and denying it the joys of youth. Her outrage was translated into a pacifism that rejected the legitimacy of war and led her to devote herself to campaigning for international agreements to end war. Many liberal Protestants attached themselves to pacifism at the same time. Most famously, Reverend Dick Sheppard created a mass movement in the 1930s as he argued for "Pacifism" (which he spelled with a capital *p*) as the logical outworking of Christianity. Similarly to Vera Brittain, his was a movement that referred back frequently to the horrors of World War I. He suggested that Britain should lead the way in unilateral disarmament.[40] But, as Reinhold Niebuhr persuasively argued, such theology was infected with "a moralistic sentimentality which neglects and obscures truths in the Christian gospel."[41] It lacked a grasp of the impact of sin in human relationships, displaying a naïve optimism in the possibilities of advanced humanity to overcome violence. Thus for example Sheppard argued that "if we renounce war, we have the opportunity of building a civilization which shall endure."[42] Other pacifists of this era naively hoped that modern international organizations such as the League of Nations (a precursor to the United Nations) could avert war. These writers assumed that the various theories and proposals they called "Pacifism" were the same as Christianity. As Niebuhr astutely observed, such Christians essentially

38. Cortright, *Peace*, 8.

39. Brittain, *Testament of Youth*.

40. Sheppard, *We Say "No"*.

41. Niebuhr, *Why the Christian Church Is Not Pacifist*, 30.

42. Sheppard, *We Say "No"*, 167. Also revealing of the naivety of this pacifism was his statement "I doubt very much whether Hitler's Reich is planning a war of revenge" (ibid., 95–96).

share the same belief system as rational, liberal atheists and "make Christ into the symbol of their faith in man."[43]

Nor is gospel peace the same as "nonviolence." This, like pacifism, is a modern term and is a strategy of political action that uses mass, citizen-led nonviolent tactics to force policy changes. Examples include strikes, boycotts, and noncooperation, as epitomized most famously in the movements spearheaded by Mahatma Gandhi and Martin Luther King, Jr. It is based on a theory that even brutal regimes depend on the cooperation of the population and thus can be weakened if this cooperation is withdrawn.[44] It has been described as "a force more powerful"[45] and for a relatively new idea has certainly enjoyed some remarkable successes. But it does not always "work": the killing of a Christian by the forces of Satan is not a failure; rather, the Bible sees faithful endurance unto death as a victory. Christians can and have legitimately and effectively used nonviolence, but it is not the same as Christianity.[46]

Unlike pacifism, gospel peace is based solely on God's revelation to humanity through Jesus Christ, testified to in the Bible. I believe it makes sense rationally, politically, theoretically, theologically, and philosophically and thus speaks compellingly to our age: but sinful humanity has only been able to attain knowledge of it through God's free disclosure of it to us in scripture. This gospel peace allows no place for trying to kill our enemies. As Robert Clark said, to the objection that nowhere does the teaching of Jesus rule out the slaying of one's enemies in combat, "It is difficult to imagine how this teaching *could* have been expressed more clearly."[47]

While this was clear to the officer interviewing Tony Campolo, Christians have not always understood it. In fact, they have often fought tooth and nail against it. In a perceptive analysis of how the church evades acting biblically, Danish Christian thinker Søren Kierkegaard said, "The

---

43. Niebuhr, *Why the Christian Church Is Not Pacifist*, 14.

44. Sharp, *The Politics of Nonviolent Action* (3 vols.).

45. Ackerman and DuVall, *A Force More Powerful: A Century of Nonviolent Conflict*.

46. That being said, Martin Luther King, Jr. did see nonviolence as being particularly Christian, in that it was able to accommodate love for the enemies he was opposing. Thomas Jackson argues that King's social democratic nonviolence was an alternative both to Marxism, which undervalued the individual, and to Black nationalism, which was often violent and left no room for genuine enemy love and reconciliation. See Jackson, *Civil Rights to Human Rights*, 4.

47. Clark, *Does the Bible Teach Pacifism?*

Bible is very easy to understand." What is difficult is to put it into practice: "You say, if I do that my whole life will be ruined. How would I ever get on in the world?"[48] Therefore, suggests Kierkegaard, we turn to Bible commentaries and interpretations to protect ourselves from having to act as radically as the Bible demands that we do. As Glen Stassen observes more recently, this "evasion" is exactly what theologians do so often with the New Testament teaching to love our enemies.[49] Thus, for example, US theologian Don Carson, an outspoken supporter of George W. Bush's "war on terror," could argue that loving our enemies in fact might mean having to "take them out" (a euphemism he uses for killing them), as "war can be a form of love." Carson justifies this by asserting that a soldier who gives his life in a just war displays "at least a pale echo of Jesus' self-sacrifice."[50] The Lord Jesus, who repudiated the use of violence against his enemies? The Lord Jesus, who expressly forbade his followers from using violence to rescue him? The Lord Jesus, whose example of enemy love was understood by the apostles as binding on our behavior (1 Pet 2:1–23)? Carson's lamentable arguments and tortured reasoning painfully illustrate Kierkegaard's hard-hitting but incisive observation that "Christian scholarship is the church's prodigious invention to defend itself against the Bible." Instead of playing such evasive games, Kierkegaard counsels, "Take any words in the New Testament; forget everything except pledging yourself to act accordingly."

Carson thinks that war can be an expression of Christ's love: but he does not stop to ask what war is. What *is* war? Scholars commonly define a war as a conflict resulting in at least one thousand battlefield deaths. It is clearly not individuals fighting each other for immediate survival needs: that is common across the animal kingdom. Rather, it is an extended and calculated use of violence by one group against another to achieve a desired outcome. It needs organization to prosecute it and commitment to sustain it. War seems to have arisen in our history with the development of human society from hunter-gatherer to agricultural, which produced permanent settlements and stores of wealth that could be raided for gain and thus needed defending.[51] As anthropologist Margaret Mead put it in

---

48. Kierkegaard, "Kill the Commentators!," 201. Other Kierkegaard quotes in these paragraphs are derived from the same source.

49. Stassen calls this move a "hermeneutics of evasion" and sees that it is increasingly being challenged by biblical scholars. Stassen, *Just Peacemaking*, 34.

50. Carson, *Love in Hard Places*, 112, 19.

51. Keegan, *War and Our World*, ch. 2.

the title of a famous essay, "warfare is only an invention—not a biological necessity."[52] It is a social activity almost unique to humans (it can be argued that ants practice a form of it). Its essential goal is, as scholar Nigel Hunt puts it, "to inflict harm on the opposition, with the specific intent of making them suffer so much that they cease fighting and surrender. This has been the case for thousands of years and, though some claim that war can be fought 'surgically,' with minimum damage to life, this is fallacious. Without physical and mental harm occurring to the enemy or to civilians . . . it would not succeed in its aim."[53]

War, at basis, is thus a calculated strategy to keep hurting another group of people until you hurt or frighten them enough to make them do what you want. As such it is simply incompatible with the New Testament command to love enemies. Nineteenth-century Baptist preacher C. H. Spurgeon wrote that "it is an ill sign when a man dares not look a scripture in the face" but instead "endeavours to make it mean something less sweeping in its demands."[54] The incongruity of theologians using Christ's example of enemy love to call for us to kill our enemies is startling. Jesus loved his enemies and taught his followers to do likewise; and the apostles, when they eventually realized that this meant being harmed by them rather than harming them, taught us to do likewise. The church's function (as we shall consider in detail in the final chapter) is not to support one side or another in a war but to be the window through which God's present and future gospel peace can be seen. The church by its nature can never sanction war, because war is a manifestation and a consequence of sin. Rather, the Christian response to war is this: be the church! Preach the gospel! Make peace in the love and power of God!

Yet, the objections to this seem weighty. Doesn't the Old Testament show that God allows his followers to take part in wars? Don't some New Testament passages suggest likewise? Don't Jesus' teachings refer to private, individual dealings, not national or international affairs? What about church tradition and "just war" teaching down the ages? Don't we have a duty to support the state, because it is mandated by God to enforce justice? And isn't this teaching impractical in the real world—a world of bad people who do bad things unless stopped, a world of Adolf Hitler, Saddam Hussein, and the Islamic State?

52. Mead, "Warfare Is Only an Invention."

53. Hunt, "Health Consequences of War," 294.

54. Spurgeon, Treasury of David, 2:389.

These objections are serious and important, and deserve careful consideration. This is the task of the remaining chapters of this book. Nonetheless, its conclusion is simple: the Bible is our highest source of authority, and the biblical record is clear. We must love, not fight, our enemies. We respond to war not militarily but by being the church (an alternative community to the warmaking powers of the world), preaching the gospel, and practicing gospel peacemaking. The historical record attests that when the church has adhered to this message, it has brought good to the world and honor to the faith. When it has abandoned it in favor of crusades and just wars, it has sometimes brought short-term political advantage to a church in one country, but long-term shame and harm to the name of the gospel. Across churches throughout the world a new stage of the Reformation is jettisoning medieval Roman Catholic just war theory and reclaiming this gospel teaching. Just as over the past two decades the broad evangelical church has recovered the biblical truth that God's heart for justice for the poor must be translated from words into actions, so now it is awakening to the realization that this applies equally to biblical teaching on peace. I believe that because of this we may be standing on the threshold of one of the most exciting moments in church—and therefore human—history.

2

Doesn't the Bible Permit Warfare? Part I
The Old Testament

The Bible is "a book of war, a book of hate." These sound like the words of an anti-Christian propagandist, but they are not. They are the cry of an activist in the so-called US "Christian Identity" movement.[1] This is a group of American militias whose activities, conducted in the name of Christ and America, have included the creation of armed communities in remote compounds and the murder of doctors who perform abortions. Most infamously, a link has been alleged between them and the blowing up of a federal building in Oklahoma in 1995 that killed 186 people. These people draw heavily on Old Testament texts to justify their actions.

But this use of the Old Testament to justify contemporary violence is not confined to marginal criminal sects. In November 2004, US military chaplain Kenny Lee held a service in a makeshift chapel in Iraq to mourn the deaths of eight marines in combat that week and to bolster the survivors for an assault on the beleaguered city of Fallujah. "Have I not commanded you?" he read from the book of Joshua, the supposed biblical archetype for a military conqueror. "Be strong and courageous. Do not be terrified; do not be discouraged, for the Lord your God will be with you wherever you go."[2] Is such use of Old Testament military

---

1. Juergensmeyer, *Terror in the Mind of God*, 145–46.

2. Peterson, "US Troops Prep for Fallujah Fight." Speaking of violence in the Old Testament, Richard Dawkins writes that "the ethnic cleansing begun in the time of Moses is brought to bloody fruition in the time of Joshua, a text remarkable for the bloodthirsty massacres it records and the xenophobic relish with which it does so" (*God Delusion*, 208).

discourse justified? *Had* God commanded the marines to attack Fallujah, and was he really with them?

As the previous chapter hinted at and as the next chapter will show, the New Testament provides scant support for those who wish to justify Christian participation in warfare. It is not surprising, therefore, that those church leaders who have sought to align themselves with states or rulers and bless their military action have frequently turned to the Old Testament instead. Here, Yahweh is clearly portrayed as the "Lord of Hosts" (or armies), the God who goes before Israel in battle. In Psalm 144 David sung, "Blessed be the Lord my God, who trains my hands for war . . ." Indeed, Kerry Noble, formerly a leader of a now-defunct Christian militia known as The Covenant, the Sword, and the Arm of the Lord, quoted Exodus 15:3, "The LORD is a man of war," to justify the existence of that militia.[3] This chapter will ask, is this reasonable? Can we use Old Testament texts to justify Christian violence today?

This is an important question because one of the strongest arguments against religion today used by the "New Atheists" is that it causes violence. The Old Testament "is one long celebration of violence," writes Stephen Pinker in his influential book on the decline of violence in history; his seven-hundred-page text begins with a lengthy overview of the multiple histories of violence in the Hebrew Bible.[4] Pinker claims that "the scriptures present a God who delights in genocide, rape, slavery, and the execution of nonconformists, and for millennia whose writings were used to rationalize the massacre of infidels, the ownership of women, the beating of children, dominion over animals, and the persecution of heretics and homosexuals."[5]

He cites the estimate of one researcher that approximately 1.2 million deaths from mass killings are described in the Bible—not including the flood of Noah's day. Pinker concludes that Christians today pay lip service to the Bible as a symbol of morality "while actually getting their morality from more modern principles."[6] His charge must be taken seriously and can be countered, and it is important to respond to it. That is part of the purpose of this book. But in so doing we need to address another charge that critics of Christianity and some liberal Christians

3. Juergensmeyer, *Terror in the Mind of God*, 145–46.

4. Pinker, *Better Angels of Our Nature*, 6–12.

5. Ibid., 676.

6. Ibid., 12.

themselves make: that if we cannot use the Old Testament texts to justify Christian violence today, does this mean that over time our idea of God has changed, from a vindictive and violent warrior to a loving, peaceful savior?

Two main arguments from the Old Testament are made by Christians to justify war. The first is to compare their country to biblical Israel, the ancient people chosen by God with a special mission for the good of the world. This view was enormously influential in some countries up until the 1940s, but, although it persists in a few places today, the 1914–45 world war catastrophe has made this theology fall from fashion. In its place, a second argument has achieved preeminence: that God allowed fighting and killing in the Old Testament, proving he is not against it in principle; so there may be circumstances when Christians can fight in wars today. Both of these arguments have been widely used to justify Christian participation in warfare. This chapter will argue that neither is tenable when tested against Holy Scripture.

Chosen People Syndrome—Britain and Germany

The first main argument that exponents of Christian participation in warfare make from the Old Testament is to suggest that their modern nation-state is somehow peculiarly chosen by God, as Old Testament Israel was, and can therefore be justified in acting as ancient Israel did by fighting wars. Although widely discredited now, it is worth a brief consideration. In a splendid book on the history of the idea in Britain and the United States, Clifford Longley terms it "chosen people syndrome" and regards it as very dangerous indeed.[7]

"Chosen people syndrome" has peculiarly affected Britain in the past. Oliver Cromwell was often compared to Gideon, the ideal Christian ruler who refused to be made king but remained the "judge" of his people. Cromwell's troops charged into battle—against other Christians—with the war cry of the Israelites against the Midianites and the Amalekites from the book of Judges: "The sword of the Lord and of Gideon!" (Judg 7:18 KJV). The sacking and massacre of Jericho was cited as divine sanction for Cromwell's sackings and massacres at Drogheda and Wexford in 1649.

---

7. Longley, *Chosen People.*

The idea of Britain as a latter-day Israel outlasted Cromwell. In the mid-nineteenth century, George Croly said, "There is the strongest reason to believe, that as Judea was chosen for especial guardianship of the original revelation, England has been chosen for the especial guardianship of Christianity."[8] In the same century, John Wilson argued that Jesus was really an Aryan, and that "the lost sheep of the house of Israel" are none other than the English.[9] Lord Ashley, later the seventh Earl of Shaftesbury and a leading evangelical and social reformer, was a prominent parliamentary advocate of Christian rectitude in imperial dealings (he opposed the opium trade with China, for example). In 1844 he expressed anger at French aggression near the disputed island of Tahiti, stating that responsibility for its "regeneration" had been "given to our people as a triumph of the cross."[10]

The First World War saw the high noon of this type of argument. John Handcock, in a 1916 booklet called *God's Dealings with the British Empire*, wrote, "We are God's chosen people, his inheritance, the salt of the earth, his loved ones, his glory, the people He delights in, his sons and daughters."[11] Against those who were bemused at this language, Dawson warned, "Let us not fall into the old mistake of counting Jewish history as sacred and English history as secular. . . . You cannot shut up God in a section of time or a corner of the globe." It was observed that the Kaiser was 666 months old when the war began, supposed proof that he was like Sennacherib and Antiochus Epiphanes, ancient persecutors of God's people, Israel.[12]

Bishop Winnington-Ingram of London, who had been pro-German before 1914 but gained infamy during the war for his bellicose sermons, cited Judges 5:23 in support of British entrance into the war. If God cursed a small region of Palestine called Meroz for not helping Deborah and Barak fight the Canaanites, he would, reasoned the bishop, curse England if it did not help Belgium. He omitted to mention that until relatively recently, the Church of England had been cursing Belgium for its ruthless slaughter of up to eight million Africans in its Congo empire.

8. Croly, *The Apocalypse of St. John*, quoted in Wolffe, *God and Greater Britain*, 17.

9. Juergensmeyer, *Terror in the Mind of God*, 33.

10. Cited in Wolffe, *God and Greater Britain*, 216.

11. Cited in Hoover, *God, Germany, and Britain*, 69.

12. Most of the examples in this and the subsequent two paragraphs are taken from Hoover, *God, Germany, and Britain*, chs. 5 and 6; some material is drawn from Marrin, *Last Crusade*, ch. 3.

He also quoted from Isaiah 49:2, asserting that England was a "polished arrow" in the quiver of the Almighty whose armies would do his bidding, just as Israel's had done before.

But it was not only British clergy who fancied themselves as the true sons of Israel. Taking the story of David and Goliath, German preachers liked to compare David to little Germany, pluckily standing against the tyrannical giant of England who, these preachers reminded their congregations, had the largest empire the world had ever seen. These accounts depicted the U-boat as the modern equivalent of David's sling, with which God would slay the English! They continued that just as Gideon had defeated a superior force in Judges 7, and Luther had stood alone against the pope, so would Germany again stand up to the forces of evil, this time embodied in the rapacious British Empire. Both German and British preachers compared the enemy nation to Assyria, biblical Israel's foe. Tolzien justified the German invasion of Belgium and Poland by comparing them to the Philistines whom Israel supplanted. Other pastors described Germany as "the Israel of the new covenant." Otto Hattenschwiller said that since the atheistic revolution the French had no fear of God, and so Germany, which feared God, was fighting irreligion, defending Christianity against the godless French.

This attempt to understand modern Europe using an Old Testament map was entirely subjective and without any scriptural warrant at all. It was also immensely tragic, with devout Christians on each side urging men on to slaughter their brothers and sisters. In the aftermath of the war, with a general revulsion against the slaughter of trench warfare for hazy political ends, the folly of this distortion of scripture was widely recognized.

The theological objections are more weighty still. The whole teaching of the Apostle Paul, in core texts such as Romans and Ephesians, shows that "the New Israel" is not Britain, or Germany, or the modern State of Israel, or any other nation-state. Rather, it is the church that Christ founded with his resurrection, a church that draws people from every tribe, tongue, and nation and breaks down the old ethnic barriers of division by uniting in Christ former enemies. The fundamental division is now between the church and the world, not one territorial state and all others. It is now the church, not the Davidic kingdom of Israel, that is the key instrument in God's working out of salvation history.[13] It is

---

13. It is not that the church has replaced biblical Israel in God's purposes but rather that God has had one people in history and one way of salvation, through the atoning

no doubt flattering for a state to believe that it is the chosen instrument of God for salvation, and the New Israel. It may be convenient for a government seeking a justification for war. But it is also blasphemous.

The New Israel—the United States?

The belief that their country and military is particularly blessed by God and called by him to exercise a special role in world history has largely disappeared among the peoples of Europe. However, across the Atlantic, "chosen people syndrome" has been more resilient. It has an old pedigree, going back to the founding of the American colonies by religious exiles seeking a "promised land." God's providence was used to justify the genocide of Native Americans and the theft of their land. Later on, similar arguments were used to justify the seizure of Mexican land.[14] It was enshrined in American political practice and culture from the earliest days of the republic. For example, in his first presidential inaugural address, George Washington said, "No people can be bound to acknowledge and adore the Invisible Hand which conducts the affairs of men more than those of the United States."[15]

However, although the First and Second World Wars largely cured Europe of "chosen people syndrome," the idea that a certain nation-state is specially chosen by God still persists in the United States—indeed, it has enjoyed something of a revival in recent years. This is partly due to the influence of certain trends in evangelical end-time theology, encouraged by the foundation of the State of Israel in 1948 and the Israeli victory in the 1967 war against neighboring Arab states. From the late 1960s onward, right-wing TV evangelists such as Pat Robertson and Jerry Falwell, whose shows enjoyed enormous popularity, rose in influence. They believed that the modern republic of Israel was prophesized in books such as Daniel, Ezekiel, and Revelation, and that "Gog and Magog" was the Soviet Union, against whom the United States had a divine mission to militarily support Israel. Using a particular and controversial form of end-time theology, they believed that Christ's one-thousand-year reign

---

blood of Christ. Jews had a unique role in history leading to the Messiah, and will one day all come to have faith in him. The church is Israel renewed and restored but now enlarged to embrace people of all nations. See Sizer, *Christian Zionism*.

14. Anzaldúa, *Borderlands, La Frontera*, 29.

15. Quoted in Longley, *Chosen People*, 24.

on earth would follow the battle of Armageddon (in modern Israel), an inevitable nuclear confrontation to usher in God's kingdom.[16] Therefore, they concluded, anyone who advocated arms control treaties or peaceful resolution of Cold War conflicts was opposing Christ.[17]

United States president Ronald Reagan had been influenced by these theologies earlier in his political career and as president frequently used language suggestive of "chosen people syndrome." For example, in an address to the nation supporting the Contra terrorists in their campaign to destabilize the Nicaraguan government and replace it with a regime friendly to US business interests (a conflict in which thirty thousand people died), Reagan said that "the Almighty" had a reason for placing the United States where it is, to help bring freedom to the world. By supporting the Contras, Reagan proclaimed—using a well-known messianic prophecy from Isaiah 6—America was demonstrating that it was "still a light unto the nations."[18] In his farewell presidential address, he described America as "a shining city set on a hill." This was a reference to the Sermon on the Mount—Jesus' exposition of a radical new ethic for the coming mystical kingdom. Yet Reagan applied it not to the church, but appropriated it to a dubious foreign policy episode in the life of his particular country, the United States.

During his presidency, George W. Bush pushed this language to new levels. In his inaugural address, he referred to Virginia statesman John Page, who wrote to Thomas Jefferson, "Do you not think an angel rides in the whirlwind and directs the storm?" Bush went on to say, "We are not this story's author, who fills time and eternity with His purpose. . . . This work continues. This story goes on. And an angel still rides in the whirlwind and directs this storm. God bless you all, and God bless America."[19] He has unambiguously declared that God is fighting on the side of the United States in his "war on terror." Calling for the nation to pray to God soon after 9/11, he declared,

> The course of this conflict is not known, yet its outcome is certain. Freedom and fear, justice and cruelty, have always been

16. Their end-time theology is known as "premillennialism." For more, see ch. 8, p. 232.

17. Halsell, *Prophecy and Politics*. For more on militaristic readings of biblical prophecy, see the section of this book "Eyeing the End Time," ch. 8, p. 231–35.

18. Ó Tuathail and Agnew, "Geopolitics and Discourse," 196–97.

19. Quoted in Longley, *Chosen People*, 9–10.

at war, and we know that God is not neutral between them. (Applause.)

Fellow citizens, we'll meet violence with patient justice— assured of the rightness of our cause, and confident of the victories to come. In all that lies before us, may God grant us wisdom, and may He watch over the United States of America.[20]

Concluding his book on "chosen people syndrome," Longley argues that nations that suffer from it are a potential threat to others. This is because they feel intensely righteous and are convinced that the moral justification of their actions lies in their unique status. As Longley says, "If 'an angel rides in the whirlwind and directs this storm,' as John Page wrote to Thomas Jefferson, then George Bush's conclusion is correct: 'We are not this story's author, who fills time and eternity with His purpose.' Is this not an oblique way of warning the world: to stand in America's way is to resist the will of God?"

In the Darmstadt Statement of 1947, leading German theologians recognized the damage done to the church and the world by confusing the progress of their country with the advance of God's kingdom. They said, "We went astray when we began to dream about a special German mission, as if the German character could heal the sickness of the world. In so doing we prepared the way for the unrestricted exercise of political power, and set our own nation on the throne of God."[21]

It is time that the few remaining states that cling to a notion of their military might being the especial tool of God's kingdom-building purposes on earth also reached such a conclusion. There is neither theological nor historical justification for mapping the political geography of the Old Testament onto the modern world. When this has been done, it has invariably fostered arrogance, bred bad theology, and brought disrepute to the gospel as violence is done in its name.

The Laws of War: From Moses to the Burning Bush

In January 2003, Andrew Motion, the British poet laureate, or royal poet appointed by the monarch, broke with tradition by penning a short poem sharply critical of Her Majesty's government, "Causa Belli." Prime Minister Tony Blair was about to take Britain into war with Iraq, ostensibly

---

20. Bush, "Address to a Joint Session of Congress and the American People."

21. Darmstadt Statement, para. 2, cited in Hockenos, *Church Divided*, 193.

to disarm the country of its threatening "weapons of mass destruction." Informed critics (who would be proven right by the course of events) insisted that this threat was nonexistent, believing it to be a pretext to fight a war for other reasons. Motion succinctly summed up these reasons as "elections, money, empire, oil, and Dad,"[22] the latter term referring to George W. Bush's infamous repeated description of Saddam Hussein as "the guy who tried to kill my dad."[23] Motion's poem cast doubt on the motives behind the planned US-UK invasion of Iraq, reflecting widespread public debate about whether the cause was just and, hence, the war legal.

Proponents of Christian violence today point out that just the same concerns can be found in the Old Testament. God laid down for the Israelites precise and detailed rules about when they could go to war and how they should conduct themselves in warfare. They argue that God has not changed, and as he allowed war in the Old Testament, he must therefore still allow it today. Therefore, they conclude, Christians are permitted to partake in the contemporary form of warfare as practiced by states such as Britain and the United States—within certain rules. These rules (known as "just war theory," to be discussed in ch. 5) include provisions such as the insistence that we must strive to minimize civilian casualties, use violence proportional to the aim, and undertake war only as a last resort under proper authority. The idea of Britain, America, or whoever being a latter-day Israel having now been widely discredited, this is the major argument for the rightness of Christian participation in warfare that is made today from the Old Testament.

If the Old Testament provides a model for Christian soldiers, we must not just say that "God allowed war in the past so must still allow it today." Rather, we must take those scriptures seriously by looking in detail at what they say and applying that to our own context. That is what we will do for the rest of this chapter: and, as this chapter shows, closely studying God's word here shows how untenable it is to use the Hebrew Bible to justify Christian violence today.

The clearest section on the conduct of warfare in the Old Testament is contained in Deuteronomy 20, where Moses lays out the principles and rules of conduct for warfare. It begins with these words:

> When you go to war against your enemies and see horses and
> chariots and an army greater than yours, do not be afraid of

---

22. Produced in full by Ezard, "Poet Laureate Joins Doubters over Iraq."

23. Greenberg, "Fathers and Sons: George W. Bush and His Forebears."

them, because the LORD your God, who brought you out of
Egypt, will be with you. . . . The LORD your God is the one who
goes with you to fight for you against your enemies to give you
victory. (Deut 20:1, 4)

This introduction immediately presents advocates of modern
warfare who use the Old Testament rules to back up their case with a
major problem. The remaining "just war theorists" in the church today
have constructed an elaborate framework to allow any country to decide
whether their war is "just" and to encourage them to inflict the minimum
violence and cause the minimum suffering necessary. However, the Old
Testament rules had quite the opposite purpose. As these verses show,
these are not an objective code of international conduct that any side
could use equally. Rather, they assume that God will divinely give victory
to one side only—here, the side that was fighting what just war thinking
today would have to condemn as an unprovoked, genocidal war of aggressive territorial acquisition.

Modern readers struggle to understand these rules of warfare because they misunderstand their intention. They had an entirely different
purpose from the rules of warfare to which we are accustomed today.
They were *not* designed to create a system to limit the number or in-
tensity of wars, as the modern international rules of war are. The Old
Testament saw warfare as an act of worshiping God. The chief goal of
this worship through warfare was not politics or justice or power, but
holiness and faith before the Lord. In particular, the *conduct* of warfare
was intended to produce and demonstrate faith in God for security; the
intended *outcome* of warfare was holiness before God.[24] The remainder of
this chapter will look at these two principles at work in three of the many
rules of war: on treatment of prisoners, use of military technology and
strategy, and the formation of military alliances.

Three Rules of Old Testament Warfare

First Rule—Vanquished Foes

A first Old Testament rule of war regards treatment of vanquished
foes. There were in fact two laws for the treatment of the inhabitants of

---

24. Although he does not use these terms in these ways, this understanding of the
rules of war in the Old Testament is informed by Kreider, *Journey towards Holiness.*

conquered land. For those cities outside the promised land, the Israelite armies were to approach the city and offer terms of peace in exchange for accepting slavery. If the cities refused this offer, all the men were to be killed, and the women, children, livestock, and everything else to be taken as plunder (Deut 20:10–15). If certain beautiful women attracted the desire of the conquerors they could be taken and forced to be wives until their abductors ceased to be pleased with them (Deut 21:10–14).

For cities within the promised land, however, the Israelites were instructed to be utterly merciless: "Do not leave alive anything that breathes. Completely destroy them" (Deut 20:16–17). This was taken deadly seriously by the commander of the invading army, Joshua. For example, following the capture of Jericho, Achan disobeyed by keeping back a robe and some silver and gold that he plundered (Josh 7). God was so angry that he had Joshua kill Achan, his whole family and all their livestock, and then burn the corpses along with the plunder, his tents, and all their possessions. Why this severe sentence? The answer is that the intended outcome of this warfare was *holiness*. In Deuteronomy 20:18, Moses explained to the Israelites that total genocide is required; otherwise the survivors "will teach you to follow the detestable things they do in worshipping their gods." The writer of Joshua records that, at the destruction of Jericho, the people "devoted the city to the LORD and destroyed with the sword every living thing in it—men and women, young and old, cattle, sheep and donkeys" (Josh 6:21).

This word "devotion" is in Hebrew *herem,* or "the ban"—a purifying act of worship to God.[25] The colossal destructiveness of this warfare was not about politics, or self-defense, or justice, or economic or geopolitical advantage, but about holiness. It is common in warfare today to hear Christian leaders call for restraint—for minimizing enemy civilian casualties and damage to civilian infrastructure, treating prisoners of war humanely, protecting cultural heritage, and certainly refusing to engage in wholesale ethnic cleansing or the sexual molestation of women. According to the Old Testament rules of warfare, that attitude is so evil that those who practiced it in the conquest of Canaan had to be destroyed along with all their families and worldly goods.

---

25. Nidditch, *War in the Hebrew Bible,* chs. 1 and 2.

Second Rule—Military Weakness

A second rule of warfare that Yahweh called on Israel to follow was one of intentional military weakness. This was to force Israel to rely upon the miraculous saving intervention of God, and never think that human military strategy, bravery, skill, training, alliances, or technology had won them victory.

This principle is shown clearly in the first military encounter that the children of Israel faced in the scriptures, as Pharaoh bore down on them at the Red Sea. As the people trembled at the approach of the Egyptian armies, Moses said to them, "Do not be afraid. Stand firm and you will see the deliverance the LORD will bring you today. . . . The LORD will fight for you; you need only to be still" (Exod 14:13–14). The "battle" was won when God parted the waters, allowing his people to pass through, and then closed them on the pursuing forces. A great victory was won without Israel lifting a sword. The songs that Moses and Miriam sang following the battle, extolling the greatness of God in defeating his enemies (Exod 15), would have been very different had Moses defeated Pharaoh with a cunning trap and the brave resistance of his warriors.

This principle of intentional military weakness in anticipation of a miracle to ensure that all the credit for victory was God's is shown repeatedly throughout the Old Testament. In the first battle in which the Israelites actually engaged in combat (against the Amalekites), victory was only assured so long as Moses held his arms aloft (Exod 17). When he grew tired, Aaron and Hur held his arms up for him and thus secured victory. This was probably one of the oddest actions by a military commander in the history of warfare! Again, the point is the same: the glory goes to God, not to Moses.

The Old Testament records other seemingly bizarre military strategies. In Judges 7 Gideon defeated the Midianites, but before the battle God told him to drastically reduce the number of soldiers by only choosing men who lapped water with their hands. This was not because these men were more civilized and thus made better soldiers but rather to make a weaker force that would demonstrate to the world that victory came from God, not human strength. We read in 2 Chronicles 20 that Jehoshaphat defeated Moab and Ammon by sending the worshippers into battle before the soldiers, and the Lord miraculously set ambushes. These examples characterize warfare in the Old Testament: intentional military weakness by bizarre and eccentric preparations and strategies that were intended to force people to depend on God to fight for them, so that all the glory for victory went to God. The *conduct* of warfare was intended to produce faith in God and ensure that all the glory and praise for victory went to him alone, not military heroes. Modern British and American warfare, which depends upon carefully thought out strategies developed at military colleges and through battlefield experience aimed at gaining an advantage over the enemy, are utterly unlike any form of warfare advocated in the Old Testament and, indeed, would be judged by it as sheer blasphemy.

This strategy of intentional weakness demanded the eschewal of military technology. The most prized and feared items of military hardware in Old Testament times were cavalry and chariots, which could cause immense destruction and swing the outcome of a battle. As having such an advantage could make the Israelites trust in themselves rather than God, it was obviously not allowed to them. Thus Joshua assiduously saw that horses captured from the enemy were hamstrung and chariots burned to prevent the risk of being tempted to use them (Josh 11:6). Samuel warned the Israelites that if they disobeyed God and asked for a king, a sign of the king's oppression of them would be his acquisition and deployment of military hardware (1 Sam 8:11–12). Isaiah proclaimed, "Woe to those who . . . trust in the multitude of their chariots, and in the great strength of their horsemen, but do not look to the Holy One of Israel, or seek help from the Lord" (Isa 31:1). Micah announced his great vision of coming salvation by declaring that on the day of salvation, along with destroying witchcraft, God would "destroy your horses from among you and demolish your chariots" (Mic 5:1). This intense prophetic dislike of horses and chariots is not some quirk: it is only explicable by understanding the principle of intentional military weakness to ensure reliance on, and glory to, God. It was an either-or option; you could not be true to God and try to win wars through superior forces: "Some trust in chariots and some in horses, *but we* trust in the name of the Lord our God" (Ps 20:7).

The British and American militaries boast proudly about their wonderful weaponry such as laser-guided cruise missiles, stealth bombers, thermobaric devices, and remotely controlled drones that allow them to pummel their enemies with near impunity. Such a strategy on the part of Israel would be regarded as just as evil as the sin of witchcraft by the Old Testament, because the effect is the same: to transfer trust for security away from God to something else. When Joshua took Jericho (Josh 6) he was not to send in warriors first but silently send the priests ahead of the crowd as it walked around, until the walls miraculously fell down. Imagine a modern British or American general beginning the invasion of some Asian or Middle Eastern state by sending in "leaders of the faith communities" ahead of armor and airstrikes! It sounds ridiculous because there can be no equivalent whatsoever between the Old Testament rules of war and modern warfare.

Third Rule—No Alliances

The third rule of Old Testament warfare that we shall consider is that the Israelites were utterly forbidden to make military alliances with other states. This mirrors the rule on intentional military weakness. The prophets vehemently denounced alliances with neighboring states, particularly Egypt, Babylon, and Assyria, the powers that Israel and Judah found themselves sandwiched between for much of their history. As Isaiah explains, "Woe to those who go down to Egypt for help . . . but do not look to the Holy One of Israel, or seek help from the Lord" (31:1). Engaging in military alliance made them trust people rather than God, and the divine intention for the *conduct* of warfare was that it should produce *faith*.

A clear example is provided by King Asa of Judah. In 2 Chronicles 14, at a time when he was passionately pursuing religious reform at home, he showed admirable faith in God for deliverance when the vastly superior forces of the Cushites attacked him. God honored his faith with a miraculous victory. A few years later, however, in 2 Chronicles 16, when King Baasha of Israel came up to besiege Judah, Asa's faith wavered. He sent money to Ben-Hadad, king of Aram, to form an alliance. No doubt he did this praying to God that it would work, but God was angry and did not give Asa the victory he desired. Our modern concept of alliances, of forming "coalitions" in the "international community" or even the United Nations, of standing "shoulder to shoulder with our allies," is, according to Old Testament laws of warfare, wicked apostasy and sheer rebellion against God.

Same Old Rules?

Some Christians argue that, as God endorsed warfare in the Old Testament, it must still be an acceptable practice for Christians today.

However, if we make that argument, we cannot be selective: we must treat scripture consistently and look seriously at what it says. We must argue for merciless genocide, the plunder of possessions, forced slavery of the vanquished and the sexual appropriation of captured women. We must insist that wars are not undertaken to advance political or economic or strategic aims, and certainly not to achieve international justice through the implementation of UN Security Council resolutions, but that only unprovoked, genocidal wars of territorial aggrandizement undertaken as acts of worship to Yahweh are acceptable. We must also ban the use of any item of military technology that would give an advantage over the enemy and denounce the formation of alliances with any other state as blasphemy. We must insist that unarmed priests lead into battle a force that has intentionally been made weaker than their opponents in anticipation of Yahweh's miraculous military interventions for victory, rather than strategy, tactics, or training—which we must scorn as ungodly. We must hold that this applies to only one state, the state that Yahweh has identified as his, and identify which state that would be. Bishops and other religious leaders who comment on war must cease calling upon their governments to treat prisoners of war and civilians well, but instead strictly instruct soldiers to massacre them. And we must declare that any deviation from this is apostasy that must be mercilessly punished by death of the offender and his entire family.

Of course, no Christian would advocate this type of warfare today. It is contrary to all our moral senses, to all international law, Roman Catholic "just war theory," and cherished codes of conduct such as the Geneva Convention. We feel that it is utterly unlike the way Jesus and the apostles lived and taught us to deal with our enemies. If we claim to treat scripture seriously, we cannot use the Old Testament to justify Christian participation in modern warfare.

Has God Changed His Mind about Warfare?

We have seen in the previous section that the rules of warfare in the Old Testament are so contrary to our notions of civilized warfare that they would be impossible for us to contemplate putting into action today. Part of the reason is that they are so unlike the teaching and practice of Jesus and the apostles, who, as we saw in the previous chapter, loved their enemies and allowed themselves to be overcome rather than hurt them first. But this creates a problem. Does that mean that God has changed, or that Moses and Joshua were simply primitive and have been superseded by the evolution of values? Non-Christians use what they describe as this apparent discrepancy between Old and New Testaments to attack Christianity and the truth of the Bible. Liberal Christians commonly also suggest there is such a discrepancy—for example, the often insightful Jacques Ellul admitted that he found the wars in the Hebrew Bible "most embarrassing."[26] Even Christians who hold scripture in higher regard may be troubled by it and may subconsciously harbor an image of the Old Testament God who is warlike and angry, and the God of Jesus who is peaceful and loving. Does this mean that God has changed?

These are legitimate questions and the apparent tension needs taking seriously. However, any suggestion that God has changed, or that the Bible reflects merely human ideas about God, is false. The Bible is the divine revelation of the unchanging God. To understand why this objection is a false problem, we must return to the explanation of the purpose of warfare in the Old Testament. The *conduct* of warfare was intended to produce and demonstrate faith in God for security; the *outcome* of warfare was intended to lead to holiness before God. How are these achieved in the New Testament?

Faith in Old and New Testaments

According to the apostles, faith in God for security, the product of the *conduct* of Old Testament warfare, is, after the death and resurrection of Jesus, no longer to be achieved through trusting in God's miraculous intervention to kill the enemies of Christians. In 1 Peter 2:21–25, Peter invokes the example of Christ, who did not retaliate when attacked but "entrusted himself to him who judges justly"—God. We are to trust God for security, risk ourselves on him, and trust that he will rescue us when we so need it. The disciples followed this pattern faithfully; beaten, imprisoned, attacked, they sometimes ran but never fought back. What they did do was trust that God would protect them. They experienced many miraculous escapes, but sometimes God did not deliver—some disciples were killed in the end. That is God's business: ours is to obey his command to depend upon him—rather than our own violence—to

26. Ellul, *Anarchy and Christianity*, 13.

advance the kingdom. As we do that, as we prove God's faithfulness in our experience, we grow in faith—just as the Old Testament Israelites did as they weakened themselves in battle and stepped out in faith in a living God. Here, it is instructive to read the accounts of Christian missionaries to Africa and Asia in the nineteenth century. They are filled with stories of these brave Christians facing violence, who trusted God for protection, and in so doing not only saw their own faith grown but presented a remarkable testimony to those to whom they were trying to preach the gospel.

One such example is that of John G. Paton. He was a missionary to the New Hebrides Islands in the South Pacific.[27] He worked among people whose culture was violent. They had been badly abused by other whites and were thus, understandably, extremely hostile to him. Many of the friends he made among them were killed. But he refused either to leave or to use violence to protect himself. Many times people tried to kill him. But as his biographer put it, he never thought "of revenge or of shooting in self-defense. He trusted only in the Lord who had placed him there and to whom had been given all power in heaven and in earth."[28] His patient work and example of a holy life eventually led to people accepting Christ. Litsi Soré was one person who became a believer through the work of Paton. Queen of the Aniwans, her husband was killed by the chief of the neighboring Tannese people. Rather than organize a retaliatory expedition, as might be expected of a leader, she devoted her life to living among and spreading the gospel to the Tannese.

An instructive example closer to home is that of Tom Skinner, a 1970s African-American preacher. As an angry young man and disturbed teenager resentful at the injustices that his community suffered, he turned to violence as a way to ground his identity. When still a teenager, he became the ruthless leader of a notorious New York gang; he claimed to have knifed twenty-two people, without a trace of remorse. One night, he was listening to the radio as he planned a strategy for what he claimed would be the largest street battle that New York had ever seen. The broadcast was about Jesus. He was stunned to learn, as he put it, that God had taken Tom Skinner and put him (his sinful nature) on the cross, and that Jesus had shed his blood to forgive Tom Skinner's sins, deliver

---

27. This and the subsequent example are cited in Megoran, *War on Terror*, 78–80. Used with kind permission of InterVarsity Press.

28. Legg, "John G. Paton," 314.

him from death, and give him new life. He prayed there and then, committing his life to Christ.[29]

Nonetheless, there remained the not inconsiderable matter of the gang. The next day there was a meeting of the gang; Skinner had planned to brief them on strategy for the upcoming battle. He told his dumbfounded audience about what had happened, that he had encountered Jesus and that he was leaving the gang. That was brave, as no one left that gang alive—he had personally made sure of that. Yet no one moved as he stood up and walked out past the seated gang members. A few days later he met a rival in the gang, who had said he had tried to get up and knife him but was rooted to the spot—and others had experienced the same inability to move. That was God's miraculous, intervening, saving power. He quickly developed a ministry of preaching and reaching out to gangs, seeing numerous killers saved in the fullest sense of the word, turned from death to life. He did not withdraw from his world, even though it was full of temptation and danger. Neither did he use violence to protect himself. Rather, his transformed and holy life, lived by the Spirit's power, amazed his former friends and enemies and proved infectious to them. He depended on God's miraculous power for deliverance from danger—the same power that God used to bring the walls of Jericho down.

These two examples show exactly the key themes of Old Testament warfare correctly applied in the New Testament context. That is, ordinary people empowered by the Spirit to lead holy lives that are attractive to others and transformative of the world around them, relying not on human means but on faith in a God who intervenes to save his people for their protection.

Holiness in the Old and New Testaments

The intended *outcome* of Old Testament warfare was holiness, as we saw above. In the New Testament, holiness is still desired by God for his people. However, it is no longer to be secured by separating ourselves from the world and destroying anything that could come near and pollute us. On the contrary, Paul urged the believers not to withdraw from the world because of its ungodliness (2 Cor 5:9–11) but rather to keep their holiness and live—as the Lord Jesus put it—as "salt and light" (Matt 5:13–14), without hiding the light or losing the saltiness. Outsiders are no longer

29. This story is retold in Skinner, *Black and Free*, 12.

to be seen as threats that must be destroyed or excluded but as potential members of the church who are to be overcome by love and brought into our new holy nation.

Here, a note on language illustrates the point even more clearly. As we saw earlier in considering the conquest of Canaan, a city to be destroyed was declared *herem* and dedicated to God under "the ban" (see above, 34). The New Testament equivalent translation of the Hebrew *herem* is the Greek *anathema*—excluded, banned, or "excommunicated." In the letters to the Corinthians (1 Cor 5:1–11; 2 Cor 5:1) the punishment on a sinner is that he is to be declared *anathema*, temporarily excluded from the fellowship of believers so as not to pollute it, but with the aim of restoring the sinner to proper practice and full fellowship (2 Cor 1:5–11; Gal 6:1).[30] This was the standard New Testament punishment on unrepentant sinners from among the believers (following the Lord's teaching set out in Matt 18:15–20), and its general fall out of practice is to be much regretted. The goal was not to destroy the sinner but temporarily to remove him in order to demonstrate the error of his ways, leading to repentance and restoration.

Thus, the Old Testament principle of destructive warfare to ensure holiness is replaced by the New Testament principle of excommunication, with the goal of reconciliation. God is just as concerned as ever to protect the holiness of his chosen people, and ensure their justification, but now he does it in a better way.

One might reasonably ask at this point why this change occurred. Paul's clearest explanation of the relationship between the law of Moses and the Gospel of Christ is in Galatians 3 and 4. He memorably likens the law to a schoolmaster (or, as Tom Wright wonderfully translates it in today's language, "the law was like a babysitter"[31]), a supervisor to keep us in check until we were mature enough to do right without its strict rules—that is, until the light of the gospel era dawned. The law was good, but it was given as a temporary measure in an era before the general outpouring of the Holy Spirit. Because Christ died and rose again and has washed us clean in the new birth, the Holy Spirit now dwells in us, and we know God in a more intimate and powerful way than the people in the Old Testament did—we can "live by the Spirit." Those ancient believers needed to be kept holy by staying separate from nonbelievers, and their

---

30. Marshall, *Beyond Retribution*, 149–62.

31. T. Wright, *Paul for Everyone: Galations and Thessalonians*, 39.

kingdom was a tiny and exclusive part of the earth's surface. They only saw Christ from afar, and so they needed the strict oversight of a schoolmaster. We are infinitely more blessed—we are part of the kingdom of God ushered in by Christ. This kingdom covers the whole earth, and it advances by the sanctifying power of the Spirit working through believers everywhere. To justify war from the Old Testament is to hanker after the law when we have the gospel; it is to "turn back to those weak and miserable principles" (Gal 4:9)—the very tendency that Paul wrote the book of Galatians to confront.

Progressive Revelation and Warfare in the Bible

We have seen that the Old Testament rules on warfare existed not to allow states to pursue political, economic, security, or legal goals (such as correcting injustice) but to promote faith in God and produce holiness. They were part of the law of Moses and have no place in the new covenant ushered in by the death and resurrection of Christ. Warfare served a limited purpose for a limited period and is now superseded. To hanker after it would be as anachronistic as attempting to reintroduce animal sacrifices to atone for sin or to reconstruct the temple as a site of Christian worship.

Thus the argument that Christians can take part in war because God approved of it in the Old Testament can only be made if the Old Testament is grossly twisted out of all reasonable context. However, even the assumption that God wholly approved of war in times past is not as clear as it may seem. The Old Testament shows God disliked violence, and successive prophets made this increasingly clear.

David himself is a prime example. At the head of Yahweh's army, David did kill, and by God's help: but the very idea of Israel having a military king to lead them into battle "like the Gentiles had" itself was a rejection of God's kingship, something they were never meant to have (1 Sam 8:19–20). The David phenomenon was never meant to happen. Samuel warned them that if they had a king, he would bring hardship on them by oppressing and militarizing them (1 Sam 8:11–13). This came true. The rule of David's son, Solomon, was so oppressive to the people that as soon as he was dead, "all Israel" challenged his son, Rehoboam, to "lighten the harsh labor" or otherwise they would reject the House of David (2 Chr 10). Even though he seemed to be doing God's will, David was not allowed to build a temple for God because he had become unholy by virtue of the wars he had fought. God made this clear in delivering to him the devastating news that "you are not to build a house for my name, because you are a warrior and have shed blood" (1 Chr 28:3). David's warring was incorporated into Yahweh's purposes by a gracious God who condescended to meet humanity in its fallen state. However, this was always a gracious paradox, and David's very participation in warfare left him permanently tainted and unable to serve God fully. It clearly was not the best way. Indeed, in reference to divorce, Jesus explained to his hearers that Moses had permitted it "because your hearts were hard" (Matt 19:8). This is a holy mystery, but our Lord implies that the Old Testament law was a gracious concession to wayward humanity for the limited period until Christ came to fulfill the law, rather than as an expression of his holy character.

In the end, David's kingdom would be re-established, taught the prophets, but in a way very different from that in which David established his. Ezekiel warned of the punishment coming on Israel and the nations because they "spread terror in the land of the living" (Ezek 32), but in the valley of the dry bones (ch. 37) he spoke graphically of the great hope of the resurrection of Israel, which is a reference, in the first instance, to the church that would be founded by Christ. This would be under "David" (v. 24), but, unlike the first David, it would be with a covenant of everlasting peace (v. 26). When the enemies of God ("Gog") would see this and attack an unsuspecting people (Ezek 38:11), then they would stand and see God deliver them by his mighty power (v. 19), not by their taking up arms. This latter glorious kingdom of David would not be soiled by God's people shedding blood, as the former one was.

David's case is not isolated in the Old Testament. Theologians describe a "progressive revelation" in the Old Testament—not that God changed, but that the true nature of the Messiah became clearer as prophetic history advanced. Reformed theologian Charles Hodge explains the "progressive character of divine revelation" thus: "What at first is only obscurely intimated is gradually unfolded in subsequent parts of the sacred volume, until the truth is revealed in its fullness."[32] Although generally overlooked in traditional Reformation formulations, central to this was the place of violence. There was a sense that war and violence and sacrifice were stopgaps that the Messiah's coming would supersede. This was faint at first but grew clearer as the gospel age neared. However,

---

32. Hodge, *Systematic Theology*, 1:446.

even as far back as Moses the people understood that killing in war was not an altogether holy act. Thus in Numbers 31, Moses instructed the Israelites that all Midianites must be killed (except female virgins, who could be kept along with animals) but that *anyone* who has killed must purify themselves.

In another example, it seems unambiguous that God told Jehu to kill Ahab: "This is what the LORD, the God of Israel, says: 'I anoint you king over the LORD's people Israel. You are to destroy the house of Ahab'" (2 Kgs 9:6–10). Jehu did just that in a massacre at Jezreel. Later, however, God said via Hosea, "I will soon punish the house of Jehu for the massacre at Jezreel" (Hos 1:4). Did God change his mind, or did one of these prophets get it wrong? No. Hosea and the later prophets clearly saw that God "desire[s] mercy, not sacrifice" (Hos 6:6); they were given a clearer understanding of the mercy and grace of God than had been revealed at the time of Jehu. This was because they had a clearer vision of the Messiah. These prophets proclaimed that the Messiah would abolish all weapons and bring in a reign of everlasting peace (Zech 9:9–10; Mic 4:1–5). In glimpsing the glory of the coming new covenant, Hosea announces God's declaration, that "bow and sword and battle I will abolish from the land, so that all may lie down in safety" (Hos 2:18).

But it is Isaiah who is the prophet with the fullest picture of Christ in the Old Testament. He saw, by the Spirit's revelation, that the Messiah child to be born would be the "Prince of Peace," whose reign and peace would have no end (9:6–7). He would destroy the army boots and battle fatigues of the soldiers (v. 5). Isaiah sees that this will happen not by might, nor power, but by the suffering death of the defenseless servant, who had himself "done no violence" to his enemies but instead died for their justification (53:9). The progressive revelation about the evil of warfare and violence was part of the glorious revelation about the true nature of the coming kingdom of the Messiah. To look forward to Christ, for the Old Testament prophets, was to look forward to the end of the age of violence. This was revealed incrementally.

To take seriously the Old Testament message on violence, we must reckon with the progressive course of biblical revelation, how what at first was only intimated became gradually unfolded in subsequent parts of scripture. Hodge writes that "the progressive character of divine revelation is recognized in relation to all the great doctrines of the Bible."[33]

33. Ibid.

Peace must be no exception. Taking the scriptures as a unified whole in this way undermines the arguments of those who would justify modern Christian violence by oblique references to the Old Testament. A close reading of the place of warfare in the Old Testament is vital for an integrated understanding of scripture. It takes the Bible itself seriously as a unified whole. It is essential to demonstrate the falsehood of the charge that there is some contradiction between an Old Testament God of war and a New Testament God of love. To answer a charge made by opponents of the faith,[34] it proves that Christianity, properly understood, does not lead to warfare and violence (thereby distinguishing it from Islam and Judaism, which, in not recognizing the fullness of Christian revelation, remain mired in this problem). When we realize that this is not true, it becomes even more exciting to be part of his kingdom. To live in the light of the new covenant is to joyfully proclaim that the age of sacred violence has been superseded by the "gospel of peace," which is indeed good news to a warring world.

We can see by this that it is not admissible to argue, as some liberals do, that because revelation was progressive in the Bible it remains progressive today and thus we could allow violence in the supposedly new context of twenty-first-century globalization. This entails the view that the Bible does not anticipate changed contexts of, say, Christians being in political power or of international institutions like the United Nations. Evangelicals reject such an approach to scripture. God's requirements for his people on violence as a means of action have changed from the Israel of the old covenant to the church of the new covenant. But these contexts are covenantal: revelation in scripture has ended with the closing of the canon. God has made no new covenant with humanity since our Lord broke bread and drank wine with his disciples at the Last Supper.

To use the Old Testament's wars as an argument for Christian warfare today is totally inadmissible by any acceptable evangelical standard of biblical interpretation. Such a strategy down the ages has been used by extremists and those on the margins of the church, and today is the preserve of radical militia or terrorist groups such as the Christian Identity movement.[35] Rather, as John Goldingay observes about the Hebrews' conquering of Canaan, "Israel itself never saw God's commission to dispose of the Canaanites as a precedent for its relationships with other

34. See, for example, S. Harris, *End of Faith*, ch. 3.
35. Barkun, *Religion and the Racist Right*.

people."[36] Traditional, mainstream evangelical theology has recognized that the proper application of such scripture today is not to take up "the weapons of the world" but rather to use weapons that have "divine power to demolish strongholds"—in other words, the proclamation of the gospel (2 Cor 10:3–5).

Conclusion: The Law and the Gospel

Throughout history, Christians anxious to find a way to justify their participation in the wars of their state have performed all manner of bizarre tricks of biblical interpretation. They have replaced the word "Israel" in the Old Testament with "Britain," "America," or "Germany," their exegetical barbarities justifying all manner of imperialistic ones. They have removed the unique Old Testament battles from their proper context in the Law of Moses and suggested that they in some way justify Christian participation in warfare in the gospel era. They have done this because the New Testament contradicts any attempt to use the name and teachings of Christ to promote the bloody ambitions of empire builders or the noble causes of just warriors on earth.

But this will not do. As Walter Chantry points out, "Israel was a nation of God's people. There is no such political body on the earth today."[37] No country enjoys the covenantal relationship with God that ancient Israel did. God's holy people is now visible on earth as the church. Neither can we apply the rules that Moses gave his people to our wars today—they were for genocidal wars of unprovoked territorial acquisition, accompanied by the killing or enslavement of all prisoners, and undertaken by divine assistance that precluded any use of military technology, strategy, tactics, or alliances. Warfare in the Old Testament was not about economic strength, strategic advantage, or international justice, but was intended to produce *faith* by its conduct and *holiness* as its outcome. It was fulfilled with the gospel age when the outpouring of the Holy Spirit enabled believers to enjoy both these spiritual gifts in greater measure through faith in Christ. As the time of Christ drew nearer, prophets were given greater glimpses of the gospel of peace, and it became increasingly clear that this involved an end to violence by believers. It also became clear that violence was only ever a temporary tool of the "schoolmaster"

36. Goldingay, *Joshua, Judges and Ruth*, 4.
37. Chantry, *God's Righteous Kingdom*, 112.

of the law until grace and truth came in Jesus Christ (John 1:17) and that it always polluted, that it was never God's heart for his people.

To use the Old Testament to make a case for Christian participation in warfare is to misunderstand the relationship between the law and the gospel in God's salvation plan for history. The writer to the Hebrews described the law as "only a shadow of the good things that are coming," realities that would be found in Christ (Heb 10:1). The laws on warfare in the Old Testament were part of this. It is no more reasonable to use the Old Testament to make the case for Christian participation in warfare today than it is, say, to claim it mandates the reintroduction of animal sacrifices, temple worship, or Levitical dietary regulations. But this can be put more strongly. To read the Old Testament and hanker after violence as a way to ensure God's justice and holiness on earth today is to prefer the law to the gospel; it is effectively to deny the life, death, resurrection, and ongoing ministry of Jesus Christ. It is, as bishop and commentator J. C. Ryle said of those who try to reintroduce Old Testament ceremonial practices today, "to light a candle at noon-day."[38] We have something much better.

---

38. Ryle, *Expository Thoughts on Matthew*, 197.

3

Doesn't the Bible Permit Warfare? Part II

The New Testament

Saint Paul was a military contractor, patriotically supporting the expansion of the Roman Empire, and this shows that Christians should fight to advance our countries' imperial wars today.

At least, this is what a prison chaplain told British Christians imprisoned in Wandsworth Jail for refusing to fight in World War I. Attempting to persuade them that when Jesus taught us to love our enemies he really meant we should kill them, he claimed that "St. Paul had been an army tent contractor who was proud to do his bit for the empire."[1] Therefore, the reverend implied, the mistaken young men should wholeheartedly throw themselves behind Britain's war efforts and thus fulfill the call of Christian discipleship.

Of course, this claim was groundless. We read in Acts 18 that Paul stayed and worked with fellow tentmakers Aquila and Priscilla while in Corinth. In 2 Thessalonians 3:7–10 he explained that he made tents so as not to be a burden on his hosts and to set a good example of hard work. The suggestion that he was patriotically attempting to support the expansion of the Roman Empire (which was oppressing his own, Jewish people) through strengthening its military machine was a fiction invented by the chaplain to attempt to give scriptural support for his own national prejudices. Yet perhaps we should not be too hard on the chaplain: one *cannot* use the New Testament consistently to make an argument for Christian participation in warfare. This chapter looks at the ways that some people have attempted to do so over the centuries.

---

1. Cited in Marrin, *Last Crusade*, 160.

The first chapter argued that Jesus taught us to love our enemies even when they invade our country and try to harm us, emulating the love that God poured out on us, his undeserving enemies, in justifying us by grace through Christ's death and resurrection. He instructed his followers to be peacemakers, calling them to a radical discipleship that imitates the enemy love he modeled on the cross. The apostles built up a church that adhered to these principles, proclaiming "the gospel of peace" by uniting old enemies in a new community that demonstrated the reality of God's salvation. Non-Christians commonly recognize this in Jesus' teaching and use the church's subsequent failure to follow it as an indictment of Christianity. However, there are Christians who do not accept this, and claim instead that some New Testament passages open the way for Christians to kill their enemies in warfare. In this chapter, I will look at some of the more popular ways today that Christian leaders have used scripture to try to make an argument that is the opposite of what is apparently taught.

Proof Text—or Pretext?

Late medieval Bohemia was terrorized by a radical Christian sect known as the Adamites. This group believed that the sword must go throughout the world until it was cleansed of evil. To do this, they made nocturnal sorties in which the entire population of a village would be killed. This "Holy War," as they called it, was justified with a quotation from the parable of the Ten Virgins: "At midnight the cry rang out: 'Here's the bridegroom'" (Matt 25:6).

It is an oft-repeated dictum in evangelical circles that "a text without a context is a pretext." Had the Adamites studied Matthew 25 carefully they would have understood that it was a challenge to both the Israel of Jesus' day and to us to be ready and not miss what God is doing in Christ,[2] and thus they would have been deprived of a pretext for the brutal murder of neighboring villagers. Although an extreme example, Christian history is littered with shocking and unjustifiable uses of decontextualized proof texts to serve as pretexts to justify violence. It is worth examining a few of the more egregious ones used in recent times.

An often used text by those trying to build a case for Christian participation in warfare is drawn from the Lord Jesus' statement in his

---

2. T. Wright, *Matthew for Everyone, Part 2*, 131–35.

discourse on the destruction of the temple that, until the end of the age, "there will be wars and rumors of wars" (Matt 24:6–7). Doesn't this indicate that war would be a normal part of human history, and therefore Christians are meant to support one side or the other in these wars? It is important to note that this text in no way suggests that Jesus approves of these wars or advocates taking part in them. For example, in the same passage Jesus says there will be "earthquakes, famines and pestilences" (Luke 21:11). Should we therefore strive to oppose famine-relief efforts, hinder the work of polio vaccination campaigns, or close down research on communicable diseases? I work in a geography department: should my colleagues abandon seismological research and the attempt to build earthquake-resistant buildings for cities on tectonic fault lines such as San Francisco and Tokyo? These hypothetical scenarios demonstrate what extreme violence is done to this scripture in misrepresenting Jesus' words to make a political point about warfare. Similarly, in this same discourse Jesus said that false prophets will appear (Mark 13:22) and that children would betray their parents (Luke 21:16–17). Yet no one would suppose that Christians ought not to oppose such terrible things through prayer, sound teaching, instruction, and (in the case of false prophets) excommunication. These things will happen because of sin, but by no stretch of the imagination are Christians therefore mandated to welcome their appearance or to participate in them.

Matthew reports that, when asked whether it was lawful to pay taxes to Caesar (Matt 22:17), the Lord Jesus drew attention to the emperor's face on the coins and replied, "Render unto Caesar the things that are Caesar's." Various commentators have suggested that this extends to military service. For example, St. Augustine attempts to infer that because taxes were used in part to pay soldiers' wages, Christ was indirectly condoning war by allowing the payment of taxes to Caesar (Matt 22:21).[3] This argument forgets both the context of the age and of the passage. In that age, this tax money was used to support a system whose leader (Caesar) was claimed to be a living god. If the passage is an endorsement of Caesar's military, it is also an endorsement of his godhead. But it is neither. Such argumentation is an example of poor use of scripture and logic. As for the context of the passage, the Pharisees were trying to trick Jesus. His response was not "an answer, for all time, on the relationship

---

3. See Cox, "Christian Churches of God Working Paper 110."

between God and political authority," but "a strategic outflanking move."[4] His response avoided both bringing on a confrontation with the Romans before the time was right and losing credibility with the people. It also showed the Pharisees up as hypocrites: they had a coin, showing that they themselves were using the blasphemous object. To use this text to argue for Christian participation in warfare is to remove it from its context and twist it to very different ends. It is unsound biblical exegesis.

In the broader context of the New Testament, obedience to earthly rulers is never unconditional. In Acts 5:29 the apostles told the Sanhedrin, "We must obey God rather than men." The New Testament affirms that we only obey the authorities if their commands do not contradict Christian teaching (Acts 4:19–20). Our Lord's enigmatic reply in Matthew 22 says nothing about whether military service is one of those services we owe the authorities. As we shall see in the next chapter, the early church believed that it was not, and many believers were martyred for refusing to render this service to Caesar.

It is not only Jesus' sayings but also his actions that have been taken out of context to make a case for Christian endorsement of military violence. In a dramatic account in Luke 19:41–48, we learn that as Jesus entered Jerusalem for the last time, he went straight to the temple and cleansed it by driving out traders. This passage has sometimes been used to claim that Jesus supported violence and thus, by extension, Christian participation in the military is acceptable. Even a cursory glance shows this is not the case: there is no textual evidence that either man or beast was killed or even hurt. More significantly, the context of this passage shows how invalid a militaristic reading is. A careful study of Luke's gospel narrative shows that the temple features highly in it, as a symbol of the old order whose authority Jesus was challenging in ushering in the new age. Cleansing the temple was a symbolic messianic act that immediately provoked the question, "By what authority are you doing this?" (Luke 20:1–2). Like all the examples we have considered here, it is only by removing this text from its context that a New Testament argument can be made for Christian participation in warfare. But that is not an authentic way to understand biblical texts: it is misusing the Bible as a pretext.

4. Ibid., 87–88.

Didn't Jesus Teach Personal Not Political Morality?

Even advocates of Christian militarism often recognize that their position is at odds with the life and teachings of Jesus. So to get round this they commonly suggest that Jesus taught a "private" rather than "public" morality. By this count, the teaching about "loving your enemies" only applies to private disputes in, say, the home or workplace, and does not apply to "public" enemies such as the soldiers of another country.

This argument is unsustainable in the light of contemporary scholarship on the social context of the gospels. The idea of a division between the religious and the secular, between a privatized sphere of a personal relationship with God and life with other people in the public sphere, originates in the seventeenth century as modern states emerged in opposition to the various feudal and ecclesiastical entities that preceded them.[5] It was certainly alien to Jesus' times, sixteen hundred years earlier. As Horsley writes, "The Palestinian Jewish people at the time of Jesus did not deal in such abstractions as 'the individual' and did not have a 'religious' sphere of life separate from the political dimensions of their common life."[6] In a land seething with protest and revolt under foreign oppression, when he spoke of "enemies" Jesus' listeners would naturally think immediately of the Romans. Even the examples Jesus uses of not resisting an enemy refer to public conflicts when your enemies take you to court (Matt 5:40) or legally demand forced labor (v. 41). This latter injunction to "walk an extra mile" shows that he was thinking of military occupation, as a Roman soldier had the right to force anyone to carry a load for one mile. Jesus' teachings on loving enemies embrace both private and corporate enemies.

This can be clarified by reflecting on what Jesus meant when he said, "You have heard that it was said, 'Love your neighbor and hate your enemy'" (Matt 5:43). The other quotations he gives are all from the Old Testament, but there is no corresponding law instructing hatred: on the contrary, Moses' law enjoined kindness to one's Jewish enemies—such as in Exodus: "If you come across your enemy's ox or donkey wandering off, be sure to return it" (Exod 23:4). A Jew hearing this would likely have thought immediately of national enemies. As the Philistine-slayer David said in Psalm 139:21–22, "Do I not hate those who hate you, LORD . . . I count them my enemies." Likewise, the exiled Israelites indulged in

5. Cavanaugh, *Myth of Religious Violence*, ch. 3.
6. Horsley, *Jesus and the Spiral of Violence*, xi.

murderous fantasies about killing the children of Babylonians in revenge for their exile in Psalm 137:8–9: "Daughter Babylon, doomed to destruction . . . happy is the one who seizes your infants and dashes them against the rocks." Earlier, the book of Numbers enjoined Israel to "treat the Midianites as enemies," which meant to "kill them" (Num 25:17). When Jesus refers to hating enemies, he is probably referring to the Old Testament attitude and practice of violence against Israel's national rivals.

Jesus Christ claimed that he came not to abolish the law but to fulfill it (Matt 5:17), and one of the ways that he did this was by ruling out exceptions. Moses' law contained compromises with human nature. Thus, as we saw in chapter 2, the seventh commandment against adultery was compromised by the permission of divorce, which Jesus said Moses only gave because of the hardness of our hearts (Matt 19:8). Jesus abolished this exception, thus fulfilling the law. The ninth commandment against lying was compromised by the existence of oaths, allowing people to think they could be less than honest at certain times: so Jesus repudiated this exception (Matt 5:33–37). The sixth commandment against killing had numerous exceptions, too, which Jesus likewise repudiated, even in regard to national enemies—be they Midianites, Babylonians, Romans, or, I suggest, Germans, Russians, Iraqis, Afghans, Britons, and Americans. Killing the enemies of one's state was no longer an option for God's people: they had to be loved.

The idea that the New Testament can be divided between private morality (which does apply to us) and political/public morality (which does not apply) depoliticizes the significance of Jesus Christ. It confines him to private areas of our lives and excludes him as irrelevant from the big questions of our times. Why should this understanding of the Lord Jesus have arisen? Richard Horsley and Ronald Sider give two different but complementary answers to this question.

Horsley reckons that this depoliticization is uniquely connected to the influence of modern Western individualism on our understanding of the Bible. It is, he suggests, due to Western assumptions about "religion" and "politics" as separate spheres and to a Western individualism that sees Jesus as a private figure dealing with individuals not groups. He also points to the particular scientific orientation of liberal Western scholars, who reduced Jesus to a purveyor of wise sayings by sifting out anything not considered reasonable.[7]

7. Horsley, introduction to *Jesus and Empire*.

Ronald Sider and Richard Taylor suggest that it is the influence of liberalism in eroding our understanding of the church that is responsible for the idea of a dualism between private and public morality. They focus on the work of Reinhold Niebuhr, an important US public theologian in the first half of the twentieth century. His best-known book, *Moral Man and Immoral Society*, contends that individuals are less selfish and wicked than social groups.[8] He regards the church as an example of a social group—and like any group it is unable to practice Jesus' ethics about enemy love. Sider and Taylor believe that herein lies the problem with his work: Niebuhr's "church" is not Jesus' new, Spirit-filled, messianic community but simply another human institution. They write, "In Niebuhr's thought, the church is a weak, pale reflection of the Spirit-filled New Testament community of transformed believers; the kingdom is entirely transcendent and future; and the Holy Spirit is almost nonexistent. Does this not smack of liberalism?"[9]

Sider and Taylor contend that this is why Niebuhr does not believe that the church can put Jesus' teachings into practice. But people said of the early church, "See how they love one another."[10] Christians can and should live in the Spirit, not the flesh—in their homes, at work, in the marketplace, and in international spheres. This is because they have been delivered from the dominion of the old age into the kingdom of his beloved Son (Col 1:13); they have access to a power that no other social group does. Of course, sin still lingers in our fallen world. Paul never argued that because this sin lingers it is acceptable for Christians to fornicate, lie, and steal. Why then should it be acceptable to choose to ignore the New Testament teaching on loving our enemies? Whereas Niebuhr said that Jesus' teaching on loving our enemies will not apply to Christians until the millennium, Sider and Taylor pointedly reply, "We do not believe that God intends Christians to wait until the millennium to obey the Sermon on the Mount."[11]

We should also be suspicious of the political motives of those who argue that Christian morality is for the private sphere, not the public sphere. In January 1934, Reich Bishop Müller issued a decree that he pretended was needed to restore order in the German Evangelical Church,

8. Niebuhr, *Moral Man and Immoral Society*

9. Sider and Taylor, *Nuclear Holocuast and Christian Hope*, 179.

10. Tertullian, *Apology* 39.7.

11. Sider and Taylor, *Nuclear Holocaust and Christian Hope*, 132.

many of whose pastors were growingly critical of Nazism as unchristian. This decree became known as the "Muzzling Order," because it forbade ministers to say anything in their sermons about the church controversy. Müller ordered churchmen to preach nothing but "the pure gospel." This was resisted by theologians such as Karl Barth, who insisted that the gospel *is* political. The British evangelical tradition of social reform— epitomized by reformers like William Wilberforce (see below, ch. 5)—has always rejected the contention that there are separate spheres of public and private morality and that the gospel does not speak to public sphere morality.

The idea that the Lord Jesus taught "private" not "public/political" morality is a politically dubious reading back onto the scriptures of Western philosophical and sociological assumptions and an associated liberal theology. Evangelicals must reject these modern, Western, liberal interpretations of the Bible, while at the same time not confusing the church for a peace movement or similar. The argument that Jesus' teachings were intended for our private lives only is impossible to sustain from scripture. If Christianity is true, we cannot privatize it into a separate compartment of our lives for Sundays and "quiet times" and say that it does not work in other spheres of life. The Bible has the very truths that a warring world needs to hear—truths about how to live our entire lives in the world God has given us. And he has given the church all the spiritual power it needs to live out the "gospel of peace" as testimony to the salvation achieved by Christ on the cross.

Haven't Circumstances Changed?

A cousin of the argument that Jesus taught only "personal morality" is that the circumstances facing Christians today are so different from those facing our Lord that the New Testament opposition to warfare does not apply to us. This is an argument commonly made over the past 150 years by liberal theologians. One example is Albert Schweitzer in his early twentieth-century book, *The Quest of the Historical Jesus*. Schweitzer argued that Jesus taught a radical "emergency" or "interim ethic" for the time between his day and the inauguration of the kingdom of God. As this did not happen as quickly as he thought, so the argument goes, the impractical injunctions of radical teaching such as the Sermon on the

Mount (Matt 5–7) and the Sermon on the Plain (Luke 6) are no longer binding on Christians.[12]

That circumstances have changed since the time of Christ is undeniable. Christians of every age are called to reconsider with prayerful imagination what the teachings of our Lord say to the new issues of that day. But the suggestion that Christ and the earlier Christians did not anticipate a time that would make those teachings unworkable should be anathema to any Bible-believing Christian. Scripture was given by the God who sees the end from the beginning. In his defense of scripture as the more authoritative guide to Christian conduct than church tradition and the writings of theologians, the late eighteenth-/early nineteenth-century Newcastle preacher James Murray said in his *Sermons to Asses*, "It has been often affirmed, that our circumstances are much altered since the times of Christ and his Apostles, which is an undoubted truth; but this does not, I hope, infer that the laws of Christ's kingdom have undergone any alteration."[13]

The Model Soldier?

For all our democratic leanings, our modern culture is one of hero worship. Children play with toys and computer games of their favorite superheroes from film or sport, teenagers pin posters of pop stars on their walls, and adults buy magazines with the latest celebrity gossip. Christians avidly read biographies of reformers, saints, missionaries, or martyrs. In doing this, we imply that we not only admire these people, but approve of their lives.

Exactly the same argument has been made to justify Christian involvement in warfare. After all, didn't John the Baptist, the Lord Jesus, and the Apostle Paul either personally admire some soldiers or at least assume that their military profession was compatible with following God? This has been argued by Chris Seiple. Seiple, a former Marine, is president of the US-based Institute for Global Engagement, an exciting Christian organization that promotes interreligious dialogue and peacebuilding. He is also an advocate of Christian participation in the military

12. I have relied for this argument on Stein, *Method and Message*, 97–98.

13. J. Murray, *Sermons to Asses*, 10. My thanks to Alastair Bonnett for bringing this rare text to my attention.

and of just war theory (see ch. 5), although one who is careful not to claim that the Bible unambiguously and definitely teaches that.

Seiple argues that because John the Baptist apparently told soldiers at baptism to be content with their lot (Luke 3:14), he therefore endorsed soldiering as a vocation for Christians today. However, all three pieces of counsel that Luke records John giving were about *economic* justice, probably chosen to frame Jesus' announcement of Jubilee themes in his "Nazareth sermon" in Luke 4. The identity of the "soldiers" is unclear. It seems unlikely they would have been Roman soldiers, because John's was a very Jewish movement for renewal of a Jewish nation at a time of crisis. They are more likely to have been temple guards, but that is not clear. Furthermore, as a prophet of the old covenant God made with Moses, John was preaching to people who had not yet entered the gospel era. In his book on John the Baptist in the context of contemporary Jewish activism, Robert Webb concludes that John's movement rejected violence, along the lines of some other prophetic renewal movements in Palestine at the time.[14]

Seiple lines this incident up with others in the New Testament that, he claims, cast a positive light on soldiering. He mentions Jesus' pleasure at the faith of a centurion (Luke 7:9), the conversion of fellow centurion Cornelius as the opening of the church to Gentiles (Acts 10:34), and reads Philippians 4:22 to mean that "Paul suggests that members of Caesar's Praetorian Guard had converted."[15] Seiple calls these references a "commentary" on the role of organized violence[16] and concludes that the "New Testament times were comfortable with the international order of the day and that the military had a natural place therein as the sustainer of it."[17] This is a bold claim, but Seiple's choice of texts is arguably too narrow and selective to support it. If so desired, the New Testament material can also be mined to tell another, darker story about the military. The Roman governor with his soldiers and the Jewish authorities with security guards subject to him are repeatedly shown as responsible for heinous injustices such as the "slaughter of the innocent" (Matt 2:13–18), the execution of the Baptist (Matt 14:1–12), the massacre of the Galileans (Luke 13:1), and the flogging, murder, and arbitrary arrests of the apostles (as recorded

---

14. Webb, *John the Baptizer and Prophet*, 62.

15. Seiple, "Wars and Rumors," 43.

16. Ibid.

17. Seiple, "Guns, Government, & God?"

throughout the Acts of the Apostles, e.g., 12:1–4). The most sustained description of the operation of the military is the graphic account of their arrest, humiliation, torture, and murder of Christ himself, which is the extended focus of each of the four gospels. Marshall argues that the New Testament bears eloquent testimony to the darker side of judicial power and violence. Quoting Acts 4:26–27, he stresses that followers of Jesus must reckon with the sobering fact that "the kings of the earth took their stand, and the rulers . . . gathered together against the Lord and against his Messiah," employing the full force of the finest judicial systems in the ancient world, backed by military power, to do away with him.[18] Taking Seiple's logic in a different direction, one could argue that as the portrayal of the military in the Gospels is overwhelmingly negative, this is an argument against the military being an acceptable profession for followers of Jesus. That would be abusing the text, however, because in reality, none of these passages is primarily about soldiering and the military. There is no "commentary" on warfare in the New Testament, and certainly not one that presents the military in a positive light.

He Never Said *Not* to . . .

> There was a young man from Ealing,
> Who sat on the bus to Darjeeling;
> It said on the door,
> "Don't spit on the floor,"
> So he stood up and spat on the ceiling!

Over the years, I have enjoyed hearing about outrageous claims for damages made in courts. I imagine that most of these are either gross distortions or "urban myths," but they nonetheless act as a critique of the perceived extent to which the law can be used to absurd ends. My favorite example is of a woman who allegedly sued the manufacturers of a tumble dryer for not explicitly stating in the instructions that her pet cat should not be (safely) dried off in it! Much as we might sympathize with the distraught pet owner, we cannot help feeling that the claim is somewhat disingenuous: we assume that any sensible person would not do what she did, and realize that no one can legislate for every possibility. And we also know that for cases like the objectionable man from Ealing, it is

18. Marshall, *Beyond Retribution*, 8.

impossible to preempt the person who is determined to evade the spirit of the law by a cunning misinterpretation of its letter. We instinctively know that there is something dishonest and disingenuous about "the argument from silence," that is, the claim that something is allowed and good because it is not explicitly condemned.

Unfortunately, Christians have not always been free of the same tendency when handling scripture. For example, that some slave owners in the Bible were referred to in positive lights was used as an argument for slavery by nineteenth-century Christians in the United States.[19] The "argument from silence" should always be treated with suspicion.

The same "argument from silence" has sometimes been used by Christians attempting to justify Christian participation in warfare. The classic texts used in this way relate to two centurions in the New Testament. In Luke 7 Jesus is amazed at the unnamed centurion who recognizes Jesus' authority: Jesus holds his faith up as the best instance in Israel. In Acts 10, the centurion Cornelius is held up as a true worshipper of God and the first named Gentile convert. Brearley observes that neither Jesus nor the apostles told these people to leave the army and suggests this is an endorsement of the military profession for followers of Jesus.[20]

This "argument from silence" is a weak one. In general terms, there are many activities that Jesus did not explicitly condemn but that we can understand from the broad thrust of New Testament teaching would be unchristian (for example, rape, bribery, and extortion). It would be a very unsound principle to argue that apparent silence on an issue assumes positive moral approval.

Returning more specifically to the centurion of great faith, it is true that Jesus did not condemn his soldiering. But equally we do not know that he did not condemn his soldiering: much more might have occurred in exchanges between them than is recorded in the text. We know nothing of his later life: whether he became a follower of Jesus, continued soldiering, or eventually left the military after working through his newfound convictions. Nor do we know whether he wasn't part of the detachment that arrested Jesus when his former supporters turned against him.

Such speculation where the text is silent is fruitless. As a Gentile, he would not even have been a candidate for joining Jesus' group of

19. Clark, *Does the Bible Teach Pacifism?*
20. Brearley, *Does God Approve of War?*, 88–89.

disciples, so the question of what he had to do to become a follower of Christ was not a real one.

The military occupation is not the theme of this passage. It is the man's faith, not his profession, that Jesus praises. The man himself is not even named and is important only in so far as he demonstrates true faith—and glaringly shows up the lack of it in Jesus' enemies among the Jewish religious leaders. In this context, the use of a Roman soldier is a masterful way to force the point he is making. Jesus used social anathema such as prostitutes, tax collectors, and Samaritans to illustrate his message of the kingdom, but in no way does this suggest he approved of their actions. For his Jewish hearers, Roman soldiers were similarly beyond the pale: not only Gentiles, but the very defilers of God's holy land and the oppressors of his people. What better way to illustrate the lack of true faith in Israel?

If Brearley and others are to make an argument from silence about his soldiering, they must also be consistent in considering aspects of being a centurion. As a man of this rank he would almost certainly have owned slaves—and probably would have used female slaves as concubines. Can we assume that Jesus' failure to condemn that is approval? If arguments for Christian soldiering, or Christian slavery, or Christian concubinage have to be based on what Jesus *didn't* say, then those arguments must be regarded as being very weak, even desperate. Jesus repeatedly and frequently condemned the desired use of violence by his disciples, enunciating universal principles about "putting away the sword" and imitating God's bountiful love to us by loving our enemies unreservedly. The apostles faithfully passed this on in their epistles, providing rigorous theological arguments grounded in the doctrine of justification by faith, as we saw in chapter 1. The New Testament is clear that followers of Christ were not to take the only route to political violence open to them and take up arms against their enemies, but were to love them.

This argument from silence is akin to the argument that the Bible has nothing to say about war, because the church should not mix with politics. Such a view is as dangerous as it is unbiblical, because it allows corrupt rulers to escape being held to account by God's standards. It is also the refrain of tyrants down the centuries. For example, in 1626, when the Chilean Synod of Santiago excommunicated slave traders, it was accused by the Spanish crown of meddling in business outside its competence.[21]

21. Cavanaugh, *Torture and the Eucharist,* 254.

In 1934, the Nazis' so-called Muzzling Order forbade German ministers from discussing political controversies in their sermons, ordering them to preach nothing but "the pure gospel." South African ministers were told not to question apartheid in their sermons. The list goes on. The view that Christianity should not address violent social problems like slavery, war, and racism is a great error. It is an error that hinges on the modern distinction between "religion" and "politics" that was unknown to biblical writers. Martin Lloyd-Jones criticizes the view that the Bible is "exclusively a textbook of personal salvation." That is doubtless one of its central themes, he says in a sermon on why God allows war to occur, but "ultimately the main message of the Bible concerns the condition of the entire world and its destiny. . . . That is why it starts with the creation of the world rather than the creation of man."[22] If war is our age's scourge, the gospel is its solution—as it is the diagnosis and remedy of all sin.

What's in a Metaphor?

The Apostle Paul sometimes used martial metaphors to depict the spiritual struggle of the Christian life—in 2 Timothy 2, for example, and in his famous discourse on "the whole armor of God" in Ephesians 6. As Paul wrote some of his letters while in prison, where his guards were Roman soldiers, they were an immediate source of suggestive imagery. A friend of mine once said that Paul's use of martial metaphors shows that he was comfortable with the military, and that is "significant" as a justification for Christian participation in warfare. However, this is a simple misunderstanding of the function of language. A metaphor is, by definition, *not* meant to be taken literally: it uses a commonly understood image to explain something entirely different, and goes no further. Anyone who assumes that use of a metaphor meant literal approval of the original image, to be consistent, would run into all sorts of problems in interpreting other passages of scripture. The Bible illustrates spiritual realities with images of a drunken man arising from a stupor (Ps 78:65), a dishonest judge who needs badgering for results (Luke 18:6), a corrupt master who reaps where he does not sow (Luke 19:20), and a thief in the night (Matt 24:43). Yet it would be absurd to suggest that the Bible thus commends alcoholism, judicial corruption, looting, or nocturnal theft! These are

22. Lloyd-Jones, *From Fear to Faith*, 9.

used to illustrate spiritual truths—fearing the wrath of God, the power of prayer, the importance of being prepared for the return of Christ, etc.

Paul himself, a man who reveled in language, enjoyed metaphors, which he drew from the contexts that people of his day understood—such as farming, sport, and soldiering (all in 2 Tim 2:3–6). But he intended them only to serve as metaphors. For example, in Philippians 3:12–14, he compares the Christian life to a race, the prize being everlasting life. However, this metaphor only works so far—only one person wins a race, but many attain to the life eternal. In the rest of the letter, he makes it clear that he wants as many of the Philippians as possible to also "win" that race. If this metaphor were to be read as a prescription for real life, then it would have to be taken as an endorsement of noncompetitive sports, of awarding equal prizes to everyone who manages to finish!

This is of course ridiculous, yet that is precisely what those who argue for soldiering being a profession acceptable to Christianity on the basis of military metaphors do. Paul compares the Christian to a soldier in some circumstances, when he wants to stress values such as determination in the face of attacks of the devil and single-minded devotion to the cause of the gospel. The use of metaphors is not an endorsement of soldiering, athleticism, animal husbandry, drunkenness, dishonesty, or whatever, no more than it is a disapproval of them: it is a linguistic device and ought to be recognized as such. In case anyone really should misunderstood his use of soldiering metaphors, Paul insisted with the utmost clarity that "although we live in the world, we do *not* wage war as the world does. The weapons we fight with are *not* the weapons of this world" (2 Cor 10:3–4).

Thus, the use of military metaphors implies no positive endorsement of the military. In fact, it may be that these metaphors actually subvert military thinking. For example, using a military metaphor, the writer of the Epistle to the Hebrews calls Christ "the captain of their salvation" (Heb 2:10). Yet, exactly opposite to a military leader, he was made "perfect through sufferings," gaining victory over his enemies by surrendering to them. Certainly, some values of a soldier—endurance, loyalty, obedience, and the like—are to be emulated. But perhaps we can redeem these abilities and use them for good instead of evil. Indeed, "much of Paul's key terminology is borrowed from and turned back against imperial discourse."[23] Thus, for Rome, Caesar was the "savior"

23. Horsley, *Jesus and Empire*, 133.

who by his armies had brought "salvation" and "peace" to the world, and in whom people were meant to have "faith" as their "Lord," honored and celebrated in the assemblies (*ecclesiae*) of cities such as Philippi, Corinth, and Ephesus. Paul was depicting Jesus as the alternative or real emperor of the world.[24] His use of military language and metaphors in doing this underlines how radically different Jesus' kingdom was from the empire of Caesar, an empire that was upheld by armed force. To think that by using a metaphor the New Testament endorses the literal reality is to display a basic inability to grasp the rules of language. To use martial metaphors to endorse militarism is to do what Hoover accuses World War I theologians of doing in finding arguments that the British or German cause was one God approved of: it is to rummage "through the Bible irresponsibly, tearing passages from their contexts, wresting statements to the destruction of a sound hermeneutic."[25]

Prayer and Personal Revelation

The leader of a significant mission organization once told me that although his reading of scripture was such that he could not "imagine a position where God could authorize the use of force," he would remain open to the "direction of the Holy Spirit" to the contrary. For evangelicals who regard scripture as the clearest form of the revelation of the Holy Spirit to us, the idea that insights gleaned through private prayer could trump scripture is disturbing. Prophecy must be tested (1 John 4:1), and the chief test is "the law and the testimony," namely, scripture (Isa 8:20 KJV).

Quite apart from that crucial principle, the history of the church is filled with a melancholy series of incidents of individuals using "prayerful discernment" to confirm conclusions and prejudices they held from elsewhere. A suitably grisly example is the slaughter of Connecticut Pequot Indians by the English in 1636. A disreputable English trader was killed by unknown assailants. The English blamed the Pequots, without evidence, and used it as opportunity to destroy the tribe and seize control of a lucrative bead trade. Whereas Native American warfare was based on tactical skirmishes that avoided much killing, the English strategy was calculated genocide. They surrounded the Indian camp and burned it

---

24. Ibid., 134.

25. Hoover, *God, Germany, and Britain*, 133.

down, shooting or stabbing the men, women, and children who managed to flee the inferno. Most of the five hundred people inside were killed. Two months later, the English pursued refugees into swamps, where they surrendered. The men were bound and thrown to their deaths in the ocean, while the women and children were enslaved. An English officer, Captain Underhill, scorned the pleas of his shocked Indian allies to grant mercy to the vanquished foe. Prominent Puritan preacher Increase Mather emphasized the power of prayer in the victory, and wrote of the destruction of the camp, "The Lord burnt them up in the fire of his wrath, and dunged the ground with their flesh, it was the Lord's doing, and it was marvelous to our eyes."[26]

It is easy with hindsight to look back and condemn such obscenities. But had Mather depended on the careful interpretation of scripture, rather than his own interpretation of God's actions, he would not have reached the conclusion that he did. It is frequently dangerous and always inadmissible for Christians to claim private revelation in order to override the teaching of scripture. Had the church maintained the New Testament condemnation of the use of violence, the shameful oceans of blood that can be reckoned to its account would not have been spilled.

Not Peace, but Swords?

In January 2010 a political storm occurred when it was revealed that gunsights widely used by the US and UK militaries in wars in Iraq and Afghanistan were inscribed with biblical passages. One inscription on the Advanced Combat Optical Gunsight, used on the Sharpshooter rifle, read "JN8:12," a reference to the Lord Jesus' statement in John's Gospel, "I am the light of the world." The US-based manufacturer, Trijicon, which was founded by a devout Christian, defended this practice by saying that the company runs to "biblical standards" and that it engraves scriptures on its weaponry "as part of our faith and our belief in service to our country."[27]

What the rifle is to the twentieth-century soldier, the sword was to his first-century counterpart. The Gospel accounts contain two of our Lord's sayings about "swords," which proponents of Christian participation in

26. Shapiro, *Violent Cartographies*, 4–7.
27. BBC, "Gunsights' Biblical References Concern US and UK Forces," January 20, 2010, http://news.bbc.co.uk/go/pr/fr/-/1/hi/world/americas/8468981.stm.

warfare have used to make their case. The first is Matthew 10:34, when the Lord Jesus said, "I did not come to bring peace, but a sword." Thomas Aquinas uses this text to justify Christian participation in warfare against what he terms an "evil peace."[28]

This is, frankly, shocking biblical exegesis. As Martin Lloyd-Jones writes on this verse, "When our Lord said that, he did not mean that he had come into the world to make nations fight one another. Of course not!"[29] In the following verses, the Lord Jesus explains that this means turning members of the same family against each other (vv. 35 and 36), so that "anyone who loves his father or mother more than me is not worthy of me" (v. 37). The context was increasing divisions among the Jews over the claims of Jesus, and Jesus' insistence that they must choose between him and everything else they hold dear if it should come between them. It is metaphorical: about setting priorities, and showing how allegiance to him must come before even cherished family bonds. Jesus was saying that his new humanity would unite people from a wide variety of communities, inevitably dividing those communities. This is a glorious truth—the church breaks down family/tribal divides and, in Christ, unites former enemies. This may involve painful decisions. People from Muslim backgrounds, who are commonly disowned by their families and cold-shouldered by society when they decide to become followers of Jesus, are all too aware of how painfully true these words are. "Sword" is an apt metaphor for what they feel.

However, if "sword" here is not being used metaphorically, but is actually discussing the real use of fatal violence, then this argument must be made consistently. That would mean that this is not referring to organized political violence (warfare) but to the actual killing of biological family members, possibly in a brutal form of civil war. Nowhere is this preached in the Bible as a command to Christians. Indeed, Paul insists that "anyone who does not provide for their relatives, and especially for their own household, has denied the faith and is worse than an unbeliever" (1 Tim 5:8). The Lord and the epistle writers frequently refer to the Decalogue as a source of enduring authority,[30] which, of course, includes the command to honor one's father and mother. To suggest that Jesus was allowing his followers to partake in warfare is inadmissible from the text and makes a travesty of any coherent notion of biblical interpretation.

28. Thomas Aquinas, *Summa Theologica*, Question 40.

29. Lloyd-Jones, *Authentic Christianity*, 82.

30. Chantry, *God's Righteous Kingdom*.

The second passage in the gospels sometimes used to argue that
Jesus endorsed warfare is Luke 22:36, when Jesus said to his disciples, "If
you don't have a sword, sell your cloak and buy one." Loraine Boettner
uses this passage to make a case that it is legitimate for Christians to participate in warfare. This is difficult to imagine: does the Lord Jesus really
mean that two swords is "enough" (sufficient) for military resistance to
the Jewish authorities, and then sufficient to overcome the Roman gar-
rison in Jerusalem? Boettner argues that Jesus was advising his followers that they had better be armed to defend themselves on "missionary
journeys that they were to make over long distances and among hostile
people."[31] However, although the book of Acts devotes considerable space
to recording some of the disciples' long and dangerous missionary journeys, there is no evidence in it at all that they were ever armed.

These words have long puzzled and divided commentators, offering
explanations from those of Boettner's above to the argument that swords
were routinely carried by farmers and travelers to protect them from
wild animals. But the standard principle of interpretation is to explain
obscure texts in the light of clearer ones. In John 18:36 Jesus explicitly
told Pilate his disciples did not fight, and we saw in chapter 1 that Jesus'
kingdom movement was very different to armed contemporary ones.
More clearly, we know that when Peter did use a sword in self-defense
later that evening, Jesus rebuked him explicitly (Matt 26:52). Thus the
meaning is unlikely to be an endorsement of violence. As ever, we find
clarity by considering this verse in its immediate context. Commenting
on this passage, the nineteenth-century Evangelical Anglican Bishop J. C.
Ryle wrote, "It is safest to apply these remarkable words in a proverbial
sense."[32] He interpreted them as warning that the servant of Christ ought
to work hard to do the master's work, and expect trouble and hardship in
carrying it out. Tom Wright agrees: for him, Jesus was making one last effort to prepare his disciples for the hardship that would soon befall them.
Throughout his time with them, the disciples frequently misunderstood
his spiritual allusions and metaphors, and this continued right until this
point. In proffering two real swords, they failed to grasp that "sword"
indicated hardship. Thus when Jesus says, "That is enough!" according to

31. Boettner, *Christian Attitude to War*, 23.
32. Ryle, *Expository Thoughts on Luke*, 413.

Wright, "he is wearily putting a stop to the entire conversation, in which at every point they seem determined to misunderstand him."[33]

The word "sword" is used occasionally in the gospels to represent actual military action: the weapons of the men who came to arrest Jesus (Mark 14:43), and his warning that Jerusalem would suffer destruction if it did not adopt his way of peace (Luke 21:24). It is also used metaphorically to mean great anguish and trial. Thus, as Simeon prophesied over the infant Jesus when he was presented at the temple, he nonetheless warned the joyful Mary that "a sword will pierce your own soul too" (Luke 2:35). This was not a prophecy that she would be stabbed to death, but rather that her heart would be broken over her son—which, undoubtedly, was the case as she watched him bleeding to death on the cross. But in no case is the word "sword" used to allow Christian violence. When our Lord was arrested, one of his companions "reached for his sword, drew it out and struck the servant of the high priest" (Matt 26:51). Jesus emphatically commanded him to "put your sword back in its place . . . for all who draw the sword will die by the sword" (v. 52). Simply looking carefully and consistently at the context of each instance of the use of the word "sword" in the gospels dispels any idea that these passages endorse Christian use of lethal weapons against their enemies.

This was the position of the twentieth century's most influential Protestant proponent of the idea that Christians can fight in just wars, Reinhold Niebuhr. In his classic 1940 essay "Why the Christian Church Is Not Pacifist," he gave short shrift to those who argued the just war position from the life and teachings of Christ. "Nothing is more futile and pathetic," he wrote, than using scattered texts in the gospels about whips in temples, buying swords, bringing "not peace but a sword," and the like, to justify Christian participation in warfare.[34] As he put it, "What could be more futile than to build a whole ethical structure upon the exegetical issue whether Jesus accepted the sword with the words: 'It is enough,' or whether He really meant: 'Enough of this' (Luke 22:36)?"

We have seen throughout this chapter that scattered verses from the New Testament are sometimes taken out of context to make arguments for Christian participation in warfare. Such usage amply illustrates the wise old adage that a text without a context is a pretext. This has particularly been the case when discussing our Lord's metaphorical references to swords. But the most substantial and serious argument for Christian

33. T. Wright, *Luke for Everyone*, 226.
34. Niebuhr, *Why the Christian Church Is Not Pacifist*, 15–16.

involvement in warfare, and the one preferred by Niebuhr, is made from a passage that also uses the imagery of swords: Romans 13:1–6. We will consider that in the next section.

Romans 13: The Warrior's Proof Text?

At Michaelmas 1498, John Colet (1467–1519), Dean of St. Paul's Cathedral, delivered a series of lectures in Oxford on Romans 13:1–6. This was a landmark moment in biblical studies because Colet argued that an understanding of the context of the first-century Roman Empire was necessary to fully appreciate the message of Christ. He concluded that the passage showed traditional church teaching on "just war" was unfounded. Arguing that Romans 13 was rather an admonition for those living under tyranny not to rebel and thereby invite violent repression, he said,

> It is not by war that war is conquered, but by peace, and forbearance, and reliance on God. And in truth we see that by this virtue the apostles overcame the entire world. . . . This [peaceful contending with evil persons] was alone used by those first soldiers of the Church, who fought under the banner of Christ, and conquered gloriously.[35]

Colet's choice of Romans 13 to make the historic Christian argument against participation in warfare highlights the battle over this text. Ironically, Romans 12:14—13:6 has been championed by some as the proof text *against* Christian participation in warfare, and by others as the proof text that Christians *may* rightly take the sword in just wars or crusades. For example, in his introductory devotional commentary on this passage in the usually excellent Welwyn Commentary series, Stuart Olyott writes that a "career in the armed services is a most honorable task for a Christian man."[36] Such use of the passage has declined since the end of Nazi Germany, where churches used it to justify accommodation with the Hitler regime, but before that it had a long history of justifying various Christian wars. Indeed, Lee Griffiths claims that "it is the text that has been misused most often to justify Christian participation in horrendous bloodshed."[37] With such a checkered pedigree, before looking at what

---

35. Cited in Musto, *Catholic Peace Tradition*, 113.

36. Olyott, *Gospel as It Really Is*, 124.

37. Griffith, *War on Terrorism*, 33.

these six verses *do* argue, it is therefore as well to clear up a few historical misunderstandings by examining what they do *not* say.

What Romans 13 *Doesn't* Say

First, this passage is not considering war but the limited violence of the administration of civil justice. Paul's word that is rendered "sword" is *machaira*, a long dagger that was the symbol of the authority to administer justice, not of warfare.[38] Perhaps a modern British equivalent would be a policeman's truncheon, or the sword held by the famous scales of justice above London's High Court; a US example might be the bas-relief of Justice cradling a set of scales, seen on the base of a lamppost outside the Supreme Court Building in Washington DC.

Second, it does not suggest that Christians could or should be involved in the wielding of this "sword." Indeed, seen variously as members of a Jewish sect or a new upstart religion, Christians would have been at the margins of the governing authorities, and more commonly its victims. Rome did not consider its subject peoples as being obliged to offer military or police service. There is no indication that Paul considers the possibility that his readers would have been at anything other than the receiving end of this "sword." John Howard Yoder argues that Paul's letter to the Romans assumes Christians cannot wield the sword. In Romans 12:19 Christians are told never to exercise vengeance but to leave that to God, and in Romans 13:4 the authorities are identified as exercising that function which the Christian was to leave for God. Thus, the vengeance or wrath of God displayed in the sword of the state is recognized as that function which Christians were explicitly told *not* to exercise.[39] However, by the same token it should be observed that Paul does not explicitly rule out the possibility that Christians could wield this sword: it was probably his assumption that his readers were not wielding it.

Third, Romans 13 does not teach us that we must obey everything that the ruling authorities insist upon, including our participation in their exercise of violence. If this were the case, the apostles who declared to the Sanhedrin that they would obey God not humans (Acts 4:18–20) would have been in error. Likewise, Paul's insistence to Timothy that there is only one God (1 Tim 2:5) would have brought him into conflict with an

38. J. H. Yoder, *Politics of Jesus*, 203–4.
39. Ibid., 198.

empire where worship of the Roman gods and the emperor himself was part of state practice. From the Israelite midwives in Egypt who resisted and deceived the Pharaoh's order to kill baby boys (Exod 1), to Daniel and his friends in Babylon refusing to obey immoral laws and worship state power (Dan 3 and 6), the Bible holds up various godly individuals who disobeyed state power when it was exercised contrary to God's will.

Fourth, this text does not explicitly state that God approves of the actions of the authorities as they wield the sword. The Roman Empire was brutal and savage, killing many Christians—including apostles. Paul is under no illusions about this. Indeed, his reference to the authorities as God's "servant" echoes the Old Testament depictions of Babylonian warrior-king Nebuchadnezzar as "my servant" (Jer 43:10), the blood-thirsty Assyrian hordes poised to sack Israel as "the rod of my anger" (Isa 10:5), and Persian conqueror Cyrus (Isa 44:28) as God's "Shepherd." These were godless, wicked, bloodthirsty, and imperial tyrants whose violence against Israel and Judah is held up in the Psalms as the epitome of evil (for example, Ps 137) and who themselves came under God's judgment for the very violence that God used to chasten Israel (Jer 25:12). The prophets were in no way suggesting that God approved of what these men did, but simply that even the worst of tyrants cannot escape God's providential overrulings. The authorities that exist have been "lined up, used by God in the ordering of his cosmos"—as Yoder puts it, no more suggesting that God approves their actions than a librarian does the books that she is shelving.[40]

Fifth, it does not teach us to do whatever the government tells us, including fight in its armies. We are certainly to be subordinate to the powers and authorities, but Yoder terms this type of submission a "revolutionary subordination."[41] We are not to submit to the state's demand to worship the emperor or to refrain from worshipping or preaching Christ; but we are to be subordinate to the punishment that this disobedience will entail, and not rise up in violence against it. Paul himself provided a clear example of putting this into practice. The last section of the book of Acts contains an account of Paul's trials before various Roman authorities, some of whom were obviously corrupt (Acts 24:26). Paul subordinated himself to the process, cooperating with the trials, addressing with respect those judging him (Acts 26:1–3), and seeking to use their legal

40. Ibid., 202.
41. Ibid., chs. 9 and 10.

procedures such as an appeal to the emperor (Acts 25:11) and asserting his rights as a citizen (Acts 22:25) to procure justice. Vernard Eller
suggests that by subordinating themselves to Roman justice—even when
it was manifestly unjust and subjecting Christ and his followers to violence—Jesus and Paul were in fact demonstrating love of their enemies.[42]

Sixth, it does not give us "a theory of the state"—a blueprint of how
it should operate or of how Christians should relate to it. This is a term
used by political scientists to describe the basis on which state power is
organized and operates. John Moses, former Dean of St. Paul's Cathedral
and a man much experienced in thinking and working through the relationship of the church and the state, concludes that the New Testament
contains no "theory of the state."[43] He claims there is an "ambivalence" in
the pattern of Jesus' ministry on the question of how his followers are to
relate to the ruling authorities—only a handful of scattered verses, such as
Jesus' enigmatic comments on paying taxes (Matt 22:15–22). Elsewhere,
Paul (e.g., in Rom 13) was not thinking about "constitutional or juridical
questions" about church and state, but was rather pastorally concerned
with helping his readers work out what it meant to follow Jesus in their
own contexts.[44]

Indeed, from the perspective of a political theorist coming at the
scriptures, the historical emphasis placed on six verses in Romans 13 as a
single edifice to build a theory of the state is remarkable. Other New Testament passages that could equally be used as a basis for "a theory of the
state" paint a very different picture. For example, Matthew 4:8–9 suggests
that the state is controlled by Satan, not Christ. In Revelation 13, writes
John Stott, "The state is no longer seen as the servant of God, wielding his
authority, but as the ally of the devil."[45] The New Testament paints a grim
picture of the exercise of state power, with the police repeatedly shown to
be responsible for murders of righteous individuals or mass slayings of
the innocent (for example, Matt 2:16; Luke 13:1). The New Testament's
most sustained description of the operation of the enforcement powers
of the state is the account, found in all four gospels, of the arrest, trial,
torture, and execution of Christ. The finest judicial systems of the ancient
world are shown employing their full power to do away with the righ-

42. Eller, *Christian Anarchy*, 196–204.
43. Moses, *Broad and Living Way*, ch. 3, "Theories of Church and State."
44. Ibid., 34–36.
45. Stott, *Message of Romans*, 343.

teous Messiah.[46] Their mistreatment and torture of the Son of God are portrayed in unsettling detail, in more than five hundred verses. These texts need to be held alongside each other, yet a handful of verses from Romans 13 have, without warrant, been prioritized as representing some theory of the state.

Sixth, this passage does not refer to the "international" or war-making capacity and activities of a given authority. It is about that authority conducting affairs in its own territories. It is not about war with other authorities. That is not to say that it cannot legitimately be extended to that topic, but simply that Paul does not do that here; it is not what he was considering.

Lastly, this passage does not justify rebellion or invasions to overthrow unjust rulers. Some theologians have argued that this passage does not ordain a particular government as such, but the idea of proper government. By extension, when a government ceases to govern properly, Christians can wage armed rebellion against it. Variations of this perspective can be seen from the Zwingli and Calvin strand of the Reformation, through Oliver Cromwell and the American Revolution, to anticolonial liberation thought in the twentieth century. However, there is nothing in the text itself to support this argument.

Romans 13:1–6 is therefore not about war, nor does it endorse the activities it describes as suitable for Christians to participate in. So, what *is* it about?

What Romans 13 *Does* Say

We have seen that in Romans 13:1–6 Paul is presenting neither a "theory of the state" to please political scientists, an argument for Christian participation in warfare to please just war theorists, nor a pamphlet to enable the ardent revolutionary or military coup plotter to know when he should strike. It does not permit us to declare who is God's choice for an election. It does not suggest that God approves of certain governments and disapproves of other ones, nor does it indicate that Christians should take part in the retributive system. Like the bottom of an ancient ship that has become so covered with barnacles that the hull can hardly be seen, this little text has been encrusted with all of these readings and more that have been added to it over the centuries.

46. Marshall, *Beyond Retribution*, 8.

So what message *does* it give us? It tells us that no earthly power escapes God's overruling sovereignty, that he orders the earthly authorities to bring about justice on the earth, and that Christians are not to hinder this process but are to submit to it, for conscience's sake.

As John Colet realized five centuries ago, the context in which Paul was writing is crucial to grasping his meaning. Jews were increasingly restive under Roman rule, with seething resentment feeding the violent revolutionary movements whose tactics the Lord Jesus had warned Jerusalem from following (see ch. 1, p. 5 onward). The expulsion of Jews from Rome (Acts 18:2), the city to which Paul was writing, might have been part of this dynamic. They are not to assume that because Christ will return soon they can dismiss the structures of administration. They are not to assume that because God is greater than Caesar they can disregard the governance of Caesar. Writing to Christians in Rome, Paul may well be warning them not to revolt as the Jews in Palestine did. "Paul's basic purpose," write Sider and Taylor, "was to make sure that Christians in Rome exercised nonretaliatory love toward hostile government officials" at a time of persecution.[47]

Vernard Eller makes this argument pointedly. He reminds us that it is important to remember that the chapter divisions are medieval insertions not part of the original letters. He observes that Romans 13:1–8 is part of a passage that begins in Romans 12:14.[48] In that part of Romans 12, Paul repeatedly urges his readers to love their enemies and live in peace with all, not being overcome by evil but overcoming evil with good (vv. 14–21). This is his main topic. Then he introduces the "governing authorities," in Romans 13:1, as "an example of those to whom it will be most difficult to make the obligation apply—but whom God nevertheless commands us to love, even when our natural propensity most strongly urges us to hate, resist and fight them." As we saw in chapter 1, the Roman authorities brutalized the Jewish people, including Jewish followers of Jesus. So "Paul is using the governing authorities as a test case of our loving the enemy—even when doing so is repugnant to our innate moral sensibilities." Jewish followers of Jesus are not to fight a just war or humanitarian intervention against their repugnant enemy but to emulate Jesus by loving them and submitting to their rule.

47. Sider and Taylor, *Nuclear Holocaust and Christian Hope,* 169.

48. Eller's discussion of Romans 12:14—13:8, and the quotes in this paragraph, can be found in Eller, *Christian Anarchy,* 196–204.

If this reading is correct, there is thus no suggestion in Romans 12–13 that Paul is "legitimizing" Roman or any other rule, no more so (as we saw above) than Isaiah and Jeremiah saw the tyrannies of God's "servants" Nebuchadnezzar or Cyrus as "legitimate" or especially backed and blessed by God. Nor is there any hint that Christians should take part in the administration of the criminal justice system, even less so in warfare. Rather, as far as it serves higher ends, they are to submit to the exercise of "the sword," for conscience's sake. It is ironic that this text has been given the opposite meaning and made what Yoder calls "the classic proof for the duty of Christians to kill."[49] This has only been possible by removing it from its context and attaching to it a whole range of unwarranted assumptions and theories. If it is the classic text used in support of Christian participation in the military, it is also the classic illustration of the old adage that a text without a context is a pretext!

Conclusion: A Simple Choice

Rhondda Williams, minister of Union Church, Brighton, during the First World War, wrote that although individual people may reach different conclusions about the rightness or wrongness of some particular conflict, "The relation of the Christian ethic to war admits to my mind of no controversy. . . . [War] is the antithesis of Christianity."[50] In his services he refused to curse the Germans or pray for victory. He recorded that many soldiers attended his services during the war, afterwards some of them writing to him that "the Union church service was the one thing they looked forward to all the week, the one bright spot in the troubles of the time." Throughout the war, Williams "kept the antinomy between Christianity and war, and maintained that nothing could ever reconcile them." This tension existed, he argued, because even if the cause that took you to war is just, "war means that you must, if you can, deal out more destruction to your enemy than he can deal out to you—that, surely, is the antithesis of Christianity."[51] In contrast, the twentieth century's most influential Protestant proponent of the idea that Christians can fight in just wars was Reinhold Niebuhr. He had earlier advocated liberal pacifism, which he had rejected by the time of World War II as he came to see

49. J. H. Yoder, *Politics of Jesus,* 202–3.

50. Rhondda Williams, *How I Found My Faith,* 172–73.

51. Ibid.

how naïve it was. By 1940, he wrote that the ethical teaching of Jesus was "absolute and uncompromising" and leaves no space for violence—in a text that then went on to argue that it was not "immediately applicable" to modern Christians.[52] I think Niebuhr was wrong that Jesus' teachings do not apply to us: he reached that conclusion on the basis of particular theories of international politics that were popular at the time. He went from one extreme (pacifism) to the other (just war theory), in each case by making the classic mistake of interpreting the Bible through the culture of his own age, rather than interpreting his age through the Bible. Nonetheless, it is significant that the man who wrote the most influential attack in recent times on the idea that warfare is incompatible with Christianity unequivocally accepted that this was the position taught and lived by the Lord Jesus himself.

Indeed, it is impossible to take a consistent evangelical approach to biblical interpretation and yet still use the New Testament to justify exchanging our crosses for swords. You can have war or Christianity, but not both. People who reach the opposite conclusion generally do so because they start with the unacknowledged assumption that violence is regrettably necessary in a chaotic world. In effect, they say that the way of Christ could not possibly work in what they consider to be "the real world." Such reasoning is informed more by the culture in which they live, and particular theories of power and international politics, than by scripture. This has been one of the greatest dangers facing the church throughout the ages.

But the New Testament teaches us to see reality differently. Christ and the apostles commanded us to love our enemies and refuse to use violence on them, as the "gospel of peace" builds a kingdom uniting people from all nations and demonstrating kingdom values of justice, peace, and joy in the Holy Ghost (Rom 14:17). The church is an alternative peacemaking community to the warring powers and authorities. We are presented with a straight choice: accept the teachings of Christ in their totality, or reject them as being insufficient to cope with the evil realities of our age. While the implications are tremendous, the choice is uncomplicated. As for me, I am with the Reverend Williams. On Easter Sunday 1918, the week he learned that his own precious son was killed in the slaughter of trench warfare, with churches on both sides proclaiming that theirs was a "just war" (see page 96 onward), he preached a sermon

52. Niebuhr, *Why the Christian Church Is Not Pacifist*, 15–16.

restating New Testament gospel peace, titled "The Life-Giving God, a Greater Reality than the Death-Dealing Forces of the World."[53]

53. Rhondda Williams, *How I Found My Faith*, 174–75.

4

Hasn't the Church Allowed Soldiering? Part I
The Early Church

But as in a dream
Which one partly controls, I shrink
From an unholy church and all
Its accretions; I rebound, I
Contrive to circumnavigate
Its monstrous, twisted edifice.[1]

The scientist Henry Disney wrote the poem from which these words are taken after shooting a cat. Now, cats are no doubt loved by God as part of his creation, but nonetheless the reader may feel that these musings sound a little too anguished. The context, however, is important—he actually mistook the cat for an enemy guerrilla soldier while on night sentry duty. A former colleague of mine, he was conscripted as a young man into the British Army to put down an anticolonial uprising in Cyprus in the late 1950s, during one of the last gasps of the British Empire.

His opponents were Greek nationalists, aided and led by the Greek Orthodox Church. The British side was succored by Anglican chaplains. Sickened by such Christian support of violence, he turned against the church. Happily, he was later to regain his faith, minus the "accretions"— the unbiblical additions that allowed the church to justify warfare. Nonetheless, that opposing groups of warriors were succored by different branches of the church illustrates a major objection to the claim made throughout this book, that warfare is incompatible with the profession

1. "Faith under Fire," in Disney, *Lapsed Atheist and Other Poems.*

of Christian faith. Undoubtedly, as this example shows, the church *has* allowed and even at times encouraged warfare down through the ages. The Protestant tradition does not accept church teaching or tradition as more authoritative than scripture: nonetheless, the way in which the Holy Spirit has guided our forerunners in the faith to interpret scripture should not be dismissed lightly.

Although acknowledging through much of church history that the majority of churches have permitted their members to fight and kill in warfare, this chapter and the next show that this has not been universal. Far from it. Indeed, for centuries the early church resolutely opposed war and violence of all kinds, instead embracing the positive teaching and practice of gospel peace inherited from the apostolic church. This was to change as the Roman Catholic Church was co-opted by the late Roman Empire and invented "just war theory" to adapt to the new circumstances. This was a novel theology based on pagan ethical philosophy, and it enabled the church to allow its members to participate in the empire's wars. Although the church's embrace of "just war theory" increased its political influence in the short term, the effects of this move away from apostolic Christianity have been disastrous to the world, the church, and to the reputation of the gospel. This chapter will look at the how the early church taught and lived—and eventually abandoned—the gospel of peace. The next chapter will look at how gospel peace has increasingly reasserted itself since that time, and especially with the Reformation.

The Early Church

The historian Albert Marrin said that the Church of England's passionate support of the First World War inevitably raised the question whether Christians could kill their enemies. He stated that the early church fathers "would have had absolutely no difficulty answering this question. They would have denied absolutely that recourse to the sword was permissible to the follower of Christ."[2]

The early church was made up of imperfect people like us; its teaching and practice is not finally authoritative for us—scripture alone is. Nonetheless, the early church in its second and third generations was led by men who had been personally taught by the apostles and who lived in a world close to that in which Christian faith emerged. For example, in

2. Marrin, *Last Crusade*, 9.

the second century Irenaeus wrote that Christians "have changed their swords and their lances into instruments of peace, and they know not how to fight." Irenaeus was personally instructed in the faith by Polycarp, who in turn was discipled by John, the beloved disciple of Jesus Christ.[3]

Of particular significance is that, until the fourth century, the church was subject to legal persecution and exclusion from political power. It thus occupied the same marginal position that characterized the first followers of Christ. No major Christian writer approved of participation in warfare before the fourth century. On the contrary, all who wrote on the subject disapproved of the practice. As Ronald Bainton put it in his classic summary of the early church's position on warfare, "All of the outstanding writers of the East and West repudiated participation in warfare for Christians."[4]

The institution of warfare and Christian participation in it were unambiguously condemned by leaders and theologians of the early church. Lactantius (c. 240–c. 320) described Christians as "those who are ignorant of wars, who preserve concord with all, who are friends even to their enemies." "It will not be lawful for a just man to serve as a soldier," he declared, as "it is always unlawful to put to death a man, whom God willed to be a sacred animal."[5] Origen (c. 185–254) stated, "It was impossible for Christians to follow Mosaic law in killing their enemies."[6] Cyprian, who died approximately four years after Origen, equated war with murder and insisted that "the hand that has held the Eucharist must not be stained with blood and the sword." Asking rhetorically, "How will a Christian take part in war, nay, how will he serve even in peace?" Tertullian (c. 160–c. 225) asserted that "Christ, in disarming Peter, ungirt every soldier." This rule extended from the military to other violent spheres, wrote Athenagoras, forbidding Christians to attend the circus games.[7] On the same grounds, Christians likewise opposed abortion and capital punishment.

One of the earliest "apologies" (defenses of the Christian faith) was written by Justin Martyr in AD 155–157. He considered the rejection of violence taught by Christ as a glorious demonstration of the Christian

---

3. Clarkson, *Doctrines and Practice*, 6, 22.

4. Bainton, *Christian Attitudes toward War and Peace*, 73.

5. Lactantius, *Divine Institutes* 6.20.

6. Remaining quotes in this paragraph cited in Barrett, *The Orthodoxy of Pacifism*.

7. Driver, *Christians Made Peace with War*, 24.

faith, as something to boast of. He said that Christians, who once were "filled with war, and mutual slaughter, and every wickedness, have each through the whole earth changed our warlike weapons—our swords into ploughshares, and our spears into implements of tillage—and we cultivate piety, righteousness, philanthropy, faith, and hope, which we have from the Father Himself through Him who was crucified."[8]

The early church leaders saw this gospel peace as a demonstration of the reality of the Messiah having come. Jewish critics charged that if nothing had changed in the world, the Messiah could not have come according to Isaiah's prophecy that "they will beat their swords into plowshares, and spears into pruning hooks. Nation will not take up sword against nation, nor will they train for war anymore" (Isa 2:4). Christians responded by saying that the world had in fact changed; it was transformed in the people of the Messiah who live according to law of Christ, and there was no longer any violence in the church. In the church, claimed Eusebius,[9] the messianic vision of the prophets has already begun to be fulfilled. Although the whole world would not recognize this until the last day, believers had no reason to excuse or disregard the new way of peace that marked this kingdom begun by Christ.

This gospel peace was not only affirmed by Christians: it was attested to by their enemies. Writing in 178, the pagan philosopher Celsus charged the Christians that "if all men were to do the same as you, there would be nothing to prevent [the king's] being left in utter solitude and desertion, and the forces of the empire would fall into the hands of the wildest and most lawless barbarians."[10]

These were not merely the statements of bishops or theologians: they were codified in the rules that governed the life of ordinary church members. One example is the *Apostolic Tradition* associated with Hippolytus (c. 170–c. 236), an important teacher in Rome. It seems to have been the basis for many other church orders over the following two centuries, and it expressed a certain consensus. It listed occupations forbidden for those seeking church membership, including brothel keepers, participants in gladiatorial combat, idol makers, astrologers, and prostitutes. The *Tradition* states that "the catechumen or faithful who wants to become a soldier is to be rejected, for he has despised God." This drew from theological

8. Justin Martyr, *Dialogue with Trypho* 110.

9. Driver, *Christians Made Peace with War,* 27.

10. Ibid., 38.

WARLIKE CHRISTIANS IN AN AGE OF VIOLENCE

objections to not only military violence, but also to the violence of civil power: "If someone is a military governor [has the authority of swords], or the ruler of a city who wears the purple, he shall cease or he shall be rejected."[11]

That Christian profession or the military profession were understood as contradictory alternatives is shown most dramatically in the lives, or rather deaths, of the so-called military martyrs. These were believers who paid the ultimate price for their decision to follow Jesus.[12] "I cannot serve because I am a Christian," said Maximilian on March 12, AD 295, refusing induction into the Roman army in North Africa. He explained that he could not accept the seal of the Roman army, because he had accepted the seal of Christ, "whom all Christians serve: we follow Him as the Prince of Life." He was executed by the Romans. Three years later, Marcellus, a centurion in the Seventh Legion in Spain, was executed for throwing down his weapons during a military parade. He replied to his interrogators that "it is not fitting that a Christian, who fights for Christ his Lord, should be a soldier according to the brutalities of this world." Around a century later, the young Martin of Tours was also martyred. He was conscripted at a time when he was undergoing instruction in the Christian faith. This instruction was preparation for baptism. After serving in what he described as a "nominal fashion," he requested release, declaring, "I am a soldier of Christ. It is not lawful for me to fight." This stand for the orthodox position of the early church—that is to say, the complete rejection of violence—led to his execution. The early church believed that Jesus and the apostoles taught that warfare was incompatible with being a disciple of Jesus—and Christians frequently paid the ultimate price rather than compromise this principle.

Onward Christian Soldiers?

That Marcellus was a centurion, however, indicates that there *were* Christians in the army at the period when church leaders were declaring that killing, legalized or otherwise, was a practice that was contrary to Christian teaching and practice. Indeed, historical evidence supports this— it is well known that the Roman army was an important route for the

11. *Apostolic Tradition of Hippolytus*, 16.1–16.

12. Examples in this paragraph are drawn from Driver, *Christians Made Peace with War*, ch. 8.

arrival of Christianity in Britain. Does this indicate that some Christians did consider military service to be compatible with Christian profession?

Until the mid-to-late first century, there is no firm evidence of Christians serving in the army, but from that time on we see a gradual increase. However, that this did not necessarily mean approval of killing is seen in the *Apostolic Tradition* of Hippolytus, which implies that participation in the army did not inevitably entail combat or the infliction of capital punishment. When engaged in support practices such as road maintenance and mail services, soldiers who refused to take the military oath and therefore become involved in killing might, it appears, have been given leave to remain in the army.[13] It is also the case that many people would have been converted while in the army and taken time to decide to quit. A modern parallel comes from the life of someone I met. He spent months of agonizing before deciding to disobey orders and refuse to continue serving in the South African army, as he slowly worked through the Christian implications of committing violence in support of apartheid.

Nonetheless, the number of Christians willing to engage in lethal soldiering did increase. But this does not mean approval by the church. Throughout history we observe a tension between teaching and practice of Christians, which may be a sign of human weakness and a failure by the church to properly teach and discipline its members. We see this in other areas of life besides military service. One example is the area of sexual purity. We learn from Paul's letters to the Corinthians that Christians were involved in unchristian sexual conduct. We see this today from modern surveys that show significant proportions of US evangelical churchgoers engaging in sexual activity outside of marriage.[14] This does not mean that it is or ever was generally regarded as legitimate for Christians.

Significantly, no major writer justified Christian violence before the fourth century. Tertullian noted that some Christians did indeed take part in the military, but insisted that this was incompatible with their true profession: killing any person, he taught, whether in war, punishment, or abortion, was a devil-inspired crime against God. Railing against the hollowness of military victory, he wrote, "Is the laurel of the triumph made of leaves, or of corpses? Is it adorned with ribbons, or with tombs? Is it

13. Ibid., 50.
14. Sider, "The Scandal of the Evangelical Conscience."

bedewed with ointments, or with the tears of wives and mothers? It may be of some Christians too; for Christ is also among the barbarians. Has not he who carried [a crown for] this cause on his head, fought even against himself?"[15]

Some modern advocates of Christian participation in warfare have argued that the early church opposed militarism because the military involved idolatry. By this they mean that military oaths were taken to Caesar, and as he was regarded as a god, Christians could not take such oaths. This was certainly a concern to Christian leaders. Tertullian, in his 211 treatise *On the Crown* (the first piece of Christian writing dedicated solely to the question of Christians and the army), accused Christians in the ranks of the army of pretending that they could be servants "of two masters, of God and Cæsar."[16] Tertullian was undoubtedly concerned at the idolatry that he saw this involved, but he expressed a more fundamental belief that soldiering was incompatible with being a believer. "Shall it be held lawful to make an occupation of the sword, when the Lord proclaims that he who uses the sword shall perish by the sword?" he went on to argue. In stark language, he described Christian involvement in the military as "the very carrying of the name over from the camp of light to the camp of darkness."[17]

Furthermore, the martyrdom of Martin of Tours (discussed above) occurred in the late fourth century. By this time emperors were (at least nominally) Christian, and Christians were tolerated in the army. Thus, Martin could not have been objecting to ritual idolatry. Although there were grey areas in some cases, the overwhelming understanding of orthodoxy in the early church was that killing was incompatible with Christian profession. Summarizing the writing of the early church, Clive Barrett concludes that the rejection of war, violence, and soldiering "is the only acceptable position for orthodox Christians. . . . [It is] not an option for a few, it is mainstream Christianity."[18]

Of course, the teaching and practice of the early church cannot be taken as another canon of scripture. It contained many examples of what we would now regard as heresy, and practices that to our eyes look strange and peculiar. For example, the doctrine of the Trinity, which became so

15. Tertulian, *The Chaplet, or De Corona*, ch. 12.

16. Ibid.

17. Ibid., ch. 11.

18. Barrett, *The Orthodoxy of Pacifism.*

central to mainstream Christianity, took some centuries to be formulated. However, we must be precise with language here. The doctrine of the Trinity was arguably the culmination and consummation of centuries of thought and scriptural exegesis. In contrast, the fourth-century church's acceptance of warfare (see the section on just war theory, below) was in sharp contrast to what had gone before: it was a stark reversal of the doctrine and practice of the apostolic and early church.

The rejection of warfare and the commitment to peaceful alternatives were understood by the early church as being true to the teaching and example of Christ and the apostles. They formed a core component of the identity of early Christianity. As we shall go on to consider, they were also integral to evangelism.

Peace as Evangelism

In 2005, thirty-year-old US single mother Kari Smith auctioned advertising space on her forehead on the Internet auction site eBay. The winning bidder, online casino GoldenPalace.com, paid Ms. Smith $10,000 for her to have their website permanently tattooed in black block letters on her forehead. Explaining that she was doing it to pay for her child's education, she told a journalist, "It's a small sacrifice to build a better future for my son."[19]

I remember someone in my church youth group shaving a cross shape in his hair, but I have not heard of Christians adopting this extreme form of display in their evangelism. For Christians, calling people to repentance and faith in Jesus Christ is one of the primary tasks of our lives in the present age. In a thought-provoking book on evangelism in the early church, historian Alan Kreider asks how it was that the church grew so rapidly over so many centuries after the resurrection of Jesus. It was not, he concludes, public preaching or "attractive worship." In times of persecution the former was impossible and outsiders were generally not present at secret meetings. Even unbaptized believers were commonly excluded from parts of the service anyway.[20] Nor was it "mission-oriented structure" or even prayer for the unconverted—such concepts and language are not present in the texts and liturgies of the early believers. (Kreider is silent on the issue of forehead advertising, but I think we can

19. Falk, "Mom Sells Face Space for Tattoo Advertisement."
20. Kreider, *Worship and Evangelism in Pre-Christendom.*

rule that out.) Rather, he argues, it was a type of lifestyle that showed Christ to the unconverted. This occurred as believers lived compelling and uncompromising lives, like their master. And central to that lifestyle and witness was peace.

Jesus' message was seen as inspiring, challenging, and alluring to the world by early fathers such as Origen and Justin Martyr. In particular, Christians testified that pagans were drawn to the Sermon on the Mount. "The idea that these were hyperbolic demands which were 'unfulfillable' never occurs in their writings," writes Kreider. "And no teaching was repeated more by the Christians, or more pondered by the pagans, than Jesus' command to love the enemy."[21] Justin noted that pagans were turning to the gospel attracted by Christians whose lives were distinctive. He boasted of the Christians, "We who hated and destroyed one another, and on account of their different manners would not live with men of a different tribe, now, since the coming of Christ, live familiarly with them, and pray for our enemies, and endeavor to persuade those who hate us unjustly to live comfortably to the good precepts of Christ, to the end that they may become partakers with us of the same joyful hope of a reward from God the ruler of all."[22]

In his assessment of how Christianity spread so rapidly in the early church, the historian Robin Lane Fox said that it proclaimed an attractive message that spoke to the weak points of Roman culture.[23] One of those he identified as peace—in a time when war and violence were seen as the norm, and even celebrated, the Christian gospel of peacemaking was immensely attractive. No wonder it drew people flocking to Jesus, and to this community of like-minded followers of him.

What did that look like in practice? Fortunately, we have historical evidence of various examples. Thus in the mid-third century the Christians in Carthage had been subjected to what Pontius in his *Life of Cyprian* terms "an unusual and violent rage of a cruel persecution" that "laid waste God's people." This was followed by a deadly outbreak of a "dreadful plague" that afflicted the city, leaving it strewn with carcasses.[24] Many people fled, but Bishop Cyprian urged the believers not to save themselves, but to remain in the city and help those in need—that is,

21. Ibid., 11.

22. Justin Martyr, *First Apology*, ch. 14.

23. Lane Fox, *Pagans and Christians in the Mediterranean World*.

24. Pontius the Deacon, *Life and Passion of St. Cyprian*, paras. 8–9.

those who had been persecuting them. According to Pontius, Cyprian preached to his flock that "there was nothing wonderful in our cherishing our own people only with the needed attentions of love, but that he might become perfect who would do something more than the publican or the heathen, who, overcoming evil with good, and practicing a clemency which was like the divine clemency, loved even his enemies."[25] The Christians therefore stayed and treated and fed their suffering persecutors. This was a genuine example of real enemy love, of turning the other cheek and demonstrating how different from worldly conceptions of self-preservation, justice, and revenge is the grace and love of God. This led to a great growth in the church in Carthage.

Another instructive example is from the life of John Chrysostom, who was born in Antioch circa 347. When the Roman emperor levied a war tax on the city the population rioted, destroying statues of the emperor. The authorities executed rioters in a violent reprisal. John preached twenty-one sermons during Lent 387, and many people came to listen to him. He said that while destroying statues was not a crime, destroying a human being, made in God's image, was. He helped bring reason to rioters, and Christian leaders interceded with the authorities to prevent further executions. An extract from the text of one of John's sermons, on Matthew 10, the sending out of the twelve disciples, is instructive. He said that Jesus sent them out unarmed "that they may learn that this system of war is new. . . . When the sheep get the better of wolves, and receiving a thousand bites, so far from being consumed, do even work a change on them, [then] a thing far greater and more marvelous than killing them [has occurred]; . . . and this being only twelve while the world is filled with wolves."[26]

For John, real enemy love, standing up to one's enemies in love and continuing to demonstrate Christ to them, was at the heart of witness to the world. With men like Cyprian and John Chrysostom, no wonder the gospel spread so rapidly!

But it was not simply leaders teaching ideas from the front. In his analysis of early church evangelism, Kreider argues that the worship of the church shaped individuals and communities that were distinctive peacemakers. The process of catechizing baptismal candidates "weeded out" those who were not prepared to follow Christ's teachings. For

25. Pontius the Deacon, "The Life and Passion of Cyprian."

26. Egan, *Peace Be with You*, 38–39.

example, the *Apostolic Tradition* insisted that a candidate in the military had to leave the military, promise not to kill (i.e., undertake noncombat roles), or be prevented from being baptized. Those who joined the military after already beginning the process of baptismal preparation had to be rejected as candidates.

Along with this, elements of worship such as the "kiss of peace" were important. This was not merely the gesture that "the peace" has become in many churches today; it obliged people to sort out ruptures in relationships before communion. It was a statement of radical equality that also helped teach and foster a sense of a distinctive community that acted differently from others: it practically taught Christians what peace looked like.

The extent to which Christians demonstrated this gospel peace enemy love was seen as a litmus test of the true practice of the faith. In a sermon, Clement (c. 150–c. 215) said, "When, for instance, they hear from us that God says, 'It is no credit to you if you love those who love you, but it is to your credit if you love your enemies and those who hate you,' when they hear these things, they are amazed at such surpassing goodness. But when they see that we fail to love not only those who hate us, but even those who love us, then they mock and scoff at the Name."[27]

For the early church, Jesus' teaching about loving our enemies as God loved us, and putting that into practice, was seen as compelling and immensely attractive, and at the heart of evangelism. In an age when the state saw war as an instrument of policy to bring about good, and when violence was celebrated in the entertainment of popular culture, the Christian gospel was radical and liberating. For early Christians, the passages of Isaiah 2 and Micah 4, which speak of swords being beaten into plowshares with the coming of the Messiah, were important reference points, and the worship and life of the community was seen as a proof that the Messiah had come and that his Spirit was upon them. Conversely, a failure to live up to this teaching was recognized as a poor testimony to the faith. However, this understanding of the gospel and the New Testament took a dramatic U-turn in the third and fourth centuries, and this is associated with the name of one man—Constantine.

27. Quoted in Kreider, *Worship and Evangelism in Pre-Christendom*, 38.

The Constantinian Reversal

The early church followed the teachings and examples of Christ and the apostles in embracing peacemaking enemy love as the orthodox position for all believers. The modern church, generally, does not. When, and why, did this fundamental change occur?

Of course, such changes do not occur overnight. They are part of long processes. But a useful starting place is AD 312. According to his biographer Eusebius, Bishop of Caesarea, the Roman emperor Constantine had a dream in which he saw a fiery cross and heard the words, "Conquer by this."[28] Believing this was God speaking to him, he made the cross his military standard and began the process of decriminalizing Christianity and aligning it with the state. Sunday became the legal day of rest, special favors were given to cities that converted en masse, imperial funds were given to churches and pagan temples destroyed. "Within a generation the church went from being a counter-cultural sect to being the established state church. It went from being a persecuted minority to a persecuting majority," argues Tim Chester.[29] After Constantine's death, this process eventually led to Christianity being the only permitted religion in the Roman Empire. Christianity was made the official religion of the empire by the emperor Theodosius in AD 380.

One part of this shift was that the church changed its theology and practice to accommodate this new alliance with imperial power by allowing its members to inflict violence for the state and join the military. In his overview of the historical evidence, Thomas Clarkson, the leading force behind the British evangelical movement to abolish slavery, wrote, "Thus in the first two centuries, when Christianity was purest, there are no Christian soldiers upon record. In the third century, when it became less pure, there is frequent mention of such soldiers. And in the fourth century, when its corruption was fixed, Christians generally entered upon the profession of arms, with as little hesitation as they entered upon any other occupation."[30]

The significance of this is hard to overstate. Before Constantine, to be a Christian was to be part of a minority and to suffer the costs that this entailed; by the end of the fourth century, not to be a Christian was to be in a minority in the Roman Empire, and to suffer the disadvantages

28. Eusebius, *Vita Constantini* 1.28.
29. Chester, *Good News to the Poor*, 152.
30. Clarkson, *Practice of the Early Christians*, 16.

that Christians had themselves endured not so long before. In the early centuries, Christians were forbidden by the church to fight in the army as well as being in danger of execution by the army if discovered; after Constantine, by a law established in AD 416, *only* Christians could serve in the Roman army. A new entity, "Christendom," a church-state alliance exercising power over a defined geographical area in which everyone in it was cajoled to be "Christian," was born.

Social transformation is complicated, and it would be foolish to attribute such a dramatic shift to one dream alone. Changes in attitude were already occurring, and Constantine accelerated them. Nonetheless, this seismic shift in theology, teaching, and practice can be dated to the fourth century. Why did it occur? Certainly, although we can never know his true thoughts on the matter, Constantine's own religious experience played a role. However, some historians consider that he did not convert personally until late in his rule, and continued supporting and protecting pagan religions alongside Christianity, exploiting them all for his political interests.

Setting aside the political benefits that the Roman Empire enjoyed by its new alliance with the institutions of Christianity, why did the church take such a dramatic reversal in direction? Again, the reasons are complicated. Growing numbers prompted a reconsideration of church-state relations. The radical ethical and moral standards of the early church became more lax and this allowed a process of compromise to commence. However, theologically, it appears that leading Christians confused the approaches of the Roman state and the new settlement with the eschatological fulfillment of biblical prophecy.

An example is demonstrated in Eusebius' description of Constantine organizing a meeting for church leaders in 326:

> About this time he completed the twentieth year of his reign. On this occasion public festivals were celebrated by the people of the provinces generally, but the emperor himself invited and feasted with those ministers of God whom he had reconciled, and thus offered as it were through them a suitable sacrifice to God. Not one of the bishops was wanting at the imperial banquet, the circumstances of which were splendid beyond description. Detachments of the bodyguard and other troops surrounded the entrance of the palace with drawn swords, and through the midst of these the men of God proceeded without fear into the innermost of the imperial apartments, in which some were the emperor's own companions at table, while others reclined on

couches arranged on either side. One might have thought that
a picture of Christ's kingdom was thus shadowed forth, and a
dream rather than reality.

Eusebius confuses here the imperial splendor of a violent empire
for God's kingdom. This was a world away from the early church, for
now the church was being seduced by wealth and weaponry and access
to the powers and authorities, rather than understanding itself as an alternative community of God's people living by radically different laws.[31]
Eusebius made further grand claims of this nature. He asserted that the
Roman Empire was successful in its wars against other nations because
Christ was born under its rule. He claimed that prophecies of the Messiah's reign of peace from Isaiah and Micah were being fulfilled by the
Romans: "That which the prophets foretold has been fulfilled precisely.
The various independent governments were destroyed by the Romans;
and Augustus became the sole master of the entire universe at the very
moment when our savior came down to earth. Since that time, no nation
has waged war on another nation, and life is no longer squandered in the
former confusion."[32]

Of course, it followed from this that if the Roman Empire were
God's kingdom built on earth, then its wars were God's wars. Indeed, Eusebius believed that the defeat of Rome's enemies could be attributed to
God's intervention.[33] When the war was Christ's war, there was clearly no
longer any question as to whether Christians might fight in the military.
Whereas the early Christians had held it to be a great sin for Christians
to harm their enemies, and Tertullian had scorned the celebration of
military "glory," Athanasius preached the opposite: it is "praiseworthy to
destroy the enemy. Accordingly not only are they who have distinguished
themselves in the field held worthy of great honors, but monuments are
put up proclaiming their achievements."[34]

This process of revisionism required some highly imaginative leaps
in biblical exegesis. Cyril, in the early fifth century, tackled the prophecies in Isaiah 2 and Micah 4 that the Messiah's reign would see "swords
beaten into plowshares." The militarism of the Roman Empire surely
presented a difficulty to those who would endorse it as Christ's kingdom

31. Eusebius, *Vita Constantini* 3.15.

32. Quoted in Driver, *Christians Made Peace with War,* 27.

33. Ibid., 80.

34. Ibid., 78.

on earth—it most certainly was *not* beating its swords into plowshares. Cyril said that swords had been beaten into plowshares because "many peoples were . . . conquered by Roman weapons and so converted."[35] What he meant was that Roman/Christian swords had beaten *other people's* swords into plowshares—hardly the first image conjured up by the prophets' announcements!

From our vantage point, and with the benefit of hindsight, we can see that this was a monumental blunder. Wars did not cease and universal peace did not reign, and the Messiah did not return. Indeed, the "glory that was Rome" itself faded and crumbled. It was a highly ethnocentric judgment: Eusebius could claim that the Romans ruled "the entire universe" only because he was ignorant of the true size of the earth and the multiplicity of its peoples. But perhaps we should not be too hard on the Christians of this period. Subsequently, countless people down the ages have been overly impressed at victorious warring empires and have mistaken the high dramas of their day for the biblical last times. We have thus learned to be more circumspect in the interpretation of apocalyptic scripture. Nonetheless, the error of the fourth- and fifth-century theologians was not easily undone, and it had far-reaching practical consequences. Driver is so bold as to claim that "the church has never fully recovered from this move."[36]

The Constantinian reversal had practical as well as theological consequences. With almost everyone now formally a "Christian," the expected moral and spiritual standards were lowered for the masses. Whereas the post-apostolic early church had commonly expected people to be discipled before being baptized, the post-Constantinian church came to reverse that order, to make it easier for the masses in state and public to enter the church. Clergy and monks were expected to lead a life of exemplary holiness, and so were still forbidden from fighting. Ordinary church members, however, were excused these more exacting requirements, enabling them to live at a lower level of holiness. The radical demands of holiness and love that in the early centuries characterized the church as a whole were now confined only to a tiny minority of what might be termed professional Christians.

Similarly, ex-soldiers were originally prohibited from becoming priests—a ban that recalled scriptural teaching, such as God's prohibiting

---

35. Quoted in Kreider, *Worship and Evangelism in Pre-Christendom*, 44.
36. Driver, *Christians Made Peace with War*, 37.

David from building the temple due to his having taken the lives of others (see ch. 2, pages 43–44). Eventually, even this was abandoned. Jerome reflected on this period that the church "increased in influence and wealth but decreased in virtue." These changes were not necessarily the cause of this decay in Christian spirituality, but its consequence. The church changed its convictions and theology to accommodate itself to the practice of Christians enjoying unprecedented power, prestige, and wealth.

Conclusion: Abandoning Gospel Peace

Thus we have seen that from the fourth century the church, co-opted for political reasons by the Roman Empire, abandoned the apostolic commitment to gospel peace. These changes were certainly neither unlamented nor uncontested. For example, Basil, who succeeded Eusebius as bishop of Caesarea, said that "military courage, and the triumphal arches erected by a general or the community, exist only through the magnitude of murder."[37] However, as Driver put it, in Constantine's century a new "alliance of mutual self-interest and interdependence between state and church, the sword and the cross, had been laid."[38] Where the church had previously understood the cross as an alternative to the sword, now it came to see it as its partner. This new interdependence of sword and cross was such a radical reversal of centuries of Christian practice and teaching that it demanded a whole new theology. This new theology came to be known to history as "just war theory" and will be examined in detail in the next chapter.

As it is well-nigh impossible to construct a consistent argument for Christian support of and participation in warfare on the basis of sound biblical interpretation as understood within the evangelical tradition, its advocates therefore commonly resort to appeals to church history. But to do that, they cannot go back *too* far into church history, and certainly not to the history of the early church. For there, as we have seen, the church for centuries resolutely carried on the apostolic teaching of gospel peace—that God's kingdom was built through the infectious holiness of enemy love as God's Spirit enabled his people to faithfully follow the teaching and practice of the Prince of Peace. To follow their Lord faithfully in this way the early church forbade its members from being

37. Ibid., 78.
38. Ibid, 57.

soldiers, stood against infanticide and gladiatorial games, even barred former soldiers from holding church office, and taught its members to embrace martyrdom rather than betray their Lord by abandoning these principles. It was this uncompromising holiness that witnessed so powerfully to an age addicted to violence. And it was its undoing in the Constantinian settlement that so diluted the power and witness of the church, striking a blow from which the church is only now, after some seventeen centuries, beginning to recover. The next chapter will continue this story by showing how the medieval church invented a theory of the "just war" to explain how it abandoned the apostolic witness against war, but how in turn the modern church has been jettisoning just war theory and returning to gospel peace.

5

Hasn't the Church Allowed Soldiering? Part II

The Medieval and Modern Church

On January 10, 2010, the archbishop of Canterbury, Rowan Williams, joined the Greek community of Thanet, in southern England, for the forty-sixth annual "Blessing of the Seas" ceremony. The congregation gave thanks that the sea yielded its produce, and prayed for another productive year of fishing. On January 11, 2010, volunteer coastal warden Tony Sykes reported that thousands of dead crabs had washed up on the Thanet coastline. "Environment experts were mystified," reported a local news agency![1]

This coincidence is amusing, hinting that the church's sincere efforts to engage usefully in the affairs of the world could have disastrously adverse effects. I suggest that something similar happened with the church's eventual abandonment of gospel peace and its adoption of novel theories and theologies to justify participation in warfare. This has meant that, in the minds of millions of peoples throughout history, the Christian church has become associated with violence. It has hidden the Prince of Peace behind the armies of his followers, who as often as not have been fighting and killing each other in wars that both sides believed to be just. It has brought more suffering to the world, not less—and all too often exacerbated and excited rather than suppressed or quelled the martial spirit.

The previous chapter showed how the early church resolutely maintained the New Testament teaching and practice of gospel peace, and concluded by noting how this was abandoned with the "Constantinian reversal." This chapter picks up that story, showing how the church

1. As reported in *Private Eye*, 22nd January–4th February, 2010.

justified this reversal through "just war theory." However, although it came to be part of the official teaching of the Roman Catholic Church, and was adopted by some churches that in other respects broke from it in the Reformation, this theory was always opposed by significant numbers of Christians. This chapter shows how gospel peace repeatedly challenged just war theory in medieval and modern times. The Reformation accelerated this process. Although war remained a blind spot for many of the early Reformers, who uncritically carried over Catholic teaching on this area, as Christians have gradually returned to scripture they have increasingly come to reject unbiblical church dogma about just wars. In fact, we may be entering a period in which the idea of just war is largely displaced within evangelical circles, and authentic gospel peace moves once again to the center stage of church life and teaching.

Justified Warfare

Most animals *fight* to control territory in order to secure food supplies, attract a mate, and reproduce. However, humans are the only ones that *war* (some scientists argue ants are an exception). War is the calculated use of violence by one group against another over an extended period of time to achieve a desired outcome. Thus warfare needs to be organized. As anthropology documents, not all societies in human history have manifested this social practice of organizing themselves for warfare. Those that do have tended to develop cultural codes to regulate it. These generally address two aspects: *when* war can begin, and *how* it can be conducted. The rules governing how wars are fought may be desired by leaders to prevent war from becoming too expensive and thus taking the shine off their glory, or they may spring from moral beliefs about an imperative to reduce harm to human beings. Whatever the rules governing warfare, and in spite of a wide variety of cultural practices, "[t]he tale of the just war," argues political geographer Paul Reuber, "is as old as mankind."[2]

Many different cultural codes regulating warfare have been developed by humanity, but this chapter will give particular attention to the one that has been most closely associated with Western (especially Catholic) Christianity since the post-Constantinian period, the "just war tradition." This was a complex set of ideas borrowed from classical

2. Reuber, "Tale of the Just War," 44–46.

pagan philosophers and ethicists and developed by Catholic theologians from the fourth century. From the sixteenth century its development was largely carried forward by more secular thinkers in international law. However, because it was the precursor to modern international law on warfare, and because its premises are shared by some major Christian denominations today, it is worth considering in detail. Indeed Charles Reed, an influential thinker in the Anglican Church and author of books on the subject, has argued that a recovery of just war theory should be the basis of the church's engagement with the state on issues of international conflict, and a vehicle to restore the church's relevance in an age of its decline.[3]

The Catholic tradition of just war theory draws on a variety of cultural influences. Its foundation was laid by pagan Greek and Roman thinkers such as Aristotle and Cicero, who discussed just causes for war and the necessary authority to declare it. The later Roman Christian leaders Ambrose and Augustine adopted and adapted this, drawing on both Hebrew and Christian scriptures to add that wars must be fought with the right intention. Jewish thinkers, such as the philosopher Maimonides, contributed by identifying different types of just war. From medieval German knights came codes of chivalry about just conduct in battle. At the same time, the idea of noncombatant immunity developed, extended from church lands and property to all who were unable to bear arms. There was no smooth linear development. For example, from the fall of Rome to around the tenth century, earlier just war traditions in Europe were largely forgotten. By the fifteenth century these often contradictory ideas from multiple sources coalesced into a broadly recognizable cultural consensus.[4]

Just war theory traditionally distinguishes between two sets of rules.[5] The first concerns "just resort to war," or *jus ad bellum*, to establish the criteria by which a war may be begun or joined. Five criteria are commonly advanced. The war must have a *just cause*, that is, self-defense against an unlawful attack, or the righting of wrong and the re-establishment of peace. A "just cause" would not include seizing territory or natural resources. Second, it must be waged by a *right authority*. A

3. Reed, *Just War?*

4. Material and arguments in this paragraph are drawn from D. Johnson, "Just War Tradition in Western Culture."

5. The material in the rest of this subsection is drawn from Megoran, "Militarism, Realism, Just War, or Nonviolence?"

group of people such as criminals, rebels, or private militias cannot band together and start a war on their own initiative, even if the cause is just. In the contemporary state system as codified by the United Nations, established governments acting in self-defense or the United Nations Security Council are regarded as the only right authorities. Third, the proper authority must have a *right intention*. It is one thing to identify a just cause such as resisting the invasion of an ally, but if the authority is only using that as a mask for the real purpose of securing natural resource access, for example, then the intention is not just. Likewise, vengeance is not a just intention. Fourth, there must be a *reasonable chance of success*. Even if the intent is just, it is not just to launch a war that has little chance of succeeding, as the expected good results of the war must outweigh the evil of war in the suffering and destruction that it brings. Finally, war must be launched as a *last resort*, when all other avenues of resolving the conflict have been exhausted.

The second set of criteria is known as *jus in bello*, or "just conduct in war," and is about the actual conduct of war once it has begun. Two requirements are commonly stipulated in this category. The first is *discrimination* between legitimate and illegitimate targets. Thus civilians and noncombatants such as medics and chaplains are not to be purposely targeted for attack, although if they are killed as the indirect result of an attack on a military target, then that is not regarded as a crime (the so-called law of double effect). Likewise, prisoners of war must not be executed or poorly treated. Second, force used must be *proportional* to the aim, and only that firepower strictly necessary to secure one's objective must be used—even against military personnel.

At its best, just war theory is about continual ethical reflection on the morality of a war, and is not a set of boxes that a politician can tick to establish if a war is "just." Just war theory is a dynamic and evolving tradition, and thinkers such as Mark Evans have recently proposed the addition of a third category to these two traditional ones: *jus post bellum*, or "justice after war." By this count, a war can only be considered just if the victors put sufficient planning and effort into stabilizing the situation and restoring order and well-being after any war, and if they foster processes of reconciliation and forgiveness.[6] Some writers have suggested that this must involve installing functioning democracies.

6. M. Evans, "Moral Theory," 13.

It should be apparent that these criteria are highly demanding. Even if a war has been justly begun, it may subsequently become unjust by virtue of the way it is fought. Far from celebrating it, the presumption of just war theory is against war: "History knows of no just wars," writes just war theorist and theologian Oliver O'Donovan.[7] "A just war," writes Hayden, "is not to be regarded as a good thing *per se* but as the lesser of two evils."[8] Just war theory is thus a moral framework formulated to aid statesmen and stateswomen in practical reasoning in the murkiness and confusion of the real world.

The Secularization of Just War Theory

A significant weakness of medieval just war theory was that it was often unequally applied to Christians and non-Christians. For example, the Second Lateran Council of 1139 forbade the use of the crossbow against Christians, but allowed it against nonbelievers. Therefore from the early modern period, European thinkers increasingly secularized it, removing such monstrosities. That is the basis of today's notion that the same basic rights can be claimed by everyone.

Writing in 1530s Spain, professor Francisco de Vitoria said that as the inhabitants of the "New World" did not know Christian revelation, they could not be blamed for not accepting the authority of the pope, but were still humans and must be treated in accordance with certain rules. In effect, he shifted the basis of just war theory to "natural law" that could be taken as applying to everyone by virtue of their being human. From the late nineteenth century, this became codified in a series of international "laws." In 1863, during the American Civil War, the "Lieber Code" was drawn up by Dr. Franz Lieber on the request of Abraham Lincoln to stop Confederate soldiers being mistreated. Lincoln calculated that this risked leaving them permanently disaffected with the Union and would make future pacification of the South harder. Conventions in St. Petersburg (1868) and the Hague (1899 and 1907) were held to limit the types of weapons that could be used, in order to protect the coffers of warring states by limiting the development of expensive armaments.[9] Other important landmarks, such as the 1928 Paris Treaty that outlawed war

7. O'Donovan, *Just War Revisited*, 13.

8. Hayden, "Security Beyond the State," 171–72.

9. Robertson, *Crimes against Humanity*, 183–85.

except in self-defense, and various Geneva Protocols outlawing poison gas and protecting prisoners of war, have meant that the regulation of warfare has moved from the church to the state and inter-state organizations. Nonetheless, although just war theory has thus lost its former political relevance, some theologians have continued to work with it as a way of guiding the church's response to war.

Trials and Tribulations of the Just War

Although some Christian churches have long held to variants of just war theory, it has never been without its critics within and without the church. Indeed, over recent decades it has been subjected to unprecedented critical appraisal. In the next section we shall focus on particularly Christian objections. But first, we shall consider some more general problems with the just war tradition.

The questioning of just war theory in the twentieth century has been precipitated in part by the development of new military technologies that, some people argue, have rendered this medieval theory obsolete. These changes have made it very difficult to apply the principle of "proportionality," and also "discrimination"—not intentionally harming noncombatants. In the total war of conflicts such as the 1939–45 world war, it could be argued that almost every section of the civilian population may be involved in the war effort and thus cease to be noncombatants with immunity from attack. Similarly, it is hard to see how nuclear weapons could be used without entirely ignoring the demand for proportionality. As Anthony Harvey, an Anglican expert on the subject, argues, "There are serious difficulties in applying Just War principles with any stringency to modern armed conflicts."[10]

One of the most profound objections to just war theory is that it justifies the status quo. It allows those countries that have gained wealth through violence and military expansion to stay rich by preventing the structurally disadvantaged countries and stateless peoples from seeking to redress the balance through the same methods. As Lee Griffith observes, Augustine did not generate a theory of just piracy or just revolution: just war theory was shaped by the nature of his allegiance to the Roman Empire and identification with its ruling classes.[11] Similarly,

10. Harvey, *Demanding Peace*, 70.
11. Griffith, *War on Terrorism*, 20.

medieval theologian Thomas Aquinas argued that because excess wealth is given by God for the purpose of passing it on to the poor, if the rich do not give it to the starving then they have a right to steal it rather than die.[12] However, he did not develop this insight into a more explicit theory allowing poor people or kingdoms to pursue the same goal through warfare. It is thus hardly surprising that just war theory tends to be advocated by those who are comfortable with the current system, and even benefit from their place in it. This applies to theologians and churchmen who gain a sense of importance, security, and identity from institutions such as their national militaries, or from feeling that they are listened to, important, and thus "relevant."

Another factor that has crippled the practical exercise of just war reasoning is the impossibility of policing it in a world ruled by self-interested nation-states. The international lawyer Geoffrey Robertson QC, in his book *Crimes Against Humanity*, is extremely cynical about this current incarnation of just war theory in the international laws on war. He calls the numerous conventions on ending wars a "graveyard of good works." They are useless because states know that they will be the final arbiters of whether their actions will be defined as unjust/illegal or not. Indeed, the deeming of an action as "illegal" is an act of power, and in reality it is the states with the most muscle that get to determine the law in accordance with their own political interests. Carpet-bombing of German civilians by the US and UK in World War II, or of Cambodian civilians by the US in its Southeast Asian wars, clearly contravened the Hague Rules of Aerial Warfare—yet these powerful nations escaped any sanction. Under corporate pressure, the George W. Bush administration, contends Robertson, refused to allow inspections of biological weapons that would annoy the US pharmaceutical industry.[13] The 1949 Geneva Convention on the treatment of prisoners of war stipulated that they must be "quartered under conditions as favorable as those for the forces of the detaining power," given a wage equivalent to a norm stipulated in Swiss Francs, be allowed to pray and smoke, and even provided with a musical instrument of their choice. Robertson considers these rules "ludicrous," as they make demands on captors to give captives what most third world armies themselves lack.[14] He reckons that the continual ac-

---

12. Thomas Aquinas, *Summa Theologica*, II-II, q. 66, art. 8.

13. Robertson, *Crimes Against Humanity*, 199–200.

14. Ibid., 197.

cruing of such conventions has probably contributed to the jettisoning of the whole edifice, including the most basic decencies. Cynics might say, he suggests, that it is not the victims of war that have benefited from the Geneva conventions, but rather the diplomats who enjoyed years of conferencing in pleasant surroundings drafting them, and the Swiss tourist hospitality industry that hosted them.

It could also be argued that the modern laws on war (the secular offspring of just war thinking) repeat and even magnify the potential destructiveness of their Catholic predecessor. A prominent figure in the creation of a normative law of war based on natural justice, Grotius, argued that a war could be just not only when injury has occurred, but that "war is lawful against those who offend nature," such as cannibals.[15] Citing the same crime, Gentili, using the language of "world community," defended the Spanish conquest of Latin America on grounds that the natives had committed sins contrary to human nature. Henk Houweling and Mehdi Amineh thus see secular just war theory and the modern laws of war as a doctrine of the right of "civilized peoples" to punish primitives. They suggest that the United States drew on this doctrine in exterminating the indigenous inhabitants of North America and that it can be seen in terrifying documents such as the 2002 National Security Strategy, which proclaimed that the United States had the right to attack any potential rival to prevent them equaling its strength.

Another weakness with just war thinking is that judgments about what wars and actions within wars are deemed "just" are highly arbitrary. For example, the Lieber Code considered shooting at sentinels as illegal, whereas contemporary laws of war regard them as legitimate targets for killing. One of the most hotly debated elements of just war theory today is the demand that violence be used in proportion to attaining its ends with minimum civilian casualties. During the 2003 invasion of Iraq, US Defense Secretary Donald Rumsfeld required that every US bombing raid on Iraq where thirty or more civilians were likely to be killed be passed by his office for approval.[16] The *New York Times* reported that Mr. Rumsfeld approved every single one of the more than fifty requests, but on what possible basis was the number thirty arrived at? Why not twenty-five or thirty-five, or five or 105?

---

15. Quoted in Houweling and Amineh, "Geopolitics of Power Projection," 30. Remaining material in this paragraph is drawn from this source.

16. Otterman, "The Calculus of Civilian Casualties."

Michael Walzer is the most widely read modern authority on just war theory, yet his work provides numerous examples of arbitrary and highly debatable judgments. For example, he considers civilians working in a munitions factory as legitimate targets, but not civilians working in a factory producing food for the military.[17] The reason for this apparent discrepancy is not clear. Or take another example, from World War II: in 1944, forces murdered eighty German prisoners of war in retaliation for the execution of eighty of their prisoners. While Walzer considers such retaliation generally unjust, he allows it in this case because it ended the practice, deterring the Germans from such executions in the future. Ultimately, Walzer identifies the "supreme emergency" when, to ensure the survival of the state, it is just to suspend the rules of war—soldiers killing unjustly for the sake of justice, as he puts it.[18] On this basis, he argues that the terror bombing of German cities in 1941 was just, as Nazism needed defeating, but it had ceased being just by 1943 because Britain was clearly winning the war. One might equally well argue that the Germans would have been justified to do the same to Britain to prevent the supreme emergency of the extinguishing of their state. Ultimately, the attempt to flesh out what just war reasoning looks like in practice simply underlines just how subjective it is.

It is, arguably, this circularity that is the greatest weakness of the just war tradition. By definition, almost anyone fighting in a war (except perhaps mercenaries) thinks that their cause is just. Using traditional just war arguments, Iraq could claim that its 1990 invasion of Kuwait was just,[19] and the United States could assert that its 1991 expulsion of Iraq from Kuwait was likewise—both Iraq and the United States citing just cause, namely, to right a wrong that could not otherwise be corrected. In World Wars I and II, both Germany and Britain used the language of just war to attempt to claim the moral high ground. In the 2000s, both Osama bin Laden and George W. Bush used variants of just war reasoning to legitimate their violence against the other. Just as one person's freedom fighter is another person's terrorist and one person's war criminal another's patriotic hero, so one person's unjust war is another's just war.

17. Walzer, *Just and Unjust Wars*, 9.

18. Ibid., ch. 16.

19. Kuwait was allegedly extracting Iraqi oil at a disputed boundary, and its overproduction was depressing the world oil price, preventing Iraq from recovering from its war with Iran—a war that arguably protected Kuwait from potential Iranian aggression.

The sixteenth-century Christian scholar Erasmus observed dryly that in practice a just war "means any war declared in any way against anybody by any prince."[20] As 1930s Labour Party leader George Lansbury astutely observed, when war breaks out, "Christians of all denominations and all nations discover that God is on both sides," that their side has the just cause.[21]

Holiness and Just War Theory

In spite of theoretical justifications for Christians killing other people in just wars, Christian Europe was haunted by a deep sense of discomfort that it had compromised the holiness of the church by blessing warfare. The argument that war may be a "lesser evil" for the result of a great good fits uncomfortably with the New Testament's uncompromising call to holiness. Paul tackled this general principle head-on in Romans 3:8. "Why not say—as some slanderously claim that we say—'Let us do evil that good may result'? Their condemnation is just!" thundered the apostle. Therefore even formal church positions on just war have never completely eradicated the sense that there is something deeply unchristian about warfare and the "lesser evil" argument. The sense that one could not kill, even in just wars, and remain holy has never gone away from the church. Three institutional arrangements in the medieval Catholic Church, and its Reformation successors, reflected this.

First, clergy were forbidden from bearing arms, a tradition that largely continues to the present day. For example, J. G. Simpson, canon and precentor at St. Paul's Cathedral during World War I, opposed the recruitment of ordained men as soldiers, arguing that as they were peculiarly entrusted with the word of Christ, "padres had a duty to represent ideal humanity."[22] Presumably, by implication, Canon Simpson believed that the duty to represent ideal humanity as Christ intended it did not extend to lay Christians, who could aim at a lower level of holiness. This is a deeply unscriptural view of the church, but it is one that pervades Christendom. Even today some churches give their ministers titles such as "His Holiness" or "The Reverend," implying that these office holders have attained or expect to attain more reverence and holiness than a

20. Quoted in Musto, *Catholic Peace Tradition*, 131.
21. Lansbury, *My England*, 180.
22. Bourke, *Intimate History of Killing*, ch. 9, "Priests and Padres."

member of the laity, who is permitted to commit "lesser evils" such as killing their enemies.

Second, in movements like the eleventh-century Peace of God and Truce of God, certain days of the week, holy festivals, and seasons were designated where warfare was forbidden. Rowan Williams observes that this was ludicrous, but far less absurd than people "who could in principle kneel side by side to share the communion of Christ's body and blood, also planning revengeful slaughter against each other."[23] It was ineffective, but its real importance was the recognition that real holiness only existed in the absence of warfare, that people could not really be holy when they were fighting.

Third, participation in warfare was formally regarded as polluting in the church's "penitential" manuals. These were guidelines for those hearing confession that enjoyed their heyday in the ninth century. They listed what type of penance had to be performed for every sin and are thus an insight into what the church regarded as sinful. For example, the *Penitential of Columban*, dating to around 600, prescribed three years of unarmed exile surviving only on bread and water for those who killed. Most penitentials considered killing in war a sin and demanded at least forty days of penance, and people were expected never to take up arms again. The *Old Irish Penitential*, dated to around AD 800, regarded killing in battle alongside murder, revenge in a blood feud, and the killing of offspring. It required penance of one and a half years.[24]

Sometimes the demands for penance after warfare were quite precise. Following the Battle of Hastings, the Norman Council of Westminster drew up the *Establishment of Penance* in 1070 for the victors—one year for each man who killed in battle, forty days for each who wounded, and three days for those who did not see combat. Even noncombatant involvement was thus regarded as sinful. The late ninth-century English *Arundel Penitential* required one year of penance for killing in a just war, and two years for killing in a war of doubtful legitimacy: therefore even killing in a so-called just war was regarded as polluting and sinful.[25] These texts coexisted with and undermined the operation of just war theory in the church, casting a moral shadow on all military involvement and acting to limit recruitment by preventing anyone serving more than once in the

23. Rowan Williams, *Truce of God*, 25.

24. Musto, *Catholic Peace Tradition*, 57–58.

25. Ibid., 67.

army. The reason for this is expressed in the so-called False Capitularies, a series of genuine legal texts mixed with forgeries from 847–57, which said, "Whoever sheds human blood spills the blood of Christ."[26]

These practices (clergy noninvolvement in war, seasons when war was banned, and penance for fighting in just wars) represent a diluting of the holiness of the New Testament and early church. They effectively made Christianity into a two-track vocation. Previously, every believer was expected to obey Christ's teachings by refusing to ever harm their enemies. The Constantinian shift required now that only a tiny minority of Christians (the clergy) be expected to strive to obey Christ's command to "be perfect, therefore, as your heavenly Father is perfect" (Matt 5:48), while the majority of professing Christians were no longer expected to strive after the same degree of holiness. However, setting aside certain days as holy when killing could not take place, and regarding the holiness of everyone who killed as being compromised, revealed a profound unease at the just war accommodation with violence that church elites had made. Writing centuries later, the Methodist preacher and leader W. E. Sangster said that war is "an abrogation of His holy will."[27] Whatever else it professes with its mouth, in its heart the church has always known that, and its embrace of just war theory has in practice thus generally been half-hearted and inconsistent.

The Christian Questioning of Just War Theory

Medieval Christian unease with just war theory became more acute when outsiders challenged them on it. For example, in the ninth century, Saint Cyril was sent by the church to evangelize the Turks. He made little progress, and one of the principle reasons was the familiarity of Muslim scholars with the Christian Scriptures, Christian practice, and the yawning chasm of violence between them. Their scholars objected to Cyril:

> Your God is Christ. He commanded you to pray for your enemies, to do good to those who hate you and persecute you and to offer the other cheek to those who hit you, but what do you

---

26. The Crusades seem to mark the decline and eventual termination of this practice. In 1095, calling for what would later be termed "the First Crusade," Pope Urban II declared that "whoever, out of pure devotion and not for the purpose of gaining honor or money, shall go to Jerusalem to liberate the Church of God, let that journey be counted in lieu of all penance." War for God's cause became its own penance.

27. Sangster, *They Met at Calvary*, 75.

actually do? If anyone offends you, you sharpen your sword and go into battle and kill. Why do you not obey your Christ?[28]

Why not indeed? Cyril struggled to respond and his reply—that while Christians endure personal offense, they consider it noble to assist each other in battle—was unconvincing. However, not everyone felt as able as Cyril to defend just war theory. Indeed, as the Middle Ages wore on and the bloody consequences of the church's adoption of justified warfare theory became clear, Christians increasingly questioned the wisdom and rightness of jettisoning the early church's belief. The just war consensus became increasingly questioned.

However, even to speak of a "consensus" having existed in the first place is probably to go too far. In his monumental 1919 survey of the early church's attitude to warfare, Cadoux reported that the official church's transition to militarism was not universally accepted. For example, the mid-fourth-century *Testament of Our Lord* forbids a soldier to be baptized unless he leaves military service, and an Egyptian Church order contained the same ruling, with the modification that if a soldier is received into membership, he is forbidden to kill.[29]

This theology reasserted itself at different periods throughout the Middle Ages. For example, a church Council meeting at Narbonne in 1054 declared, "No Christian shall kill another Christian, for whoever kills a Christian undoubtedly sheds the blood of Christ." Cardinal Peter Damian wrote that "in no circumstances is it licit to take up arms in the defense of the faith of the universal church: still less should men rage in battle for its earthly and transitory goods."[30] In fact, historian H. E. J. Cowdrey states that there is no evidence that the just war theory teachings of Augustine had any influence on the church in the latter part of the eleventh century, but rather a pre-Constantinian mood against justified warfare reasserted itself.[31]

The papal drive for crusades at the end of the century seemed to trump that mood, justified as they were by just war theory.[32] However, while supported by many Christians, these monstrous adventures seem to have prodded some back along the tracks of the New Testament

28. McTernan, *Violence in God's Name*, 63.

29. Cadoux, *Early Christian Attitude to War*, 259.

30. McTernan, *Violence in God's Name*, 60.

31. Ibid.

32. Coates, *Ethics of War*, ch. 2.

church. Criticizing crusading in his 1266 *Opus Maius*, Roger Bacon urged Christians to follow the example of the early church, and eschew killing: "Nor are unbelievers converted in this way, but killed and sent to hell. Those who survive the wars together with their children are more and more embittered against the Christian faith because of this violence and are indefinitely alienated from Christ and inflamed to do all the harm possible to Christians."[33] As the Muslim opponents of Cyril had suggested four centuries earlier, Christian violence is not only directly contrary to the teachings of Christ, but is actually a dreadfully bad testimony to those to whom one is trying to bear witness of the "gospel of peace."

Precisely as just war theory became reconsolidated by theologians in the later Middle Ages in support of the Crusades, popular opposition to just war theory mushroomed. For example, Huzmann of Speyer saw the papacy as illegitimate because it espoused violence in the form of just war theory. In 1085 he wrote a pamphlet making this point, and declared, "It is Christian to teach, not to make war; to endure injustice with patience, not to avenge it. Christ did nothing of the kind, and neither did any of his saints."[34] At the time of the early crusading movement Peter the Venerable, abbot of Cluny, wrote to Bernard of Clairvaux, who was known for his support of the Crusades, insisting that "the Church has no sword. Christ took it away when he said to Peter, 'Put back thy sword.'" He believed that the Holy Land should indeed be won for Christendom again, but by preaching, persuasion, and conversion—not war.

This attitude toward violence was exemplified in the lives of many church leaders. Bishop Boniface of Crediton was a missionary to the violent, pagan Franks and had a tremendous reforming influence on Frankish culture. In 754 he resigned as a bishop and returned to missionary work, this time among the Frisians of northern Europe. When attacked by a band of them, his followers prepared to defend themselves by force. However, he said, "Sons, cease fighting. Lay down your arms, for we are told in scripture not to render evil for good, but to overcome evil by good." The bishop and his followers were all martyred.

This opposition to just war doctrines was not simply scholars writing learned treatises or bishops undergoing brave deaths. On the contrary, mass popular peace movements emerged, returning to the teachings of the Bible and celebrating gospel peacemaking. Huge numbers of people

33. Siberry, "Missionaries and Crusaders, 1095–1274," 108–9.

34. This and the remaining examples in this section are drawn from Musto, *The Catholic Peace Tradition*, chs. 6 and 7.

became involved. A notable example is the "Great Alleluia," which was partially a reaction to war in northern Italy's city-states. Apparently spontaneously, although often encouraged by wandering preachers, thousands of people gathered to search for alternatives to war. They expressed their piety through sermons, processions, devotions, and other demonstrations, and participation in them spread rapidly. At the Plain of Pasquara, Verona, on August 28, 1233, Musto reports sources claiming that four hundred thousand people of all classes gathered to demonstrate for an end to war and to call for peace and reconciliation. Similar events occurred with the later Bianchi of northern Italy. Beginning in a series of visions to peasants, they wore white robes, lived simple lifestyles, and moved to initiate reconciliation and peacemaking, repentance, forgiveness of enemies, and a return to peace. Their long processions moved from city to city in large groups, with their arrival marked by scenes of high emotion and reconciliation. By the time that they reached Rome in September 1399, one chronicler claims, their number had reached two hundred thousand.

Numbers reported in medieval sources cannot be regarded as accurate statistics; nonetheless, these are remarkable figures and suggest a movement seen by contemporaries as large and significant. While not more than thirty thousand people were involved in the First Crusade, by 1450 six hundred thousand belonged to the Third Order of Franciscans, who eschewed use of violence and participation in the military. Musto observes that historians have given much more emphasis to the smaller, less important, and less reputable group of Crusaders than to these massive popular peace movements—movements that might have been more representative of Christianity at the time than those that espoused just war theory. Indeed, by the end of the thirteenth century popular Christian rejection of warfare had become so widespread that for the 1272 Second Council of Lyons, Pope Gregory X requested briefings from all over Europe on opposition to war. The report survives to this day and lists people from all walks of life and all levels of society. It details forms of protest from mass peace movements to poetry. Its aim was not to extol the peacemakers but to find ways of dealing with public opposition. Nonetheless, ironically, it persists to quietly refute the claim that the church has always supported war.

The Reformation and the Undoing of the Just War

A Catholic professor of church history told me about a visit he once made to a US military college to give a lecture on just war theory. After his talk, he was introduced to a group of (Protestant) military chaplains. They told him that they had never been taught just war theory because it was Catholic. Their observation highlights the often marginal role that just war thinking has played in Protestant churches. Indeed, the Reformation set in motion a process of questioning just war theory that has, over the centuries, led more and more churches and theologians to reject it altogether in favor of gospel peace.

Why should it be that the Reformation redoubled attacks on the concept of "just war theory"? We have seen in chapter 1 that gospel peacemaking modeled on the grace of God to his enemies (sinful humanity) lends itself to the doctrine of justification by faith more easily than does just war theory. However, it is perhaps in the question of authority and the balance between the Bible and church history that gospel peace can be most clearly seen to chime with the concerns of the Reformation. The Catholic advocate of just war theory James Turner Johnson has observed that it has been of less interest to Protestant theologians compared to their Catholic counterparts in recent decades. He offered the explanation that this is because Protestants have tended to give more weight to the Bible than to church teaching.[35] He did not mean that he approved of this, but it inadvertently highlights a major obstacle for Protestants, and in particular evangelicals, in accepting just war theory. That problem is that as just war theory is apparently contrary to both Old and New Testaments, the biblical texts must be accommodated to a very alien set of ideas.

This problem is clearly exampled in one of the most forthright statements advocating just war theory by a British Protestant in recent years: the 2004 book *Just War?*, written by senior Anglican thinker Charles Reed. Reed is a liberal who regards just war theory as necessary to augment scripture. He writes that "between Old Testament militarism and New Testament pacifism stands the just war tradition," a tradition that "seeks to bridge the gap between the Old and New Testament."[36] Reed thus considers the Old and New Testaments contradictory and regards a theory imported from classical paganism by medieval Catholicism as

35. J. T. Johnson, "Just War Tradition in Western Culture," 24.
36. Reed, *Just War?*, 9, 59.

necessary to "bridge the gap" between them. This language reveals a low regard for both the authority and the integrity of scripture, and is anathema to evangelicals who see no "gaps" in the Bible that are in need of filling by humanly conceived notions. As argued in chapter 2, there is no contradiction between the two testaments, and to set one up as Reed does is a misunderstanding. Scripture contains, in the words of the Westminster Confession, "all things necessary for [God's] own Glory, man's salvation, Faith and Life." The evangelical position is that if scripture lacks just war theory, it is not because of an oversight by biblical writers, or because they did not anticipate our context, but because the Lord God Almighty did not consider it necessary for life and godliness. In fact, he gave us something much better.

The Protestant Reformation took a number of directions. These had many elements in common and often included a return to the Bible as the chief source of Christian authority, the stripping away of traditions and customs that interposed between the believer and Christ, a thirst for holiness, and personal experience of conversion. Some of the reformers adopted traditional Catholic just war teaching. They included Calvin, the Church of England, and Luther, who famously said that "the pacifism of Jesus was no more binding on his followers than his celibacy or his carpentry." Other reformers, including the Hussites, Anabaptists, and Quakers, rejected just war theory as yet another Catholic addition to the scriptures; as the Swiss reformer Conrad Grebel argued, the gospel did not need to be defended by violence.

George Fox, founder of the Quakers, was an example of this latter group. Following a dramatic experience of conversion precipitated by his recognition of sin in himself and in the church, he became utterly given over to preaching and building the kingdom of God. Although he sympathized with his theology, he refused to support Oliver Cromwell's army in the English Civil War, because he had rediscovered biblical gospel peace. He recorded in his diary the response that he gave to Cromwell's military recruiters when they invited him to join the New Model Army: "I told them I knew from whence all wars arose, even from the lusts, according to James's doctrine; and that I lived in the virtue of that life and power that took away the occasion of all wars."[37]

John Woolman, a New England follower of Fox a generation later, developed this theology and practice further. His dedication to the gospel

37. Fox, *Journal*, 54.

lead him to articulate one of the earliest rejections of slavery in North
America, and also a powerful statement of gospel peace. He not only refused to become involved with wars between England, the settlers, and
France, but when war between the white settlers and the Native Americans broke out, he chose the radical move of worshipping with Christian
Indians rather than seeking to kill them. Quoting heavily from scripture,
he argued that the gracious design of the Almighty was to send his Son to
finish transgression and bring about peace, a process whose outworkings
could already be seen but were not yet finally complete. He located his
movement as part of the "Reformation from Popery" begun by earlier
reformers who started a process that they had been unable to complete.[38]
For men such as Woolman, driven by a desire to proclaim the unadul-
terated gospel, jettisoning medieval Catholic just war teaching was an
essential part of the Reformation.

Present-day Quakerism has, regrettably, significantly departed
from the evangelical roots of these illustrious forebears, in no small part
because it underplays Fox's regard for scripture and overemphasized his
teaching on personal spiritual discernment. But there are many theologically conservative Protestant churches that have always adhered to, or
have rediscovered, gospel peace. For example, I worship at Heaton Baptist Church in Newcastle. In 1609 John Smyth, founder of the first Baptist
church in Britain, formulated, as part of the Reformation's solidification
in Britain, a confession of faith that agreed Jesus called Christians to follow "his unarmed and unweaponed life."[39] This spirit was manifest in the
many comments on war by the English Baptist church's greatest figure,
Charles Haddon Spurgeon, who in the nineteenth century exercised a
remarkable gospel ministry in Britain and beyond. Spurgeon abhorred
war, decrying it as "the sum of all villanies."[40] He was an implacable and
vocal opponent of British imperialism and militarism all his life, appalled
at how "England, at set seasons, runs wild with war lunacy, foams at
the mouth, bellows out 'Rule Britannia,' shows her teeth, and in general
shows herself like a mad creature."[41]

He was just as scathing of foreign powers. Writing an open letter
to Emperor Napoleon III and Kaiser Wilhelm under the pen name John

38. Woolman, *Journal of John Woolman*, 167.

39. Smyth explained that this meant they were not permitted to hold offices of state
that required harming others. See Dekar, *Healing of the Nations*, 21.

40. Spurgeon, "Periodical War Madness," 148.

41. Ibid., 145.

Ploughman, he scorned the leaders of France and Prussia as worse than common ruffians and urged them, "Before the deep curses of widows and orphans fall on you from the throne of God, put up your butcher knives and patent men-killers, and repent."[42] He was no mere critic of war: he passionately believed that "only let the gospel be preached and there shall be an end of war," and thus dedicated his life to preaching the gospel and building the church.[43] Whereas the world wages war, Spurgeon argued, the authentic task of the church is rather to "evangelize the masses, carry the truth of the loving God to their homes, preach Jesus and his dying love in their streets, and gather men to his fold," as soul-saving aims a blow at the root of the war spirit.[44] Albert Meredith observes that his theological principles ensured that "he never failed to be appalled at the shocking spectacle of nations resorting to arms and seeking to destroy one another" and that he "never failed to condemn the outbreak of hostilities. There was not a single instance in which he supported violence or warfare."[45] As this book has argued, Spurgeon's position is the inevitable conclusion of a consistent conservative evangelical exposition of scripture, yet in most biographies his views on war have received less attention than his various theological debates or even theologically unimportant issues such as his literary use of humor or the venues he chose for preaching.[46]

Many Baptists departed from the stance of John Smyth's congregation as echoed by Spurgeon, a departure associated with the marginalization of the scriptures that Spurgeon vociferously opposed in the so-called Downgrade Controversy.[47] However, the example of Baptist origins is far from unique. In fact, when new churches emerge that take the scriptures as their first rule, rather than the strictures of tradition, and passionately seek the illumination of the Holy Spirit as they search the Bible in order to learn to lead a holy life, they are often pointed inexorably to gospel peace. This is perfectly illustrated by the wonderfully named "Peculiar People," a group of churches that flourished in the English county of Essex in the nineteenth and twentieth centuries and in 1956 changed their by-now

42. Spurgeon, "John Ploughman's Letter on the War," 354.

43. Meredith, "Social and Political Views," 94–95.

44. Nettles, *Living by Revealed Truth*, 500–501.

45. Meredith, "Social and Political Views," 92.

46. For example, Carlile, *C. H. Spurgeon*; Dallimore, *Spurgeon*; I. Murray, *The Forgotten Spurgeon*. Notable exceptions to this rule are Meredith, "Social and Political Views," and Nettles, *Living by Revealed Truth*.

47. See Spurgeon's *Autobiography*, vol. 2, *The Full Harvest, 1860–1892*.

anachronistic name to become part of the Fellowship of Independent Evangelical Churches.[48]

The Peculiar People grew out of the conversion experience of James Banyard, born in 1800 to a plowman. To the despair of wife and family, he was somewhat given to drink and petty crime. He was converted through a growing conviction of sin that only Christ's death and resurrection could atone for, and with the realization that only the indwelling of the Holy Spirit could produce real holiness. He set about preaching in his home area, a message that we must be born again, receive the baptism of the Holy Spirit, and advance in holiness. He quickly attracted a group of followers who went on to set up rural chapels all around Essex and surrounding counties. These were characterized by vibrant worship—Bible reading, hearty hymn-singing, clear and direct preaching, and passionate prayer by all men and women present.

In the early days a few church rules were formulated but not written down, as Banyard would allow no books to be used except the Bible. As this group of new, unlearned and uneducated disciples of Jesus gathered together, they pored over the scriptures for rules of conduct. What they developed looked, unsurprisingly, like the New Testament church. They met every day at 5 a.m. before work for prayer, as well as some evenings and most of the Lord's Day. At these meetings "brothers and sisters . . . offer[ed] their thanks, praises and requests to God the Father." They also resolved that they would "accept no money for preaching, make no laws, have no book of rules, but the Word of God."[49] Their religious life was marked by simplicity of life, sharing of possessions, a passion for holiness, and a zeal for evangelism.

Unencumbered by church tradition, they turned to the Bible for guidance on all aspects of life and conduct. In choosing a name for themselves, they selected the frequent description of God's people in the Old and the New Testament as a "peculiar people".[50] Similarly, like the early church, their life was characterized by divine healings. This was not an imported theology but simply based on their plain reading of scripture. One of their number, William Perry of Southend, had been ill with consumption for years, unable to work and finding no help from doctors.

48. This discussion is taken from Sorrell, *The Peculiar People*. See also Pearce and Durham, "Patterns of Dissent in Britain."

49. This is a quote from an 1882 account of the Peculiar People, recorded in Sorrell, *Peculiar People*, 19–20.

50. See, for example, Deut 14:2 and 1 Pet 2:9 in the King James Version.

One morning when praying, God impressed upon him the words of James 5:14–15: "Is anyone among you sick? Let them call the elders of the church to pray over them and anoint them with oil in the name of the Lord. And the prayer offered in faith will make the sick person well; the Lord will raise them up. If they have sinned, they will be forgiven."

He convinced two of the brothers to take him to worship, whereupon he asked Banyard to anoint and pray for him according to the scriptures. Banyard was reluctant initially as this was new to him, but did so. He was instantly healed, and as proof walked the twelve miles home, ate a good meal, and went to work the next day—none of which he had been able to do for years. Other healings followed, and the church became known for spiritual healing.

Exactly the same holds true for the church's attitude to war, which it was forced to confront with the outbreak of World War I in 1914 and compulsory conscription in 1916. Historic debates about just war theory were unknown to these ordinary, simple believers, so they did what they always did—looked prayerfully to the scriptures. Unsurprisingly, after a whole Council met together, they issued the following statement:

> The Council of the Peculiar People believe and maintain that War and Bloodshed is the work of Satan and absolutely contrary to the principles of the religion of Our Lord and Saviour Jesus Christ and the teachings of the New Testament. . . . We may not and cannot take human life nor engage in any work that requires taking the Military Oath.[51]

They resolved to pray for and support conscientious objectors, who were advised to seek employment in industries other than munitions. The church was persecuted for its position: for instance, Ernest Hockley of Barking, a Sunday school teacher, was sentenced to ten years hard labor for standing by his deep-rooted conviction that "war is contrary to the teachings of Jesus Christ." There was internal debate in the church about whether its members could accept noncombatant military service (in the Army Medical Corps, for example). The church steered people to reject it, but allowed it for conscience's sake. Come World War II, however, the church issued a clear statement of total noninvolvement.

The Peculiar People offer a great insight. When God's people seek to listen to his voice and follow the New Testament pattern of Christian living, unencumbered by regard for pagan theories like just war and

---

51. Sorrell, *Peculiar People*, 51–52.

unhindered by positions of power in society that make them bend theology for a seat at the table of the good and great, they reach the conclusion, with Mr. Hockley, that "war is contrary to the teachings of Jesus Christ." A similar example, from North America, is given by the Church of God in Christ, the largest Pentecostal denomination and fifth-largest Protestant denomination in the United States. Deeply rooted in the Bible-based church culture of the American South, it is theologically and socially conservative, opposing abortion, homosexuality, and the ordination of women. It also abhors war and instructs all its members not to enlist or otherwise engage in acts of war. In March 2003, the church's Board of Bishops wrote a letter to President Bush, opposing the planned invasion of Iraq on gospel principles.[52]

Since the beginning of the Reformation, a slow but steady rise can be charted in the growth of gospel peace and the rejection of warfare in the Protestant church. This has often been fitful. For example, in the aftermath of World War I, the Fellowship of Reconciliation, an interdenominational Christian German-British voluntary organization that sought to resolve conflicts between nations without resorting to war, gained much support not only from traditional peace churches but also from the clergy of mainstream Protestant denominations. This movement was interrupted as Europe was engulfed in the nationalist fervor of World War II. However, the sentiment returned with even greater force after the war, and since then the number and importance of Protestant theologians who have questioned or rejected just war theory has steadily grown. Seven reasons for this will be considered next.

Why the Reformation Leads to the Rejection of Just War Theory

We have thus seen that Protestant churches have been less likely to accept Catholic just war teaching and that the Reformation birthed new denominations that in some cases wholly rejected it. It is helpful to think of the Reformation not simply as a sixteenth-century movement for moral, theological, and institutional reform of the churches in western Europe[53] but as an ongoing process of continually purging the visible church of Jesus Christ of human traditions that hinder its really being church.

52. Megoran, "Militarism, Realism, Just War, or Nonviolence?" 483.
53. McGrath, *Christian Theology*, ch. 3.

In the twentieth and twenty-first centuries the rejection of just war theory has increasingly spread into mainstream Protestantism as it has wrestled with the practical questions thrown up by US/UK foreign policies. There have been seven particular spurs to this latest stage in the process of Reformation.

The first is the vigor and spread of evangelicalism at the expense of liberal Protestant denominations in the Anglo-American world[54] and, through this influence, the whole globe. Evangelicals take the Bible as their first rule of faith and conduct, which has occasioned greater scrutiny of the scriptural material on war in both testaments. As chapters 2 and 3 argued, this makes it difficult to sustain a commitment to so unbiblical a tradition as just war theory. As we saw in chapter 1, it is difficult to accommodate just war theory to the doctrines of grace. It fits well with a Catholic emphasis on works or a liberal view of humans as relatively good and progressing slowly towards civilization, but not with the reformed insistence that without God humans are utterly lost and can only be justified (put right with God) through his unmerited grace made possible by the death and resurrection of Christ.

The second has been a belated realization of the damage done to the church and the world by just war theory. A popular posting in various Internet forums in the first decade of the twenty-first century was the following:

> Over the centuries, billions of people have fallen prey to religion run amok. How many Jews and Gypsies suffered in Nazi concentration camps while churches in Germany turned their heads? How many people were murdered in the Crusades during the Middle Ages—in the name of God?

Most of the arguments used against religion in the work of the so-called New Atheists are weak, revealing a poor understanding of both science and religion—take, for example, Richard Dawkins' bestseller *The God Delusion*.[55] When Dawkins' *God Delusion* attacks Christians for using their faith to support violence over time, however, the book is at its most compelling.[56] Such critiques have long concerned thoughtful

54. For an excellent and respected account of this, see Marsden, *Fundamentalism and American Culture.*

55. Dawkins, *The God Delusion*. For a good rebuttal of the argument that science and religion are contradictory (especially when it comes to the topic of creation), see Alexander, *Rebuilding the Matrix.*

56. Dawkins, *God Delusion*, ch. 7.

Christians. In particular, as we shall see in the next two chapters, the way that just war theory brought disrepute to the gospel as it was used by all sides to such disastrous effects in the First and Second World Wars has served to diminish its popularity as a satisfactory source of authority for Christians.

It is important to observe that this damage to the reputation of the church and (far more importantly) to the Name of Jesus has been done as much by Protestants as by others. It will not do simply to dismiss the Crusades and inquisitions as solely the product of Roman Catholic just war theory. The Protestant Reformation was accompanied by violence. This was not merely the violence of its more radical wings[57] but of its mainstream. In a sixty-five-thousand-word treatise, *On the Jews and Their Lives*, Luther advocated violence against Jews—including destroying their homes and synagogues and threatening their leaders with death if they continued to preach Judaism (see below, ch. 7, 182–83). Luther could have ensured that the Reformation made a clean break with medieval Catholic European anti-Semitism; instead he entrenched it, contributing to its horrific culmination in the twentieth century. Luther also advocated the killing of Christians who argued that infant baptism was unbiblical. The Reformation's other main leader, John Calvin, had a similar attitude toward "heretics," most infamously ordering the execution of scientist and theologian Michael Servetus because of his unorthodox views on the nature of God.[58] As we saw in chapter 2 (above, 26–31) and as we shall see in chapters 6 and 7, Protestant churches have consistently supported and fanned the flames of war to the present day. The mounting evidence of the harm done by the churches' adherence to just war theory is causing the evangelical church to realize that it is unbiblical and thus to reject it.

The third was the invention of nuclear weapons and the threat of global annihilation. If a single bomb or missile could kill thousands of people, then the traditional parameters of just war theory were rendered redundant by the prospect of superpower war. As historian Iain Maclean observes, "The reality of total war and the sense of urgency conveyed by the threat of nuclear holocaust from the 1950s onwards led to a radical questioning of the whole just-war theory."[59] This also led to placing greater stress on peacemaking in order to avoid the possibility of war.

57. Ellul, *Anarchy and Christianity*, 18–23.
58. Pinker, *Better Angels of Our Nature*, 141–43.
59. Palmer-Fernandez and Maclean, *Encyclopedia of Religion and War*.

Fourth, the success of organized nonviolent opposition to violence and tyranny neutralized for many people what had been a decisive, if unscriptural, reason for supporting just war theory: that nonviolent gospel peacemaking "did not work in the real world." Furthermore, Gandhi's opposition to the British Empire (informed by Tolstoy's writings about Jesus and peace), Martin Luther King Jr.'s Christian-based civil rights actions, and Catholic-informed mass protests of 1989 that brought down Eastern European Communist regimes were all, implicitly or explicitly, inspired by gospel teachings. The systematic study and practice of these methods was very new, but already experience seemed to validate faith.[60]

Fifth, the evangelical church is increasingly recovering the conviction that the gospel is relevant for all of life, not only personal salvation and individual morality. This is in part an extension of engagement with questions of social justice. This was established within evangelical circles by the social/political action of the British evangelicals of the late eighteenth and early nineteenth centuries. Central to this was the so-called Clapham Sect, a group of devout and wealthy evangelical politicians, clergy, and activists who settled in the Clapham area of London and collaborated on a range of political and social actions. William Hague calls the Clapham Sect "one of the most extraordinary and influential coalitions British society had ever seen."[61] They combined fervent passion for holiness and scripture with a deep conviction that Christian principles were relevant for the broader life of the society as well as the individual. Their chief achievement was the abolition of the slave trade within the British Empire, in the face of great opposition; they were led in this effort by William Wilberforce and fellow evangelical Thomas Clarkson. Of this trade, historian David Brion Davis writes, "Since we now know that New World slavery was very productive and profitable, and that abolishing the slave trade and slavery was generally contrary to economic self-interest . . . one can argue that abolitionism produced the greatest moral achievement in human history."[62]

But the slave trade was not an isolated campaign. William Wilberforce frequently spoke out in Parliament and elsewhere against other forms of violence, including the widespread use of capital punishment and cruelty to animals. Slavery was integral to the emerging imperial

60. The first sustained study of this phenomenon, Gene Sharp's *The Politics of Nonviolent Action* (3 vols.), was published only in 1973.

61. Hague, *William Wilberforce*, 217.

62. Davis, "Should You Have Been an Abolitionist?," 56.

system, and this group was also critical of Britain's wars against France that were prosecuted in part to maintain and extend that system. Wilberforce conveyed the antiwar sentiments of this group to his friend, Prime Minister William Pitt.[63] Thomas Clarkson developed a more thoroughgoing Christian critique of war. In a study of the early church, he argued that at a period when "the lamp of Christianity burnt pure and bright," the early church "held it unlawful for Christians to bear arms."[64] Clarkson was, personally and through his writings, influential in the establishment of the very first peace societies, the New York Peace Society (1815) and the British Society for the Promotion of Permanent and Universal Peace (1816). The former was set up by David Dodge, whose 1812 pamphlet *War Inconsistent with the Religion of Jesus Christ* was influenced by Clarkson.[65]

Thus British evangelicalism had a profound effect in reducing violence in Britain and around the world. However, in contrast late nineteenth- and early twentieth-century Protestant liberalism put the cart before the horse. It argued that real Christianity was social action to cure the ills of the world. The so-called liberal social gospel movement of the early twentieth century was led by Walter Rauschenbusch, a German Baptist minister who ministered in a terribly deprived area of New York. His acquaintance with poverty led him to question an evangelicalism that wanted to save the souls of poor people but had nothing to say to the social systems that made people poor, and he ended up by rejecting the theology of the atonement.[66] Instead, he argued, Jesus bore the sins of the world "not by imputation, nor by sympathy, but by direct experience."[67] His death, so the argument went, revealed "social sins" such as religious bigotry, militarism, and the corruption of justice. Liberal theologians in his wake pinned future hopes for world peace on international organizations and social change. This received a fatal blow by two world wars.

Liberalism was not merely hopelessly naïve about politics and human nature; it made grossly innaccurate assumptions about the biblical doctrine of atonement. That God "loved us and sent his Son as an atoning sacrifice for our sins" (1 John 4:10) is the core gospel message, yet

63. Cortright, *Peace*, 27.

64. Clarkson, *Doctrines and Practice*, 21.

65. See also Barrett, *Subversive Peacemakers*, ch. 1.

66. Keller, *Generous Justice*, xii.

67. Rauschenbusch, *Theology for the Social Gospel*, 250.

this new liberalism saw it as an incitement to war because it supposedly demonstrated a violent God. This book has shown that this is a grave error, and it is worth repeating the argument of earlier chapters here. First, the cross shows the utter sinfulness of humanity and thus removes any human presumption to exercise righteous violence over another. Second, by taking the punishment of sin on himself, Christ broke the cycle of retaliatory violence—it finished at Calvary. Third, the apostles expressly took the example of Christ making atonement on the cross as an example of how to treat our enemies—by loving, not striking back. The mass collapse of the liberal pacifist movement with the outbreak of World War II was a demonstration of the false promise of liberalism as a response to war. It showed the limitations of discipleship without the power of the cross. Although liberalism continued to exert a malign influence in many seminaries in the postwar period, the pastoral limitations of detaching social and political action from the radical transformation of biblical Christianity has led to its decline.

This waning of liberalism's influence has allowed evangelicalism to recover the belief of its eighteenth- and nineteenth-century ancestors that the gospel is the hope for *both* individual sinners standing before a holy God *and* a sinful world. The widespread celebration in British churches in 2007 of the work of William Wilberforce on the bicentennial anniversary of the abolition of the slave trade was a healthy sign that evangelical churches, having seen off or adapted to the challenges of liberalism, are confident to rediscover the insights of Wesley, Wilberforce, and others that the gospel provides the most perceptive diagnosis of the ills of modern society and also its most powerful remedy. And they have increasingly (although not universally) realized that this remedy is found in the radical gospel rejection of war and Christ's alternative kingdom, not obscure medieval just war doctrines.

A sixth factor that has led to the questioning of just war traditions by evangelicals has been the great growth in evangelism. When everyone was assumed to be a Christian by virtue of christening and confirmation in a church, evangelism was an empty concept. Evangelicalism rejected the idea that being born in Britain or America and being made a member of the church as an infant meant someone was a true Christian, and instead sought evidence of personal conversion. An important part of this was the growth of missionary work outside the traditional domain of "Christendom." The eighteenth-century evangelical revival in Britain was the beginning of the recovery of the Great Commission to preach the gospel to all nations.[68] Hand in hand with this has been a slow discovery that the association of the gospel with the politics and culture of imperial armies and colonial administrations has hindered its reception by those being subjugated by them.

This was put to me forcibly by a senior figure in one of the largest evangelical/charismatic mission agencies. He has worked not only in training Western missionaries to work in the Middle East, but also alongside Evangelical Arab Christians, and has fostered sensitive and meaningful relationships with Jewish and Muslim leaders. His experiences proved to him that the legacy of Christian just wars in the Middle East was one of the biggest stumbling blocks to Muslims coming to faith in Christ. As he put it to me, "Once we start saying that we, speaking as Christians, find authority from Christian theology and biblical principles to support our government as it bombs and kills them and their families, how on earth do we start talking to them, face to face, about Jesus and their need for him?"[69] It becomes impossible. This fact is easily ignored by theologians and churchmen who live and work in the West and who see the gospel through the lens of their engagement with politicians and public in a single nation-state. It is ignored by more liberal churchmen who hold that the church's job is to dialogue with those of other faiths not try to win them for the gospel. However, as the church recovers its great mission to evangelize the whole world, it has simultaneously realized that just war theory is a hindrance to this mission. The rejection of just war theory and the recovery of the early church's understanding of the gospel is thus being driven to an extent by evangelical missionaries, and spread as they report home.

The seventh and final reason for evangelicalism's increasing rejection of just war theory is the decline of "Christendom." Christendom is the idea, sketched out in the previous point, that everyone in a certain land was a Christian and that everything outside those lands was pagan. It is deeply unscriptural, as it merges the kingdom of God with the kingdoms (and republics!) of this world, and, as we have seen in the previous chapter, it proved disastrous for spiritual religion. The nineteenth and twentieth centuries saw the decline of Christendom. In my own sphere, education, this has brought many benefits. For example, in Britain people who were not communicant members of the Church of England were

---

68. Tiplady, *World of Difference*.

69. Anonymous, personal communication.

formerly barred from taking university degrees. The lifting of this bar was fairer in a diverse society and also meant that participation in university Christian circles increasingly resulted from a passion for Jesus rather than a formal university stipulation. The decline of the church as indicated in falling attendance figures is not the decline of Christianity, but the decline of an unscriptural Christendom. In order for Christendom to work, the church had to create a version of just war theory to support the ruler's wars; with the end of Christendom the church is freed from having to make such uncomfortable accommodations, and thus the church is freer to question and jettison distortions from the old order, including just war theory.

As a result of these processes, the advocacy of gospel peace and the resistance to just war theory that has always existed within the church is increasingly moving from the margins to center stage among Protestant denominations. Canon Anthony Harvey has written that such developments "may even impel Christians to recognize that the centuries-old involvement of the church in warfare has been a form of apostasy from its faith in the non-violent redemption wrought by Christ," and their culmination may be gospel peace "becoming the norm for the churches instead of a minority movement within them."[70] The importance of this development cannot be underestimated. Eileen Egan suggests that fifteen hundred years ago a dramatic shift occurred when "the Roman and the Galilean clashed on the issue of justified warfare, and the Roman prevailed." Now, however, she observes that a changeover in the opposite direction is occurring, from justified violence to the nonviolence of Jesus, claiming that "this turnaround is as important to history as that which occurred fifteen hundred years earlier."[71]

Why Has the Church Endorsed Violence?

In his autobiography, the United Kingdom's former Lord Chancellor, the late Lord Hailsham, a Christian, sardonically wrote, "The civil wars . . . the pogroms, the crusades, the sackings, the holy wars, are not, one would think, good advertisements for the divine society, inspired by the Holy Spirit, against whom we are expressly told the gates of hell shall

70. Harvey, *Demanding Peace*, 84–86.

71. Egan, *Peace Be with You*, xii.

not prevail."[72] A man from a very different background yet who shares citizenship in the kingdom of Heaven with Lord Hailsham is Allan Boesak, a black theologian and anti-apartheid leader in South Africa.[73] Yet he reached the same conclusion: "Who could have imagined that the church, which bears the name of him who said, 'Love your enemies,' and 'Put up your sword,' would devise a 'theology of just war,' bless battleships, pray over bombs, [and] bend the knee before politicians who justify the murder of children?" he wrote in amazement.[74] Both these men realized that the Constantinian adoption of just war theory has in numerous ways meant the church has added to the violence of the world. Perhaps more than any other human addition to the gospel, just war theory has served to discredit it in the eyes of the world. Indeed, the historian of religious violence Mark Juergensmeyer considers it remarkable that just war thinking still occupies so important a place in Christian understanding of the use of violence.[75] Why has it proved so persistent in the church?

There are numerous answers to this question, many of which have been discussed thus far in this book. These include the confusion of the Roman Empire with the kingdom of God, modern nationalism's negation of the unity of allegiance to the kingdom of God, the relegation of biblical authority to traditions taught by people, the influence of Hollywood (see ch. 6), and a theological failure to grasp the political implications of the doctrine of justification by faith. However, it is important to remember that doctrines are adopted and supported by individual people. As we have seen in this chapter, just war theory has been far more popular among church elites than laypeople. Four factors in particular explain the peculiar addiction of church elites to just war theory.

The first is *class* and *privilege*. Until very recently, bishops in Britain have traditionally been drawn from the aristocracy. In a famous World War I sermon, Professor H. E. J. Bevan praised war because it "destroys the artificial barriers between class and class."[76] He meant that having an enemy was a good way to unite the poor behind the rich in a nation, dissipating the class tensions in Britain at the time that were propelling the Labour Party forwards and presenting a challenge to the comfortable status quo. This is hardly a Christian argument but, regrettably, has been

72. Hailsham, *Door Wherein I Went*, 43.

73. Ackerman and DuVall, *Force More Powerful*, 348.

74. Boesak, "Word to the Living," 49.

75. Juergensmeyer, *Terror in the Mind of God*, 225.

76. Longley, *Chosen People*, 201.

all too common in the reasoning of clerical elites. As the historian Marrin observes, the church became embedded in its association with the state, leading to power and prestige that was conditional on its never straying too far from society's prevailing values and interests.[77] Put crudely, if churchmen routinely adopted a position of gospel peace, they would not be invited to hobnob at high table with the top dogs.

The second factor is closely related to this—the desire for *relevance*. In his defense of just war theory, the Anglican Church's Charles Reed stated that its "value lies in its ability to set out an ethical framework which enables churches to contribute to discussions on war in a way that ensures that they are heard."[78] I was told by an influential church leader whom I interviewed that because his denomination took a position on a certain UK war "we were taken seriously," and that maintaining just war theory "enables us to be heard."[79] Again, that misses the point. To be "salt and light" in the world is the church's calling, but it comes with a warning: if the salt loses its saltiness, it is worthless. At the time of the Vietnam War, President Nixon refused to even meet church leaders who questioned its wisdom, but those who supported it found the doors of the White House wide open.[80] This presents a great temptation to Christian leaders: whether to tone down the Gospel and be wined and dined by the great or to present it in all its uncomfortable truth and be left outside the gate. Cyril Garbett, a mid-twentieth-century archbishop of York who willingly took on propaganda roles first for and then against the Soviet Union as British policy toward it changed, wrote in his diary in 1945, "I am much better known and have more influence than I had in 1939, but I doubt if I am nearer to God and if I have more *spiritual* influence."[81] What a tragic testimony from a Christian leader. The gospel is inherently relevant by virtue of its being God's revelation to sinful humanity, but "relevance" in the sense of being received by the government is a poor informant of theology. Do we want to be seen as "relevant" because we cozy up to newsmakers by adjusting our theology so they like what we say, or because we proclaim God's truth, no matter how uncomfortable that makes politicians around us? Allan Boesak writes that in apartheid South

77. Marrin, *The Last Crusade.*

78. Reed, *Just War?*, 33.

79. Anonymous, interview, London, May 2003.

80. J. Gill, "The Political Process of Prophetic Leadership."

81. Quoted in Kirby, "Archbishop of York and Anglo-American Relations."

Africa "the voice of the church was heard, not because it was connected to power but because it spoke *truth*." He adds that the church "is no longer the strong voice of a strong nation. And that is good."[82] In the Magnificat Mary declared that God "has filled the hungry with good things but has sent the rich away empty" (Luke 1:53). Too often the church hierarchy would rather associate with the powerful than with the poor, and just war theory enables them to do this: but that is not where Christ is.

I suspect that a third factor behind the popularity of just war thinking is the gratification that comes from seeing dramatic, violent action to confront evil. In 2009 director James Cameron released his Oscar-winning futuristic movie *Avatar*. It depicts the struggle between a greedy Resources Development Administration (RDA) mining corporation and an indigenous race of forest dwellers on the planet Pandora whose habitat the miners want to destroy in pursuit of the mineral "unobtainium." In the inevitable Hollywood final battle scene, it appears as if the advanced private security forces of RDA—whose commander, Colonel Miles Quaritch, is a caricature of unfeeling, racist evil—have won, but suddenly the forest fauna rises up and defeats them. It is an immensely satisfying moment: injustice resolved by righteous violence, by the just war. But it is not Christian. In contrast, a quintessentially Christian response to violence is depicted in the haunting 2010 film *Of Gods and Men*. Set in the Algerian monastery of Tibhirine, it depicts the life of French Trappist monks and how they decide to respond to the rising violence between the Algerian army and Islamic rebel groups during that country's civil war. Rather than flee to safety in France, or accept the offer of protection by government soldiers, they choose to remain in a life of prayer, worship, and provision of medical care for all. They love their enemies more than their own lives. In contrast to the Hollywood ending, their eventual martyrdom appears to be a defeat. But it was a victory like that Christ won on Calvary, and, by God's mercy, those men who came out of that great tribulation are even now part of "a great multitude which no one could count, from every nation and all tribes and peoples and tongues, standing before the throne and before the Lamb" (Rev 7:9).

The knowledge that evildoers have been "brought to book" evokes deep moral satisfaction. This is only right—God is a God of justice. But we need to separate pleasure in proper *ends* from pleasure in improper *means* (violence). What might that look like? No one who witnessed them live on television screens can forget the jubilation of East Germans surging across the Berlin Wall as nonviolent demonstrations, significantly informed and led by Christian churches, overthrew the totalitarian East German regime in 1989.

The fourth and final factor that has lead so many clerics and theologians—as well as laypeople—to adopt and persist with just war theory is a more subtle one: *worldview*. In his study of how early twentieth-century geopolitical thinkers and policy formulators made war more likely, Polelle wrote that "geopolitical thought led its believers to be resigned to the necessity of violent international conflict."[83] War is always a choice: there is no circumstance where it is inevitable, but the belief that it is can easily become a self-fulfilling prophecy. Hence the common-sense assumption that in a world of violence, where "dog eats dog," we must be violent too. Reasoning like this led influential American Christian groups in the 1980s to advocate the escalation of the Cold War and military buildup, on the assumption that as war with the USSR was inevitable, America should fight it on its own terms.[84] In the aftermath of the Second World War, some US military strategists argued for a pre-emptive nuclear war on the Soviet Union before it managed to develop nuclear weapons. The assumption was the same: war is inevitable, so it is best to fight it on our terms at a time of our choosing. Such an assumption is the precise opposite of Christianity, which teaches (Rom 12:2) that we should not be conformed to the thinking of the world, but be transformed as our minds are renewed in accordance with God's perspectives—and then act as peacemakers. As Tolstoy wryly put it, to reject Christian peace because the world is violent "is as though drunkards when advised how they could become sober, were to reply that the advice was unsuitable to their alcoholic condition."[85]

Conclusion: Church History and the Rejection of Violence

Evan Wright was a journalist "embedded" with an elite reconnaissance platoon of US marines as they invaded Iraq in 2003. His harrowing account of the war and the behavior of the belligerents, *Generation Kill*, details numerous incidents of savagery on the part of what he calls these

83. Polelle, *Raising Cartographic Consciousness*, 145.
84. Dalby, *Creating the Second Cold War*.
85. Tolstoy, *Kingdom of God Is within You*, 57.

"ultraviolent" US forces. He recounted how Marines regularly murdered wounded Iraqis, refused medical care to critically wounded prisoners, and took pleasure in killing and destroying. For this unit in particular, whose job was to speed ahead of advance attacks and effectively spring ambushes set for the main force, killing was their raison d'être, what they got high on, and even their motto.[86] However, despite initial impressions, he does not paint a picture of mindless brutality. On the contrary, he reports that the Marines constantly debated the morality of their actions. A sergeant in the platoon told him that he had consulted with his priest about killing. The priest had told him it was all right to kill for his government so long as he didn't enjoy it. As the killing proceeded, the sergeant told his men, "If we did half the s**t back home we've done here, we'd be in prison." By then, the sergeant recounted, he'd reconsidered what his priest had said about killing. "Where the f**k did Jesus say it's OK to kill people for your government? Any priest who tells me that has got no credibility," he said scornfully.[87]

For all his crudity of language, the Marine sergeant grasped what numerous refined churchmen down the ages have tragically failed to see. That is, advocating the killing of one's enemies is utterly contrary to the commandments of Christ and can only ever discredit his name and his cause. In 2004, Tom Frame, bishop to the Australian armed forces, issued a remarkable statement of repentance for his endorsement not only of recent Australian military backing of the US and UK but for his institutional role in support of war in general: "I continue to seek God's forgiveness for my complicity in creating a world in which this sort of action was ever considered to be necessary," he said.[88] The bishop's confession hit the nail on the head. The issue is not whether one particular war is "just" or not but how, in making such judgments, Christians have legitimized and perpetuated the institution and practice of warfare. In so doing, they have revoked and reversed the clear teaching of Christ and the apostles, and the practice of the apostolic and early church.

Scholar Michael Northcott has described the Constantinian adoption of just war theory as the moment when "Christianity was turned from its non-violent and anti-imperial origins into an imperial cult." He deems it "a tragic deformation of true Christianity" that the church needs

---

86. E. Wright, *Generation Kill.*

87. E. Wright, "Dead-Check in Falluja."

88. Frame, "Forgive Me, I Was Wrong on Iraq."

to work to reverse.[89] It is true that the church has often allowed its members to take part in wars. However, this is not an argument for Christian participation in war. On the contrary, the cumulative fallout from this dreadful mistake only underlines the wisdom of New Testament gospel peace. Just war theory, on which Christian involvement in warfare is largely based, is intended to make wars less frequent and less destructive. Most of its advocates believe war to be a regrettable evil, albeit one necessary for the pursuit of justice in a fallen world. However, that is to miss the point: it is simply not *Christian*. It may be a far higher ethic than that of plundering or "might is right," but it is a far lower ethic than that of Christ. The argument that Christian participation in warfare is justified because the church has allowed it in the past is unconvincing in the light of scripture, reason, and history.

Under the conviction that just war theory is both fundamentally unchristian and damaging to the cause of the gospel, large numbers of Christians down the ages have either rejected it altogether or expressed profound unease with it. These have included theologians, church leaders, and laymen and women. The number of such dissenters from just war theory has never been greater than at the present time. Like the medieval church's espousal of the idea that the sun revolved around the earth, or the later opinion that lightning rods protecting buildings were impious because they resisted the judgment of God, just war theory was an alien accessory added to the gospel by the church over time. Like these other beliefs and superstitions it would seem ludicrous—had it not been so pernicious. It is one of the last vestiges of a corrupted medieval church that the Reformation is finally ditching. As we shall see in chapter 8, this may be ushering in one of the most exciting periods in church history for many centuries. Before that, however, it is necessary to address the question that haunts Anglo-American Christian reflection on war and peace: what about Hitler?

89. Northcott, *Angel Directs the Storm*, 12.

6

What about Hitler? Part I
What Was the Second World War?

When applying for permission to enter the United States of America, foreign visitors like me are required to answer the following question: "Have you ever been or are you now involved in espionage or sabotage; or in terrorist activities; or genocide; or between 1933 and 1945 were you involved, in any way, in persecutions associated with Nazi Germany or its allies?"[1]

Quite apart from the obvious question about whether anyone would own up to one of these activities had they actually perpetrated them, I was struck when entering the United States recently by the oddity of the question. Why should an event that occurred more than sixty years ago be singled out for special attention, when it is far more likely that an arrivee has been implicated in some more recent atrocity that was not specifically named? The answer lies in part with the peculiar place that the Second World War has found in modern American and British cultural senses of national identity.

The Second World War has come to occupy such a unique place in Anglo-American self-understandings that it has even come to replace scripture as the cornerstone of reasoning for many British and American Christians. Many Christians realize intuitively that the spirit of Christianity is against warfare, and know that the New Testament teaching and examples of Christ and the apostles leave no place for violence. Yet they struggle to square this with the existence of bloody tyrants such as Adolf

---

1. Department of Homeland Security, US Customs and Border Protection, I-94W. Nonimmigrant Visa Waiver Arrival/Departure Record. As of April 2010 (and online September 2012).

Hitler and reluctantly conclude that for worshippers of God doing justice must demand even engaging in warfare to protect the innocent. Thus the question, "What would you do about Hitler?" becomes used as a "trump card" by those who assume that the only Christian answer to war is more war. This is such an important issue (and such a serious problem) that two chapters are devoted to it. Whereas the next chapter looks at the Christian churches and resistance to Hitler, this chapter revisits the historical record to challenge the assumption that the existence and actions of warlike tyrants, quintessentially represented by Adolf Hitler, justify Christians going to war in defense of justice. It suggests that the Second World War depicted in countless Hollywood films, a simple world of honest "goodies" and despicable "baddies" and clear moral choices between them, is not the real Second World War of history. It argues that when Hollywood rather than the Bible, and Hitler rather than Christ, exercise a greater influence on our ethics and theology, then the choices we make in the world our bound to be unchristian.

The Second World War

The Second World War has an extraordinary place in modern British and American senses of national identity. The cultural importance of the war is visible everywhere. In his witty memoir, *Achtung Schweinehund!*, Harry Pearson engagingly describes growing up in postwar Britain on a diet of Second World War films and plastic Airfix self-assembly model kits of planes and tanks, endlessly refighting the good war against evil Germans with his friends.[2] In July 2007 the British television broadcaster Sky TV screened an epic "100 greatest war films" program; three of its top four films—*Saving Private Ryan*, *The Great Escape*, and *Schindler's List*—were Second World War films.[3] It was also demonstrated in a 2002 BBC television show vote for "Great Britons," when the British public was asked to nominate the greatest British person of the past millennium: the Second World War leader, Sir Winston Churchill, topped the poll. It was famously parodied by the peerless British comedian John Cleese, in his 1970s portrayal of Basil Fawlty in the BBC television comedy *Fawlty Towers*. Cleese played an uptight British hotelier unable to follow his own

2. Pearson, *Achtung Schweinehund! A Boy's Own Story of Imaginary Combat*.
3. Sky television, UK, 07/07/2007.

advice to his staff in dealing with German guests: "Whatever you do, don't mention the war!"

The war's ongoing importance is far from simply cultural. Its contemporary political relevance has been underlined in recent British and American foreign policy, especially the leading role that the two states took in the wars against Iraq in 1991 and 2003. Leaders of both countries have spoken of these wars as yet another example of the "special relationship" between the two countries that was founded in the Second World War. For example, in 1990–91, in the face of international skepticism over his planned attack on Iraq following its invasion of Kuwait, President George H. W. Bush likened the fate of Kuwait in 1990 to that of Czechoslovakia in 1938. He said that those who opposed the war were "appeasing the dictator," a direct reference to Chamberlain's failed policy of trying to engage Hitler diplomatically.[4] His son, President George W. Bush, made similar insinuations in attempting to persuade the world to support his wars against Afghanistan in 2001 and Iraq in 2003. The allusion was misleading, of course: having failed in an eight-year-long struggle against neighboring Iran, Saddam Hussein's large but weak conscript army was in no state to launch a war of regional, let alone world, conquest. Nonetheless, this tactic worked in persuading the American public to support these dubious wars, even though in both cases major claims about Saddam's actions, capabilities, and intents were subsequently proved to be fraudulent.[5]

Why is it that World War II, of all modern wars, exerts such an enduring cultural influence and enjoys such remarkable political importance? Part of the answer must be the enormous scale of conflict and that it affected the lives of so many who molded the postwar period. Doubtless too, as Richard Evans put it, it is because of the probing moral questions that it raises about the possibilities for human destructiveness, the potential consequences of militarism and discrimination, and the dilemmas of conformity or resistance.[6] But there remains far more fascination with the war in Britain and the United States than in most other countries, even countries that were more seriously and more directly affected, such

4. Ó Tuathail, "Effacement of Place?," 17.

5. The fraudulence of claims in 2003 that Iraq possessed "weapons of mass destruction" is well known. For a summary of fraudulent claims and deception by the US and Kuwaiti governments in 1990–91, see Pollock and Lutz, "Archaeology Deployed for the Gulf War," 265.

6. R. Evans, *Third Reich at War*, 764.

as the Soviet Union and France. Part of the answer, therefore, is that for Britain and the United States, World War II is more than a victorious historical conflict or a moral lesson: it is what scholars of geopolitics call an "identity myth."

By this, they are not of course claiming that it did not really take place. Rather, they mean that this version of it occupies a special place in our present-day understanding of who we are, a self-understanding that continues to influence how we make sense of the world and who we are in the world. This identity myth is of two entirely innocent states united together in a titanic and absolutely just struggle for freedom against pure evil embodied in Nazi Germany, fascist Italy, and imperial Japan—that they delivered the rest of the world from. No other conflict in our history plays the same role, or so greatly shapes the way that we—Christian or otherwise—think about war in our own times. Geopolitician Gearóid Ó Tuathail describes this version of World War II as a "feel-good war,"[7] a gratifying and clear-cut storyline of beleaguered freedom desperately struggling against rampant evil, with us as the "goodies" and them as the "baddies." This "script," as Ó Tuathail calls it, makes the answer to the question "what about Hitler?" obvious. Significantly, it also makes the answer to the question "what do we do about people whom we compare to Hitler?" equally obvious.

Although such a script undoubtedly makes for good speeches and good films, does it make good history and good theology? In this chapter, I will argue that it does not, and that it has trapped Christians into thinking about war through the worldview of the British and American World War II identity myth, rather than the biblical worldview. It is very difficult for a modern Briton or an American to look critically beyond this identity myth. But unless we do that we will never allow our minds to be molded by the Bible's story, rather than Britain's story; by Adam's story, rather than America's.

What Was the Second World War?

World War II, as portrayed in accounts such as the respected *Times Atlas of the Second World War*,[8] is seen as a series of battles, invasions, and counter-invasions between the so-called Axis and Allies. Germany and

7. Ó Tuathail, "The Effacement of Place?"

8. Keegan, *The Times Atlas of the Second World War.*

its principal allies, Italy and Japan (the "Axis"), sought to carve out large empires for themselves by invading and subjugating numerous other countries. The "Allies" (principally Britain, the United States, and the Soviet Union; some historians would add France) resisted this aggression in a truly global struggle that left few parts of the world untouched. The war came to an end on September 2, 1945, when, last of the Axis powers to hold out, Japan finally surrendered. An estimated fifty million people died in the most destructive war thus far in human history.

The horror of the Second World War, however, was not simply that of great powers clashing and causing enormous loss of life. The Axis countries maintained rule of both their own states and conquered territories through a ruthless reign of terror that suppressed dissent and resistance. Even more insidiously, they propagated beliefs in racial superiority that led Nazi Germany to attempt to systematically annihilate whole populations whom they regarded as subhuman. These included gypsies, homosexuals, and the mentally and physically handicapped, but their principal target was Jews. Jewish populations—first in Germany and subsequently in the territories that Germany and its allies ruled or overran—were initially identified as being different through visible markers such as badges, then were subject to theft or destruction of property, and eventually were singled out for mass murder. Murder took place on a chillingly calculating scale of industrial killing in death camps like Auschwitz, where modern achievements of Europe-wide transport systems were coordinated by educated men and women carefully running bureaucracies to wipe out Europe's Jews. This bequeathed the world a frightening new word: *genocide*. But most Jews died outside of these camps: in fields and woods, or in their homes, streets, and synagogues. In occupied and Axis-allied East Europe, often small numbers of German officers oversaw gangs of Ukrainians, Latvians, Hungarians, and others, who murdered their Jewish neighbors and looted their possessions, fueled not only (or not even) by anti-Semitism but by drink, the promise of booty, and a debauched culture of power and prostitution that fed off this new wealth.[9] In many cases, the Jewish populations of whole villages were rounded up and either shot on the spot or herded into synagogues and burned to death. For example, in the village of Byelaya Tserkov, near Kiev, the German army rounded up several hundred Jewish men and women, and shot each in the head. Ninety of their children, from babies

9. Stone, "Beyond the Auschwitz Syndrome."

to age six, were shut in a building for three days without food or water, lying in fly-covered excrement. After three days they were taken to the edge of a wood, shot, and cast into a mass grave.[10] Some German soldiers and citizens were uncomfortable with this massacre, and the extent to which the German populace knew about the scale of the Holocaust remains a topic of scholarly debate. Nonetheless, accounts of individual German soldiers and their allies reveling in the sadistic invention of cruel ways to torment their murder victims abound.

Bruno Bettelheim, an Austrian Jewish psychologist who survived the Dachau and Buchenwald camps to write his penetrating analysis, *The Informed Heart*, describes how the existence of the camps and the threat of being arrested and taken to them allowed the Nazi regime to disintegrate the entire personality of adults across the whole of Germany. For example, the replacement of traditional handshake greetings with the Nazi salute meant that numerous times each day an anti-Nazi must make the Nazi symbol or face almost certain death in camps, thus destroying his self-dignity. Or, children were encouraged to inform on parents who expressed any anti-Nazi views. Few children did so, but the knowledge that some did terrorized parents, breaking trust and reducing the personal dignity that they obtained from being masters of their own homes. By numerous similar measures the Nazi state created such an atmosphere of fear for the general population that they not only obtained compliance, but many people even felt such relief when they were finally summoned to Gestapo headquarters (and therefore death) that they willingly went rather than sought to escape, claims Bettelheim.[11]

The brute fact of this unbelievably terrible regime, and the estimated 5 to 6 million Jews who died at its hands, can be pitted against the argument above that World War II acts simply as an "identity myth." Surely, the face of evil shown in the Holocaust makes it easy to answer the question, "What do you do about Hitler?"—stop him, and those like him, at all costs. This was the answer eventually reached by the German Christian Dietrich Bonhoeffer, who was executed in April 1945 for his part in a failed plot to kill Adolf Hitler. For many British and American Christians, the conclusion that Bonhoeffer and his co-plotters arrived at is the correct one: it was undesirable but nonetheless necessary in a fallen

10. R. Evans, *Third Reich at War*, 229–30.
11. Bettelheim, *Informed Heart*, ch. 7.

world to prevent the forces of evil, when embodied in warmongering tyrants like Hitler, from running amok.

Can this conclusion possibly be challenged? Yes, it can, and to begin our challenge we need to ask an apparently obvious question, but one that is very difficult to answer: when did the Second World War begin?

When Was the Second World War?

In order to answer the question of *what* the Second World War was, it is useful to ask when it began. At first, this appears an obvious question. It began on September 1, 1939, when Germany under Hitler invaded Poland, and when Britain and France, honoring treaty commitments, declared war on Germany. Over the following six years more and more states became embroiled in the largest and most destructive conflict the globe has ever known.

That is a British perspective. For the American public, the war with the Axis powers began on December 7, 1941, when the Japanese launched a surprise attack on the US Pacific Ocean naval base in Pearl Harbor. For the Soviets, what they call the "Great Patriotic War" began on June 22, 1941, when Germany reneged on a treaty agreement and attacked the Soviet Union. For the Chinese, the war began in 1937 with a full-scale Japanese incursion. Likewise, for the Ethiopians, it began on October 3, 1935, when the Italians invaded their homeland.[12]

So, when did the Second World War begin? How about March 23, 1899?

On that date a bizarre coronation took place. Malietoa Tanu, wearing an ill-fitting British naval officer's dress uniform and borrowed canvas shoes, was crowned king of the Pacific islands of Samoa, under the protection of British and American naval guns. The celebrations were short-lived as the followers of Mataafa, a German-backed candidate, sought to overthrow him. In the end British and American force prevailed, and an international commission subsequently divided Samoa between German and American rule, with the British receiving compensation elsewhere.[13]

---

12. Incidentally, out of a general sympathy for colonialism and also a leaning to fascism, the "British-Italian Council for Peace and Friendship" supported the Italian invasion of Abyssinia (Ethiopia), through a campaign in the UK, arguing that Italian motives were primarily humanitarian. Whittal, "Colonial Fascism," 46.

13. Boot, *The Savage Wars of Peace.*

It would be absurd to date the origins of the Second World War to a relatively minor dispute in a remote Pacific island in the late nineteenth century. However, the Samoan episode is one of many that illustrates the expanding imperial power rivalry whose eventual climax came in 1945. In the nineteenth century and first half of the twentieth century, superior military technology was allowing the "big seven"—Britain, France, Germany, Italy, Russia (later Soviet Union), Japan, and the United States to frantically build expanding empires outside of their territorial homelands by subjugating other peoples and states.

Two characteristics of this imperialism can be noted, which are true for all seven countries. The first was that it was about extending territorial control for the benefits of economic exploitation. The second was that it was justified by a belief in the inherent inferiority of the conquered peoples. This inferiority was expressed in arguments about the civilizational or racial or ideological superiority of the imperialists, and sometimes too by recourse to claims of divine providence. This potent mix led to a form of warfare and conquest that was unimaginably cruel and savage. It resulted in the annihilation of peoples by the millions, whether Irish, Africans, and Indians at the hands of the British; Chinese at the hands of the Japanese; or Jews at the hands of the Germans. It is no coincidence that these big seven countries were the main protagonists of World War II, for, in truth, this clash of 1914–45 was the inexorable outcome of the process of competition put in motion a century earlier. In the following sections, we will consider the imperialism of some of these competitors in this "game." There is not space to discuss Russia, which, under both the Tsars and the Soviets, was using violence to build an empire in the Caucasus, Central Asia, and the Far East. Neither is it possible here to consider Italy, which, under Mussolini, was doing the same in Southeast Europe and North and East Africa; nor likewise France, whose empire covered Asia, Africa, and the Americas. So, we will look at the story in so far as it concerns the other four of the seven: Britain, the United States, Germany, and Japan.

Britain

We are not a young people with *an innocent record and* a scanty inheritance. We have engrossed to ourselves . . . *an altogether disproportionate* share of the wealth and traffic of the world.

> We have got all we want in territory, and our claim to be left in
> unmolested enjoyment of vast and splendid possessions, *mainly
> acquired by violence, largely maintained by force*, often seems less
> reasonable to others than to us.

This paragraph was written by future Prime Minister Winston Churchill,
in a paper submitted to his cabinet colleagues in 1914 explaining the
need for an increase in military expenditure. The italicized phrases were
judiciously removed from the version made public in his book *The World
Crisis* in 1920.[14] It is easy to see why parts of his startlingly candid description of Britain's place in the world were seen as not fit for public
consumption.

Britain's quest for greatness and empire was an old one. England
had lost its first empire in France in the Middle Ages, then its second in
North America with the American War of Independence at the end of
the eighteenth century. In the nineteenth century it built a third, focused
on India but including possessions in other parts of Asia, Africa, Ocea-
nia, the Mediterranean, and the Caribbean. This quest for greatness and
empire would drive it into fatal competition with Germany between 1914
and 1945 and is one of the most disturbing and shameful aspects of the
country's history.

In 1877 the ex-president of the United States, Ulysses S. Grant, departed for a grand tour of Europe and Asia.[15] *New York Herald* journalist John Russell Young accompanied him and reported seeing famine in
British-controlled areas of Africa, India, and China. He wrote, "English
influence in the East is only another name for English tyranny." British
rule in India was "despotism . . . mighty, irresponsible, cruel." Five million
people had died of starvation there in the preceding three years, while
Britain was extracting enormous sums of money from its most profitable
colony.

That famines had occurred across such a wide area was not a coincidence. Climatologists now know that the El Niño effect, a periodic
change of the ocean's temperature that can lead to drought or freak flood-
ing, triggered a number of major droughts in the nineteenth century.
These events weakened peoples in Asia and Africa: rather than assist
these populations over which they had assumed responsibility, colonial

14. Chomsky, *The New Military Humanism.*

15. Material for this and the subsequent two paragraphs is drawn largely from
Davies, *Late Victorian Holocausts.*

powers such as Britain used El Niño as an opportunity to increase and extend their influence.

For example, in 1877, seeking to exploit the suffering of people during a famine in southern Africa, Prime Minister Benjamin Disraeli dispatched Sir Bartle Frere as a high commissioner. He made war on weakened independent African kingdoms and societies such as Khosa, Bantus, and Boers. However, he underestimated their desire to be free, and when sixteen hundred British troops were lost at Isandlwana in 1879, the empire struck back in revenge with a systematic policy of burning homes, seizing cattle, and destroying the economic foundations of the Zulu society.[16] Drought was taken as an opportunity to create poverty by British policy in southern Africa: people who refused to support the British were made destitute by not having their land returned after the famine had passed.

But it was India that suffered most at this time. By the late nineteenth century British industrial goods were increasingly uncompetitive in the world market, so India was forced to purchase them. By 1910, for example, two-fifths of UK finished cotton goods and three-fifths of railway exports, pharmaceuticals, electrical products, and books were exported to India, even though the government of India could have bought them more cheaply elsewhere. The British went to extraordinary lengths to maintain this system. They imposed a "Salt Tax" on India, which Roy Moxham calculates in the mid-nineteenth century meant that while the Indian peasant would have to pay two months' wages for his yearly salt requirements, the Chinese peasant to the north would only have to pay two days' wages.[17] To enforce this, the British obviously had to prevent salt smuggling from China, so they planted a "customs hedge" on an embankment twenty feet high and forty feet wide stretching 2,300 miles across northern India. This hedge was one of the greatest constructions in human history, yet also "a monstrosity; a terrible instrument of British oppression."[18] Such was the wealth from what can be considered one of history's greatest protection rackets that twelve thousand men were employed to patrol the hedge. In 1930 Gandhi chose the Salt Tax as the issue with which to confront the British government in his campaign of civil disobedience.

16. Ibid., 102.

17. Moxham, *Great Hedge of India*, 170. The 1910 export statistics in this paragraph are taken from Davies, *Late Victorian Holocausts*.

18. Moxham, *Great Hedge of India*, 222–23.

India was also vital to British investment, financed by the export of cash crops such as opium, cotton, wheat, and rice. The effects of these arrangements were devastating for India. Development was held back as India was unable to purchase the highest-quality goods at lower prices on the world market. Cash crops meant basic food production for Indian people was inadequate, while mass irrigation for those crops undermined traditional irrigation systems used for food and created conditions ideal for the spread of diseases such as malaria. A crippling 25 percent of the Indian government's expenditure was on Britain's wars (with China, for example), whereas Victorian England never spent more than 3 percent. Indian wealth was manipulated to keep UK interest rates low and thus promote British investment, leading to a collapse in the value of the savings of ordinary Indians.

The impact of these policies was what Davis pointedly calls a "holocaust." British politicians and public opinion tolerated the deaths of up to one million people in its closest colony, Ireland, in the famine of 1845–47, but this figure was multiplied many tenfold in the case of India, where the death toll during the droughts of 1876–79 and 1896–1902 is estimated between twelve and thirty million. It was not that they were killed by droughts. Documents show that the impact of a similar drought in 1661, before British rule, was less severe because the Emperor took measures such as opening the treasury, giving aid, importing grain and distributing it either freely or cheaply, and temporarily reducing taxes. Likewise, in 1743–44 Qing dynasty China avoided famine during an El Niño drought by good organization of aid and redistribution of wealth: tellingly, the same drought led to mass starvation in Europe. British viceroys of India such as Lord Curzon allowed huge grain exports to England in the middle of mass starvation. Surplus grain existed either in India or elsewhere in the empire, and British railways and shipping meant that it could be distributed speedily if needed: a political decision was made that Indians should die so that Britain should keep enjoying the benefits of luxury.

But suffering on such an unimaginable scale did not elicit sympathy from British and other imperial powers but rather greed for further opportunity. The dry years of 1881–91 brought famine to India, Korea, Brazil, Russia, and the Horn of Africa. Failing monsoons across the tropics at the end of the nineteenth century brought hugely destructive epidemics of malaria, bubonic plague, dysentery, smallpox, and cholera that culled millions from the ranks of those whom famine had already weakened.

European empires, the United States, and Japan "rapaciously exploited the opportunity to wrest new colonies, expropriate communal lands, and tap novel sources of plantation and mine labour. What seemed from a metropolitan perspective the nineteenth century's final blaze of imperial glory was, from an Asian or African viewpoint, only the hideous light of a giant funeral pyre."[19]

Enlightened English people were appalled. William Digby, a chronicler of the 1876 Madras famine, speculated that when "the part played by the British Empire in the nineteenth century is regarded by the historian fifty years hence, the unnecessary deaths of millions of Indians would be its principal and most notorious monument." But, for the most part, Britons patriotically sang the words of Benson's early twentieth-century popular hymn to Britain: "Wider still and wider shall thy bounds be set / God, who made thee mighty, make thee mightier yet."

Our consideration of British imperialism began with the eye-opening exposure of Winston Churchill's candid admission of the violence and injustice of imperialism. On May 14, 1840, another future prime minister of Britain, William Gladstone, wrote in his diary, "I am in dread of the judgement of God upon England for our national iniquity towards China."[20] Well he might dread: by military power (especially wars of 1839–42 and 1856–58) and diplomatic trickery, throughout the nineteenth century Britain forced China to accept opium and derivative imports (such as heroin) from British India. Indeed, from 1832 to 1872 the proportion of income to British India's coffers obtained from this wicked trade jumped from one-eighteenth to one-seventh. In 1879 alone a staggering eighty-seven thousand chests of opium were exported to China, which Mike Davis calls the "biggest drug transaction in world history."[21] By 1870 a House of Commons motion to condemn this trade was heavily defeated, with Gladstone himself now supporting it as important for the economy of Britain.[22]

In 1927 the poet Muhammad Iqbal, reflecting on the consequences of just such appalling European imperialism in Asia, wrote, "Europe's hordes with flame and fire / desolate the world entire."[23] But Iqbal's ge-

19. Davies, *Late Victorian Holocausts*, 6–7.
20. Beeching, *Chinese Opium Wars*, 164.
21. Davies, *Late Victorian Holocausts*, 300.
22. Beeching, *Chinese Opium Wars*, 164, 331.
23. Houweling and Amineh, "Geopolitics of Power Projection," 68.

ography was too limited: it was not just Europe. Britain, France, Russia, and Germany used force and trickery to oblige a weakened China into unfair trading agreements, but they were joined in slicing up the cake by Japan and the United States. All these powers variously competed or cooperated in a game that would inexorably lead to, and temporarily be settled by, the Second World War. As the examples discussed in this section such as Samoa and China reveal, the United States was as thoroughly implicated in this imperialism as were its future World War II allies and enemies, and it is to the United States that we turn now.

The United States

In 1845 the United States was engaged in a war with Mexico, after which it took half of Mexico's territory. In opposing this, a former New York congressman envisaged what for him was a frightening future for an imperial America: "Contemplating this future, we behold all seas covered by our fleets; our garrisons hold the most important stations of commerce; an immense standing army maintains our possessions; our traders have become the richest, our demagogues the most powerful and our people the most corrupt and flexible in the world."[24]

Such opinions were generally dismissed: America was a democratic republic not a European-style empire, or so the argument went, and its wars were in the name of freedom. However, while its leaders did not use the word *empire*, from the declaration of American independence in 1776, they pursued a policy remarkably similar to that of Britain's—extending formal or informal territorial control for economic gain, based on the belief of their inherent superiority.

In the decades following independence, this expansion was principally on the North American continent. Millions of Native Americans were annihilated as the white Americans grabbed their land in a westward push. President Theodore Roosevelt summed up popular attitudes toward the "redskins" by saying, "I do not go so far as to say that the only good Indians are dead Indians, but I believe nine out of ten are, and I shouldn't inquire too closely the case of the tenth."[25]

Sociologist Michael Mann, in his disturbing book *The Dark Side of Democracy*, records how America's supposedly enlightened politicians

24. Quoted in Horsley, *Jesus and Empire*, 39.
25. Quoted in Houweling and Amineh, "Geopolitics of Power Projection," 34.

and thinkers saw the Indians whose territory they were stealing. Thomas Jefferson wrote that the "barbarities" of Native Americans "justified extermination." Theodore Roosevelt said that their "extermination was as ultimately beneficial as it was inevitable," and George Washington instructed his generals to attack the Iroquois and "lay waste all the settlements . . . that the country may not be merely overrun but destroyed." This was put into practice, ruthlessly. For example, in 1867 Indians raided for horses and killed four whites. In response, some Tucson residents attacked an Apache village unconnected to the raiders, killing 144 of the inhabitants, only eight of whom were men; many of the women were raped first. *Denver News* congratulated the killers, adding, "We only regret that the number was not double."[26] Even Nazi Germany was never as publicly candid about its systematic slaughter of comparable numbers of Jews.

This policy continued through wars with neighboring Mexico, whereby the United States grew from a relatively small territorial base on the eastern seaboard of the continent to cover much of North America within a century. In his harrowing account of the conquest of Texas between 1820 and 1875, which he subtitles *Ethnic Cleansing in the Promised Land,* Gary Anderson describes how government and citizens not only sought to subdue native lands for their own economic use, but to completely exterminate the native populations. They simply would not accept Native Americans living in their territory. The notorious Texas Rangers were encouraged by the state's government "to attack Indian villages filled with women and children—the usual victims of ethnic cleansing. Rangers killed indiscriminately, they robbed, and they raped. Their goal was to spread terror so that neighboring Native groups would leave."[27]

As biblical scholar Richard Horsley observes, within a few decades after the declaration that "all men are created equal," the United States had killed or expelled virtually the entire native population from east of the Mississippi River, "climaxing a historically unprecedented process of ethnic cleansing."[28]

This genocidal expansion of America did not stop at its present borders. In 1823 President Monroe declared what became known as the Monroe Doctrine—that the United States regarded the entire American

26. Mann, *Dark Side of Democracy,* ix, 91–92.

27. Anderson, *Conquest of Texas,* 8.

28. Horsley, *Jesus and Empire,* 137.

hemisphere as its backyard and would not tolerate the presence of European imperial meddling. Max Boot calculates that between 1800 and 1934 the US marines alone staged 180 landings abroad as part of the United States' "savage wars of peace," many of which were in Latin American and Caribbean countries, in support of US commercial interests.[29] In the early twentieth century Britain recalled its Caribbean fleet squadrons as it felt increasingly threatened by Germany, and the United States replaced Britain in the region as the dominant naval power.

As the nineteenth century progressed and much of the Americas fell under US sway, the United States sought to extend its control westward into the Pacific. We have seen earlier how the United States brought half of Samoa under its domination. But a major moment was the United States' war with Spain in 1898. The rump of the Spanish Empire, which had once controlled most of Central and South America and parts of Asia and Africa, had been struggling to control its last major territories, the Philippines and Cuba. As Philippine rebel victory and national freedom were imminent, the United States intervened, allegedly to assist the anti-imperial war, but actually to take control of the country for itself. Four thousand American soldiers died, but some modern scholars estimate that almost a million Filipinos perished in the genocide that this invasion unleashed, mainly of disease and starvation as the United States ruthlessly put down almost a decade of resistance for independence.[30] The final settlement saw Spain cede control of not only the Philippines but also Guam and Puerto Rico to the United States. In a particularly dirty deal, America recognized the Japanese imperial takeover of Korea in exchange for Japanese recognition of its conquests of the Philippines and also Hawaii, another Pacific kingdom that saw its monarchy toppled by the United States (in 1893) in its westward expansion.

In 1993, exactly a century later, Congress issued a formal apology for the overthrow of the Kingdom of Hawaii.[31] But, as with the case of British imperialism, there was some domestic dissent at the time of the overthrow by those horrified at the injustice of the act. Mark Twain was ashamed at the war, saying that the stars and stripes of the American flag ought to be replaced with a skull and crossbones.[32] Such criticism

29. Boot, *The Savage Wars of Peace*.
30. Hamilton-Paterson, *America's Boy*, 37.
31. Weyeneth, "Power of Apology," 10.
32. Hamilton-Paterson, *America's Boy*, 37.

was brushed aside by the initiator of the war, President McKinley, who said that the United States had been acting "in the interest of civilization, humanity, and liberty," and further expounded,

> We were obeying a higher moral obligation, which rested on us and which did not require anybody's consent. We were doing our duty by them, as God gave us the light to see our duty, with the consent of our own consciences and with the approval of civilization. . . . It is not a good time for the liberator to submit important questions concerning liberty and government to the liberated while they are engaged in shooting down their rescuers.[33]

Mark Twain's was not the only dissenting voice. Senator Henry Cabot Lodge, a critic of "manifest destiny," said that the United States had a "record of conquest, colonization, and territorial expansion unequalled by any people in the nineteenth century."[34] And, as with Britain, this was based on twin props of violent territorial expansion for economic gain and a belief in the inherent superiority of the imperialist. As we shall see in the next section, the same holds true of those countries that would be termed the "Axis" powers.

Germany

Compared to Britain, Germany was a relative latecomer to overseas imperialism, but what it lacked in history it sought to make up for in effort. Germany was consolidated as a state following its grabbing of land from various neighbors whom it defeated in battle, such as Denmark in 1864 and France in 1871. By this time it had established a substantial European homeland. From this base, Germany sought to accelerate the quest to have its own "place in the sun," as Kaiser Wilhelm put it, alongside the other imperial powers. It built up an extensive empire in Africa, seizing territories including present-day Namibia, Rwanda, Burundi, and Cameroon. In Asia it acquired island chains such as the Marshall, Solomon, and Caroline islands. It also gained treaty concessions in China.

As with its rivals such as Britain and America, these policies were undertaken in the name of civilization but often with immense brutality. For example, in 1904 the Hereros people in German South-West Africa

33. Chomsky, *New Military Humanism*, 76–77.
34. Quoted in Horsley, *Jesus and Empire*, 140.

(Namibia) rebelled against harsh colonial rule. The German military commander, General von Trotha, ordered the Hereros to leave Namibia or be killed, issuing the following declaration:

> I, the great general of the German troops, send this letter to the Herero people. . . . All Hereros must leave this land. . . . Any Herero found within the German borders with or without a gun, with or without cattle, will be shot. I shall no longer receive any women or children; I will drive them back to their people. I will shoot them. This is my decision for the Herero people.[35]

Many Hereros were massacred with machine guns. Others had their wells poisoned and then were driven into the desert to die. Estimates put their death toll between 35,000 and 105,000 people. At a remembrance ceremony in 2001 Germany's ambassador expressed "regret" for the genocide but ruled out meeting Herero demands for economic compensation, which Herero Paramount Chief Kuaima Riruako insisted was "an effort to regain our dignity and help us restore what was wrongfully taken away from us."[36]

The First World War was disastrous for Germany. Rivals Britain, America, and Japan grabbed its overseas empire, while neighbors like Denmark and France took large swaths of adjacent land controlled by Germany. The postwar settlement conferences of Versailles imposed punitive sanctions on Germany, including hefty reparations and loss of territory.[37]

This settlement was intended, in the words of a leading contemporary British geopolitical advocate of imperialism, Sir Halford Mackinder, to "reduce the German people to its proper position in the world."[38] Mackinder was an arch advocate of British imperialism and paranoid that the global supremacy of the country would be threatened by rising German power,[39] especially if it could expand eastwards.[40] Nonetheless, although Germany had its imperial wings clipped, the expansion of powers that had emerged as victorious continued unabated. As well as seizing

35. *BBC News*, "Germany Regrets Namibia 'Genocide,'" http://news.bbc.co.uk/2/hi/africa/3388901.stm.

36. Ibid., para. 9.

37. Fleure, *The Treaty Settlement of Europe*.

38. Mackinder, *Democratic Ideals and Reality*, 203.

39. Blouet, *Halford Mackinder*, especially ch. 8.

40. Mackinder, "The Geographical Pivot of History."

lands from Germany in Africa and Asia, France and Britain snapped up more territories from the defeated Ottoman Turks. The United States continued to use its military to extend its influence in Latin America and elsewhere. Russia was busily developing an economic heartland in its recently acquired possessions in Central Asia and Siberia. Even Italy was expanding in North Africa.

Germans, understandably, feared for their future fate with their neighbors expanding and growing when Germany itself was forced to remain weakened at its reduced size. A postwar German school textbook included three maps showing Germany imprisoned, dismembered, and, with the relative weakness of the German army compared to its neighbors, highly vulnerable.[41] Unsurprisingly, this provided fertile ground for the rise of Nazism, which promised to reverse these losses and protect the fragile German people. This movement was given intellectual support by the work of a group of scholars, led by professor of geopolitics General Karl Haushofer, who created a vision of future German strength. Haushofer developed the concept of *Lebensraum*, or "living space." This was the idea, popular in Europe and America after Darwinism, that states were living organisms that needed to expand or die.[42] These scholars argued that just as Germany's numerous rivals were expanding, so too the German state needed *Lebensraum* or it would fall behind in its competition with other states. They said, however, that Germany should not now try to seek overseas greatness as Kaiser Wilhelm had done, but rather should expand its territory in Central Europe.[43] This was exactly what Hitler did, and it was popular with many Germans because it was understood as a just and necessary way to defend Germany by doing exactly what its rivals and persecutors were doing elsewhere.

Japan

As with Germany, Japan was another relative latecomer to the imperial game. Until 1853 the Japanese had maintained a policy of isolation from the outside world. This was ended in that year when US Commodore Matthew Perry sailed four warships into Tokyo Bay and threatened to

41. Heffernan, *Meaning of Europe*, 136–37.

42. This idea was outlined by Ratzel, "The Laws of the Spatial Growth of States." For Haushofer himself, see Haushofer, "Why Geopolitik?"

43. Ó Tuathail, *Critical Geopolitics: The Politics of Writing Global Space*.

shell the city, thereby massacring its vulnerable population, unless Japan opened trade with the West. Within a few years such "gunboat diplomacy" forced the Japanese to sign unequal trade treaties with a number of Western powers. Understandably alarmed at the threat of growing American and European imperialism, in the last quarter of the nineteenth century they undertook a major project of modernization, industrialization, and militarization.

In the two decades before the First World War, Japan began building an empire. Successful wars against China and Russia allowed it to seize territory on the Asian mainland (including Korea) and some offshore islands. During the First World War Japan took advantage of Germany's distraction to join Britain and the Allies in declaring war on Germany. It seized—and, after the war, kept—some of Germany's colonial territories, such as German New Guinea and treaty territories in China. Warily viewing American imperial expansion in its vicinity, it recognized American control over the Philippines as a concession for being allowed to maintain possession of Korea.

Beginning in 1930 the Japanese launched an undeclared war on China, invading Manchuria in 1931. In 1937 this was renewed with a full-scale invasion and war. The course of this war is reconstructed in Iris Chang's harrowing account of the Japanese conquest of the Chinese city of Nanking in 1937. In "six weeks of terror," hundreds of thousands of Chinese were killed following the fall of the city. Numerous specific incidents were recorded by foreign missionaries, which are too distressing to recount here in detail, but broad "strategies" can be outlined. Sport was made of novel and mass killings. Japanese officers lined up civilians and raced each other in competitions to see who could behead the most in the shortest period of time. Women and young girls were repeatedly raped and then their bodies sexually mutilated before being murdered.[44] Eventually, Japan was forced to surrender its conquests in China and elsewhere with its final defeat in 1945.

Imperial Competition, Not Goodies versus Baddies

On July 29, 1921, General Billy Mitchell of the US Army Air Service led a force of heavy bombers in a simulated bombing raid on New York, picking out landmark buildings. After landing, he declared to the carefully

44. Chang, *The Rape of Nanking*.

assembled press corps that the twenty-one tons of bombs his planes simulated dropping would have paralyzed the city. Using new onboard
technology developed by Kodak, the raid was filmed and rushed for
distribution in cinemas around the country the next day. As he repeated
these theatricals in other cities, newspapers struggled to outdo each other
in gory accounts of the destruction that would have occurred had these
raids been real rather than simulated.[45]

These stunts were organized and funded by US chemical weapons companies disappointed that, as they saw it, the premature end of
World War I had not allowed them to sufficiently profit from the conflict.
They were designed to swing public opinion away from antiwar pacifist
sentiment, as part of a campaign to persuade the government to fund
a massive buildup of weapons of mass destruction (heavy bombers and
chemical weapons) for a possible future confrontation with Germany
or Japan. Germany and Japan, seeing these claims in public and fearing a massive buildup of this attack capacity explicitly intended to attack
them, responded by building up their own forces. German and Japanese
governments used this US arms buildup to scare their own populations
into supporting a similar militarization drive. For example, Germany was
saturated with images and writings showing their total vulnerability to
potential allied bomber aircraft carrying poison gas. Eight-foot dummy
bombs were hung up in city centers to visually demonstrate the threat.
Thus, corporate-funded American propaganda helped provoke an arms
race that made World War II more likely. Danger became a self-fulfilling
prophecy.

Such histories, like the histories considered thus far in this chapter,
challenge the British and American "identity myth" of the Second World
War as being about good "Allies" fighting for freedom, democracy, and the
liberation of the Jews against an evil "Axis" hell-bent on world conquest
and genocide. Rather, the war that ended in 1945 was the culmination
of numerous local wars in different parts of the globe that came together
as part of the nineteenth-century imperial clash for world dominance
between the "big seven" countries. These countries were very different,
with different systems of government, religions, ideologies, and ways of
making war. But all had two characteristics in common over this period.

The first was the desire to extend territorial control for the benefits of economic exploitation. This was variously through both formal

---

45. Jenkins, *The Final Frontier: America, Science, and Terror.*

annexation of territory and informal pressure to force countries to trade on favorable terms. It included the naked grab of other people's land but also economic legislation and tariff regimes that excluded other countries from taking advantage of trade opportunities within certain territories. Thus in 1930 the Smoot-Hawley legislation in the United States raised import duties, and in 1932 the Ottawa Agreements created a system of imperial preference within the British Empire.[46] Such measures pushed out German companies, putting the country at an economic disadvantage and thus increasing pressure for it to expand elsewhere. These economic measures reflected similar social developments at the same time. In a monumental book described by *History Today* magazine as "the definitive account of the Nazi economy,"[47] Adam Tooze examines the economic foundations of Nazi foreign policy. Hitler's wars, he argues, were not based on his admiration of imperial Britain, or a visceral hatred of the Soviet Union, but were essentially challenging the United States to global dominance.[48] Thus Hitler knew Germany was fighting a proxy war with the United States, whose support of Britain and the USSR was crucial for the survival of both. In 1939 and 1940 he knew he had to break the United States' western European allies, Britain and France. Although he succeeded in conquering much of western Europe, he still lacked the basic industrial base to compete with the United States. Even though he used essentially slave labor from concentration camps to keep production costs down, his factories were still often only working at half their capacity due to a perpetual oil shortage resulting from the Royal Navy's blockade. Therefore, he invaded the Soviet Union to gain control of its oil resources, which would have helped him compete with the United States. He was not able to secure them, and eventually lost the war. The Second World War was a clash for global dominance between self-interested imperial powers.

The second characteristic common to all the big seven countries in this imperial clash was a belief in the inherent inferiority of the conquered peoples. This was expressed in arguments about the civilizational, racial, or ideological superiority of the imperialists, or by appeals to divine providence. All the powers involved professed to be working for the good of conquered peoples. The Japanese professed an intention to establish an

46. Blouet, "The Imperial Vision of Halford Mackinder."
47. Stargardt, "The Wages of Destruction."
48. Tooze, *The Wages of Destruction*.

"earthly paradise" and to protect Manchurians from "Chinese bandits."
Hitler claimed to be conducting an operation "filled with earnest desire
to serve the true interests of the peoples dwelling in the area" by protecting minority rights. US President McKinley said of the 1898 US seizure
of Cuba that it was done "in the interest of civilization, humanity, and
liberty" and "in the name of humanity."[49] US President Theodore Roosevelt said of the conquest of the West that "the most ultimately righteous
of all wars is a war with savages," establishing the rule of "the dominant
world races." Germany fought a racial war of extermination to cleanse
large stretches of land from racial inferiors; European settlers in North
America and Australasia had done likewise;[50] indeed, Nazi propagandists
said that they were only following in the Americans' footsteps. Whether
by appeals to "manifest destiny," God, ideology, civilization, or even the
interests of the conquered people, the big seven countries committed
mass genocides against those conquered peoples whom they regarded
as inferior. It is not without reason that sociologist Michael Mann writes,
"Murderous ethnic cleansing comes from our civilisation and from people, most of whom have been not unlike ourselves."[51]

This is *not* to conclude in the advocacy of relativism. To compare
is not the same as to equate. As Niebuhr wrote, "If it is not possible to
express a moral preference for the justice achieved in democratic societies, in comparison with tyrannical societies, no historical preference
has any meaning."[52] That Stalin, Roosevelt, and Churchill beat Hitler and
Mussolini was undoubtedly better for humanity than if they had lost.
British and American democratic systems worked better than German
and Italian ones. It is true that examples can be found of American gloat-
ing in public over the massacres of native populations that was candid
and unrestrained. However, popular national morality in Britain, while it
generally celebrated imperialism, would never have condoned the public
lionizing of warriors vying with each other in a competition to see who
could behead more prisoners of war that gripped Japan in 1937. Politicians in Britain and America led their countries in nationalistic wars
without recourse to the thugs that Mussolini and Hitler used to subvert
the democratic process. There is no equivalence in scale or culpability

49. Chomsky, *New Military Humanism*, 75–77.
50. Henk and Amineh, "The Geopolitics of Power Projection in US Foreign Policy."
51. Mann, *The Dark Side of Democracy*.
52. Niebuhr, *Why the Christian Church Is Not Pacifist*, 40.

between British/American wars in the twentieth century and German crimes at the same time. The freer media of democratic societies allowed a scrutiny of, and debate over, government policy to racial inferiors that the tightly controlled propagandistic media of Nazi Germany never offered its public. American and British and Soviet genocides, although at times intentional, were never carried out with the same industrial, calculating, centrally planned ruthlessness that marked Hitler's genocide of Jews and others, arguably the lowest point to which any of the big seven descended. What is significant is that all of these outrages were part of a great system of imperial competition for economic and political survival and supremacy, justified by a belief in the superiority of the imperialist power, that led to the horrendous devastation that came to an end in 1945. Various localized imperial conflicts became a truly global one by 1941, when the British oil blockade on Germany led it to invade the USSR, and an American oil and raw materials embargo on Japan provoked its attack on the United States. A myriad of small conflicts became a global one.

Alliances during this period shifted like sand. In 1853 Britain and Russia went to war, and again in 1918 Britain invaded Russia and intervened in the civil war. By 1939 Britain was planning Operation Pike, an aerial attack on Russia (by then the Soviet Union), which, along with Germany and Slovakia, had invaded Poland in 1939 and was Nazi Germany's oil lifeline.[53] However, between 1941 and 1945, Britain and the Soviet Union were allies. Nonetheless in 1944 Winston Churchill, whose stated objection was the "elimination of Russia," ordered plans to be drawn up for hundreds of thousands of British and American troops, backed by one hundred thousand rearmed Germans, to unleash a surprise attack on their war-devastated Eastern ally, while the RAF would bomb Russian cities from bases in northern Europe.[54] But this so-called Operation Unthinkable, which would have plunged the war-weary British population into yet another war for supremacy, was true to British form. For example, in the Napoleonic Wars at the start of the nineteenth century, Britain allied with Germany against France; in 1914–45 it allied with France against Germany. In World War I, Japan joined Britain and the United States against Germany, but by 1941 had allied with Germany against these former allies. In 1812 Britain fought against the United States at the same time as it fought with German states against France,

---

53. Osborn, *Operation Pike.*

54. Aldridge, *Hidden Hand,* 58–59. Documents were declassified in 1999.

but by 1916, it was fighting with the United States and France against Germany; and so on. Power politics dominated and alliances shifted with perceived interests. The Second World War was a bloody clash of grubby and sordid imperial interests. On closer scrutiny, World War II makes a less appealing basis for the Anglo-American identity myth than Hollywood and school history books would have it.

United States and Britain—Our Finest Hour?

At this point it may be objected that although it is certainly true that all sides in World War II were fighting for economic strength and survival, it is not true that those were the *only* motivations. Surely, Britain and America were fighting against the monstrous evil of Nazism for the defense of civilization and the protection of the Jews?

This is the way in which the war was packaged for future generations, but how well does it account for policy decisions at the time? This contention can be tested in four ways: by examining Britain's relationship with the Soviet Union at the same time, British and American policy towards the Jews, how the allies actually fought, and how we treated some Nazi war criminals after the war who were deemed to be useful in the new Cold War against the Soviet Union. On all these counts, the idea of the US and UK experiencing their finest hours as they fought a noble war can be questioned. It may well be that individual soldiers and politicians were wholly or in part motivated by noble ideals. That is beyond the scope of this chapter. But considering the following four arguments, it is difficult to assert that World War II was "our finest hour."

Britain and the USSR

In the twentieth century statues of Lenin were built—and toppled—across the socialist world. Perhaps the oddest of all was the one that went up in London. From 1941 to 1945, when Britain found itself allied with the Soviet Union against Hitler, there was widespread pro-Soviet feeling in Britain. Fierce anti-Bolshevik sentiments that had propelled Britain into an invasion of Russia in 1918 in a failed attempt to prevent a Communist takeover evaporated as local authorities, both Labour and Conservative controlled, held pageants, festivals, and exhibitions that were pro-Russian. The government even supported the building of a statue of

Lenin in London.[55] This bizarre alliance was in spite of everything we knew about Stalin's Soviet Union, a country that by 1941 had murdered its own citizens on a scale unprecedented in world history and in 1939 had contracted an alliance with Nazi Germany that, as Stalin said approvingly, was "cemented in blood."

In 1943 news broke of the mass execution of Polish military personnel and civilians by the Soviet Union in the Katyn Forest in 1940, when the German army discovered and publicized the graves. Winston Churchill privately believed the German claims were true but collaborated in a Soviet cover-up in order not to upset relations with Britain's wartime ally. But this was just the tip of the iceberg.

The nature of the Soviet Union was well known by the late 1930s. Beginning with Pontic Greeks in the 1930s, whole ethnic groups that were unfortunate enough to have come under Soviet rule and the peculiar personal dislike of Stalin were forcibly relocated from their homes to other parts of the Soviet Union. When the Chechens were moved, herded by massed ranks of Red Army troops for immediate shipment to different parts of the Soviet Union, those declared "non-deportable" such as the old, sick, and pregnant were rounded up and summarily executed. Thousands died on the journey, and a quarter of those who survived the deportation to Kazakhstan died of hunger within five years.[56]

If mass racial violence against minorities decimated some ethnic groups, Stalin attempted nothing less than the total extermination of the Christian faith. In 1929 an All Union Congress of Militant Atheists took place, which stepped up the closing of churches, the persecution of priests, and the desecration of buildings and icons.[57] Communists killed priests and lay Christians in broad daylight, along with their families: the murdered included a staggering 670 bishops, 20,000 members of religious orders, and 25–30,000 priests[58] in a wholesale attempt to destroy the Christian faith.

Even these atrocities were dwarfed by a genocide of which Graham Smith said, "It is hard to think of a worse crime perpetrated by an imperial

---

55. BBC Radio, "Fallen Heroes," August 17, 2004.

56. Michael Casey, "About the Central Asian Link to Those Boston Bombers," *Registan*, April 19, 2013, http://registan.net/2013/04/19/about-the-central-asian-link-to-those-boston-bombers/.

57. Conquest, *The Harvest of Sorrow*.

58. Chandler, *Presences Felt*, 22.

power."[59] In a deliberate terror-famine of 1932–33, so ably exposed by journalists such as Malcolm Muggeridge in British papers, some 8 million Ukrainians and Kazakhs were killed by bureaucratic procedures that deliberately prevented the poor from obtaining food. Food was confiscated in order to reach quotas, while officials knew that this was killing people. Robert Conquest reports how one woman was sentenced to ten years' imprisonment for "stealing" a hundred ears of grain from her own plot, a fortnight after her husband had died of starvation.[60] She was one of the "lucky ones." Starving people were shot as they tried to take rotting food left in piles by the road as it was being packaged for export, and even using the words *hunger* or *famine* could lead to accusations of "counter-revolution" and thus death following show trials.

If this was not evidence enough of the Soviet Union's wickedness, something of its nature could be glimpsed by considering the enemies it attracted. A little-known regiment of the German army was the Turkestan Legion, inaugurated in 1942. Consisting mainly of Uzbek, Turkmen, Kazakh, Kyrgyz, Karakalpak, and Tajik former prisoners of war, it fought alongside the Nazis against its colonial oppressor, the Soviets.[61] That a Muslim Asian regiment should see Stalin as worse than Hitler—nay, see Hitler as a potential liberator of their homelands—is revealing.

Winston Churchill once described the Bolshevik rulers of the Soviet Union as "the most horrible tyranny and brutality the world has ever seen."[62] It is equally famously reported that he defended his alliance with Stalin by joking that if Hitler invaded Hell he would make an alliance with the Devil. The alliance with Stalin was not far short of that. We willingly allied with one state headed by a tyrant whose ideology we abhorred, a state that committed mass murder of its own people and invaded Poland, against another state headed by a tyrant whose ideology we abhorred that likewise committed mass murder of its own people and invaded Poland. What was the difference between them? Only this—that, at that one moment in history, one of those states presented a threat to the interests of the British Empire, and the other offered a lifeline. Predictably, London's statue of Lenin was demolished soon after the war when our relationship with our erstwhile Soviet allies soured and we switched allegiances

59. Graham Smith, "Post-Colonialism and Borderland Identities," 4.

60. Conquest, *Harvest of Sorrow*, 226.

61. Andican, *Turkestan Struggle Abroad*.

62. Cited in Osborn, *Operation Pike*.

again to ally with—of all people—the reconstructed German state against them.

Abandoning the Jews

In allying with the USSR, Britain and the United States knowingly joined forces with up until then the state that had committed the worst mass murder in modern history. But, it may be objected, the morality of the Second World War is proved in our combating a regime that committed the Holocaust against the Jews. The belief that we were fighting for Jewish rights, however, is a retrospective one. Public knowledge of German atrocities against Jews was limited, and in truth not only were the British and American governments largely indifferent to them, but actively obstructed attempts to rescue European Jewry as a distraction from the aim of defeating Germany. For example, in an interview with Sam Harris, Mark Riebling, who researched the history of the Vatican's spy network during World War II, claimed that during the war "you find British and US diplomats begging Pius not to denounce the genocide of the Jews, fearing this would also expose Soviet atrocities against the Poles."[63]

This sordid abandonment is chronicled in David Wyman's sobering historical study of the United States and the Jewish question in the Second World War, aptly titled *The Abandonment of the Jews*. By November 1942 America was presented with authenticated information on the systematic mass murder of European Jewry. President Roosevelt initially delayed the release of this information, and then did not act for over a year. Public opinion was not mobilized to pressure for more action, due to the failure of the US media to properly publicize the Holocaust, the near silence of US churches, and rabid anti-immigration and anti-Semitic sentiment in the United States. Roosevelt was forced into eventual action only to avert an election scandal about nonrescue, establishing the War Refugee Board to coordinate the rescue of Jews and others. His support was half-hearted, making only meager resources available to it. Numerous specific requests for rescue assistance were made to the US and British authorities but were turned down. Only twenty-one thousand refugees were allowed into the United States during the whole course of America's war.

63. "Rethinking 'Hitler's Pope': A Q&A with Mark Riebling," September 28, 2015, https://www.samharris.org/blog/item/rethinking-hitlers-pope.

Documents show that both the British and American governments were reluctant to pressure the Axis powers to release Jews, as they feared this would put pressure on their immigration policies, and rescue would divert vital resources from the war effort. Wyman claims that "Franklin Roosevelt's indifference to so momentous an historical event as the systematic annihilation of European Jewry emerges as the worst failure of his presidency."[64] At least, however, he concludes America's record was better than that of Britain's "abysmal" performance: the British government saw the War Refugee Board as an election-year gimmick and actively obstructed its plans.[65]

Discussing a number of concrete proposals that were made at the time, Wyman carefully rebuts all the arguments that "nothing could have been done." The United States and Britain could have put considerable pressure on the Axis powers, especially their minor allies who realized by 1942 that the war was lost, to release Jews, and also could have made it clear that their mistreatment would be punished after the war but their good treatment would grant them subsequent leniency. This might have encouraged the SS to halt the mass deportations and massacres earlier than it did (in 1944). The developed Allied propaganda networks of leafleting and broadcasting could have been used to warn Jews what was occurring—many willingly sent their families to Auschwitz thinking it was a benign internment camp. Auschwitz's infrastructure could have been bombed relatively easily, as by 1944 American bombers were regularly striking nearby industrial facilities. Indeed, in that year the United States rejected Jewish requests to bomb gas chambers and rail connections to Auschwitz in order to slow its murderous machinery. Funds and logistical support could have been provided to the Jewish underground agencies to assist escape—for example, money to bribe border guards. Neutral countries could have been encouraged to take more Jews by the offer of funds and postwar removal—an assurance that Switzerland sought in vain from the United States. Shipping could have been provided to rescue Jews. For example, in summer 1943 an opportunity arose to take five hundred Jewish children from the Balkans if the United States could provide a ship within one month. Bureaucratic delays in the State Department meant that this opportunity was missed. But throughout the war the British and Americans evacuated vast numbers of non-Jewish refugees, moving

64. Wyman, *Abandonment of the Jews*, xi.
65. Ibid., 334.

Poles, Spanish loyalists, Greeks, and others to safe camps all around Asia, Africa, and the Americas.

In 1944 the British backed out of an agreement to transport 630 Jewish refugees from Spain to a camp near Casablanca, yet at the same time were moving thousands of non-Jewish refugees from Yugoslavia to Egypt. There was plenty of neutral shipping that could have been used, too, such as the half-empty Portuguese liners that crossed the Atlantic unhindered throughout the war. Wyman concludes that a substantial commitment to act could have saved large numbers without compromising the war effort: "The Nazis were the murderers, but we were the all too passive accomplices."[66]

Wyman may be overstating his case in describing the United States and United Kingdom as "accomplices." But his claims that they hindered and obstructed attempts to rescue Jews should lead us to question romantic postwar ideas that the British and the American effort was driven by opposition to the evils of the Holocaust. Adding a personal note to this damning indictment, Wyman identifies himself as a Christian and judges the church harshly:

> The Holocaust was certainly a Jewish tragedy. But it was not *only* a Jewish tragedy. It was also a Christian tragedy, a tragedy for Western civilization, and a tragedy for all humankind. The killing was done by people, to other people, while still other people stood by. The perpetrators, where they were not actually Christians, arose from a Christian culture. The bystanders most capable of helping were Christians. . . . American Christians forgot about the Good Samaritan.[67]

Killing Decently?

On the sixtieth anniversary of Victory in Europe Day, BBC Radio Four's *Today* program ran an interview with a German woman who was a survivor of World War II. She recalled the final weeks as US fighter planes would fly over the countryside, gunning down farmers at work in their fields. She spoke of her relief at the end of this terror, when sudden death

66. Ibid., ix.
67. Ibid.

stalked so constantly that she did not know from day to day whether she would live or die.[68]

As we saw in chapter 3, just war theory demands that for a country to fight a just war, it must not only have just reasons to enter the war, but its conduct must be just. The German lady's testimony above that this was not the case is repeated *ad infinitum* throughout the war. The clearest examples are the Allied bombing of German and Japanese cities. For example, in 1945 one raid on the German city of Dresden destroyed fifteen square kilometers of inner city, or 24,861 of the 28,410 houses. Although accurate figures are difficult to generate, some estimates claim that Anglo-American bombing of Germany killed some 600,000 people, almost ten times more than German bombing of Britain did, and made around 7,500,000 homeless. Antipersonnel weapons and tactics were developed to assist the killing, such as delayed action bombs and second strikes with fragmentation bombs to harass firefighting and rescue work. More people died through heat, lack of oxygen, and carbon monoxide poisoning than as a direct result of the bomb blasts, and the allied raids were carefully planned to ensure maximum civilian death.[69] Behind all these figures are of course real people, made in God's image. Otto Müller, a policeman in Hamburg during the RAF terror raid in 1943, reported moving through the streets of the burning city when he saw a little girl about the age of his own daughter. "Her face was black with soot except for two streams of tears which were running down her face," he recounted. "She was dragging her little dead brother behind her; the right side of his face was already scraped smooth. She had been wandering around aimlessly for three days."[70]

Due to the more fragile nature of their homes and also to the type of weapons available to the Americans, the Japanese suffered even more. One attack on Tokyo, on March 9 and 10, 1945, destroyed more than forty square kilometers and killed an estimated one hundred thousand people. US planes hunted down fleeing civilians to drop bombs on them and napalmed the rivers to cut off escape routes. A report filed at the time by the US Strategic Bombing Survey concluded that "probably more persons lost their lives by fire at Tokyo in a six-hour period than at any time in the history of man."[71] These raids were meticulously planned by

68. BBC Radio 4, *Today*, May 5, 2007.

69. Hewitt, "Place Annihilation."

70. Middlebrook, *Battle of Hamburg*, 374.

71. O'Neill, "U.S. Firebombing of Tokyo in 1945 Killed 100,000."

educated people who used maps of the cities and meteorological reports to carefully calculate exactly where firebombs should be dropped to create firestorms that would kill the maximum number of people, generally civilians in poor and densely populated working-class communities. Robert McNamara, who would later rise to be the US defense secretary, was one such strategist in the firebombing of Japan. He later admitted that had the United States lost the war he would likely have been tried as a war criminal.[72] Freeman Dyson, who worked for RAF Bomber Command planning the destruction of Dresden in February 1945, likewise subsequently wrote, "If we had lost the war, those responsible might have been condemned as war criminals, and I might have been found guilty of collaborating with them."[73] Letters and journals of Allied pilots who took part show that many were traumatized and plagued with guilt all their lives for what they had done. One British airman who took part in the RAF's raid on Hamburg wrote, "When I volunteered for aircrew, I had a romantic notion of air fighting. I did not foresee the slaughter that ensued. Whatever statesmen and braided air marshals may say and write, it was barbarous in the extreme. 'Whoever harms a hair of one of these little ones . . .' I expect no mercy in the life to come. The Teacher told us, clearly. We disobeyed."[74]

Certainly, Germany and Japan were on no higher moral ground than the Allies. Had they possessed the means to use such tactics and weapons, only the most naïve person would doubt that they would have used them as willingly as the Americans did. Furthermore, the saturation bombing of German and Japanese cities reflected changes in the moral climate. Aldous Huxley observed that when the city of Magdeburg was sacked by Tilly in the Thirty Years' War in 1631, the massacre sent shockwaves around Europe. These reverberated in the writing of thinkers and the memories of populations for decades. When it was similarly devastated by an RAF raid on January 16, 1945, it was simply accepted as the sort of thing that regularly happens.[75] It is also true that Churchill's policy of devastation bombing produced controversy in Britain[76]—but possibly not as much controversy and opposition as some of Hitler's more destructive policies (like euthanasia) provoked in Germany.

72. Flint, *Introduction to Geopolitics*, 162.

73. Dyson, Review of *Von Braun*, 11.

74. Middlebrook, *Battle of Hamburg*, 349. The airman is referring to Matt 18:5–6.

75. Huxley, "War and Nationalism," 84–85.

76. Bell, "Obliteration Bombing."

This was mass murder from the air, but countless veterans' journals dispel the myth that the allied forces generally fought decently on the ground. For example, Edgar Jones, a US soldier in the war, wrote acerbically, "What kind of war do civilians suppose we fought, anyway? We shot prisoners in cold blood, wiped out hospitals, strafed lifeboats, killed or mistreated enemy civilians, finished off the enemy wounded, tossed the dying into a hole with the dead, and in the Pacific boiled the flesh off enemy skulls to make table ornaments for sweethearts."[77]

Thus, whether dropping bombs from great heights or exchanging bullets at close quarters, the Allied forces intentionally killed vast numbers of German and Japanese civilians and soldiers, and frequently in ways that would be classed as "war crimes" were they done by Germans and Japanese. Of course soldiers, victims, and historians know this is the case. Contrary to the image given in 1950s movies, politicians' speeches, and the books of theologians, the British and American war conduct was far from our finest hour.

Spooks and Rocket-Men

A final but generally overlooked act in the Second World War that questions the "goodie-versus-baddie" narrative is the way in which Britain and America treated a number of Nazis deemed valuable to future war efforts. The high-profile Nuremberg trials of war criminals delivered thoroughly deserved punishments on many who had perpetrated some of the century's most horrendous crimes. But a lesser-known and grimier chapter in this period relates to how we treated some German Nazis and Italian fascists considered useful in the emerging conflict with our erstwhile ally, the Soviet Union. Historian of the intelligence services Richard Aldridge has detailed how the British and American secret services actively recruited skilled German Nazi and Italian fascist agents for this new conflict—for example, re-employing senior Gestapo officers who had good knowledge of the Soviet Union.[78] But it was for those deemed able to help provide high-technology weaponry that the Allies were most willing to overlook past misdemeanors.

77. Quoted in Bainton, *Christian Attitudes toward War and Peace*, 247.
78. Aldridge, *Hidden Hand*, 197.

The most revealing example is that of aeronautics engineer Wernher von Braun.[79] One of the few areas where German military technology excelled that of the Allies was rocketry. Rocket-propelled fighter planes and unmanned bombs such as the V-2 were never available in sufficient quantities to be militarily useful, but technically they outclassed anything that the British or Americans were able to produce. Their chief designer was the brilliant Wernher von Braun, and as the Nazi regime collapsed the Americans and Soviets both sought to capture him, his collaborators, and his technology. The Americans reached him first and took him to the United States, where his expertise was employed in creating a new generation of fighter jets that would see service in the Korean War. His pivotal work later in the US space exploration program, leading the team that landed men on the moon, would make him one of America's most celebrated scientists of the century. He was one of some one hundred German scientists brought to the United States after the war.

However, during World War II von Braun's German rockets were made at the Mittelwerk factory, a vast underground complex manned by slave labor from the nearby Dora concentration camp. This institution was supervised by the SS, the most criminal part of the Hitler regime. Von Braun visited the factory and was aware of the atrocities, and even became a member of the Nazi Party and the SS. It is probable that he joined both out of opportunism, seeing the cost of building weapons for them as worth paying for the future benefits to humanity of his scientific discoveries. Nonetheless, his importance as a high-value asset clearly outweighed, in American calculation, his culpability in the Nazi genocide of Jews. Indeed, the US government sought to downplay this history. Should not all this material lead us to question the popular narratives that we have about the Second World War?

Conclusion: Not a Good War

In 1942 Subhas Chandra Bose, the leader of the rebel Indian National Army, which fought alongside the Japanese against the British,[80] met with Adolf Hitler to solicit help for a war of liberation from British oppression. Bose's hopes were dashed by the Führer, who dismissed him, taking the view that Indians needed to be civilized by further British rule. Nonethe-

79. Neufeld, *Von Braun*.
80. Ackerman and DuVall, *Force More Powerful*, 109.

less, that Hitler was seen by some not as the embodiment of evil but as a potential liberator should alert us that there was more to the Second World War than school history books and patriotic war films tell us.

The Second World War depicted in these books and films is what geopolitical thinker Gearóid Ó Tuathail described as a "feel-good war" when a dictator was stopped, free nations fought together, and British and American publics and militaries were united in their finest hour to secure the promise of a new world order. As we have seen in this chapter, however, Ó Tuathail argues that "complex histories and the realities of place were overwhelmed and effaced by a script which lifted the conflict from its actual geographical and historical co-ordinates."[81] In his book *The Pursuit of Power*, McNeill wrote that nineteenth-century Europe "launched itself on a self-reinforcing cycle in which its military organization sustained, and was sustained by, economic and political expansion at the expense of other peoples and polities of the earth."[82] World War II was the culmination of this cycle.

Furthermore, to protect our imperial interests against Hitler, Britain and America made a diabolical alliance with modern history's greatest mass murderer, Stalin. We exhibited shocking double standards in obstructing attempts to rescue European Jewry from the Holocaust, largely abandoning them to their fate. In the conduct of the war we perpetrated some of the worst crimes in history. And in its aftermath, we sheltered numerous Nazi and fascist war criminals deemed useful to us in the new "Cold War" with the Soviet Union when our cynical alliance with them broke down. The facts belie the comfortable myth that we fought a good war for noble reasons. From the perspective of an outside observer, black American historian W. E. B. Du Bois, the Allied-German wars of the first half of the twentieth century revealed "the real soul of white culture" and were the consequence of "jealousy and strife for the possession of the labor of dark millions, for the right to bleed and exploit the colonies of the world."[83]

Sixty years after the end of the Second World War in Europe, the German ambassador to London, Thomas Matussek, caused a stir by saying that he thought British people had an ill-informed "obsession with the Nazi period" and were more preoccupied with it than countries like

81. Ó Tuathail, "The Effacement of Place?"

82. Quoted in Jenkins, *Final Frontier*, 94.

83. Quoted in Kearns, *Geopolitics and Empire*, 128. The Du Bois quote refers specifically to the First World War.

Poland that actually suffered occupation.[84] His comments caused an out-cry, but he had hit on something—that it is very difficult for Britons (and Americans) to think about the Second World War in any way that departs from the schoolboy textbook and Hollywood film idea of "goodies versus baddies." The real story is more complicated, as real life inevitably is. The Second World War was the culmination of more than a century of impe-rial struggle between America, Britain, France, Germany, Russia, Italy, and Japan. As we have seen, the relative strength of these powers waxed and waned and their alliance structures shifted and changed as they com-peted or cooperated for dominance.

The church should have known how to view this titanic clash, for although it looked mighty to humans, in God's eyes "the nations are like a drop in a bucket" (Isa 40:15). Preaching on this theme, Martyn Lloyd-Jones wrote, "Nation after nation has risen only to fall": nations opposed to God's rule may have great temporary success, they "may apparently bestride the universe, but as certainly as their star arose it will go down," for, as Lloyd-Jones reminds us, the Bible assures us that one day "the earth will be filled with the knowledge of the glory of the LORD as the waters cover the sea" (Hab 2:14). Therefore, he continues, "God forbid that we should trust, or commit ourselves to, any power other than God Himself, to any idols man may set up, even though they be the British Commonwealth of Nations or the United Nations!"[85]

Making the same point, journalist Malcolm Muggeridge—who re-ported on the rise and fall of Hitler, Stalin, and Mussolini, as well as the decline of the British Empire and the humiliation of the United States in Vietnam—said that hopes for peace and fears of war are, in Christian terms, "equally beside the point." As Christians, we know that "crowns roll in the dust and every kingdom must sometime flounder, whereas we acknowledge a king men did not crown and cannot dethrone, as we are citizens of a city of God they did not build and cannot destroy."[86] As we put it whenever we sing Isaac Watts' great hymn,

> Jesus shall reign where'er the sun
> Does his successive journeys run;
> His kingdom stretch from shore to shore,

84. Day, "The British Are Obsessed with Germany—and Not Always in a Funny Way."

85. Lloyd-Jones, *From Fear to Faith*, 52–53.

86. Muggeridge, "But Not of Christ," 31.

Till moons shall wax and wane no more.

Of that there can be no doubt, and it is the starting point for a Christian view of history. This should, one might expect, give the church a unique vantage point on the Second World War—that sordid drama of ridiculously self-important nations struggling for a fleeting supremacy that is bound to finally elude them. However, alas, much of the Christian church throughout the world forgot this biblical perspective and aligned itself with the armies of whichever host nation it happened to find its churches and chapels were built in. That is the topic of the next chapter.

7

What about Hitler? Part II
The Churches and the Second World War

In 1948 the renowned non-Christian philosopher Albert Camus gave a talk in which he said that the world "today needs Christians who remain Christians." He explained that while he did not share their Christian hope, he had "the same revulsion from evil." He went on that when faced with evil like that witnessed under fascism, they "should voice their condemnation in such a way that never a doubt, never the slightest doubt, could rise in the heart of the simplest man."[1]

Stirring words, no doubt, but Camus was speaking from anger at the muted condemnation of various forms of fascism by European churches. Christianity rejects the love of power and wealth, teaching and practicing instead a universal ethic of love for enemies and reconciliation of all peoples, through the cross, into a new nation transcending national boundaries. It thus ought to have had much to say to the world about fascism, as also about imperialism. Yet Camus was right. The Christian faith became hopelessly subsumed in the imperial conflict. Christians in all of the countries involved—from Britain and America on the Allied side to Japan and Italy with the Axis—supported both the imperial expansion of their states and the murderous doctrines of racial superiority that legitimized this seizure of land from other peoples.

The previous chapter argued that the 1939–45 conflict must be seen as the culmination of a great imperial rivalry with its immediate roots in the nineteenth century, but which goes back further. While Hitler and Stalin no doubt committed the most heinous crimes, all sides in this terrible conflict were guilty to some degree of greed, cruelty, and aggression

---

1. Elshtain, *Just War against Terror*, 123–24.

against weaker peoples. As this chapter will show, "just war" churches in fact played significant roles in creating the environments that allowed Hitlerism to emerge. There were exceptions, however: brave individuals and groups of believers who held firmly to historic gospel peace. It is from their examples that we begin to see that the really significant question facing Christians today is less "what do we do about Hitler?" (or whichever warmongering tyrant is currently grabbing the news headlines) as "what do we do about the type of human behavior that allowed Hitlerism to emerge?"

Before moving on to some of those heroic Christians who opposed Hitler, we will consider some of the unpleasant examples of how churches helped create the conditions for the 1914–18 and 1939–45 conflicts. As we have looked in some detail in chapter 2 at American churches and the idea of divine ordering of the United States' foreign policy, the focus of this section will be on the lesser-known stories of the Axis churches. But before that, we will briefly revisit the case of British Christianity.

British Churches and the Two World Wars

On October 25, 1901, the *Church Times* printed a critical editorial about a recent statement by the bishop of Hereford. The bishop had spoken out against the use of concentration camps, invented by the British in South Africa in their war against the Boers, who were struggling for independence from British rule. The *Church Times* wrote caustically, "Wars cannot be carried on without entailing misery, and those who strike the first blow are responsible for them. As for the present War, it is quite without a parallel for the humanity with which, on the whole, it has been conducted."

That a leading Christian publication of its day should defend the odious practice of concentration camps, in which an estimated twenty thousand people, mostly women and children, died, illustrates what Anglican Church historian Brian Fletcher argues was a general feeling among the church that British imperialism resulted in "an empire that most churchmen saw as surpassing all others because it was founded on Christian principles rather than lust for power, or profit."[2]

This sense that the interests of Christianity and the British Empire were one and the same allowed churchmen to excuse the heinous and

2. Fletcher, "Anglicanism and Nationalism in Australia," 129.

genocidal crimes considered in the previous chapter. The British were no exception, however: parallel beliefs in the churches of Axis powers like Germany and Italy held that the cause of Christianity was best advanced by the growth of their states and empires and, where necessary, the military defeat of their enemies. Together, these beliefs helped propel Europe into the bloodletting of the 1914–45 catastrophe.

As we saw in chapter 2's discussion of "chosen people syndrome," the First World War led to some particularly warlike language from the churches. For example, the preacher Billy Sunday summed this up in 1917, saying that Christianity and patriotism were synonymous, as were hell and traitors.[3] Preachers went to considerable lengths to marry Christian love with calls to kill the German. Historian Joanna Bourke found many sermons from the time that exhorted soldiers to love the German soldier while thrusting the bayonet into him, one even encouraging soldiers to say "this is my body, broken for you" or whisper a prayer of love as they killed. In closing a lecture to a senior class of divinity students at Glasgow University in 1916, Professor H. M. B. Reid praised the fact that a large number of students had enlisted because "it proved their manhood" and was living proof that the Divinity Hall was no place for slackers but "the most martial section of the University." As Bourke says, theologians and clergy did not merely sanction killing, but sanctified it.[4] She reports that one senior general said, "The Christian churches are the finest blood-lust creators which we have and of them we made free use." We must, tragically, recognize that historian A. J. Hoover was not far off the mark when he wrote, "The founder of the Christian religion said, 'Blessed are the peacemakers,' but one would never have suspected as much from the behavior of some of the clergy in the Great War."[5]

If World War I was justified as both a just war and a crusade, the defense of Britain and its empire in World War II was more commonly supported by the church in the language of just war. However, although the bloodthirsty language of crusading was certainly toned down, various key ideas were maintained—that war paved the road to peace, promoted civilization, and allowed Christian virtues to flourish.

Nonetheless, although most clergy did not seem to see a conflict of interest between Christianity and killing, soldiers often did. The First and

3. Bourke, *Intimate History of Killing*, 271.

4. Ibid., 275–76.

5. Hoover, *God, Germany, and Britain*, 120.

Second World Wars saw many cases of soldiers regarding the chaplains as hypocrites for ignoring Christian teaching. Canon Collins reported that a radio operator engaged in Operation Gomorrah, the fittingly if chillingly named mass raids on Hamburg in 1943, wrote to him and said,

> It was a nightmare experience of looking down on the flaming city beneath. I felt sick as I thought of the women and children down there being mutilated, burned, killed, terror-stricken in that dreadful inferno—and I was partly responsible. Why, Padre John, do the Churches not tell us that we are doing an evil job? Why do chaplains persist in telling us that we are performing a noble task in defence of Christian civilisation? . . . Don't let any-one tell us that what we are doing is noble. What we are doing is evil, a necessary evil perhaps, but evil all the same.[6]

This sense of an ordinary soldier that what he was doing was deeply unchristian shows that while the church institutions generally supported British wars, not all Christians were comfortable with this. Those in the mission field were perhaps more aware than others of how nationalism split the church. J. H. Oldham, one of the leaders of the Protestant mission movement, described the outbreak of World War I as a "catastrophe" and a "terrible blow" that gravely imperiled the sense of international love and mission.[7] However, in spite of such examples of a prophetic realization that the values and interests of the kingdom of God and the kingdom of Britain might clash, British churches generally supported the project of empire and its defense in the First and Second World Wars, just as they had paved the way for those wars with their support of imperialism.

Axis Churches

In 2006, a German film about a young Christian student in Nazi Germany, Sophie Scholl, was released to acclaim around the world. The film brought to more general knowledge the group of students she was a part of, known as the White Rose. This group wrote and distributed anti-Nazi pamphlets among students—an activity for which the twenty-one-year-old Scholl was executed in 1943. The film made an excellent story and reinforced the idea that many Christians fondly maintain today—that true Christians in Germany opposed Hitler.

6. Quoted in Middlebrook, *Battle of Hamburg*, 349.

7. Stanley, "Christianity and the End of Empire," 4.

There are more than one hundred schools in Germany named after Sophie Scholl,[8] but this hero status should not obscure an uncomfortable fact—that hers makes such a good story because she was so rare. Likewise, many Christians cite the case of Dietrich Bonhoeffer and his Confessing Church as evidence that true believers resisted the strange lure of the Nazis. The truth is far more unpleasant: the majority of German Christians either actively supported Hitler and his wars (by fighting in the army, for example, or by working in industries supporting it) or at least did not resist them. We are talking here about nominal Christians, of course, but also Spirit-filled, Bible-believing evangelical Protestants.

In recent years there have been many original investigations into the social history of German support for Nazism, and the results do not make comfortable reading for Christians. Historian Richard Steigmann-Gall writes that Protestantism was a better indication of support for the Nazi Party than any other factor (class, region, or gender, for example). He argues that the more pious Protestants were, the more likely they were to support Hitler. He found that the role of Protestant clergy was vital in mobilizing support for the Nazi Party, and the vast majority of young Protestant theology students in 1930s Germany were members.[9] How could this have arisen? This support did not suddenly come from nowhere but arose from a long tradition of patriotic loyalty to the state by German Christians steeped in just war theory and Luther's emphasis on the idea that God worked through the civil powers and authorities. This can be seen very clearly in World War I.

German Churches and World War I

In a fascinating study of German Christian sermons during World War I, A. J. Hoover highlights the mindset of German Christians in relation to the big imperial struggle of the time that would, eventually, culminate in World War II. A refrain in German preaching at the time was that Britain's great sin was imperialism: "Pastors mentioned the British Empire more than anything else in their sermons against the British."[10] Comparing Germany to righteous King Jehoshaphat invaded by a host of terrible neighbors but delivered through trust in God (2 Chr 20), they depicted

8. Overstreet, Review of *Sophie Scholl*.

9. Steigmann-Gall, "Apostasy or Religiosity?"

10. Hoover, *God, Germany, and Britain*, 52.

Britain as Assyria, a monster, an octopus, or a beast like those in Daniel (chs. 7–8) and Revelation (chs. 12–13) ravaging the earth with their violence.[11] This imperial beast was guilty of a multitude of sins, including the opium trade, slavery, the suppression of American colonies, African wars, and the Boer conquest. According to these accounts, Britain was also hypocritical in criticizing German militarism while maintaining a vast empire built and maintained by violence.

These were well-rehearsed criticisms of Britain made not only around the world but also by socialists and other opponents of imperialism in Britain itself. The German clergy also made specifically Christian critiques of the British Empire. They alleged that it had mistreated German missionaries in Africa,[12] thus setting back the advance of the kingdom of God for the sake of narrow imperial benefit. Theologian Adolf von Harnack argued that Germany was, ironically, actually fighting for British (Christian) interests in holding back the uncivilized hordes of secularism,[13] such as the French who had attempted to spread their anti-Christian revolution via force of arms. In September 1914, eighty of the most renowned members of religious and academic communities issued an *Appeal to Evangelical Christians Abroad*, supporting their policies and defending "the inner right of us and our Emperor to invoke the assistance of God" in saving the West from Russian barbarism. They insisted that in spite of the multiple nations arrayed against Germany, "We stand over against this raging of the peoples, fearless because of our trust in the holy and righteous God."[14]

Christian leaders argued that German claims to be the authentic defenders of the Evangelical gospel could be supported historically, as Germany, the home of the great reformer Martin Luther, was the cradle of the Reformation and the leading center of Protestant scholarship. As Johann Kessler, a pastor in Dresden, asserted, God had equipped Germany with "such gifts of the spirit and such depths of mind, that he called [her] to be a bearer of the gospel in the days of the Reformation," and his providence ensured that "God has great things in store for such a

11. Ibid., 51.
12. Ibid., 53–54.
13. Ibid., 57.
14. Marrin, *Last Crusade*, 109.

nation."[15] No wonder, then, that Germany was compared to God-fearing Joshua, betrayed by treacherous England, its unrighteous brother.

No wonder too that the German capitulation in 1918 was seen by many Protestants as a disastrous victory for materialism and defeat for the cause of God—so much so that Protestant churches declared a day of prayer and mourning when the punitive Versailles peace settlement was forced upon their humiliated nation. They refused to accept the idea of war guilt, and clergy were often at the forefront of nationalist agitation in the years that followed, smoothing the way for the rise of Hitler.[16]

German Churches and World War II

The rise to power of Adolf Hitler in 1933 was welcomed by many German Christians. They shared the sense of injustice at the peace terms imposed on them at the end of the First World War, a war in which, they believed, Germany had been on the side of right and of God. To ordinary Germans, Hitler's strong leadership and socialist policies of creating employment through infrastructural and military expenditure, and support of public health care and schooling, were a sensible and popular response to the social and economic chaos that followed World War I. Historian Wolfgang Schivelbusch has drawn comparisons between Hitler and American President Franklin Roosevelt, who led the United States out of a comparative "great depression" by a similar set of social policies known as the "New Deal."[17] Unsurprisingly, Hitler was an admirer of Roosevelt.

This support of Hitler could be found in the church echelons as well as among laypeople. One of the most prominent Lutheran intellectuals, Paul Althaus of Erlangen University, said in 1933 of the Nazi seizure of power, "Our Protestant churches have greeted the turning point of 1933 as a gift and miracle of God."[18] Protestants were not alone in this regard: the Catholic Students Union hailed "the National Socialist revolution as the great spiritual breakthrough of our time."[19]

However, the relationship between Nazism and Christianity was ambiguous. The Nazis, largely unsuccessfully, attempted to propagate the

---

15. Hoover, *God, Germany, and Britain*, 63.

16. Steigmann-Gall, "Apostasy or Religiosity?," 280–81.

17. Schivelbusch, *Three New Deals*.

18. Steigmann-Gall, "Apostasy or Religiosity?," 281.

19. Reproduced in Matheson, *Third Reich*, 26.

so-called German Faith, a neopagan alternative to Christianity. Elements of the regime such as the SS commonly viewed churches with suspicion. Nonetheless, Hitler (a Catholic) encouraged church support by presenting himself in Christian terms. He issued a policy statement on March 23, 1933, saying that his government "regards Christianity as the unshakeable foundation of our national life and morality."[20] Such language clearly resonated with Christians alarmed at the social, political, and economic turmoil of their times. Analyzing the reasons why 80 to 90 percent of the Protestant Women's Service were also members of the Nazi Party, historian Michael Phayer suggested that these women saw a dovetail of their own moral concerns with socially conservative Nazi concerns about prostitution, divorce, pornography, feminism, subversive cultural developments, etc.[21] It is thus unsurprising that when Hitler narrowly escaped assassination in Munich in November 1939, both he himself and a host of Christian leaders attributed his deliverance to divine providence.

If Hitler's domestic policies of national economic, cultural, and "spiritual" rejuvenation chimed with the interests and priorities of many Christians, his foreign policy—which resulted in World War II—arguably did so to an even greater degree. The day after war with Britain broke out, Bishop Maharens issued the following statement:

> Since yesterday our German people has been at war, fighting for the land of its fathers, for the return of German blood to German land. The German Evangelical Church has always stood in loyal solidarity with the destiny of the German people. To the weapons of steel it has added invincible powers coming from the Word of God: the power of prayer, which strengthens us for good days and ill, and the assurance of the faith that our people, that every single person within it, is in the hands of God. So at this hour too we join with our nation in intercession for the Führer and the Reich, for all the armed forces, and for everyone on the home front who is doing his duty for the Fatherland. God grant that we may be found loyal and vouchsafe to us a just peace.[22]

Little additional comment is needed, apart from Matheson's observation that while this "exaggerated servility" was not typical, "neither

20. Ibid., 9.

21. Steigmann-Gall, "Apostasy or Religiosity?," 277.

22. Matheson, *Third Reich*, 83–84.

Catholic nor Protestant churchmen felt any hesitation about lending the war their moral support."[23]

Why was this the case? To us, it seems obviously wrong, but that is the benefit of hindsight—and victor's hindsight at that. The explanation is multifaceted. As already discussed, many Germans felt an acute sense of grievance that they were denied the fruits of empire that the British, French, Russians, and Americans were enjoying, an inequality they knew was disadvantaging them in the imperial competition. Bitterness at the terms of the Versailles settlement compounded this.[24] Nationalism was rife in Europe at the time, and the default position of a majority of people—in Germany as much as elsewhere—was to support the army at times of national crisis (indeed, that sentiment persists in many countries to this day). But there was also a more particular, explicit Christian factor, which came further to the fore after the German attack on the Soviet Union in 1941. This was the belief that Germany was a bastion of Christian civilization against the hordes of secularism and atheism.

In his study of Britain and the Vatican during the Second World War, Owen Chadwick reports that some Catholics and some fascists wanted the pope, known for his strong anti-Communism, to declare the war of Germany (and its allies such as Finland) on the Soviet Union a holy crusade.[25] Later the pope was to publicly describe Hitler's opposition to Russia as "high-minded gallantry in defense of the foundations of Christian culture." Several German bishops openly supported Hitler's invasion of Russia, calling it a "European crusade." One bishop exhorted all Catholics to fight for "a victory that will allow Europe to breathe freely again and will promise all nations a new future." Dr. Kottmann, the Vicar General of Rottenburg diocese, wrote a letter to the Ministry of Internal Affairs in November 1941 protesting at the confiscation of church property. He said, "The fact that so many believing soldiers are among the lists of the fallen justifies the conclusion that . . . those believing dead heroes sought to fight against unbelieving Bolshevism."[26]

This belief was substantiated through news reports of the German advance. Alexander Werth recorded seeing a "moving" account in the

23. Ibid.

24. It would, however, be a mistake to blame the Second World War on the Versailles settlement, as it was only one among a number of factors.

25. Chadwick, *Britain and the Vatican*, 193–96.

26. "The Ambivalent Attitude of the Churches during the War, November 1941," reproduced in Matheson, *Third Reich*, 96–97.

German media of how a church in Smolensk was reopened following the Nazi "liberation" of the town. An old priest who had been unable to attend to his priestly duties for twenty-five years due to Communist persecution came out of his forced new occupation as a stonemason, donned his tattered but lovingly preserved clerical garments, and conducted his first eucharistic service in a quarter of a century.[27] With the benefit of hindsight that might seem to be simply Nazi propaganda, but can we not appreciate that to ordinary German believers it surely was a sign that the kingdom of God was being re-established and the very gates of hell (capital city: Moscow) were being stormed?

Christian Heroes against Hitler?

Although the German church widely supported Hitlerism, it is important to remember that not all Christians did—or, at least, they did not support Nazi policies to the same degree. For example, Hermann Sasse, editor of the *Church Year Book*, wrote a strong response in opposition to Article 24 of the 1920 program of the nascent Nazi Party, "The Party as such stands for a positive Christianity." Insisting that the doctrine of original sin means that the purest-born German is "as much subject to eternal damnation as the genetically gravely compromised half-caste from two decadent races," he continued that

> the doctrine of the justification of the sinner *sola gratia, sola fide,* is the end of Germanic morality just as it is the end of all human morality. . . . We are not much interested in whether the Party gives its support to Christianity, but we would like to know whether the church is to be permitted to preach the Gospel in the Third Reich without let or hindrance, whether, that is, we will be able to continue undisturbed with our insults to the Germanic or Germanistic moral sense, as with God's help we intend to do.[28]

Isolated cases of heroism were shown by ordinary believers. Franz Jägerstätter, a devout Catholic ironworker from Upper Austria, refused to enlist in the German army when called up, as he believed Christ taught his followers to love, not harm, their enemies. He was executed on August 9, 1943, a fate that he knew awaited him should he follow his conscience

27. Werth, *Moscow '41*, 128.

28. "Programme of the NSDAP, 1920," reproduced in Matheson, *Third Reich*, 1–2.

and take that course of action.[29] Likewise, Julius von Jan, Protestant pastor of Oberlenningen in Württemberg, spoke out against government-sponsored attacks on Jews: "Where in Germany is the man who cries out in God's name and in the name of righteousness, as Jeremiah did: execute justice and righteousness, and deliver the spoiled out of the hand of the oppressor! And do no wrong, do no violence, to the stranger, the fatherless, nor the widow, neither shed innocent blood in this place?"[30]

Such protestations are fascinating not because they were typical but because they were rare. Indeed, they occurred *in spite of* rather than because of the church, which in many cases sought to suppress them. Catholic Bishop von Galen spoke out boldly on euthanasia (as we shall see below) against the advice of his seniors in the church.[31] Jägerstätter was implored by Catholic priests and even the bishop of Linz to desist and support the Nazis, something that the bishop sought to conceal after the war. This was subsequently to prove an embarrassment to the Vatican when, "having difficulty coming up" with a Holocaust martyr, it later set up a commission to consider his canonization in the 1980s.[32] Similarly, when Pastor von Jan was beaten up by the SA, imprisoned, and expelled from Württemberg, church leaders not only did not protect him: they censured him for encumbering his preaching with "political remarks."[33]

If protest within the established churches was either lacking or half-hearted, what of the Confessing Church, established in the early years of the Nazi regime in response to the rise of Hitler? When I was a child, the minister of my church told me that the Confessing Church were real Christians and opposed Hitler, whereas those who supported him were nominal Christians, "unsaved." It gained a number of notable victories against the Hitler regime in the early and mid-1930s. It used the courts and mass demonstrations to reverse Nazi attempts to remove or imprison its clergy and take control of church institutions such as schools, and in 1934 it successfully scuppered Nazi plans to create a single Reich church under its rule. Pastor Dietrich Bonhoeffer was executed for involvement in the ill-fated July 1944 plot to assassinate Hitler. But does the

29. Putz, *Against the Stream*.

30. Quoted in Moltmann, *Power of the Powerless*, 82.

31. R. Evans, *Third Reich at War*, 100.

32. Hitchens, *Letters to a Young Contrarian*, 62–63.

33. Moltmann, *Power of the Powerless*, 82.

Confessing Church deserve the reputation that it has acquired in Britain and America as the voice of true Christianity against the Nazis?

Certainly, the Confessing Church played an important prophetic role, witnessing against some aspects of Nazi policy and proclaiming the kingdom of God. However, as historian Arthur Cochrane wrote, the Confessing Church was "a relatively tiny minority,"[34] and its importance should not be exaggerated. More than that, it has developed a reputation among some modern Christians that it simply does not deserve. Richard Steigmann-Gall, in his overview of books on the topic, said that many have skewed the historical record by using it to build up a picture of Christian opposition to Hitler that is exaggerated. Studies that correct this have shown the often ambivalent and sometimes even positive stance to Nazism that some in the Confessing Church took.[35]

We must not assume that Confessing Church opposition to Hitler was for the same reasons that Hollywood films and British school textbooks today decry him—that is, for launching wars of conquest and for mass murder of Jews. A more important factor was a finer point of German Lutheran doctrine on the careful demarcation of the proper authorities of church and state, which, it concluded, had been breached by Hitler.[36] Historian Shelley Baranowski observes that the Confessing Church was largely composed of people from conservative elite backgrounds who looked down on the uncouth revolutionary Hitler and his working-class thugs. It used its connections in conservative institutions that shared this disdain, like the military, bureaucracy and the courts, to try to protect its own institutions and the cultural hold of the church on German education. Yet, like these other conservative bodies, it also approved of some aspects of Nazism, such as its suppression of socialists and communists. It therefore formed a tactical accommodation with Nazism. It also shared, to an extent, elements of its anti-Semitism. Anti-Semitism was rife in the church, and as historian Kenneth Barnes records, "most Confessing pastors took the loyalty oath to the Führer."[37] Thus the church fought strongly against attempts by the Nazis to forbid the baptizing of converted Jews but was more equivocal about the rights of those who

34. Cochrane, *Church's Confession under Hitler*, 12

35. For example, Baranowski, *The Confessing Church, Conservative Elites, and the Nazi State*; Steigmann-Gall, "Apostasy or Religiosity?"

36. Hastings, *History of English Christianity*, ch. 22.

37. Barnes, "Dietrich Bonhoeffer and Hitler's Persecution," 127.

remained in Judaism.[38] Baranowski argues that the Confessing Church's opposition to Nazism was largely single-issue opposition, primarily "the preservation of the social and cultural roles of the Protestant church," and it had little to say on anti-Semitism, violence against political minorities, and imperialism.[39]

Indeed, the Confessing Church was also marked by the German nationalism of the day, as evidenced in its unwillingness to readily criticize Hitler's foreign wars. When Karl Barth, a member of the church, attacked aspects of Hitler's foreign policy—such as withdrawing from the League of Nations (a precursor to the United Nations), rearmament against the requirements of the Versailles Treaty, and the annexation of Czechoslovakia—other members of the church distanced themselves from him.[40] That Karl Barth, though a member of the church, was himself a foreigner and not a German is indicative of the role that nationalism played in the church. The same observation is true of Franz Jägerstätter, who, as we saw above, was Austrian. As Baranowski depressingly observes, "Far more Confessing pastors died on the regime's battle lines than in its jails or concentration camps."[41] She argues that the myth of the Confessing Church as real opposition to Hitler was fostered by the conservative elites (such as the Christian Democrats) who took power in the postwar years and by the Allied backers of West Germany who were anxious to establish a legitimate state to oppose Communism.[42]

Individual German Christians showed that the church could successfully resist Nazism when it chose to. Generally speaking, it chose not to; and when it did, it was usually for class-based or relatively minor sectarian interests. West Germany's postwar chancellor, Konrad Adenauer, wrote in a letter to a fellow Christian, the Catholic priest Bernard Custodis, in 1946,

> In my opinion the German people as well as their bishops and clergy bear a great guilt for the events of the concentration camps. It is perhaps true that afterwards not a lot could be done. The guilt lies earlier. The German people, including a great part of the bishops and clergy, accepted the National Socialist

38. Baranowski, *Confessing Church*, 84–85; Haynes, "King and Bonhoeffer as Protestant Saints"; Barnes, "Dietrich Bonhoeffer and Hitler's Persecution of the Jews."

39. Baranowski, *Confessing Church*, 83.

40. Matheson, *Third Reich*, 76–77.

41. Baranowski, *Confessing Church*, 88.

42. Ibid., ch. 6.

agitation. It allowed itself to be brought into line almost without resistance, indeed in part with enthusiasm. Therein lies its guilt. . . . I believe that much could have been prevented if, on a certain day, all the bishops together had publicly protested from their pulpits against all this. That did not happen and there is no excuse for it.[43]

We should be wary of being too harsh in judging German Christians. It is very difficult to stand against the tide of nationalism, and refusing to fight and thus to face personal martyrdom and the suffering of one's own family demands incredible bravery—more so than going along with the war. Peter himself denied Christ three times rather than face such a fate; and British and American Christians have proved little better than their German counterparts over time. Nonetheless, it remains the case that without the church, Hitlerism and the Second World War could not have happened in the way that it did. What an indictment of the body of Christ!

Churches in Other Axis Powers

It was not only the German Christian churches that supported their state in the imperial clash that culminated in World War II: the same is true in other Axis states and their allies. The Italian church gave support to Mussolini, for example, blessing his invasion of Abyssinia (Ethiopia) in 1935. This act of empire-building was a clear violation of the League of Nations Charter and may have killed a quarter of a million Ethiopians in a seventh-month war. Nonetheless, the bishop of Cremona, consecrating regimental flags, pronounced, "The blessing of God be upon these soldiers who, on African soil, will conquer new and fertile lands for Italian genius, thereby bringing them to Roman and Christian culture." Cardinal Schuster of Milan declared his hope that the Italian army would achieve "the triumph of the Cross . . . opening the gates of Abyssinia to the Catholic faith and civilisation."[44] It is of course deeply ironic that the bishops should regard the Italian military conquest of Abyssinia as bringing the country within the sphere of Christianity: according to the book of Acts, an Ethiopian was converted (Acts 8:26–40) before an Italian (Acts 10)!

43. Cited in Johnson, "Ice-Cold Embrace," 10. However, as Johnson observes, Adenauer himself never denounced the pogroms and death camps, nor repeated this private denunciation of his church or nation in public.

44. Hastings, *History of English Christianity*, 396.

This illustrates just how blinded the churches were by their patriotic support of empire-building nation-states.

Spain wisely remained formally neutral in World War II, but its fascist dictator, General Franco, collaborated with Hitler and Mussolini, both of whom assisted him in taking power. Franco found a staunch support base in conservative Catholicism. This was unsurprising—the anarchist-communist wing of the Republican alliance in Spain sacked churches and systematically murdered clergy. Catholics saw in Franco the providence of God defending Christian civilization against the assaults of violent atheism.[45]

Axis Christian complicity in World War II does not stop at the borders of Europe. Japanese Christians also participated in their state's imperial wars, including the Second World War: indeed, the notorious *kamikaze* suicide pilots counted Christians among their number. Japanese Christians were a weak minority, which no doubt constrained their opposition to war. But the present-day leadership of the Japanese church has not accepted this as an excuse. In 2005, on the sixtieth anniversary of the end of the war, the Primate of the Nippon Sei Ko Kai church, the Most Reverend James Toru Uno, issued a "message of peace" accepting his church's implication in the war and in "the path of imperialism and militarism which Japan had followed" since the late nineteenth century. It said, "Throughout the unfolding history of modern Japan, we in the NSKK failed to stand up for the gospel of the boundless love of God for every human life as revealed in our Lord Jesus Christ, and lacked the courage to stand up in opposition to the war."[46] The bishop continued that Japanese Christians have learned from this experience: "In particular, we have strengthened ties with the churches in Asia. Fellowship with these churches enables us to more clearly perceive our past errors in Japan, and motivates us to discover ways of living together in Christ." What a tragedy that it took the book of history, rather than the book of Scripture, to learn that lesson!

Accounts of the Axis war generally focus on Germany, Italy, and Japan. However, these powers were supported by a host of smaller states, factions within states, and peoples—from Croats and Turkestanis to Bulgarians and Latvians. Though not necessarily fascist or National Socialist, they found in Hitler a convenient ally in their own struggles for

45. Ibid., 316.

46. "August 15 Message of Peace," http://www.nskk.org/province/seimei_pdf/2005_0815_en.pdf.

freedom and justice, often against the Soviet Union. Unsurprisingly, they frequently saw their struggle against the Allies as a holy one.

A fascinating—and disturbing—example is that of plucky Finland. Its soldiers fought bravely against the Soviet invasion of November 1939, and it became an ally of Hitler from 1941 onward. In that year, as Britain cemented its controversial alliance of convenience with the atheistic Soviet Union, the archbishop of Canterbury wished "the Soviet people, and brave Russian armies" good luck in the fight. In Finland, Archbishop Kaila interpreted this as an abandonment of Christianity. Finns believed that God was on their side, helping them defend the borders of Finland, and appealed to Acts 17:26 in support of the idea that Finland's boundaries were inviolable: supposed biblical evidence that the invading Soviets were godless.[47] Pastor F. E. Lilja wrote that the struggle against Britain and Russia was "God's fight against the powers of darkness and in this fight the powers of light will win."[48] How could they reach this apparently bizarre position, that God was fighting the "Anglo-Ruskies" on the part of his special people, the Finns, and their German allies? The explanation is the same as for why Britain and Germany saw themselves as fighting a just war in God's cause. Finnish nationalism had become inseparable from the Finnish Lutheran Church, which saw Finland as a special instrument in the hand of God. After all, Finns had long sung, in the words of the Finnish Lutheran Hymnal, song number 459:

> Oh Lord, Bless the Finnish people,
> Give to it the abundance of your clemency,
> That it would be in all periods your own,
> The chosen people.
> Give us a faithful mind,
> Success for the ways of the Finnish tribe.[49]

It was only a short step from such a mindset to the idea that the Axis war against the Allies was a just war—was God's war, no less—and should be supported by Christ's people. But, as we have seen in chapter 2 and

---

47. The passage reads, "And he made from one man every nation of mankind to live on all the face of the earth, having determined allotted periods and the boundaries of their dwelling place, that they should seek God, and perhaps feel their way toward him and find him" (Acts 17:26–27 ESV).

48. Paasi, *Territories, Boundaries, and Consciousness*, 196.

49. Ibid., 199. Paasi references the 1981 edition of the hymnal.

shall see again below, British and American Christians have absolutely no place for smugness in this regard.

Christian Churches and Anti-Semitism

It may seem bizarre to us today that Finnish Christians fighting alongside the Nazis saw themselves as God's chosen people and believed that God was with them in their battle against the Allied powers. But is that any more bizarre than the British belief that God was with them in building an empire and defending it against Germany between 1914 and 1945, or the German belief that they were peculiarly God's chosen instrument? Or that French, Russian, American, Italian, and even Japanese Christians thought likewise? With some brave exceptions, the Christian churches of the nineteenth and early twentieth centuries largely supported their countries in wars to extend and then defend their territories. They played valuable roles as recruiting sergeants and morale boosters, keeping the war machines rolling. But perhaps even more insidious than this is their role in laying the foundations for the most repulsive aspect of the culmination of this period, the Holocaust.

Anti-Semitism has made ugly reappearances at different moments of Christian history. Saint Ambrose, who, as we saw in chapter 5, was an early proponent of the idea that Christians ought to ditch New Testament gospel peace for just war theory, also defended attacks on synagogues.[50] The Fourth Lateran Council of 1215 decreed that Jews should be segregated from Christians and wear distinctive gold badges, symbolizing the gold that they as a race supposedly received to betray Jesus.[51] It was the church, not the Nazis, who invented this insidious practice.

The German Reformation intensified this. Luther criticized Christians for "not avenging" the "blood of our lord" and held that they were "not at fault in slaying" Jews. He claimed that Germans were being victimized by the Jews,[52] another line that Hitler would take up rather than invent himself. Luther advised Christians on how to treat Jews: "First, to set fire to their synagogues or schools and to bury and cover with dirt whatever will not burn. . . . Second, I advise that their houses also be razed and destroyed . . . Third, I advise that all their prayer books and

50. Griffith, *War on Terrorism*, 4.

51. Ibid., 65.

52. Ibid.

Talmudic writings, in which such idolatry, lies, cursing, and blasphemy are taught, be taken from them . . . Fourth, I advise that their rabbis be forbidden to teach henceforth on pain of loss of life and limb."[53]

Otto Dibelius, who later joined the Confessing Church, was bishop of Brandenburg and anti-Jewish long before the Nazi Party came into existence. In 1933 he defended the church's refusal to stand by the synagogues by saying, "We have learned from Martin Luther that the church cannot get in the way of state power when it does what it is called to do. Not even when [the state] becomes hard and ruthless. . . . [The state] is ruling in God's name!"[54] Luther's legacy led churches to support or be indifferent to the anti-Jewish undercurrents of Christian German society that culminated in the Holocaust. Some Nazi defendants at the Nuremberg war crimes trials cited the teachings of Luther in their defense.

We might shake our heads disapprovingly, but it was the norm not the exception. Studies such as Christopher Browning's *Ordinary Men*[55] and Daniel Goldhagen's *Hitler's Willing Executioners* have shown that the belief that Germans were forced to reluctantly kill Jews and were thus in some ways equal victims of Nazism is a fantasy. Most did so willingly, feeling "not an empathetic reverberation for the suffering of others, but a hardened disdain, if not a gleeful enjoyment of it."[56] This was due to an anti-Semitism that saw Jews not only as subhuman and thus worthy of slavery or death but as irredeemably wicked and dangerous. Therefore, in this belief, Jews should not only die but up until their death be subject to unremitting pain, degradation, and suffering.[57] This was the culmination of a deep strain of anti-Semitism in German history. Historians Robert Ericksen and Susannah Heschel argue that one of the reasons for this was the importance of German churches, especially in the role they played in persuading Germans to go along with anti-Semitic Hitlerism. Through church leaders' support, they argue, "ordinary Germans were reassured that those policies did not violate the tenets of Christian faith and morality. . . . Large and powerful segments of the Catholic and Protestant churches supported Nazism with enthusiasm, under circumstances in which judicious silence would have been morally preferable and politi-

53. Longley, *Chosen People*, 108.

54. Steigmann-Gall, "Apostasy or Religiosity?"

55. Browning, *Ordinary Men*.

56. Goldhagen, *Hitler's Willing Executioners*, 457.

57. This is a central thesis in Goldhagen's book—see above.

cally more judicious."[58] Ericksen and Heschel conclude with the chilling contention that "the major reason for the murder of Jews during the course of Western history has been Christian anti-Judaism."[59]

This Christian anti-Semitism was not confined to Germany. Romania was an ally of Hitler in the Second World War, one of the many junior partners and co-belligerents of the Axis alliance (others included Bulgaria, Hungary, and Thailand). Nineteen-thirties Romania saw the spread of the "Legionary movement," an antidemocratic and fiercely anti-Semitic force with militant adherence to Orthodox Christianity. This force found much support among Orthodox priests. In 1940 its political movement launched an attack on a synagogue in Bucharest during an anti-Jewish pogrom.[60] A similar story is true of Hungary. Paul Hanebrink has argued that the notion of a "Christian Hungary" came to prominence from the late nineteenth century, encouraged and fostered by Catholic intellectuals and priests. This was an anti-Semitic concept of Hungary as a patriotic Christian society supposedly threatened by Jews, which replaced a relatively liberal society that had hitherto been inclusive of Jews.[61] Christianity not only stoked the nationalism and imperialism that produced World Wars I and II but provided the spiritual legacy of anti-Semitism that, in its extreme outworking of the Holocaust, marked the lowest moral point of the war.

Wars and Rumors of Wars

We have seen that the school textbook/Hollywood film narrative of the Second World War as a just and noble Allied response to unprovoked cruelty and aggression begun by Hitler in 1939 is a distortion of historical reality. It was rather the cataclysmic, if tragically predictable, conclusion to more than a century of naked international imperial rivalry justified by doctrines of racial and civilizational superiority and blessed by Christian churches. Jesus warned his disciples that when they heard of "wars and rumors of wars" and saw "nation [rising] against nation" they should "see to it that [they] are not alarmed," but "stand firm to the end" and ensure that the "gospel of the kingdom will be preached in the whole

---

58. Ericksen and Heschel, "Introduction," 4.

59. Ibid., 20.

60. "Obituaries: Patriarch Teoctist I," *The Times*, June 9, 2007, 50.

61. Hanebrink, *In Defense of Christian Hungary*.

world" (Matt 24:6–14). However, churches in Britain, America, France, the Soviet Union, Germany, Italy, and Japan apparently overlooked this admonition and forgot that their primary calling was to preach and embody the gospel. Instead, they became more worried that what they perceived as God's purposes through their own nation's imperial ambitions were being thwarted by his enemies, and thus threw their lot in with the military campaigns. Nationalism—anxiety over the fate of their nation—took precedence over standing firm for the kingdom of God and remaining true to the gospel.

The final act in this horrendous drama of inter-state rivalry was the bombing of Nagaski on August 9, 1945, which precipitated the Japanese surrender and the formal end of World War II. The fate of Nagasaki's Christians encapsulates how this whole cycle of violence was such a disaster for the church.

In the middle of the sixteenth century the Jesuit Missionary Francis Xavier established a Christian community in Japan. Faced with exploitative Spanish and Portuguese commercial interests, the Japanese rulers perceived Christianity as a threat and sought to stamp it out, through ostracism, torture, and crucifixions for those who would not renounce the faith. It appeared as if Japanese Christianity had been wiped out. However, in the late nineteenth century it was discovered that there were thousands of secret believers, who had been living out their faith in a catacomb existence unknown to the authorities.

As Japan modernized, the Japanese Christian community emerged from underground and built the massive St. Mary's Cathedral, the largest Christian church in the East, in the Urakami River district of Nagasaki. This was one of the landmarks that the bombardier on the plane carrying the nuclear bomb had been briefed on, and he used the cathedral to target his bomb. Gary Kohls describes what happened next: "At 11:02 a.m., Nagasaki Christianity was boiled, evaporated and carbonized in a scorching, radioactive fireball. The persecuted, vibrant, faithful, surviving center of Japanese Christianity had become ground zero. . . . What the Japanese Imperial government could not do in over 200 years of persecution, American Christians did in 9 seconds. The entire worshipping community of Nagasaki was wiped out."[62]

But the Christian tragedy of Nagasaki is not merely that of those "on the ground." Father George Zabelka, a thirty-year-old American Catholic

62. Kohls, "Bombing of Nagasaki August 9, 1945."

priest, had the dubious honor of blessing the airmen of the 509th Composite Group who dropped the atomic bomb on Nagasaki. He later said that he thought nothing of it at the time, as the airbase was regularly used for massive bombing raids and he had heard sermons from other clergy urging the airmen to continue the war. However, he subsequently visited hospitals in Nagasaki and saw the horrors of children dying of radiation poisoning. He was shocked to learn that he as a Catholic priest had ministered to those Catholic crewmen who killed their fellow Catholics in such numbers.[63] Zabelka came to dedicate his life to the peace movement, and later said, "To fail to speak to the utter moral corruption of the mass destruction of civilians was to fail as a Christian and as a priest, as I see it. Hiroshima and Nagasaki happened in and to a world and a Christian church that had asked for it—that had prepared the moral consciousness of humanity to do and to justify the unthinkable."[64]

Zabelka's observation applies to the whole conflict, not just its conclusion: the Christian church prepared the moral conscience of the world for the Second World War and eased that conscience as it fought it. The scale of Christian-on-Christian killing in Nagasaki is unique in that it occurred in less time than it took you to read the previous paragraph. But the spiritual tragedy encapsulated the whole Second World War: a grievous wound to the body of Christ and a damning indictment of the behavior of his followers.

Alternatives

At a party once I struck up a conversation with an elderly gentleman, with whom I was not acquainted, about Christian anti-Nazi resistance movements that eschewed violence. He gently interrupted me: "How can you think about resistance when crossing the road at the wrong time could lead to your death?" I asked what he meant, and he told me his story. As a young Jewish boy in wartime Germany, he and his mother were walking along a main road when, without any particular reason, she led him to cross the street and carry on up the other side. As they walked on they saw that a few hundred yards up on the side that they had just crossed from, people were being stopped and inspected to see if they were Jews— and arrested if they were. Most of his family were murdered in the war:

63. Bourke, *Intimate History of Killing*, 268–69.
64. Zabelka, "'I Was Told It Was Necessary.'"

if he had not crossed then, he would likely have been killed too. It was humbling to listen to his story. Faced with such manifest, overwhelming evil, isn't talk of gospel peace and Christlike enemy love simply "pie in the sky"? Worse, isn't it a criminal evasion of responsibility?

Part of the answer to this lies in the rest of this gentleman's story. He survived the war by being sheltered by an order of Catholic nuns. Institutions like the Catholic Church, he explained, had the ability to resist by virtue of their organizational strength. When the church used this power concertedly, remarkable results were possible. We should not underestimate the enormous pressures created in living under a totalitarian state. It would be foolish to claim that resistance to Nazism was easy, when it could readily lead to imprisonment or death. However, as the next section shows, it was possible.

Successful Nonmilitary Resistance against Hitler

An example of successful nonmilitary resistance against Hitler is provided by the amazing courage of two men, Pastors Paul Braume and Friedrich von Bodelschwingh. They were leading figures in the care work of the Protestant Home Mission during Nazi Germany. Their remarkable work produced what the historian Peter Matheson describes as "the only substantial achievement of the [German] churches during the War."[65] Through painstaking research on deaths in medical institutions, they concluded that the state was conducting a systematic and clandestine euthanasia program against people with certain types of chronic illness. They used the German legal system to break through an apparently impregnable cordon of silence by confronting ministry after ministry with horrific details of the euthanasia program. Braume was arrested, but the intervention of well-known bishops secured his release. Braume wrote in a memorandum in 1940 that "the inviolability of human life is one of the basic pillars of every state order." The intervention of Bishop von Galen, who, as we shall see below, delivered a series of stinging sermons against the program, was also significant, as Catholic nurses began to seriously obstruct the process of registration.[66] These various Christian actions in resisting and exposing what was a program secretly authorized by Hitler in 1940 led to the Nazis abandoning their policy, afraid to confront the

65. Matheson, *Third Reich*, 84.
66. R. Evans, *Third Reich at War*, 100.

churches on this question.[67] As the official Israeli Holocaust memorial museum Yad Vashem acknowledges in its display on this issue, "The operation was officially terminated in August 1941 due to protests from the churches."[68]

In both Germany and occupied Europe, there were numerous examples of selective refusal of assistance to the Nazis by government aides, the blocking of lines of command and information, mass strikes and shutdowns, and stalling and obstruction, which led to many Jews being saved.[69] The Bulgarian Jewish community was saved largely through protests of parliamentarians and the churches.[70] A good example of coordinated and effective resistance was that in Norway. In 1942 the fascist Minister-President Vidkun Quisling set out to create a corporative state on Mussolini's model and chose to begin with the schools. He established a new teachers' organization and chose as its leader the head of the *Hird*, the Norwegian SA (storm troopers).[71]

The underground resistance called on the teachers to stand against this and suggested a model for doing so. Thousands of the country's teachers wrote identical signed letters to the Church and Education Department saying they would neither join the new organization nor assist in a program of fascist education in any way.

The government threatened them with dismissal and closed schools for a month. The teachers taught in their homes, and despite censorship, word spread and tens of thousands of letters from parents poured in. About a thousand male teachers were sent to concentration camps in cattle cars, where the Gestapo imposed a terror regime on starvation rations to induce capitulation. Teachers at liberty refused to comply. Quisling is said to have raged at teachers at a school near Oslo, "You teachers have destroyed everything for me!" He gave in, and eight months after ordering their arrest, the last teachers returned home. Quisling encountered further difficulties and opposition, and Hitler ordered him to abandon his plan for the corporatist state entirely.

67. Matheson, *Third Reich*, 84–89.

68. Personal observation, June 2010.

69. Sharp, *Methods of Nonviolent Action*, 2:321–26; see also Ackerman and DuVall, *Force More Powerful*, ch. 5: "Denmark, the Netherlands, the Rosenstrasse: Resisting the Nazis."

70. According to a poster in Jerusalem's Yad Vashem Holocaust museum, seen June 2010.

71. This example is taken from Sharp, *Power and Struggle*, 1.

The year 1943 saw dramatic and effective action at the heart of Hitler's empire. The Jewish husbands of German wives were suddenly rounded up and held at a prison on Berlin's Rosenstrasse. By the early hours of the next day their wives had discovered their location and began to congregate at the gate of the detention center to protest. Family and other supporters swelled the number to six thousand. The security police tried to make them disperse, but they would not.

Gestapo headquarters was located on nearby Burgstrasse; there was no lack of manpower for the authorities to call on to fire on the crowd and swiftly end their protest. As Heinz Ullstein, one of the arrested men, was later to put it, "Scared by an incident which had no equal in the history of the Third Reich, headquarters consented to negotiate," and the prisoners were released.[72]

These examples illustrate the historian Shelley Baranowski's assertion that "the Nazi regime governed by consent."[73] When ordinary people in sufficient numbers refuse to answer the telephone in government ministries, teach in schools, bake bread, drill oil wells, make armaments in factories, mend road signs, deliver letters, repair broken water mains—that is, obey even the most mundane orders—then even the most ruthless dictator will be helpless. The more a dictator kills, the more untenable his rule becomes. Concerted and coordinated actions like those illustrated above reversed decisions taken by Hitler's regime and derailed major policies of the Nazis and their allies. They were more effective than the various failed assassination plots against Hitler hatched by Germans disgruntled with his rule.

Academic historians disagree on the extent to which mass German cooperation with Nazism was willing or coerced.[74] Long before current debates on this theme, concentration camp survivor Bruno Bettelheim argued that resistance was effectively impossible except as a bizarre anomaly because of the destruction of personality through fear.[75] However, these examples suggest more possibilities than Bettelheim was willing to allow. They raise the intriguing question of what else might have happened if Germans had protested not only the arrest of Jews when they

72. Ibid., 88–90; Stoltzfus, *Resistance of the Heart: Intermarriage and the Rosenstrasse Protest in Nazi Germany*. For a rejection of the interpretation of these events as a protest, see R. Evans, *Third Reich at War*, 271–72.

73. Baranowski, *Confessing Church*, 5.

74. R. Evans, "How Willing Were They?"

75. Bettelheim, *The Informed Heart*.

happened to be their husbands, but *all* Jews. If the majority of German women had stood protesting and risked being shot, Hitler would have fallen. The churches could have organized this, had they developed over the long term a culture of gospel peace that nonviolently but steadfastly resisted oppression. But they did not, and the regime was, ultimately, overthrown only by the violence of a devastating enemy.

The Churches and Resistance to Nazism

It is both inspiring and painful to read the examples of those Christians who successfully resisted Nazism: inspiring because they demonstrate the possibilities for resistance that existed within Nazi Europe and belie the myth that opposition to Hitler was impossible; painful because they were so limited. The position of French bishops on the fate of Jews in occupied France is instructive. In 1997 the Catholic bishops of France issued a Declaration of Repentance, recognizing that "through their silence" they had in fact acquiesced in the "flagrant violations of the rights" of Jews.[76] But was this simply self-flagellation with the benefit of hindsight: could they have done anything else? Yes, they could. By the second half of 1942 some French bishops began to speak out against collaboration with Germans in their policy of mass deportations of French Jews. This intervention convinced Marshall Pétain, the Nazi puppet leader in France, to scrap the program of stripping French Jews of citizenship to enable them to be deported to German death camps.[77] Because it wielded institutional power and was held to have authority, when the church did speak out the government had to listen—but it said little and said it late.

More pointed still is the example of the wartime bishop of Münster, Bishop von Galen, mentioned in passing above. He successfully used the German legal system to reverse certain attacks on Catholicism, such as the removal of crucifixes from schools. In the summer of 1941 he witnessed the Gestapo seizing church property and forcing nuns and priests into exile. Incensed, he returned to his home and stayed up all night writing a damning sermon denouncing their actions as theft and an attack on the kingdom of God. His sermon was delivered from his pulpit the next day. It was the first of three thunderous sermons that summer, which blasted Nazi policies on church property seizure, the encouragement

76. Adler, "French Churches and the Jewish Question," 377.
77. Ibid.

of sexual immorality, deception of the people, and euthanasia. He cited church teaching, scripture, and Germany's legal codes. His sermons were widely distributed by German Catholics and British wartime propaganda and acted as catalysts to embolden others to denounce and voice protest. This led to the cessation of the localized seizure of church property and contributed toward the ending of the euthanasia program. The Nazis, right up to Hitler himself, were incensed by his speeches, but records of internal discussions revealed they were afraid to move against him due to the need to shore up support for the war. Himmler wrote in 1944, "We couldn't settle accounts with the traitor Galen for reasons of foreign policy. We shall catch up with him later on, and the whole church with him."[78]

Bishop von Galen has been lionized by some as a heroic anti-Nazi resister, but, according to the historian Beth Griech-Polelle, this veneration is misplaced. Afraid of the charge of disloyalty, his sermons were full of blessings for the Führer, declarations of loyalty to the state, and approval of the war. More seriously, he remained silent on the fate of local Jews and Communists. Along with Pope Pius XII, he saw Communism as a greater threat to Christianity than Nazism. Thus, although Bishop von Galen was outraged by confiscation of church property, the removal of crucifixes from schools, and euthanasia against local Catholics, he was silent on the murder of non-Catholic minorities, remaining anxious to position himself as a patriot loyally supporting the war against the Allies. Griech-Polelle's conclusion is carefully argued yet damning: the bishop, like the vast majority of German Catholics, was more concerned with protecting church institutions than with universal justice and love to the outcast. As she concludes, "To those who might think my assessment of von Galen is too harsh, I would respond that I believe von Galen should be held to a higher standard of accountability because of the office he held and the beliefs he affirmed. If church leaders will not publicly witness to the truth, to act as guides for their followers' consciences, then whom should we expect to fulfill this task?"[79]

78. Griech-Polelle, *Bishop von Galen*, 88.
79. Ibid., 269.

Spotless Records?

But perhaps I have been unduly pessimistic. Was there no German church that consistently withstood both Hitler's foreign and domestic policies? There was one notable denomination that wholeheartedly and consistently opposed the Nazis. This denomination rejected the Führer cult and National Socialist extremism, did not join Nazi organizations or persecutions of minorities, and refused to take part in war-related activities. Large numbers of them were executed by the Nazis and died in concentration camps. In spite of this ferocious persecution, they remained firm in their convictions. Indeed, Bruno Bettelheim, the Jewish psychologist mentioned above who survived Dachau and Buchenwald camps, admired them as a group who showed unusual heights of human dignity and moral behavior and survived the experiences that soon destroyed others.[80] The German scholar Johannes Wrobel explained that they maintained this opposition because "they preached about a coming 1000-year reign by Jesus Christ—not by Hitler. . . . They viewed themselves as part of an international brotherhood based on Christian love."[81] What a testimony! Their identity? Jehovah's Witnesses. That the only German religious group to emerge from the war with a near-spotless record is one that, due to theological error, is rightly considered a sect and not properly Christian should be salutary to all Christians.

As this and the examples above show, it *was* possible for people to refuse to be hoodwinked by the Nazis and to find creative, nonviolent ways to resist them. Ultimately, it was honorable to bravely choose martyrdom rather than to sacrifice principles. That so few orthodox Christians were able to even conceive of this is a damning indictment of the church of 1930s and 1940s Europe. But we cannot afford to be smug. Andrew Chandler concludes his study on the Church of England's response to Hitlerism in the 1930s with the statement that he doubts whether the contemporary church would be able to withstand another Hitler today.[82]

80. Bettelheim, *Informed Heart*, 28, 115.

81. Wrobel, "Jehovah's Witnesses in National Socialist Concentration Camps," 91.

82. Chandler, "Church of England and Nazi Germany," 231.

Not Entirely a New Question

The question "What about Hitler?" is, of course, one that has been asked by Christians only since the 1940s. However, if it is seen as really asking, "What happens if Christians don't resist a violent conqueror who stands against the dearest values of our civilization?" then it is a restatement of a question that Christians have asked throughout their history. It is instructive to consider some of the examples of answers that have been given.

The classic example from the early church was the question by second-century anti-Christian pagan writer Celsus. "What if the whole world were Christian?" he asked, meaning that if Rome adopted Christianity and thus eschewed violence, how could it defend itself against barbarian invaders? That is, in effect, the same question as "What about Hitler?" when asked of modern Christians who likewise reject violence. Origen, in reply, said it was not that Christians would fight a just war in defense, but that by God's power the Christians would be delivered and the barbarians would be converted. Musto provides numerous examples of how the barbarian invasions of Rome, which eventually led to its destruction, proved just that. The overrunning of the empire inspired prayer and missionary zeal, in the power of the Holy Spirit, to evangelize and convert Europe's new non-Christian rulers.[83] As the monk Roger Bacon later argued, war against nonbelievers only hardens their hearts against Christianity and makes converting them (the ultimate goal of Jesus' Great Commission) harder.[84]

By the sixteenth century the barbarians were long converted, but Europe faced a very different challenge: Islam. The armies of the Turks were advancing on Europe. A fear gripped many, and the question of how the church should respond was an important one. A key thinker in the northern European Renaissance was the Christian humanist scholar Erasmus. In his 1517 book *The Complaint of Peace*, he made his own position on war clear:

> What do mitres and helmets have in common? What has a crosier to do with a sword? What has a Bible to do with a shield? How can one reconcile a salutation of peace with an exhortation to war; peace in one's mouth and war in one's deeds? Do you praise war with the same mouth that you preach peace and

83. Musto, *Catholic Peace Tradition*, 36.
84. Ibid., 90–91.

> Christ? Do you herald with the same trumpet both God and
> Satan? . . . What filth is the tongue of a priest who exhorts war,
> evil, and murder![85]

Instead, he recommended alternatives: checking the true causes of war, namely personal ambition and evil desires. In another publication, he explicitly addressed the Turkish threat. He reminded his readers that the early church had always opposed war, even against barbarian invasions, and suggested a pamphlet campaign against the Turks, coupled with examples of Christian virtues in an effort to convert them.[86]

The question "What about Hitler?" is a reformulation of Celsus' attack on Christianity for what he recognized—correctly—as the obvious rejection of violence of the Gospel. It is a question that has been asked down the ages. In the course of writing this book, versions of the question I have heard posed by Christians have replaced Hitler with Iraq's Saddam Hussein, al-Qaeda's Osama bin Laden, Libya's Colonel Muammar Gaddafi, Syria's Bashar al-Assad, and Islamic State's al-Baghdadi. The name changes, but the question remains the same, as do its underlying assumptions. The answer, as given by Origen, Bacon, and Erasmus, must always be this: the power of the gospel is greater than the power of any worldly potentate, and prayer and evangelism are more powerful than the weapons of the world.

If we ask, "What about Hitler?" as a way to ignore the New Testament witness against violence and to therefore justify war, we implicitly accept that the spiritual power available to Christians is weaker than the powers of this dark age. We suggest that being disciples of Jesus does not work in the real world. At heart, it betrays the idea that a country composed entirely of millions of people seeking utterly to live out Christ's radical and costly call to discipleship who would therefore not fight an invader is something not to be desired, but rather to be feared. If that is the case, we don't really believe in Christianity—so why bother with the pretense at all?

Conclusion: What about "What about Hitler"?

In his 1989 study of the psychological and emotional culture of Britons and Americans during the Second World War, Paul Fussell takes issue

---

85. Ibid., 125.
86. Ibid., 133.

with those whom he calls "the sentimental, the loony patriotic, the ignorant, and the bloodthirsty" who, as he puts it, have "sanitized and romanticized [the Allied war] almost beyond recognition."[87] In a book that, as he says, tries to "balance the scales," he uses participant biographical accounts to explore the fears, pleasures, frustrations, and experience of physical brutality of the Second World War. He writes about US marines who mutilated the genitals of Japanese soldiers' corpses and who used defeated Japanese soldiers as target practice, experiencing "intense satisfaction watching them twist and writhe when set afire by the napalm of the flamethrower."[88]

In a chapter entitled "The Ideological Vacuum" he contrasts the joyous welcome of World War I by poets such as Rupert Brooke with the resignation that greeted World War II, where biographies and letters suggest that British and American soldiers were motivated more by hatred of the enemy than by a clear sense of right and wrong. As he writes in that chapter,

> The Second World War, total and global as it was, killed worldwide more civilian men, women, and children than soldiers, sailors, and airmen. And compared even with the idiocies of Verdun, Gallipoli, or Tannenberg, it was indescribably cruel and insane. It was not until the Second World War had enacted all its madness that one could realize how near Victorian social and ethical norms the First World War really was. Unthinkable then would have been the Second War's unsurrendering Japanese, its suicides and *kamikazes*, its public hanging of innocent hostages, its calm, efficient gassing of Jews and Slavs and homosexuals, its unbelievable conclusion in atomic radiation. It was a savage, insensate affair, barely conceivable to the well-conducted imagination . . . and hardly approachable without some currently unfashionable theory of human mass insanity and inbuilt, inherited corruption.[89]

As this chapter has shown, the Christian churches, to our shame, made this possible. Historian A. J. Hoover writes that "the Great War and its aftermath helped bring the Third Reich into being. . . . Some of the key religious ideas of the war helped create a climate of opinion that made the Third Reich possible."[90] But we must go further: the spirit of

87. Fussell, *Wartime*, ix.

88. Ibid., 120.

89. Ibid., 132.

90. Hoover, *God, Germany, and Britain*, 135.

nationalism, the ideology of empire, the conviction that certain races and civilizations possessed superior values and had a divinely mandated role in the world, and the belief in just wars—beliefs that were propagated by Christian churches in *all* the belligerent nations—made Hitlerism, the Holocaust, and World War II possible. As Martin Luther King Jr. put it, "During the last two world wars, national churches even functioned as the ready lackeys of the state, sprinkling holy water upon the battleships and joining the mighty armies in singing, 'Praise the Lord and pass the ammunition.'"[91] Let us not be trapped by a romantic identity myth into the perpetuation of the creation of a world where what Fussell describes above is regarded as not only acceptable but also Christian. We do that every time we invoke not scripture but the Second World War as some sort of moral lighthouse from which to chart the uncertain sea of whichever conflict we currently find ourselves faced with.

The scripture says, "Do not conform to the pattern of this world, but be transformed by the renewing of your mind" (Rom 12:2). The idea that World War II was a simple moral clash of good versus evil rather than a struggle between imperial powers—and therefore Christians were right to set scripture aside and fight in it—is an example of the kind of error against which Paul was warning us. It is always dangerous when our theology is derived from a particular nationalistic myth about a recent war. Francis Schaeffer described the pernicious effects of the evangelical church being unduly influenced by the culture around it as "the great evangelical disaster."[92] Although he was not discussing war, I contend that the same applies here. Endless appeals to a romanticized Anglo-American myth of World War II as the touchstone for ethical reflection on war demonstrate that the church has been more influenced by Hollywood than by Holy Scripture. Church leaders have a responsibility to ensure that discipleship undoes this.

In 1940, Martin Wight, one of the leading British thinkers in international relations theory of his generation, wrote in his application for conscientious objector status that "the only method" that can overcome

---

91. King, "Knock at Midnight," 72.

92. Schaeffer, *The Great Evangelical Disaster*. I share Schaeffer's critique of liberal pacifism but note that he nonetheless supports the use of violence in some circumstances. As with many authorities I cite in this book, I think the logical thrust of his argument has to be against Christian participation in violence, but he does not reach this explicit conclusion due to some of the factors capturing Christian imaginations identified in this book.

the "demonic forces of evil that have their fullest expression in Nazi Germany, is that of Calvary."[93] Do we believe that, or would we add, "But if that should prove inadequate, temporarily shelving what we profess to believe on a Sunday morning and butchering as many of our enemies as quickly as possible before they get us first"?

93. Quoted in Thomas, "Faith, History and Martin Wight." It should be noted that Wight later changed his mind on this.

8

Conclusion—Part I

Being a Gospel Peacemaking Church

From 2001 until his death in 2011, veteran British peace activist Brian Haw maintained a one-man protest against the Afghanistan and Iraq wars outside the Houses of Parliament in London. One placard he held up said, "I think when Jesus said love your enemies he didn't mean kill them." He was right. Gospel peace—the overcoming of our enemies through loving them in the way that God loved us when we were his enemies—is at the heart of the Christian message and lifestyle. Without it, Christianity loses its role as the "salt of the earth" (Matt 5:13). By inciting war rather than making peace, it becomes part of the world's problems rather than their solution. This conclusion is not only based on the teaching and example of Jesus and the apostles. It is the evidence of the progressive revelation of Old Testament scripture and the final revelation of the New Testament. It is the thrust of evangelical/Reformed theology with its emphasis on the doctrines of creation, fall, and redemption by the death and resurrection of Jesus Christ. Although less authoritative, its wisdom is amply attested by church history and even the example of World War II. To take up weapons is not an option for a follower of Jesus Christ who has been saved by grace through faith (Eph 2:8). War is counterproductive to the cause of the kingdom of God, bringing dishonor on his name.

It is recounted that a man who had missed the church service one Sunday morning asked his wife what the vicar had preached about. "Sin," she answered. "Oh, and what did he say about it?" he inquired. The woman paused, thought for a while, and replied simply, "He's against it." Equally simply, this book has argued that war is sin and that participation in it is sinful. To ask whether the church can support war is like asking

198

whether it can support sin: the very question reveals an immediate failure to understand what the church is and what gospel it has to proclaim. The church is by definition antiwar, and to the extent that it departs from this, it departs from being the church.

But saying that Christianity is "antiwar" is like saying it is "anti-sin"—it does not tell us very much practically. Does Christian peace-making mean copying the example of Mr. Haw, decamping outside Parliament and yelling at politicians about their foreign policy as they speed past in dark cars? No. The United States and the United Kingdom launched a war against Iraq in 2003, but before then the country had been ruled by Saddam Hussein, a dictator who brutalized his own people and launched two ruinous wars on his neighbors. As a penalty the United Nations imposed sanctions; however, these sanctions did not hurt Hussein but rather contributed to the deaths of millions of ordinary Iraqis by depriving them of basic medical and sanitary supplies. Iraq was hardly "at peace." If Mr. Haw had prevented the 2003 Iraq War, the British and US populations would have continued living their rich lifestyles and the Iraqi people would have continued to suffer. As Christopher Hitchens put it, the antiwar movement risked becoming an "auxiliary to dictators and aggressors in trouble."[1] This is not "peace" in the biblical sense. As biblical studies professor Perry Yoder says, based on his reading of the Old Testament, this type of "peace" as avoiding violence while allowing injustice to continue is a "Western, middle-class luxury."[2] That is why gospel peace is different from traditional Western pacifism, just as it is different from the "cruise missile liberals" who use just war theory to advocate deploying Western military might around the world to make or intervene in wars in the name of peace.

The primary message of this book, therefore, is not "don't fight": that may sometimes be good advice, but at other times it may be unloving neglect that only allows injustice to continue. Walter Brueggemann says that "biblical faith is not romantic. It reckons with the evil, and it knows that the evil strikes at all that is crucial and most precious."[3] The message of this book is, rather, "Be the church and preach the gospel." In a violent world, this means making peace by overcoming violence in the love and power of God. That is what I call "gospel peacemaking."

1. Hitchens, "Against Rationalization."
2. P. Yoder, *Shalom*, 1.
3. Bruggeman, *The Message of the Psalms*, 74.

What, then, should churches *do* about war? What does it mean to follow the Prince of Peace in an age of wars on terror, suicide bombers, civil wars, oppressive dictatorships, and street murders? That is the topic of these two final chapters. In the first one we shall concentrate on what it means to be a peacemaking church at the level of the local congregation. Peace is something we "do" at certain times, but should be woven into our self-identities and practice as Christians. Peace should permeate our theology, our preaching, our worship, our discipleship, our celebration of communion, our praying, and our understanding of what it means to be a follower of Jesus in this age and in the end time. In the second concluding chapter, we shall look at how congregations formed by such biblical practices of worship and discipleship can go on to play peacemaking roles in the wider world.

A Theology of Peace and War

A Christian response to war must not be molded by prevailing attitudes to war, violence, foreign intervention, and the like as presented through media commentaries, politicians, and popular culture. Neither should it be based upon sets of theories derived from merely human wisdom at different times, such as just war theory. Rather, it must begin with the Bible, and in particular a biblical account of peace and war.

Peace is central to God's will for human life. In the Old Testament the word *shalom*, usually translated as "peace," refers variously to material/physical well-being, social relationships between people and nations marked by justice, and acting with integrity and honesty. The common denominator of its many meanings is well-being, wholeness, and completeness.[4] It is, Yoder continues, a "vision of what ought to be and a call to transform society"—"a far cry from seeing peace as the passive avoidance of deadly violence."[5] *Eirene*, the New Testament Greek word usually used to translate *shalom*, extends these meanings to talk about God as "the God of peace" (Heb 13:20) and the good news of God for all humankind as "the gospel of peace" (Eph 6:15). Christ, who came and "preached peace to [those] who were far away and peace to those who were near" (Eph 2:17), is himself "our peace" (Eph 2:14). Through Christ, "God has called us to live in peace" (1 Cor 7:15), and our hearts and minds are to be

4. Swartley, *Covenant of Peace.*

5. P. Yoder, *Shalom,* 5.

guarded by "the peace of God, which transcends all understanding" (Phil 4:7). This is achieved through his death and resurrection, which brings humanity "peace with God" (Rom 5:1), peace between Jew and Gentile by creating "in himself one new humanity out of the two, thus making peace" (Eph 2:14), and even ecological peace in creation (Rom 8:19–21). Christ's death and resurrection have transforming power, setting things right between old enemies: this is not achieved not through violence but through love.[6] Thus equipped, his followers find blessing in being "peacemakers" (Matt 5:9). No wonder that Paul and Peter regularly begin their letters praying "grace and peace" to their recipients. These two terms are at the crux of the gospel, and a church that emphasizes only one of them is not an authentic Christian church.

If peace is so central to God's work and will, we might well ask, "Why, then, does he permit war to afflict his creation?" The singer Edwin Starr had a 1970 hit with the (in)famous song, "War—what is it good for?" His answer (bellowed out in a manner that revealed greater conviction than musical ability) was "absolutely nothing!" Although Starr was not known for his contributions to theological debate, a version of this question has long troubled Christians: why does God allow war?

The clearest and most biblical answer to the question that I have read is given by Martyn Lloyd-Jones, perhaps the most influential evangelical preacher of the twentieth century, who to an extent was a follower of his illustrious Noncomformist London predecessor, Charles Haddon Spurgeon (see ch. 5 on his implacable denunciation of war as sin). As pastor of Westminster Chapel during the dark days of World War II, he faced the challenge of answering this question to his congregation. Lloyd-Jones observes that the actual question "Why does God allow war?" is not directly considered or raised in the Bible. "The Bible does not isolate war," he writes, "as if it were something separate and unique and quite apart, as we tend to do in our thinking. It is but one of the manifestations of sin, one of the consequences of sin."[7] God shows us the right way to live, in love of neighbor, but when we disobey him and depart from his good design for us, we inevitably bring disastrous consequences upon ourselves.

As we experience or read about the shocking acts of depravity in war and the traumas of pain, fear, and loss that it causes, war enables us to see more clearly than ever what sin is, and our need of his forgiveness and

---

6. Swartley, *Covenant of Peace*, 1–26.

7. Lloyd-Jones, *Why Does God Allow War?*, 82.

grace. God "permits and allows such things as war to chastise and to punish us; to teach us, and to convict us of our sins; and above all, to call us to repentance and acceptance of his gracious offer,"[8] writes Lloyd-Jones. The vital question, therefore, is not why God allows war but whether we are learning the lessons, repenting before God, and seeking his salvation.

We may not always—or usually—know why God allows certain wars to happen. The prophet Habakkuk asked God, when "destruction and violence" are all around, "why do you tolerate wrong?" (Hab 1:3). God's answer to Habakkuk was unexpected: that he was raising up an invading Babylonian army to punish Israel and work his purposes out for his people. As Lloyd-Jones says of this passage, "History is under divine control."[9] The centerpiece of history is God's work of establishing a new kingdom in the world, and "everything that happens in the world has relevance to it."[10] This kingdom is demonstrated in the church. As Stanley Hauerwas puts it, the church does not "have" an ethic: it *is* an ethic.[11] This means that the primary goal of the church is not to go out and build justice, peace, or whatever: when that becomes the goal, we end up justifying all sorts of questionable things such as violence, as the sorry history of just war theology and holy war in the church shows. Rather, the very existence of the church as the body of redeemed people, who have peace with God and each other and who love their enemies and seek to be peacemakers, is an alternative social reality to all the governments, armies, international organizations, aid agencies, and whatever. When every one of these "dominion[s], authority[ies] and [power]s" have been destroyed (1 Cor 15:24), the church, as the bride of Christ (Rev 19:7–9; Eph 5:25–27), will remain.

There is evidence that the incidence of traditional wars fought between countries is declining.[12] This has led some optimists to suggest that the human race may become so civilized that we might end all war as we become richer and more democratic. However, other scholars suggest that war is changing in form as technologies and the global economy

---

8. Ibid., 88.

9. Lloyd-Jones, *From Fear to Faith*, 19–22.

10. Ibid., 21.

11. Hauerwas, *Peaceable Kingdom*, ch. 6.

12. Indeed, we have seen progress: for example, the devilishly cruel tortures and lingering executions used by devout Protestant and Catholic Christians in Europe on supposed witches, heretics, traitors, and government critics before the eighteenth century are a thing of the past. See Pinker, *Better Angels of Our Nature*, 676–78.

change and that violence and insecurity remain pervasive.[13] For example, as I write this in the autumn of 2015, over the past week Islamic jihadists have shot, bombed, and executed hundreds of people in Paris, Iraq, Syria, and Lebanon, a month after blowing up a Russian passenger jet and murdering all on board.

Optimistic pacifists hope that war can be legislated or protested out of history if only we can use nonviolent strategies and develop a worldwide civilization of human rights and democracy.[14] Optimistic just war theorists hope that war will end when all the world is democratic, and in the meantime we can use military force to jostle the bad guys along in the right direction.[15] Although apparently in opposition, at root these liberal theories share a similar failure to appreciate the sinfulness of sin, that is to say, the impossibility of eliminating the potential of human societies to exhibit violence. They assume we can use our ingenuity to create and maintain mastery of ourselves and our social world into the unending future, and somehow find ways to prevent our civilization going the way of all others in history.[16] But the Bible has a much more realistic view than both these idealisms. In a provocative book, scholar Christopher Coker asks, "Can war be eliminated?" His own answer to his question is that this is unlikely, as a study of how our humanity has developed seems to suggest that we are "hardwired" for war.[17] Likewise the Bible recognizes that sin is a universal trait in fallen humanity and that war is, as Martyn Lloyd-Jones expounded, a manifestation and a consequence of sin. Sin corrupts not only our individual inner lives but also our societies, affecting our political, economic, and social systems. As the scripture reminds us, "wars and fightings" come from our "lusts" (Jas 4:1 KJV); although legislation, peace treaties, international organizations, and the like can

13. Dalby, "Peace and Critical Geopolitics"; Nest, *Coltan.*

14. See some of the examples of early pacifism cited in ch. 1 of Barrett, *Subversive Peacemakers.*

15. An unusual example of this is Dolman, *Astropolitik.* Dolman argues that until full democracy occurs, the United States needs to militarize space as a way to dominate earth and prevent any nondemocratic power from challenging the US. In their insistence that liberal democracies are in a war of survival with militant Islam, atheist writers such as Sam Harris and Christopher Hitchens make the same argument. See S. Harris, *The End of Faith,* and Hitchens, "A War to Be Proud Of."

16. Diamond, *Collapse.* Diamond's book is controversial and runs the risk of "environmental determinism" (the idea that human history is largely controlled by what happens in nature), but nonetheless makes a salutary read.

17. Coker, *Can War Be Eliminated?,* 102–3.

change habits and restrain extremes, they cannot fully change the heart. Biblical peace, as we saw above, is not the temporary cessation of warfare but complete harmony and justice in human affairs. This is unobtainable while sin stalks the earth.

However, this does not mean that we opt out of involvement in a violent world. Although "we must stand at a distance from our society, its tendencies and movements," insists Jacques Ellul, "we must never break with it, for the Incarnation has taken place."[18] This concern goes right back to creation. In his commentary on Genesis 1, David Atkinson suggests that the truth that God created a good world is the starting point for us in "trying to develop a Christian mind on many of our contemporary environmental and social questions." He writes that "our anger at terrorism and our hatred of war" needs to be traced back to its proper origins, which "are to be found in the God who makes all things, and who makes all things new. Our deep human concern for making things better is itself a reflection of the character of God."[19]

Some Christians mistrust the language of "making things better" and want to confine the Christian message to one of inner peace with God, their consciences, and possibly with the people immediately around them. At the other extreme, some try to reduce it to a social message of pacifistic antiwar activism, just war, or international diplomacy. Neither extreme does justice to gospel peace proclaimed by the Lord Jesus. Biblical hope for peace looks not to another world but to the future renewal of this world. Sin and its manifestations and consequences, including death and war, were defeated when Jesus Christ died and rose again. Because of the death and resurrection of our Lord, we know that the awful power of generals and warlords will finally be undone, that their commands are not the final word in history; we know that eventually the terror of war will no longer stalk the earth. Nevertheless, this full renewal is a *future* renewal that will be fully ushered in only when Jesus returns at the end of the age. We should declare to the oppressed the arrival of a kingdom of justice and peace, the good news of liberation, and connect it to the experiences of war and unrest around us. But we must not offer false hope of an imminent end to violence. The hope of the gospel of peace is the only hope we can offer that is guaranteed to survive the vagaries of history.[20]

18. Ellul, *Anarchy and Christianity*, 13, 26.

19. Atkinson, *Message of Genesis 1–11*, 25–26.

20. This argument is influenced by Chester, *Good News to the Poor*, ch. 11.

Preaching the Gospel of Peace

As we have seen above, war is a consequence and a manifestation of sin, and God's "response" to war is the creation of the church through the death and resurrection of his Son, Jesus Christ. What, then, is the church to do in wartime?

Although that question seems right and appropriate, the danger is that it leads us immediately to reach for superficial and nontheological answers derived from recent human experience of issuing declarations opposing war, supporting international peace conferences, and the like. The church should no more sprinkle "Jesus pixie dust" on the United Nations and peace marches than it should on just war theory. A better place to start is by asking, "What is the church to do at any time?" Again, Martyn Lloyd-Jones put this clearly: "The church's primary function is to restore men [and women] to a right relationship with God."[21]

Anglican Bishop George Bell expounds this in a classic essay originally written in 1939, where he asks, "What is the church's function in war-time?" The answer he gives is simple: "It is the function of the Church at all costs to remain the Church," that organization which is the trustee of the gospel of redemption, "the pillar and ground of the truth" (1 Tim 3:15 KJV).[22] There is no separate wartime gospel that is different from a peacetime gospel message. The church's supreme concern is for the kingdom of God, not for the triumph of any national cause, however right or compelling it may seem at the time. Neither is the church a society for merely exhorting people to have good aims or to improve international morals. The world lies in the power of the evil one, whom Christ by his cross has overcome. War is fundamentally a spiritual problem, and the gospel is its solution.

This being the case, the church's primary function in wartime is to preach the gospel. It is to explain to men and women how God made them for himself in a perfect creation; how, by human rebellion against God's good commands (sin), death came to the world; how killing and destruction are contrary to God's good will for us; and how, in God's judgment, war is a manifestation and a consequence of sin. It is to outline how God sent his only son, Jesus Christ, to demonstrate truly authentic human life, to teach us how to live, and to be an atoning sacrifice for our sins, thereby forgiving us and cleansing us from all unrighteousness. This

21. Lloyd-Jones, *Will the Hospital Replace the Church?*, 35.

22. Bell, "Church's Function in War-Time," 23.

act of gracious love opened the way to life and gave us the power of the Holy Spirit to live in holiness and peace, turning our backs on the sins of war and murder. It is to remind the world of the promise that the Lord Jesus will return in judgment to make a final end of war and every other sin, to punish all those who remained in their sin, and to remake our world in all perfection, where humans will again dwell with God and each other in peace, forever.

The early twentieth-century missionaries Mildred Cable and Francesca French wrote in the introduction to a book on their work in China, "The business which took the Authors up and down Central Asian caravan routes, was the business of the Kingdom of God in the establishment of which lies the only solution of problems whether social, national or international."[23] This is the essence of the belief behind gospel preaching: that our message is as much the solution of the problems of nations at war, as the problems of individuals in turmoil—because both have the same root, namely, sin. There is thus no "social gospel" separate from a "personal gospel."

This conviction is seen time and time again in the lives of preachers in war zones. Gladys Aylward, nicknamed "the little woman," brought many to faith by her tireless preaching of the gospel in China. She recounts that at one point during the Japanese invasion, Chinese women fleeing the fighting flooded into her compound, "bewildered, weary of war, and unhappy." So she "seized the opportunity of telling them that the great God I served cared for them and could give them peace of heart even in these awful circumstances."[24] If she had remained in Britain deliberating on whether Britain should intervene militarily to help the Chinese, or if she had stayed in safe areas under military protection, many who are now rejoicing around the throne would have gone to a lost eternity.

Likewise Henry Martyn, while heading out to India to serve as a missionary, was caught up in fighting between British and Dutch forces for control of Cape Town in 1806. Recording in his diary (a classic of evangelical spirituality) what he witnessed, he wrote that he was sickened at the scenes of death and suffering and at the British raising their flag over conquered territory. He saw this suffering as a product and demonstration of sin that spurred him on to pray and work for the gospel. He prayed that England "might show herself great indeed, by sending

---

23. Cable and French, *Through Jade Gate and Central Asia*.
24. Aylward, *Little Woman*, 71.

forth ministers of her church to diffuse the gospel of peace."[25] We learn from Martyn's example that war should not excite us to call for further involvement or intervention, still less to champion our own host nation's fortunes, but rather should increase our determination to labor for the spread of the gospel of peace. What is our first reaction to news images of war and suffering elsewhere? If it is not to see the face of sin and to pray and work for the spread of the gospel, then our understanding has not properly been shaped by biblical theology.

Gladys Aylward and Henry Martyn are inspiring, but their lives can be daunting to those of us not called to similar contexts. However, in order to be practical gospel peacemakers we do not have to leave home and travel far like these missionaries. For example, during World War II, academic and Christian speaker C. S. Lewis took every invitation he received to preach the Christian gospel in Britain with clarity and power in churches, societies, public meetings, and on the radio. His remarkable wartime radio broadcasts, subsequently published as the classic book *Mere Christianity*, have brought generations of skeptics and doubters to faith in Christ. Lewis fittingly described his frenetic preaching and speaking ministry at this time as his "war effort."[26] I would be so bold as to claim that, without literally firing a single shot, Lewis was the most distinguished British Christian soldier of the war. His example is one for the church of every generation when the world it lives in becomes convulsed by war.[27] What is an authentic Christian response to war? Preach the gospel! Be the church!

Worship

Having identified a biblical theology of peace and war, and having committed churches to preaching the gospel of peace as God's answer to war, what else can we "do" to respond to armed conflict in our world? How do we inculcate the practices and values of peacemakers both to prevent our

25. Megoran, "Henry Martyn—Iraq," 14.

26. Lewis, *Christian Way*, 14.

27. It is important to note that Lewis, like Lloyd-Jones, allowed the possibility of Christian participation in the armed forces. Here I would contend that they erred and were inconsistent with their broader theologies of sin and the church. As I argued in chapter 5, the process of reformation of Christianity from the human additions to the faith made by the medieval Roman Catholic Church is still not yet complete, and just war theory remains one of them.

churches from making the terrible mistakes of the now-fading Christendom epoch of just war, and more positively to make our congregations places that raise up new generations of gospel peacemakers?

Alan and Eleanor Kreider, in an insightful reflection on "becoming a peace church," say that *worship* is key. This might sound surprising, but they insist that we are changed through corporate worship as we meet with God and each other. We see the world in a new light, and things change on earth and in heaven as we pray. "Worship is the motor of history; it is an engine of peacemaking," they write.[28] The Kreiders suggest a number of ways in which worship—corporate praying, preaching, Bible reading, liturgies, singing, fellowship, welcoming, communion, and the like—is peacemaking. They are not necessarily exhaustive but are comprehensive, and a number of them will be considered here.[29]

First, insist the Kreiders, *we acclaim Jesus as Lord*. We assert with Paul in 1 Corinthians 8:5 that, although "there are many 'gods' and many 'lords'" in "heaven or on earth" (including emperors, kings, presidents, generals, militant demagogues, nations, elected parliaments, and the like), our highest loyalty is to Jesus—his Word is authoritative, his ways are normative. Jesus' teaching on topics that are crucial to human life such as wealth, truth, sex, enemies, and war are not the common sense of modern life. However, as we worship the Jesus revealed in scripture, proclaiming him Lord, God liberates us from such common sense. In particular, worshipping Jesus as Lord liberates us from the common-sense political consensuses about war and peace that have in the past trapped the church's imagination.

Second, *we affirm solidarity with God's global family*. The ability of governments to make war depends on their being able to mobilize a sense of solidarity with "the nation" against another nation. This is called "nationalism," and we shall return to it in more detail in the next chapter. Tragically in history national solidarities have often pitted Christians against each other. Followers of the Prince of Peace have ended up mistrusting, hating, and even fighting against each other as solidarity with their earthly host nation trumps solidarity with the church as a nation. This has led to incalculable wounds to the body of Christ. However, when

28. Kreider and Kreider, *Becoming a Peace Church*, 23. The subsequent discussion is drawn from this marvelous booklet, which is recommended to all church leaders. For an expanded version of this argument, see Kreider et al., *A Culture of Peace*.

29. The numbered points are the Kreiders', but the commentary on them is a mixture of the Kreiders' and my own.

a worship leader reminds us that our fellow believers are meeting all over the world at different times of the Lord's Day to worship him and share bread and wine in his name—and when we are reminded that we have far more in common with them than with the non-Christian members of our host nation who are shopping, playing football, gardening, or whatever at the same time—then we repudiate those values and remind ourselves that we are a holy nation of peacemakers. This has a "cosmic" power, too. Bishop Bell identified two elements to "being the church" during wartime. The first part is "to preach the gospel of Christ," as we have seen above. But the church points people to Jesus through more than just its words, and so secondly Bell claimed it is "also to witness to the universal fellowship" of the church. How does this occur? God is glorified as his great wisdom and power and love for humanity in saving the human race through the incarnation, death and resurrection of Christ are made known, magnified, and praised. Paul explains that it is "through the church" that God displays this wisdom to the "powers and authorities" (Eph 3:10). That is to say, when creation sees people from every tribe, tongue, and nation united together worshipping him, it knows that Yahweh is the true God, powerful and wise, and that the world is saved through his Son, Jesus Christ. When the church acts as the church in the world, when it demonstrates the reality of the work of the gospel by its life and words in times of war or in contexts of national or neighborhood violence, this is a tremendous witness to the gospel of Jesus Christ. Then the church becomes the window through which God's future of gospel peace can be seen.

Third, continue the Kreiders, in worship *we tell God's story*. The Bible tells stories about God and his people—for example, how he saved the Israelites from the Egyptian armies through miraculous power not military force, or how he called Abraham and Sarah to be parents of a great nation if they left their security and followed him. The world's politicians and media tell us stories such as "the only thing that works is force." In retelling God's stories (through preaching, childrens' talks, liturgies, Bible readings, songs, the Eucharist, and prayers) we celebrate a different kind of God and are less likely to be choked by our culture's stories. This is particularly pertinent as churches mark moments like Remembrance Sunday, a day in the United Kingdom when the country recalls the dead of World War I and wars since. Do we use this to reinforce the idea that British soldiers killed in Britain's wars were "our" soldiers, representing "us" in "just wars" in order to "defend" our "security"? This is a story that any country in the world might tell of its soldiers. If we tell this story, we are implicitly supporting the notion that we are a "national" church, and in so doing we make being Christian secondary to being British, American, German, Nigerian, Indian, or whoever. Instead, we should use commemoration events like Remembrance Sunday to tell the Bible's story: that war is a manifestation and a consequence of sin, that we sorry over it as we remember the dead of all wars and repent for them, and that we proclaim the alternative rule and reign of the Prince of Peace who defeats his enemies by loving them and calls us to do the same. Preach the gospel! Be the church!

It is also worth thinking about whether the symbols, images, pictures, windows, and decorations in our churches tell God's story or the world's story. Many modern churches largely dispense with this, but for older churches and cathedrals or those in "High-Church" traditions it may be an issue. Herbert McCabe wrote scornfully that "there is probably no sound on earth so bizarre as the noise of clergymen bleating about terrorism while their cathedrals are stuffed with regimental flags and monuments to colonial wars. The Christian church, with minor exceptions, has been solidly on the side of violence for centuries, but it has normally been only the violence of soldiers."[30]

Does the architecture of the places we worship in tell the story of how Christ responded to violence, or the story of how worldly kingdoms and states do?

An extension of this is, fourth, that *we sing our theology.* The songs that we sing at church, and listen to during the week and use in our private devotional lives, may inform our theology as much as preaching. To be equipped to be Christian peacemakers means that we need songs that celebrate the God of peace. How often and how well do our hymns and songs do that? Do they shape the way we understand war and violence, and likewise shape our response? Some older hymns, such as Matthew Bridges' "Crown Him with Many Crowns," do that:

> Crown Him the Lord of peace,
> Whose power a scepter sways
> From pole to pole, that wars may cease,
> And all be prayer and praise.[31]

---

30. McCabe, "The Class Struggle and Christian Love."
31. "Crown Him with Many Crowns," lyrics by Matthew Bridges (1851).

However, when modern worship songs address "peace," it is usually more of an inner sensation or about our personal relationship with Jesus. Both of those are important, but they miss the glories of the fullness of the gospel of peace that hymns like those above proclaim. This is a challenge to our contemporary songwriters.

Fifth, argue the Kreiders, taking *communion* is central to the life of a peacemaking church. At the communion service we are reminded that we all have sinned and fallen short of God's glory (Rom 3:23), but that "God made him who had no sin to be sin for us, so that in him we might become the righteousness of God" (2 Cor 5:21). This also reminds us that we are to love our enemies as God loved us when we were his enemies—through sacrificial love. For Stanley Hauerwas and Sam Wells, communion is the basic Christian response to war because "war is a counter-liturgy to the worship of God."[32] They argue that war makes sense of life: it provides a story of what is right and true (by telling us what it is worth fighting for). It reminds us that some things are more important than life itself. It binds us to others in a community of destiny (the nation). And it is a sacrifice that attempts to make the world right by dealing with evil. War thus tries to do what the gospel does, making it the gospel's greatest rival. Yet, argue Hauerwas and Wells, war's weapons are weak: they are not powerful enough to secure forgiveness of sin and eternal life. In contrast, when the church celebrates communion, it declares that the death of Jesus is the last sacrifice, the one that "finally took away sin and became the death of war. The sacrifice of the Son of God is the sacrifice to end all sacrifice. So the war to end all wars was not the Civil War or the First or Second World War: it was the cross. The dividing wall of hostility between us and God has tumbled down. The good news of the cross is fundamentally that war is over."[33] In celebrating communion, we celebrate the church as that organization which is the custodian of a more powerful and more wonderful alternative to war.

Sixth, the Kreiders also propose that it is in the local congregations that we learn the *practices of being peacemakers*. In Matthew 18:15–20 the Lord Jesus gives instructions on how to handle conflict when one member of the church sins against another. In Matthew 5:23 he reminds us that if our brother or sister may "have something against us," then that needs addressing before we can enter public worship. Conflict in

32. Hauerwas and Wells, "Breaking Bread: Peace and War."
33. Ibid., 417.

church life is inevitable, because we are sinful people. It must not be avoided, but rather handled properly within the church (we will discuss this in more detail under the topic of "discipleship," below). Acts 6:1–7 gives an example of this occurring, with the resolution of a dispute in the early church between two racial groups. In Philippians 4:2–3 Paul gives Timothy the spiritual tools and counsel to help two godly women, Euodia and Syntyche, sort out an obviously very public argument between them that was apparently affecting the church. He does not avoid the issue; he affirms their credentials as servants of Christ who are ultimately one in the Lord and urges them to reach agreement. Conflict is to be expected, and rather than ignore it, walk away, gossip and backbite about it, or suppress it, the New Testament teaches how it can be addressed and resolved. Churches should be places where we learn to be peacemakers. Are our congregations being equipped and trained for this? We can do this by good teaching on these scriptures and by employing the servies of Christian groups who can give churches and leadership teams training in handling conflict in a biblical way.

The Kreiders conclude by stating that it is during communal worship that *God shapes our vision and mission*. It is in worship that

> we encounter "the God of peace who brought back from the dead our Lord Jesus Christ" (Heb 13:20). We tell the story of God and celebrate it. We learn the ways of God and come to view these as the path to abundant living. We praise God, give thanks, intercede. Worship thus functions as a filter; it purifies us, clarifies our vision. And it empowers us: it restores our belief, re-inspires us with God's grace and vision for the world. . . . This equips us for mission. Re-visioned by our encounter with the God of peace, we go back into the world equipped with hope and vision and spiritual energy. We will be in the struggle with principalities and powers. But we will find God at work, calling people to faith, suggesting new ways forward in intractable situations, and doing the new thing. We will not go unscathed, but the God of peace will be with us.[34]

Is our corporate worship doing this? Or is it so focused on meeting emotional human needs that it risks becoming irrelevant to the concerns of living for the gospel of peace in a world of conflict? Is it even telling the world's story about "reality" and how we respond to it? As Christians we cannot be peacemakers and respond Christianly to conflict in our

34. This quote is from Kreider and Kreider, *Becoming a Peace Church*, 27–28.

churches, homes, workplaces, and communities—let alone rise to the challenges of a violent and warring world—if our corporate worship does not equip us for that. There is thus an awesome responsibility on those who lead our weekly worship gatherings by praying, preaching, speaking, choosing songs, and playing music. In so doing they will either help us be authentic followers of the Prince of Peace or hinder us.

Praying and Believing

The story is told of a Sunday school class told to write a letter to their church's missionary partner in a far-off land, but warned that because of an unreliable postal service they might not receive a response. One child thus carefully penned in her letter, "We are praying for you. We are not expecting an answer." Too often our church prayers for "peace" in whatever unpronounceable "war-torn" corner of the world has featured in the newspapers that week are recited without any real expectation that God will do anything. And yet, prayer is a crucial and distinctive aspect of Christian peacemaking. The authentic discipleship necessary to be gospel peacemakers in a violent world depends upon prayer and the expectation that God will be true to his promises as we seek him in prayer.

Peacemaking prayer involves *crying out to God for the world*. We pray that God's kingdom will come on earth as in heaven. We struggle with evil as we pray, "against the rulers, against the authorities and the cosmic powers of this present age" (Eph 6:4), knowing that our prayers are heard and make a difference (Rev 8:3–4) and that the Spirit helps us pray (Rom 8:26). "History," writes Walter Wink, "belongs to the intercessors who believe the future into being. If this is so, then intercession, far from being an escape from action, is a means of focusing for action and of creating action."[35]

Peacemaking prayer is for the world, but it is also for ourselves as peacemakers. Gospel peacemaking is distinguished from other forms of worldly peacemaking in that, as followers of the Prince of Peace who are indwelled by the Holy Spirit, we have access to the divine *power* of God as we seek him in prayer and study of his scriptures. Without this power, enemy love would be hopelessly sentimental or criminally foolish. With it we are equipped to be "peacemakers" and in so doing to demonstrate the truth that Jesus is alive and is reigning as Lord. This depends on the

35. Wink, *Engaging the Powers*, 304.

exercise of faith in the miraculous power of an intervening God, revealed in scripture and in whom we place our faith. C. H. Spurgeon writes that prayer "has ever been the defence of saints. . . . All other weapons may be useless, but all-prayer is evermore available. No enemy can spike this gun."[36]

There is no better example of the power of prayer as a Christian response to war than the life of Norwegian missionary Marie Monsen. Monsen traveled to China in the immediate aftermath of the so-called Boxer Rebellion of 1899–1901. This uprising came after decades of British, French, Russian, German, Japanese, and American infringement of Chinese sovereignty. Foreign powers had forced China to import opium (see ch. 6, 141), invaded many times, imposed unfair trade treaties, seized portions of territory in which their own citizens were given special rights, and promoted the presence of Christianity. Unsurprisingly, this led to a fierce backlash. Although defeated by military force, the Boxer Rebellion and the aggressive foreign interventions that provoked it proved very damaging to Christianity in China.

Monsen felt stirred to go to China to replace the many missionaries who had been killed. She was used powerfully by God in revival and the establishment of the house church movement, and is honored by Brother Yun in his account of the subsequent massive growth of the underground church, *The Heavenly Man*.[37] Yun writes that Monsen's importance was the example of "her sacrificial lifestyle" and that she stressed it is not head-knowledge that counts but being "radically born-again." Part of this lifestyle was her unwavering faith that as God had called her to China, he (not weapons) was responsible for her protection.

During Monsen's time in China lawlessness, brigandage, and piracy were rife. In the absence of an effective national government, warlords controlled different sections of the country, often living off the earnings of unpaid soldiers who turned to pillage for a living. Marauding groups of bandits would raid towns to kill, loot, burn, and hold to ransom. She was frequently in danger—she was shot at, taken captive by pirates, and threatened on many occasions. Yet she never resorted to reliance on arms for protection, nor did she fear. Rather, she trusted that the God who had sent her to spread the gospel of peace would deliver her.

36. Spurgeon, on Psalm 54:2, in vol. 3 of his *Treasury of David* (numerous editions available).

37. Yun, *The Heavenly Man*. Yun refers to Monsen repeatedly in ch. 1, 15–22.

For example, on one occasion she was in a town leading Bible classes, when she received news that a certain general had given permission to his soldiers to loot for one night in lieu of pay.[38] The looting was due to begin at 10 p.m., and prior to that she overheard soldiers "casing the joint" and discussing how to break into her compound. The impatient soldiers began pillaging earlier, and terrified neighbors fled to the mission station. As she crossed the courtyard, bullets were flying close by to her but she felt the Lord impress upon her Psalm 91:5, "Do not fear the terror by night nor the arrow that flies by day," updating "arrow" to "bullet." She reasoned that as "nothing happens by chance to the children of God" the Lord had directed her to be here, and she need not fear. The Chinese Christians divided themselves up among the unconverted who had crowded into rooms throughout the compound, sharing the gospel with them and leading them to faith. Though shooting, burning, and looting went on all around them, their compound was untouched.

A number of the Chinese who came to her for refuge said they saw her "protectors"—soldiers standing around on the roof and verandah: tall people, non-Chinese, with shining faces. They assumed that these were soldiers. Marie Monsen knew, however, that there had been no one standing there. Rather, she concluded, they were angels: "It came powerfully to me and showed me how little we reckon with 'the Lord, the God of hosts,' who sends forth his angels, mighty in strength, 'to do service for the sake of them that shall inherit salvation' (Heb 1:14 RV)."

Monsen was right: central to any discussion of Christian responses to violence should be the truth that we serve a mighty God who is powerfully at work in a world that he rules over. This means that Christians can be open, by the leading of the Holy Spirit, to pursue creative responses to violence that are beyond the experiences of the unconverted.

This is just as applicable in our own streets as in lawless China a century ago. When I first wrote this paragraph, in 2012, the British newspapers were dominated with the story of the conviction of two white men who, when young, murdered a black teenager in an unprovoked racist attack. The biggest domestic British news story of 2011 was widespread youth rioting and looting in the summer. In 2015 as I edit this chapter the United States has been shocked by a string of racist murders and attacks on African Americans, culminating in the murder of nine worshippers at a prayer meeting at Emanuel African Methodist Episcopal Church in

---

38. Monsen, *Present Help*, 37–39.

Charleston, South Carolina. Sadly, I imagine that, whenever you read this, the problem of urban violence is not far from the headlines. Politicians and pundits debate the causes and responses, and there is no doubt much value in what they say. But the primary explanation of violence at the individual level is the same as that at the international level: sin, a rebellion against God's righteous laws. And an authentic Christian response, whatever useful things the church may contribute to policy debate, provision of social services, and so forth, likewise relies on the extraordinary power of God to change and transform individuals and their contexts. This book has already considered a number of instructive examples, from former New York gang leader Tom Skinner (ch. 2, 40–41) to Uganda university lecturer and pastor Kefa Sempangi (see below, 227–29). Our prayers for the transformation of violent situations and the people within them are powerful.

The experiences and vocations of people like Marie Monsen and Tom Skinner may seem far removed from most of our daily lives. But the glory of the Christian walk is that God uses his mighty power in response to the prayers of his people wherever they are. Hilary Cook in her book *What Will the Neighbours Say?* gives an engaging account of moving to a new town and setting up a midweek women's prayer meeting. As a busy mom, housewife, and doctor in Sheffield, Northern England, her life was very different from that of a spinster missionary in lawless China or of a reformed gang leader in New York. But she shared the same belief in a God who was alive and working in the world. Gathering a growing group of similarly busy women (and their toddlers!) together in her front room, the often chaotic prayer and Bible study meetings became a place where people met with God and saw answers to prayers in their own lives.

She recounts the story of one member of the group asking God what to pray for, when that woman saw "a clear impression of an express train hurtling along a track that I somehow knew was in Northern Ireland," and that "there was a bomb on the train" that "was going to explode before it reached its destination."[39] She cried out to Jesus to stop the train, and in her vision did indeed see him halt it. She was not surprised to find a newspaper article soon afterwards headlined "Narrow escape for Belfast train." Police learned that an Irish Republican Army (IRA) bomb had been planted on the train and was about to go off. Frantic attempts were made to stop the train, but to no avail. The article continued that "by

39. Cook, *What Will the Neighbours Say?*, 53–54.

some strange coincidence" an error meant that a signal that should have been green was red, stopping the train in time to defuse the explosive. Prayer is more powerful a defense than anything humans can devise, and gospel peacemaking is set apart from the world's peacemaking by reliance upon it.

Because of prayer, gospel peacemaking is different from the world's peacemaking. The world relies on strategies that make sense at the human level, whether a violent invasion to topple an unjust ruler, or a United Nations–style "peacekeeping" operation, or a nonviolent mass action to effect change. Gospel peacemaking—an enemy love that transforms individuals and their contexts—relies upon risk-taking faith in a miracle-working God. It steps out in obedience to God's direction, believing that the consequences are with God and trusting him to work out his own ends. It should be obvious that this is neither easy nor cowardly. On the contrary, as Ben Witherington writes in his study of Christian responses to the violence of the powers and authorities in the book of Revelation, "Let there be no mistake: in a violent world it takes far greater strength of character to take Jesus' approach to these matters than to take up arms. The meek are not the weak."[40]

As we saw in chapter 7, the second-century anti-Christian writer Celsus argued that if the whole Roman Empire were Christian there would thus be no one to defend it against its enemies, because the early church did not countenance Christians committing violence against their enemies. Origen replied that because Christians pray against the demons who stir up war, "none fight better for the king than we do . . . we fight on his behalf, forming a special army—an army of piety—by offering our prayers to God."[41] The church makes its best contribution to society, and its most helpful interventions in a violent world, by simply and fully being the church. Prayer is an awesome responsibility we must discharge. In commenting on Paul's exhortation to Timothy to pray "for kings and all those in authority, that we may live peaceful and quiet lives" (1 Tim 2:2), John Stott writes, "I sometimes wonder whether the comparatively slow progress towards peace and justice in the world . . . is due more than anything else to the prayerlessness of the people of God."[42] The Christian peacemaker, when he or she obeys God's word, has access

40. Witherington, *Revelation*, 174.

41. Driver, *Christians Made Peace with War*, 45–46.

42. Stott, *Message of 1 Timothy and Titus*, 62.

to power and support that no general or politician can ever know. Too often we spend time arguing about abstract ideas like "just war theory" or "pacifism" because we lack faith in God's word that he will protect and bless his peacemakers. To be blessed as a gospel peacemaker it is necessary to move beyond the world's ways of thinking about peace and step out in prayerful faith. The lives of Marie Monsen, Hilary Cook, and countless others testify that that is the beginning of a royal adventure of faith. As the next section shows, we cannot always assume it is God's will to preserve our bodies, and preparation for martyrdom is an important part of church discipleship in a warring world. But the point remains: we trust God to save us from our sins; dare we also trust him to save us from our enemies?

Martyrdom

A few years ago the British satirical magazine *Private Eye* carried a cartoon that parodied the grisly Islamist suicide bomber martyrdom videos, captioned, "If Christians made martyrdom videos." Two glum Romans sat watching a Christian's being fed to the lions, declaring, "Caesar, we forgive you" and "I hope we taste nice!"[43] The cartoon reminds us that one of the defining features of Christians over the ages is that they have preferred to suffer and die for their faith, loving their enemies rather than using violence to try to harm their enemies in defending themselves. In contrast to the suicide bombers of recent al-Qaeda and Islamic State campaigns and the Buddhist nationalist Sri Lankan Tamil Tigers, Christian martyrdom involves a love for enemies and a refusal to harm them. Thus in the nineteenth century Adin Ballou defended Christian peacemaking against the objection that if a believer refused to fight back when attacked, they would be killed: "Would it not be more glorious for him to die in the triumph of non-resisting love, praying for his enemies, than to live wearing the crown of Caesar, spattered with the blood of the slain?"[44]

When confronted with Babylonian king Nebuchadnezzar's demand that they worship a gold image he had set up, Shadrach, Meshach, and Abednego replied, "If we are thrown into the blazing furnace, the God we serve is able to rescue us from it"—but "even if he does not," they added,

---

43. Unfortunately, I did not keep the cartoon so the wording may be inexact.

44. Cited in Tolstoy, *Kingdom of God Is within You*, 20.

"we will not serve your gods."[45] We saw above that gospel peacemaking is dependent upon the power of a God who intervenes in our world to support his people as they do his will. But, as the three Hebrews recognized in their defiant speech to the tyrant, that does not mean God will always act miraculously to rescue his people from death. If God always intervened to act in the way we want, that would result not in faithful trust in God himself but in a technique—it would become another form of worldly power, like Aladdin rubbing the magic lamp and summoning up the genie to do his bidding. Rather, the church has always held martyrdom as a noble calling. In the book of Revelation, those who "had been slain because of the word of God and the testimony they had maintained" are pictured as being preserved by God "under the altar" and honored with "a white robe."[46]

Being willing to love enemies and bless those who persecute—and risking martyrdom in so doing—is one of the most powerful Christian testimonies the world can see. For example, Reverend Hassan Deqhani-Tafti was a godly Iranian pastor who found faith in Christ as a young man. It was obvious to him that following Jesus and obeying his teachings meant rejecting violence. Upon conscription to the Iranian army, he arranged to meet the Chief of the General Staff and told him that because he was a Christian, he was "against fighting of any kind" and would not be "trained in killing."[47] He wrote that leading Muslims to Jesus is difficult because "how can a Muslim understand the Cross when he can still remember the Crusades, not to mention the last two world wars? . . . When Christians have taken up the sword it has been against their Lord and his ways, and they ought to repent. But taking up the sword in defense of Islam has been and still is a duty."[48]

When the Iranian Islamic revolution occurred in 1979, his church came under severe persecution. Although he narrowly survived an assassination attempt, his son was murdered and so he went into exile. In spite of this he was known for his message of love and forgiveness.[49] A similar testimony is offered by the life of his fellow Iranian believer, Reverend Mehdi Dibaj. His testimony to the peace and love of Christ led him to be

45. Dan 3:16–18.

46. Rev 6:9–11.

47. Dehqani-Tafti, *Design of My World*, 40–41.

48. Ibid., 71–72.

49. R. Harris, "Obituary: The Rt Rev Hassan Dehqani-Tafti."

sentenced to death in 1993 by an Iranian court for converting from Islam forty-five years earlier. In presenting a defense to the court, he said, "The love of Jesus has filled all my being and I feel the warmth of His love in every part of my body. . . . All the bad happenings have turned out for our good and gain, so much so that I am filled to overflowing with joy and thankfulness." He wrote from prison, "I am filled to overflowing with joy; I am not only satisfied to be in prison . . . but am ready to give my life for the sake of Jesus Christ."[50] He was subsequently released, but murdered by unknown assailants.

Brave Romanian pastor Richard Wurmbrand writes about a Christian who was sentenced to death by the hardline communist state for his faith. Before being executed, he was allowed to see his wife. His last words were these:

> You must know that I die loving those who kill me. They don't know what they do and my last request of you is to love them, too. Don't have bitterness in your heart because they kill your beloved one. We will meet in heaven.[51]

Wurmbrand learned this story from another prisoner—a former officer in the secret police. These words so impressed the officer that he too became a follower of Jesus. To love those who would hurt us, to be willing to suffer and even die because of a refusal to hate or harm our enemies, in whatever context, is honored by the church as an authentic Christian response to war and violence. We should disciple our churches to follow the examples of this great cloud of witnesses—even to death, if necessary—not to be soldiers.

Discipleship: Prohibiting Participation in Warfare

> To see a soldier a Christian is a joy; to see a Christian a solider is another matter. We may not judge another man, but we may discourage thoughtless inclinations in the young and ignorant. A sweeping condemnation would arouse antagonism, and possibly provoke the very spirit we would allay; while quiet and holy influence may sober and ultimately overcome misdirected tendencies.[52] —C. H. SPURGEON, 1878

50. Dibaj, "The Written Defense of the Rev. Mehdi Dibaj."
51. Wurmbrand, *Tortured for Christ*, 41.
52. Spurgeon, "Periodical War Madness," 148.

In 1964 British television ran a series of interviews with lay Christians on "Why I believe." In his interview, businessman and World War II veteran John Marsh spoke of the crisis of faith that the war caused for him. "It seemed to me a tragic and in fact almost criminal thing that people in different countries, professing to be Christian, should set themselves out to kill themselves in a wholesale way," he recounted. Unable to reconcile killing his enemies with loving them, he told his interviewer that "I deliberately opted out of the Christian faith for two whole years."[53] He later refound his faith, but the tragedy is that many people in his situation do not, and that others distort and deform their Christian faith to enable it to encompass killing. What is at stake here is *discipleship*. John Marsh was not cared for pastorally before the war. The church, apparently, had not prepared him to think biblically about how to handle these contrasting claims on his life from the kingdom of God and the United Kingdom: it had not taught him the ways of gospel peace. When a crisis grips a nation, it is easy to go with the flow of nationalist fervor, which sweeps our compatriots along in a tide of emotion, anger, fear, and revenge. To do the hard work of peacemaking is much more difficult because it often means standing outside and against these national narratives. It is unreasonable to expect followers of Jesus to do this if they have not been thoroughly disciplined in the ways of "the gospel of peace."

Happily, the church has many counterexamples. One is the prominent anti-apartheid campaigner and black South African Reformed minister Allan Boesak. He argued forcibly in his sermons and writings that Christians cannot confess to follow Jesus and at the same time support a regime that systematically discriminates against people on the basis of their skin color. He complained that many South African Christians, black and white, refused to read the Bible politically. To keep politics out of religion, he argued, is to "break up the wholeness of life" and put "impermissible limitations" on the work of the Holy Spirit.[54] Authentic gospel preaching "speaks to the *whole* person and to *all* of life," and therefore "relevant preaching is always political." Boesak argues that preachers must make the full consequences of the gospel clear to their congregations, without giving them a lecture on politics or, worse, preaching some particular political program. To avoid repeating the mistake of the black and white churches in South Africa, ministers and preachers have a pro-

53. Moir, *Why I Believe*, 42–43.
54. Boesak, "Relevant Preaching in a Black Context," 12.

found responsibility to show how the "gospel of peace" is relevant to the big stories of war and peace in our age.

This is best done in "peacetime." It is difficult to do from scratch during war, when passions are inflamed and congregations may have members serving "at the front." One of the great Christian stories of World War II relates to the Protestant pastor of the French village of Le Chambon-sur-Lignon, André Trocmé. He led the area in resisting first Vichy France and then the Nazis themseleves when Vichy was overrun by German forces in 1944. But this was not by joining the armed resistance, whose methods of resisting the occupation he considered likewise to be unchristian. Rather, moving from symbolic resistance to active organization, he helped create an extensive system to rescue Jewish refugees from all over occupied Europe. Trocmé himself survived time spent both in prison and on the run from the Gestapo to become an important figure in postwar Franco-German reconciliation.[55] Trocmé was awarded an Israeli state medal as one of the "Righteous Among the Nations" for rescuing Jews during the war.

Why was Le Chambon able to remain so true to the Gospel, whereas the majority of French bishops sought coexistence with the Vichy regime? Part of the answer is that Trocmé faithfully taught his parish about gospel peacemaking in the decades *before* the war, and even supported an international school for Christian peacemaking. When the war came, he was thus able to take his congregation with him on a dangerous and potentially contentious pathway of Christian resistance. It would have been virtually impossible for him to have led his parish in this direction if he had not beforehand undertaken years of painstaking instruction through teaching and example, through discipleship rooted in corporate worship.

Discipleship entails not only positive exhortation but also a negative element. Christopher Marshall argues that the Old Testament laws and punishments (frequently execution) for sinful activities that polluted the holiness of God's people find their New Testament equivalent in the teaching on excommunication. The church cannot tolerate sin that pollutes the community, and the recalcitrant offender is to be disciplined within the church and, if necessary, eventually expelled. First Corinthians 5:1–11 and 2 Corinthians 2:5–11 demonstrate a way to discipline the offender within the church by temporarily excluding him or her until he or she

---

55. Hallie, *Lest Innocent Blood Be Shed.*

repents. Matthew 18:15–20 outlines a three-stage process to implement this. The purpose was to "gently restore" (Gal 6:1) the offender.[56]

We saw in chapters 4 and 5 that the early and medieval church up until the Crusades variously disciplined its members by refusing to baptize soldiers who would not renounce the military oath, requiring penance for participation in warfare, etc. Unfortunately, this aspect of discipline is commonly lacking in today's church, even though a passion for holiness demands it. This is sadly true in evangelical as well as in other churches. In the evangelical church, the most influential handbook on pastoring over the centuries has been and remains the Puritan Richard Baxter's book *The Reformed Pastor*. Baxter exercised a remarkably influential ministry as minister of St. Mary and All Saints' Church, Kidderminster, during the English Civil War. His previously wayward parish became known for its godliness. The key to Baxter's influence was good preaching combined with regular pastoral meeting and catechizing of all parishioners. He spent two whole days every week on this latter task, with his assistants booking each family or individual for a regular hour-long slot with Baxter. An important part of this was public church discipline, which he defined as consisting in "private reproofs, in more public reproof, combined with exhortation to repentance, in prayer for the offender, in restoring the penitent, and in excluding and avoiding the impenitent."[57] His template on how to practically do this is very helpful for church leaders today in recovering a practice that has fallen sadly out of use.

However, in spite of the neglect of this discipline, William Cavanaugh shows how the Catholic church in Chile has used excommunication in an imaginative way to combat violence. In 1626 the Synod of Santiago, under the direction of Bishop Francisco Salcedo, excommunicated slave traders—provoking an age-old complaint from the king's representative that the church was interfering in matters outside its competence.[58] More recently, in 1980, seven Chilean Catholic bishops excommunicated torturers in their diocese—again to protest from the military dictatorship. In proper biblical understanding of passages considered above,

56. Marshall, *Beyond Retribution*. Pages 149–62 contain an excellent discussion of punishment within the church.

57. Baxter, *Reformed Pastor*, 105–11.

58. Cavanaugh, *Torture and Eucharist*, 254.

they referred to the "medicinal character" of this move and declared that torturers could be absolved and restored to fellowship if they repented.[59]

The worshipping community of the church must be welcoming to unconverted seekers, who without the power of the indwelling Holy Spirit are not able to live holy lives of Christian virtue and cannot be expected to. It should be endlessly forgiving of repentant sinners. However, it must keenly protect its holiness and must care for its members by following biblical teaching on church discipline for unrepentant church members. As a start, publicly known torturers, killers, warmaking politicians, and the like who are members of churches should be privately called to repent, then publicly disciplined and eventually excommunicated, as happened in Chile. Individual congregations should return to the early church practice of refusing to baptize soldiers who have not renounced warfare, and should seek evidence of repentance for participation in violence (whether in armies, paramilitaries, violent gangs, etc.).[60] This must never be done for political reasons but for the good of the sinner, with the aim of leading them to repentance and the restoration of fellowship. Similarly, parents, youth workers, and churches should not encourage children to join promilitary groups such as cadet forces. Nonetheless, there are difficult questions in less clear-cut cases that congregations will have to grapple with. How should we regard participation in military charities and army chaplaincies? Although young people should be counseled against the pursuit of military careers, what about the pursuit of occupations in nonlethal logistical support or medical roles in the armed forces? Although I do not see how Christians can legitimately work in industries that produce and sell weapons, what about employment in foreign ministry and diplomatic jobs that enable warfare? Should Christian academics and scientists engage in research about new weaponry, or write references for students wishing to apply for military jobs? Can a follower of Jesus work in a military museum that presents military history and weaponry as normal, neutral, or even as fun facets of human behavior? As we saw in chapter 4, the same early church rules that forbade participation in warfare also prohibited abortion and capital punishment (we might say that by linking opposition to war, infanticide, and execution it was "pro-life" in the fullest sense). What should a church's position on these issues be, for its parents, doctors, judges, and voters? These rules also forbade

59. Ibid., 253–54.

60. This will need to be handled differently in congregations that practice paedobaptism.

attendance at the circuses, where people fought and killed each other: should church discipline extend today to violent cultural activities such as boxing and dogfighting?

These questions do not give themselves to easy answers, nor do these practices of discipline give themselves to speedy introduction. They must be approached sensitively and through prayer and listening carefully and nonjudgmentally to each other. A new minister or a church leadership team that seeks to recover these biblical practices could not and should not simply foist them upon a congregation that has not been properly taught and disciplined about peacemaking through years of appropriate preaching and worship. Cultural context matters considerably. Different churches have different ways of doing this. In some denominations, decisions about doctrine and practice are made hierarchically and even with reference to state lawmakers. Other traditions emphasize freedom of conscience and autonomy of individual congregations. Some churches have retained effective and biblical practices of church discipline and discipleship; others have either forgotten or never had them and will need to relearn them. However decisions are made and congregations are governed, the essential point must not be missed: war and violence are always to be denounced as sinful, and followers of the Prince of Peace must be disciplined to be peacemakers.

Rethinking Victory

Practices of peacemaking worship and discipleship are aimed in the first place at glorifying God through our sanctification: making us more like our heavenly Father, whose enemy love we are to emulate (Matt 5:43–48). They are intended to form Christian character and the Christian mind, often in opposition to the common-sense understandings of the age. A major element of preaching, singing, praying, reflecting on the lives of the saints and the martyrs, and gathering around the Lord's Table is to be taught and reminded that God's criteria of victory are very different from those of the politicians or the generals. This is crucial in building congregations of disciples who follow the Prince of Peace. The examples of martyrdom that we considered above have not been remembered by the church as defeats: quite the opposite, they are honored as victories.

The death and resurrection of Jesus is, of course, the supreme reminder that in the kingdom of God what seemed a defeat was in fact

God's greatest victory in history. Paul, in 2 Corinthians 2:14, writes that God "always leads us as captives in Christ's triumphal procession." This invokes the idea of a Roman triumph. William Barclay describes the triumph as "the highest honor which could be given to a victorious Roman general." The procession made its way through the streets of Rome to the Capitol, led by state officials, senators, and trumpeters. Then were carried captive gold and treasures, paintings and models of land and buildings seized, and captive princes, nobles, and generals, who would usually be ceremonially executed in public. Priests and musicians followed. Then the victorious general himself would be drawn by four horses in a chariot. Clad in a purple toga marked with golden stars, he held an ivory scepter with a Roman eagle at its top. His family rode after him, and finally the army shouting in triumph. Granted only to generals who had won extraordinary victories over a foreign foe and extended Roman territory, it no doubt made a tremendous occasion that might happen only once in a lifetime.[61] When Paul claims this for Jesus, it is a striking reversal of image, revealing that for God "victory" is something very different from the victory of warriors. To be gospel peacemakers, we need to grasp this.

What might such a triumph look like in our age? On July 31, 1941, a prisoner escaped from the Auschwitz concentration camp, and as a reprisal the Gestapo arbitrarily selected ten men to die of starvation in an underground bunker. One of the men selected was called Franciszek Gajowniczek. The moment that he was ordered to step forward he cried out, "My poor wife and children!" No doubt to the surprise of all present, a short Polish man with round glasses stepped out of line. "I'm a Catholic priest," he said. "I want to die for that man." He continued: "That man has a wife and children, I have no one." The offer was accepted. The priest's name was Maximilian Kolbe, and he was forty-seven years old. Apparently there was a remarkable atmosphere in that starvation bunker. He led the men in praying and singing together, and they survived much longer than anyone had anticipated. After two weeks of dehydration and starvation, Kolbe remained alive. The guards wanted the bunker emptied and so they administered a lethal injection, on August 14, 1941. An orderly reportedly said that the bunker was just like a church.

So it seemed that the powers of tyranny won over God's church: wasn't the corpse a proof? But the story did not end in 1941. Forty-one years later, on October 10, 1982, in St. Peter's Square, Rome, Maximilian

---

61. Barclay, *Letters to the Corinthians*, 183–84.

Kolbe's death was put in its proper perspective. Present in the crowd of 150,000 people, together with 26 cardinals and 300 archbishops and bishops, was Franciszek Gajowniczek and his wife, Helena, his children and his children's children. Many unborn lives had been saved by that one man's sacrifice. The pope, describing what Maximilian Kolbe had done, said, "It was a victory like that won by our Lord Jesus Christ."[62]

Another victory "like that won by our Lord Jesus Christ" was shown in the life of Ugandan pastor Kefa Sempangi.[63] He studied art history in the United Kingdom and then in the Netherlands, and returned home to teach in Kampala, excited at the prospects for newly independent Uganda. But the dream soon became a nightmare as former British-backed thug Idi Amin took power. He sadistically murdered opponents and rivals and stole the wealth of ethnic minorities. As well as lecturing in art history, Sempangi became the pastor of a large church. Amin came to regard Sempangi as an enemy. This was because of the numbers flocking to his church, because Amin harbored a grudge against Sempangi for refusing his invitation to study at a UK war academy, and because Sempangi was caring for a child whose parents had been murdered by the regime.[64] The church discussed whether to use violence to defend itself, but concluded, "Of course, the Christian wouldn't take arms."[65] Instead, it trusted in God's power, preached the gospel, served the suffering, and was a shining light to the world around.

On Easter Sunday 1973, Sempangi was exhausted from hours of ministry at a large public event, and from witnessing terrible instances of cold-blooded murder that week. Coming into his church office alone, he was confronted by five of Amin's assassins. "We are going to kill you. If you have anything to say, say it before you die," said the leader, his face twisted with hatred. Sempangi wrote in his autobiography that he thought he was going to drop dead of fear. But, as he recounted, "From far away I heard a voice, and I was astonished to realize that it was my own. 'I do not need to plead my own cause,' I heard myself saying. 'I am a dead man already. My life is dead and hidden in Christ. It is your lives

---

62. Quoted by Gumbel, "Why Did Jesus Die?"

63. This example is based upon his published autobiographies and interviews I conducted with him in Uganda on May 7 and 8, 2015.

64. Interview, Kefa Sempangi, Uganda, May 7, 2015.

65. Interview, Kefa Sempangi, Uganda, May 7, 2015.

that are in danger, you are dead in your sins. I will pray to God that after you have killed me, he will spare you from eternal destruction.'"[66]

The commander of the militia band was astounded. He lowered his weapon and ordered his men to do likewise. Sempangi was so shocked when the leader asked him to pray for them that he was "speechless,"[67] and the assassin had to repeat the request! Keeping his own eyes open in case it was a trick, he prayed that God would save them from death. He described a visible transformation before him, and testified that they were not the same men who left the church building as entered it. "I saw widows and orphans in your congregation," the leader said as he left. "I saw them singing and giving praise. Why are they happy when death is so near?" Sempangi replied, "Because they are loved by God," who "has given them life."[68] As he told me in an interview, at the time of Amin people flocked to the church "because there was so much killing in the country, the only way people could find life was in the church." That is the Christian reponse to war: be the church! Preach the gospel! Make peace in the love and power of God!

However, Sempangi's authentic Christian response to war did not end there. He later went to the United States for theological training, and after Amin's fall returned to establish the Presbyterian Church in Uganda—the first reformed church in that nation—which, as of 2015, had some 250 congregations. Crucially, he responded to war by addressing its consequences and causes. The violence that Uganda had witnessed had created vast numbers of oprhans. These were children who in many cases had seen their parents brutally murdered in front of their eyes, and lived on the streets, their lives violent and twisted because of the brutality they had witnessed. Sempangi established orphanages that cared for the hardest of children, providing them with love and future opportunities. These children have in many cases gone on to transform the communities in which they later came to live.[69] As Sempangi wrote, "If Christ's redemption was total, then the message we preached must speak to the whole of human existence."[70]

66. Sempangi, *Reign of Terror, Regin of Love,* 105–7.

67. Interview, Kefa Sempangi, Uganda, May 7, 2015.

68. Sempangi, *Reign of Terror, Regin of Love,* 105–7.

69. Sempangi, *From the Dust.*

70. Sempangi, *Reign of Terror, Regin of Love,* 58.

Crucially, Sempangi's response was based on the nonviolent principles of gospel peace. As he told me,

> As Christians we don't believe in armed struggle, because that's not what Jesus taught us. Jesus had the capacity, as people came to arrest him, and Peter tried to cut off the ear of one of the soldiers. Jesus said to him, "Don't do that—I can call legions"; Jesus could command legions to fight for him, but he said this was not the time for that. This is the same thing I was sharing.[71]

If the church had supported the taking up of arms, it could never have had this testimony or this effect in the world. He fittingly titled his autobiography *Reign of Terror, Reign of Love*. That encapsulates the Christian response to war: declaring God's reign of love by being the church, preaching the gospel, and making peace in the love and power of God, in the midst of a reign of terror by the warring principalities and powers of this dark age. In stark contrast, Christians who clamor for victory in "just wars" and "humanitarian interventions" have had their imaginations captured by a worldly view of victory that is at odds with their profession of faith in the risen Lord Jesus Christ. Such people have been let down by a church that has failed to disciple them in the biblical ways of peacemaking.

At the peak of their power, people like Adolf Hitler or Idi Amin appeared to be victorious and unassailable, with the power of life and death in their hands. But their "victories" were transitory and illusory. Whereas Hitler killed himself just four years later, afraid to face justice at the hands of the forces that defeated him, the actions of Maximilian Kolbe were celebrated by a vast crowd four decades on. Idi Amin died a despised and absurd exile in Saudi Arabia, sheltered by the corrupt Saudi royal family; yet the activities of Kefa Sempangi and his church will be celebrated as the victory of the lamb in the new heavens and new earth for all eternity. In July 2015 I attended the Baptist World Alliance meeting in Durban, South Africa. Delegates from many countries faced the real threat of violence at the hands of Islamists, including the radical groups Boko Haram and the Islamic State, and wanted to know how they should respond. Reverend Dr. John Enyinnaya, the rector of the Baptist College of Theology, Obinze-Owerri, was asked this question. His reply drew rounds of applause: "Look at these issues from the angle of big picture, the kingdom of God. The Devil wants to destroy the church—and that is the one thing

---

71. Interview, Kefa Sempangi, Uganda, May 7, 2015.

he cannot achieve. God's plans will never be thwarted."[72] As he put it to me in a conversation later, "They want us to hate, but when they see us loving them it confuses them. One recently became a Christian and left the path of violence after seeing how we responded."[73]

To follow the way of gospel peace may temporarily lead to suffering, apparent setback, even death. It will not, at times, look sensible to the world. But God's victory is different from the temporary and illusionary victories of this world. That is why the church must never get too carried away in excitement about the military victories of our host nations, or get too downhearted at the apparent successes of the latest tyranny (such as the Islamic State or Boko Haram terrorizing the Middle East and West Africa, at the time of writing). This is because the world's understanding of military victory is diametrically contradictory to the New Testament's view.

No one sums up this contrast of meanings of victory better than Malcolm Muggeridge. He was one of the towering journalists of his generation, who spent fifty years reporting on some of the most cataclysmic events of the twentieth century. He saw the rise and fall of fascist Italy and Germany, Stalin's tyranny and later discrediting, the collapse of the British Empire, and American terror and defeat in Vietnam. He eventually became a Christian, impressed not by the armies and states and potentates he had seen but by humble Christians like Mother Theresa and Jean Vanier and their winsome service for Christ as they cared for the poor and the dying.[74] As he wrote in a particularly impressive passage,

> We look back on history, and what do we see? Empires rising and falling, revolutions and counter revolutions, wealth accumulated and wealth disbursed, one nation dominant and then another. Shakespeare speaks of "the rise and fall of great ones that ebb and flow with the moon." In one lifetime I have seen my fellow countrymen ruling over a quarter of the world, the great majority of them convinced, in the words of what is still a favorite song, that "God who made them mighty would make them mightier yet." I've heard a crazed, cracked Austrian announce to the world the establishment of a German Reich that would last a thousand years; an Italian clown announce that he would

---

72. John Enyinnaya, Bible study, Baptist World Alliance World Congress, Durban, July 23, 2015. Cited with permission.

73. Conversation, July 24, 2015.

74. Pearce, *Literary Converts*, chs. 29 and 30.

restart the calendar to begin with his own assumption of power; a murderous Georgian brigand in the Kremlin acclaimed by the intellectual elite of the Western world as wiser than Solomon, more enlightened than Asoka, more humane than Marcus Aurelius. I've seen America wealthier and in terms of weaponry more powerful than all the rest of the world put together, so that Americans, had they so wished, could have outdone an Alexander or a Julius Caesar in the range and scale of their conquests. All in one little lifetime. All gone with the wind. England part of an island off the coast of Europe and threatened with dismemberment and bankruptcy. Hitler and Mussolini dead and remembered only in infamy. Stalin a forbidden name in the regime he helped found and dominated for some three decades. America haunted by fears of running out of the precious fluid that keeps the motorway roaring and the smog settling, with troubled memories of a disastrous campaign in Vietnam and of the great victory of the Don Quixotes of the media when they charged the windmills of Watergate.[75]

Muggeridge concludes by reminding us that, in contrast to these absurdly pompous human kingdoms, we as Christians "acknowledge a king men did not crown and cannot dethrone" and belong to the only kingdom that is guaranteed to endure—the kingdom of God. Rather than supporting the violence of whichever host state we happen to be living in as "foreigners and strangers" on this earth (Heb 11:13), we need to remember that God's victory is very different, and that it alone will endure forever. And, like Kolbe and Sempangi, we must be prepared to dare to live—and, if necessary, to die—differently as a result. Churches should be places where Christians are discipled so that such responses to war and violence become obvious, because our understanding of victory is informed by the Bible not the world. And, as we shall see now in the final section of this chapter, that understanding of how God works in history is sharpened if we are able to focus on its end.

Eyeing the End Time

Saturday afternoons are the traditional time when British soccer matches are scheduled. In order to maximize attendance at the actual stadia, these games are not broadcast live on television. Later at night, however, the

75. Muggeridge, "But Not of Christ," 29–30.

highlights of high-profile fixtures are screened on BBC television's *Match of the Day*. So as not to spoil the pleasure of those who want to watch the matches later without knowing the result in advance, the newsreader on the early evening bulletin warns viewers to leave the room just before the football summary section of the broadcast.

As Christians struggling to respond to a world of violence and injustice, however, not only are we able to know the result in advance, to read the last chapter, but it is advisable that we do. This is because it is of great assistance in helping us respond Christianly to war and violence. The book of Revelation has been read by some Christians as containing coded clues about what will happen at "the end of the world" and when this will occur.[76] Such readings have, unfortunately, often been used by Christians to advocate the military support or attack of some or other country whose existence they think is predicted in Revelation. Loraine Boettner, in his authoritative Reformed text on the topic, argues that such an approach thrives on anxiety "in time of war or of national crisis" and is fatally flawed by the inconsistent literalism of its interpretational strategy.[77] As Kovacs and Rowland show in their study of how Revelation has been read down the ages, using it primarily to predict specific future events is historically a marginal approach in the church.[78]

A more influential strand of evangelical scholarship sees Revelation as referring not only to the final judgment, but to the powers of evil in general that oppose the church. It is likely that most immediately to the writer who received the vision, the Roman Empire was in mind. The cult of the worship of Caesar as emperor, as "the son of god" who had brought "peace" and "salvation" to the earth, was increasingly seen as integral to Roman life and welfare. Thus Revelation's proclamation of Jesus (rather than Caesar) as Lord is a profoundly political act, and one that has consequences today. For Tom Wright, Revelation's "Babylon" is a society "founded on violence"—not only the blood of the martyrs, but a system

76. For two examples, see Lindsey and Carlson, *The Late Great Planet Earth*, and Weinland, *God's Final Witness*.

77. Boettner argues that advocates of this approach take some passages literally and others figuratively and have no consistent reason for doing so. For example, if they were consistent they would have to accept that God's people literally would become "pillars in the temple of God" (Rev 3:12), would share around a real "iron rod" that they would somehow use to "rule the nations" (2:26), and would actually wash their clothes in Jesus' blood (7:14) in anticipation of his getting married and inviting them to the wedding. Boettner, *Millennium*, 8.

78. Kovacs and Rowland, *Revelation: The Apocalypse of Jesus Christ*.

of violence spanning the world, of merchants grown rich on the back of military conquest, of men and women enslaved.[79] The abiding lesson for the church is that the brutal but seductive "civilizations" and national empires from Rome down to our present day, which ensnare the world by promising luxury and delivering slavery, gain their power from the beast, Satan (Rev 12:8).

Revelation is thus about the violence that arises as a consequence and manifestation of sin, what God is doing about it, and the role of the church in bringing God's peace to his rebellious creation. It articulates a nonviolent response to the powers of evil: Christians conquer Satan's warmongering hordes "by the blood of the lamb and by the word of their testimony; they did not love their lives so much as to shrink from death" (Rev 12:11). Mark Bredin goes so far as to say that "the Jesus of Revelation is a Revolutionary of peace" who defeats his enemies by dying at their hands and who fights violence with nonviolence.[80] This is colorful language, and probably oversteps the mark by describing the Lord Jesus as a political revolutionary. However, as Joel Kovel argues, Revelation's way of thinking about politics and change has been a key text in the histories of radical struggles for justice, such as the antislavery movements.[81] Apocalyptic language, argues Joshua Searle, "is the language of human hope."[82]

Revelation was certainly a text that succored South African Christians active in the anti-apartheid movement. In his writings and sermons, Allan Boesak (see above, 221) repeatedly returns to Revelation. For him, Revelation is "much less predicting the future than contradicting the present," and the text contradicts apartheid as much as it contradicted Rome.[83] Just as Revelation exposes the violence, lies, and absurd pretense at the heart of the Roman Empire, so for Boesak it exposes the same in apartheid South Africa. In 1987 Boesak published *Comfort and Protest*, a commentary on Revelation (or, perhaps more accurately, a commentary on the apartheid regime performed through a reading of the book of Revelation).[84] He identifies specific apartheid policies and official proc-

79. T. Wright, *Revelation for Everyone*, 166.

80. Bredin, *Jesus, Revolutionary of Peace*, 223.

81. Kovel, "Facing End-Time."

82. Searle, *Scarlet Woman*, ix.

83. Boesak, "Into the Fiery Furnace," 29.

84. For a more detailed analysis of the politics of Boesak's eschatology, see Megoran, "Radical Politics and the Apocalypse."

lamations, comparing them to the Babylon of Revelation. In closing his book with a discussion of the final chapter of Revelation, Boesak quotes a poem written by Roman poet Martial praying for the safe homecoming of the Emperor Domitian:

> Thou, morning star,
> Bring on the day!
> Come and expel our fears,
> Rome begs that Caesar
> May soon appear.[85]

"The church smiles at this last desperate attempt at power and glory," writes Boesak, observing that the final chapter of Revelation hails not Domitian but the Lord Jesus Christ as "the bright morning star" (22:16). As John surveys the heavenly Jerusalem, the city of justice and peace, descending to earth to reunite symbolically God and humanity, he implores, "Come, Lord Jesus." Boesak creates a liturgical prayer from this:

> For the pain and tears and anguish must end. . . . Come, Lord Jesus.
> For there must be an end to the struggle when the unnecessary dying is over. . . . Come, Lord Jesus.
> For the patterns of this world must change. . . . Come, Lord Jesus.
> For hate must turn to love; fear must turn to joy. . . . Come, Lord Jesus.
> For war must cease and peace must reign. . . . Come, Lord Jesus.

The book of Revelation acknowledges that the tyrannical political system (Rome, apartheid, Nazi Germany, imperial Japan, the British Empire, the United States, Iraq, Libya, Boko Haram, Islamic State—wherever Babylon rears its head) is bad: in fact, it is worse than we thought. But for all its might and resources, its claims to represent civilization are nothing but lies that attempt (but fail) to conceal its violence. It does not have the final word in the human story; indeed, it will be overthrown spectacularly. Justice and peace will happen, have happened, are happening, because the empire's warmongers have been conquered by the loving self-sacrifice of Christ on the cross, and subsequently by his people.

This is put succinctly in a story (which may or may not be true) supposedly passed down in the church from the Roman persecutions of believers during the reign of Julian the Apostate (AD 361–63). In response to a sneering question from a Roman soldier, "Where is your carpenter

85. Boesak, *Comfort and Protest*, 137–38.

now?" an afflicted Christian being taken to a horrible death is said to have quipped, "Busy making a coffin for your emperor!" A few months later Julian died, and is reported to have shouted on his deathbed, "Thou hast conquered, O Galilean!" And so he had; and so he will.

Conclusion: Risk or Resurrection?

In my student days, the most popular board games in our halls of residence were *Monopoly* and *Risk*. *Monopoly* divides the board up into properties to be purchased and developed, the victor being the one who can mercilessly squeeze out their opponents by forcing them into bankruptcy. *Risk* divides a global map into segments that yield resources, the aim being to secure territories that provide resources for building armies, which one then uses to wipe other players off the board. In each case the winner is the last player standing—which often equated to the last player left awake in the early hours of the morning after a mammoth battle.

These games make for good fun between friends, but bad theology. The New Testament response to war is impossible to grasp if we understand human history as a cosmic version of such board games, where similar powers and authorities vie with each other to dominate the board and eliminate opposition. If we think that what matters most is the power of arms or diplomacy, or if we see God as another participant in the same game who simply has access to secret levers and greater powers, then we will inevitably fall back on the idea that we must advocate military force to help God and the forces of goodness win. There is neither cross nor resurrection in such a view. But because of the death and resurrection of Jesus Christ, the rules of the game have been rewritten. The updated version of the rules were issued, so to speak, when Christ died for our sins and rose again to bring us into a right relationship with God (Rom 4:25). These revised rules have removed war as a legitimate way for God's people to play the game. War is a consequence and a manifestation of sin. The church is thus always and of necessity antiwar, just as it is anti-adultery, anti-lying, and anti-greed. The church's function is to proclaim the "gospel of peace"—that God made a sinless and peaceful world; that humankind has fallen from this in its wars, violence, and murders; that God has forgiven this sin by the death and resurrection of his sinless Son, Jesus Christ, who suffered in our place that we through faith might be forgiven and be given the power to live a life of peace. The church is to call humanity in repentance away from the sin of war and instead to follow Jesus Christ; and to announce that he will return one day as judge to create a new heavens and earth marked by peace and reconciliation.

The church's job is to proclaim that message and to equip its members to be peacemakers in the world. It does this, primarily, through the disciplines of worship. As we gather in worship we must not bless warriors or cadets, pray for the success of armies, or pretend that those who died in uniform did so for the glory of God. Instead of hymning the host countries we happen to live in, we hymn Christ and his kingdom. In worship we meet and read and study and preach the Bible. We sing our theology. We proclaim Jesus as Lord. We pray and cry out for ourselves and the world. We share communion. We affirm solidarity with God's global community. We tell God's story in words, songs, prayers, liturgies, and the architecture of our buildings. We learn how to deal with conflict. We call unbelievers to repentance from sins such as violence and to faith in Jesus Christ, the Prince of Peace. We disciple believers and enforce church discipline. As we do this we are liberated from the common sense of the world's "just wars," and instead we learn the practices and values of peacemakers. We internalize the New Testament view of victory as modeled on the death and resurrection of Christ, rather than the military view of victory as the death of our enemies and our own survival. We come to grasp instinctively that, should it come to it, being martyred for loving our persecuting enemies is more glorious than receiving a medal from queen or president for killing them in a just war. It is thus in worship that we respond to war, making our congregations places that raise up new generations of gospel peacemakers. But it does not stop there: as we shall now see in the final chapter, these peacemakers are equipped by God's Holy Spirit and supported by the church to play crucial peacemaking roles in the wider world.

9

Conclusion—Part II
Making Peace in a Violent World

Discharging Our Debt to a Warring World

Some years ago an elderly American businessmen visited a small English village with an unusual gift—a new bicycle for every child. It transpired that one night, when based there with US forces during the Second World War, he stole a bicycle and did not return it. He was never caught, but the theft played on his conscience. Thus decades later, having made money in a successful career, he crossed the continents to discharge what he saw as his debt to the bemused villagers.

As custodians of the gospel of peace, we have an infinitely greater debt to a warring and violent world that we should likewise cross land and sea to discharge. In Romans 1:14 Paul makes the unusual statement that he is "obligated both to Greeks and non-Greeks, both to the wise and the foolish." In a sermon on this text, G. Campbell Morgan insisted that the church has a debt to the world, because "the gospel has been given to me for others."[1] It is always dishonorable to have the means to discharge a debt but not to do so, he contended, and "for dealing with evil and all its issues this Gospel is sufficient." This sufficiency, continues Morgan, extends to answering "the cry of war": "We have the gospel that will meet the need of the age," and withholding this supreme remedy from this supreme need is a great sin before God. "As the church discharges this debt," he concludes, "she fulfils her mission in the world."

1. Morgan, "The Church's Debt to the World."

G. Campbell Morgan was pastor of Westminster Chapel from 1904 to 1919 and again from 1933 to 1943, in between exercising an important itinerant ministry in the United States and United Kingdom. He was a contributor to the first volume of *The Fundamentals* in 1910, a landmark statement of orthodox Reformed Christianity against liberal Protestantism's attacks on scripture and the rise of the "social gospel." He was also a friend of D. L. Moody and C. H. Spurgeon, and mentor to Martyn Lloyd-Jones. Morgan thus has impeccable evangelical credentials. His preaching was marked by both its emphasis on expounding the great biblical doctrines of grace as applied to the individual before God, and also an insistence that these doctrines are the only hope for humanity in social and political life. Some Christians would balk at this, arguing that we should not mix faith and politics. It is certainly true that the church's job is not to provide a running commentary on current affairs. We are custodians of the gospel of God, not one among many pundits. However, following G. Campbell Morgan, I would contend that to the extent that we as the church fail to address the problem of war in the world, we fail to discharge the commission that God has given us. It is not good enough simply to argue, as some evangelists do today, that Christianity is exciting, true, and relevant to the individual; rather, we must insist that the Christian gospel is the only hope both for sinful individuals and a sinful, warring world.

This book has argued that God's answer to what Morgan calls the "cry of war" is simply being the church, proclaiming the "gospel of peace" (Eph 6:15; Acts 10:36). Our response to war is to be the church and to preach this gospel. The Bible diagnoses war as a manifestation and a consequence of sin and calls humanity to repentance. The death and resurrection of Jesus open the way for forgiveness and reconciliation with God. The international church, which overcomes social divisions by uniting old enemies in a new body, is God's new humanity—the cosmic demonstration that God has saved the world through Jesus Christ. The Holy Spirit enables the church to live the holy life of enemy love commanded and modeled by Jesus and the apostles, which is the authoritative pattern for how we respond to our violent enemies. This leaves no room for warfare as a legitimate Christian activity. The Old Testament saw holy war as part of the law of Moses, necessary to protect the holiness of God's people until the Redeemer should come. It looked forward to the appearance of the Savior, which would mark the end of war for God's people. With Jesus Christ's birth, life, death, and resurrection, the law—with its sacrifices, temple worship, holy war, dietary restrictions, and the like—was fulfilled, and war as an option for God's holy people went the way of prohibitions on eating shellfish and wearing clothes made of mixed materials. The early church solidly maintained this witness for centuries, refusing even to baptize soldiers who had not renounced the military oath. As a result of this uncompromising passion for biblical holiness, it grew rapidly and had great social impact on an age weary with war and deformed by violence.

However, with the political takeover of the church under "Christendom," it abandoned much of the gospel teaching and advocated just wars, crusades, and the like to deal with the enemies of the state. Just war theory tried to tack the Old and New Testaments on to a pagan legal philosophy, and in so doing ceased to be authentically biblical and thus authentically Christian. Inevitably, as with any departure from the Bible, this was disastrous for the life of the church. The name of the Prince of Peace became besmeared by churches that contributed to the violence of an already violent world. There were, however, always some churches and revival movements that held to the New Testament gospel of peace and the doctrines of grace. The Reformation saw the beginning of the turning of the tide against just war, as it sought to sweep aside the monstrous edifice of the medieval church and all that it added to the Bible. In the First and Second World Wars, Christians on all sides believed they were fighting just wars, yet their theologies made imperial wars and genocide possible. The discrediting of the churches as a result of this accelerated the process of reformation and the further undoing of Christendom. It is now clearer than ever to evangelical and other Christians that war is a sin, and it is becoming increasingly questioned whether advocating or participating in it is even an option for followers of Jesus.

There are still some Christians who hold on to the medieval Catholic idea of the "just war." Indeed, some of the Reformed evangelical authorities I have used in this book allowed the idea of Christians supporting a war. Yet in so far as they did, I contend, they were inconsistent and failed to apply the Reformation stricture of *sola scriptura* (by Scripture alone) to an accretion of the church that chimed with the medieval emphasis on salvation by works rather than the Reformation and evangelical emphasis on salvation by grace. On this point they remain more influenced by a mixture of worldly factors—including medieval Roman Catholic theology, pagan philosophy, modern international political theory, secular nationalistic views of history, and even Hollywood—than by Holy Scripture.

This view is becoming increasingly rare and discredited, however. The church is recovering the message and lifestyle of the gospel of peace, and for that reason this may be one of the most exciting periods of church history in many centuries. With the excesses of theological liberalism significantly stemmed, the church is able to recover the great truth that the Bible calls us to live lives of justice and peace in the world.

But it is one thing to recover a biblical truth; it is quite another to live it out. Our churches, with some exceptions, are barely in a state to do that. The previous chapter looked at how the worship of local congregations can inculcate the theologies and practices of peacemakers as we preach, study scripture, sing, pray, share communion, and fellowship together. In this chapter, we consider how we can go further, how we can "discharge our debt" to a world wearied by the "cry of war." We shall explore ways of doing that as citizens of countries and more generally inhabitants of a world at war. Because we have dual citizenship—we are citizens of heaven (Phil 3:20) as well as citizens of our host earthly countries—followers of Jesus are uniquely placed to be peacemakers in a violent world.

Being a National Church

More than ten thousand athletes took part in the 2012 summer Olympic games in London. Most of these participated under the banner of one of the 204 countries and territories recognized by the International Olympic Committee. Four athletes, however, were stateless and ran under the Olympic flag. They were clearly the exception. Most people belong to an earthly country. It has been an important argument of this book that in adopting the practice of war, churches around the world have too often subordinated their loyalty to Jesus Christ to loyalty to whichever host nation they happen to live in. The problem of nationalism will be considered in the next section, but it is important to remember that although our primary loyalty is to King Jesus, we have legitimate responsibilities to the communities we live in. Because the authorities are God's servants, we are to pay them the taxes we owe them (Rom 13:7); we are to pray for them that we might live in peace (1 Tim 2:1–3); and, alongside the primary obligations to love other believers and fear God, we are also to honor them as those with authority (1 Pet 2:17). In short, we are to "seek the peace and prosperity" (Jer 29: 7) of the places we live in as "foreigners and strangers" (Heb 13:11). Thus, although we can never identify with a worldly country to the extent that nonbelievers can, it is nonetheless right to care for our national communities and seek their welfare. I suggest that this in part means that we try to help them be less violent and that we help prevent or resolve their wars.

Public displays of Christian faith may be important in the United States and many African contexts, but it is sometimes said that the church in a country like modern Britain no longer holds public power. However, its importance is underlined at times of national celebration or tragedy. When disasters occur—the murder of a child, for example, or mass deaths through a terrorist attack—the nation frequently turns to the church to help it grieve (in services of mourning, for instance). At such moments, the church is well placed to speak boldly the gospel of peace.

As we saw in chapter 5 (125–26), Christian leaders sometimes argue that if the church was to condemn participation in war as sinful, it would lose the sympathetic ear of government and thus be less able to influence the world for good. This argument is absurd: it effectively says the gospel can be watered down for the sake of the gospel. The church has tried this enough times in history to know how disastrous it is. For example, in 1940 Germany defeated France, and Marshal Pétain established a nominally independent, pro-fascist French state in the south of the country, headquartered in the town of Vichy. Although the French Catholic Church opposed anti-Semitism before World War II, the bishops saw Vichy France as a chance to re-establish their position and thus fell silent on the treatment of the Jews. They gained "relevance" and the ear of the state—but at such cost![2] But more than this, the argument that to be "relevant" we need to water down the Christian opposition to war to get the ear of the state is clearly refuted by the examples of bold churchmen who *have* opposed war and have been respected by kings and rulers for this.

There is no better example of this than the early sixteenth-century Dean of St. Paul's Cathedral, John Colet (see above, ch. 3, 69). He was famous for his groundbreaking contextual exposition of Romans 13 to condemn just war theory, arguing that for true Christians "it is not by war that war is conquered, but by peace, and forbearance, and reliance in God."[3] This was not merely an academic exercise. Henry VIII, after 1510, was becoming more interested in foreign wars. According to Erasmus,

2. Adler, "The French Churches and the Jewish Question."
3. Musto, *Catholic Peace Tradition*, 113.

on Good Friday 1513, Henry invited Colet, as a respected figure in the British hierarchy, to deliver a sermon to the army. Henry had become increasingly tyrannical, and many people were afraid of expressing their views. Just war theory was being used to justify a war with France. Yet in the presence of the king, his court, and the army, Colet condemned the war. He exhorted his fellow Christians to fight under Christ's banner, that is, gospel love, and said that, in contrast, most soldiers fight under the Devil's. He called on Christians to follow Christ and not the bloody path of Julius Caesar or Alexander the Great. When the sermon was over, the king quickly rose and left, visibly shaken and apprehensive over the effect of Colet's words on his soldiers. The king summoned Colet to his chambers—they spoke, and as Colet left, the king embraced him. We should follow Colet's example and never sink so low as watering down the gospel in order to gain "relevance." In times of war, the church and the nation have been let down by timid churchmen more concerned to be relevant than to be right.

Tim Chester argues that "the desire for respectability and status weakens the power of the cross."[4] Colet's example showed that a churchman could speak the truth of Christ's kingdom of peace to a tyrant and still retain his respect and the ear of the nation. Those involved in responding pastorally to the needs of tense and suffering communities—local and national—should take those golden opportunities to do so not by watering down the Christian message but by proclaiming it gloriously and fearlessly.

Being an International Church

The seventeenth-century Christian philosopher Blaise Pascal crafted an imaginary exchange between two national enemies. "Why are you killing me for your own benefit? I am unarmed," challenges the first. "Why, do you not live on the other side of the water?" replies the second. "My friend, if you lived on this side, I should be a murderer, but since you live on the other side, I am a brave man and it is right."[5] For Pascal, the foolishness of war based on national affiliation was evidence of what he termed "the wretchedness of human existence without God," a wretchedness that could be redeemed through Jesus Christ.

4. Chester, *Good News to the Poor*, 162.

5. Pascal, *Pensées*, 44.

Pascal was reacting against an early form of what would later be called "nationalism." This is the idea that everyone belongs to a nation with whom they share common language, culture, history, and homeland, and that each nation should govern its own people and territory. This can be positive and negative.[6] It is hard to imagine democracy without nationalism: the idea that a nation should be free and that a country should be governed "by the people, for the people" (rather than by a colonial power or an aristocratic elite) was vital for the American, French, and other democratic European revolutions, and for independence movements in Latin America, Africa, and Asia. The idea that the wealthy should be taxed to subsidize health care and schooling for the poor, for example, only makes sense if we think of them as equals in one nation. But nationalism also has its dark sides: it easily sees minorities as second-class citizens and can generate fierce hostility toward other nations that is the source of much bloody warfare. An important part of being peacemakers in our world today thus lies in taming nationalism. There are three ways in which followers of Jesus can do this.

The first is by the biblical insistence that everyone is equal before God. Charles Taylor, political philosopher and Christian, contends that we have "an ineradicable sense that human life is to respected."[7] However, in a war, nationalists often regard the members of the enemy nation as less valuable than their own nation, thus justifying mistreating or killing them. The church is well placed to resist this aspect of nationalism, by its insistence that everyone is made in the image of God and thus worthy of equal respect, regardless of nation.

For example, in 1537 Pope Paul III released an official statement insisting that New World natives "are truly men" and that only Satan would want to persuade Europeans that they were "dumb brutes created for our service."[8] In 1550 the Catholic priest Bartolomé de las Casas persuaded the Spanish crown (against the arguments of slave holders) that newly conquered natives in the New World were rational human beings made in the image of God, and war therefore could not be waged against them to convert them to Catholicism. A more contemporary example of making peace by resisting nationalism through Christian consciousness and lifestyle is the "Tent of Nations," a project in a Palestinian farm in the

6. For nationalism as a positive phenomenon, see Greenfeld, "Nationalism and the Mind."

7. Taylor, *Sources of the Self*, 8.

8. Hoover, *God, Germany, and Britain*, 132.

hills south of Bethlehem. In 2010 I met the owner, Daoud, a Palestinian follower of Jesus. His farm is ringed by five expanding Israeli settlements, built on land taken from local farmers like Daoud. The Israeli government has attempted to take the land from him by declaring it unowned land, and Daoud claims that three times armed settlers came at night and tried to build a road over his land and thereby steal it, but were stopped; in revenge, they once uprooted 250 olive trees. The Israeli military have forbidden them from having running water, installing electricity mains, bringing in building materials, or constructing structures, and settlers have blocked the main access road. "The idea is to make it hard for us to exist here" so that we leave, he claimed.

Daoud explained that his family has refused to take the options Palestinians commonly choose: giving up and emigrating, resignation, or violent resistance. "We chose to stay, not to be victims—it is very important for us not to be victims." They have developed "the tent of nations" project, seeking to make their land a place of understanding, reconciliation, and peace. To this end they organize tree planting each year, getting Palestinians, foreigners, and sympathetic Israelis to undertake the work together.

Daoud's family has sought to build understanding with the settlers, inviting groups of them to visit—many have never met a Palestinian before as a human being. Daoud reported that one recently observed, "'You have no running water, but we have swimming pools'—he saw our reality as people." At the entrance to the farm is a stone with the words, "We refuse to be enemies." This project, literally surrounded by hostile enemies, is an attempt to live out gospel peace by peacefully resisting oppression while loving their enemy and insisting that he is seen not as "the enemy nation" but as someone loved by God and to be loved—and by insisting that the oppressor see them in the same way, too.[9]

It is this insistence that is one of the most attractive aspects of the Christian worldview to modern humanity. If atheism is correct, then there is no more inherent value to human life than there is to that of wasps, slugs, or algae: why not kill people who get in the way of our desire for wealth, territory, justice, humanitarian protection, or whatever? Furthermore, in a consistent atheist worldview, any struggle for peace or justice must ultimately be viewed as futile when, as our current scientific understandings would lead us to expect, life in the universe eventually

---

9. See Megoran, "War *and* Peace?"

comes to an end as the sun's energy runs out.[10] The Christian position, rather, is based on the biblical assertion that human beings are made in the "image of God" (Gen 1:27) by a loving Creator. As David Atkinson writes on this text, "Every person who crosses our path is a gift from the Creator's hands to be treasured, honored, treated with respect."[11] Or as Reverend Martin Luther King Jr. memorably put it, "Man, for Jesus, is not mere flotsam and jetsam in the river of life, but he is a child of God."[12] This Christian challenge to nationalism is one of the most compelling reasons to believe that Christianity is true and good and that atheism is not only false but dangerous.

The second way in which the gospel of Jesus Christ overcomes aggressive nationalism is when followers of Jesus identify with each other as being members of the same "holy nation" (1 Pet 2:9) more closely than they identify with the other members of the earthly "host" nation whose citizenship they may happen to hold. As many examples in this book have shown, when Christians manage to get their loyalty to their host nations in proper second place to their loyalty to their heavenly homeland, they can play useful roles in galvanizing peacemaking between their host nations.

For example, in the 1960s Polish and German bishops began meeting together regularly in a process of reconciliation. These two countries still had bitter memories and unresolved issues from World War II and were then hosts to the massed armed forces of the Cold War superpowers and their allies. Many influential groups in their home countries roundly criticized the Christians for being unpatriotic, for disregarding injustices of the past, and for seeking forgiveness. That is very difficult to do when your nation regards itself as the victim and the other side as despicable enemies. Nonetheless, this church work began a dialogue that was to help facilitate the process of the two governments signing final peace treaties in 1990 and 1991.[13] It also brought honor to the name of Christ.

Peacemaking like this is at the heart of authentic proclamation of the gospel and takes myriad forms. The ministry of the influential itinerant evangelist Gipsy Smith illustrates this. Converted as a teenager, he

10. Alexander, *Rebuilding the Matrix*, 246–47. The second law of thermodynamics would lead us to expect that eventually the universe will run out of energy, and all life will end.

11. Atkinson, *Message of Genesis 1–11*, 25–26.

12. King, "Andidotes for Fear."

13. Baum, "The Role of the Churches in Polish-German Reconciliation."

devoted his life to traveling Britain and the world sharing his testimony, singing, and calling tens of thousands to faith in the Savior.[14] Shortly after the end of the bloody 1899–1902 Boer War, he undertook a major evangelistic tour of South Africa. The country was still torn by racial tension, with hatred between the Afrikaners/Dutch and British, a hatred that extended to the churches. Smith made special effort to bring the British and Dutch Christians together. At the start of his mission they would not even share a church for evangelistic outreach. Smith argued with them that "the Christian part of the English and Dutch nations ought to be the first to show the spirit of Christ" by seeking forgiveness and reconciliation.[15] A leading politician told Gipsy Smith that his mission "will do more to bring the Churches and races together than all the politicians have done for the past three years." His mission succeeded in bringing both groups to work together to preach the gospel to all. In one poignant moment he describes how, after a meeting, a Dutch Christian brought an English South African to the Lord, while a British worker prayed with a Dutch man as he committed his life to Christ. Strikingly, these two workers had fought against each other in the war.[16] His compelling account of this trip was titled, fittingly, *A Mission of Peace*.

Gipsy Smith's example teaches us an important lesson. The authentic proclamation of the Gospel understands that war and national hatreds are manifestations and consequences of sin, out of which men and women must be called in repentance. At the same time, they are called into membership of a new humanity, the church, which came into being with the resurrection of Jesus and the outpouring of the Holy Spirit and is proof that reconciliation of people with God and each other is possible. A church that is more used to conducting evangelism based on personal needs has to recover the conviction that the Bible provides the best explanation of war and violence, and also its solution. Preaching in 1939, C. S. Lewis asked his student congregation what the point of studying in wartime was. Isn't it, he wondered, like Nero fiddling while Rome burned? "But to a Christian the true tragedy of Nero must not be that he fiddled while the city was on fire," observed Lewis wryly, "but that he fiddled on the brink of hell." As he went on to say, "War creates no new situation: it simply aggravates the permanent human situation so that we

14. Gipsy Smith, *Gipsy Smith*.

15. Gipsy Smith, *Mission of Peace*, 25.

16. Ibid., 50.

can no longer ignore it. Human life has always been lived on the edge of a precipice."[17] We must take opportunities afforded by war and violence to present the gospel of peace to the world. Today, the so-called New Atheists attack Christian faith on the grounds that it causes wars.[18] It is important to respond to this, and indeed these attacks present marvelous opportunities to invite people to hear a well-presented talk that engages with these attacks. For example, as part of a mission week one year, I saw Hull University student Christians put on a talk entitled "Does Christianity cause war?" Many students came along to the student union bar to hear the talk and ask questions. The biblical message of peace speaks with relevance and urgency to our violent times. But we can only be its spokespeople if we are living it out ourselves.

The third way in which Christian faith overcomes the violence of nationalism is by satisfying the need for purpose and meaning in life that nationalism and war have proved so seductive in offering. Nationalism allows individuals to attain fame, glory, and fabulous wealth as sportsmen and women, to be celebrated by millions of people whom they have never met but who regard them as heroes for beating the team of some other nation. This was inconceivable before the age of nationalism.

Sport may seem harmless enough, but the sinister counterpart is that glory and purpose can also be attained through violence against people from other nations who, as Pascal put it, are essentially only different because they "live on the other side of the water." In *War Is a Force That Gives Us Meaning*, his striking book about the wars he had witnessed close up, veteran *New York Times* foreign correspondent Chris Hedges records how the "plague of nationalism" can overtake apparently reasonable people as war erupts. He describes how he has seen people excuse and even revel in all manner of cruelties and injustices as they identified emotionally with "their" side in whatever supposedly just war it was engaged in. "The enduring attraction of war," he argues, is that "it can give us what we long for in life. It can give us purpose, meaning, a reason for living." He continues: "Many of us, restless and unfulfilled, see no supreme worth in our lives. We want more out of life. And war, at least, gives us a sense that we can rise above our smallness."[19]

---

17. Lewis, "Learning in War-Time," 26–27.

18. See, for example, Hitchens, *God Is Not Great*, and Dawkins, *The God Delusion*.

19. Hedges, *War Is a Force*, 3–7.

Hedges makes the perceptive comment that "war is a god." The reason that nationalism, and wars fought for the nation, give people such a sense of meaning and purpose is that at root nationalism is a form of idolatry. Historians commonly date the rise of modern nationalism to the eighteenth and nineteenth centuries. Although the idea of a nation existed earlier in some places, most states before that period were comprised of numerous different ethnic groups and were ruled by kings or other hereditary noblemen.[20] As people increasingly left the villages for new cities, the old social systems around noble-peasant relations changed, and religion's role in ordering village life declined.[21] Nationalism was an ideology that gave people a new way to rebuild a sense of community. As we have seen elsewhere in this book, Christianity was used in many contexts to support the rise of nationalism, with the idea that God had chosen a certain nation and was using it for his especial purposes. However, as political theorist Hartmut Behr argues, at this time nationalism came to be seen by some antireligious thinkers as taking the place of formal Christianity as a way of organizing society and explaining the purpose of life. Nationalism took on a religious character, the nation seen as a direct manifestation of God. An expression of this can be found in French historian Jules Michelet (1798–1874) when he writes about the French Revolution of 1789:

> People seldom sacrifice themselves for anything but what they believe to be infinite. For sacrifice they must have a God, an altar; a God in whom men recognize themselves and love one another. How then could we sacrifice ourselves? We have lost our Gods! . . . It was necessary that God should have a second period and appear upon earth in his incarnation of 1789. He then gave to association its broadest and truest form, what alone can still unite us, and through us save the world. Oh, glorious mother France! You who are not only our own, but who are destined to carry liberty to every nation, teach us to love one another in you.[22]

Under nationalism, the nation came to take on a divine, godlike role. It was believed to be what enables life, delivers happiness, and gives individuals a sense of meaning in a changing world. The nation is sacred,

20. A. Smith, *National Identity.*

21. Gellner, *Nations and Nationalism*; Hobsbawm, *Nations and Nationalism since 1780.*

22. Behr, *History of International Political Theory,* 154–56.

provides a reason for sacrifice and commitment to a cause greater than the individual, and promises eternal glory to those who labor and die in its service. To this extent nationalism, and the wars fought in the name of the nation, is idolatry, as it takes the place of God. "We belive in war more than we believe in God," observe Stanley Hauerwas and Sam Wells astutely.[23] Like any idol, the demonic power of nationalism serves death instead of life. But because the risen Lord Jesus has been exalted "far above all rule and authority, power and dominion" (Eph 1:21) men and women need not be trapped in this power—as the life of Louis Zamperini demonstrates.[24]

Born in New York in 1917, Zamperini was a champion athlete who competed for the United States in the 1936 Berlin Olympics and was tipped for success in the 1940 Olympiad. Running for his country was the greatest honor he sought. World War II ended that dream, and he enlisted in the US Air Force and deployed to the Pacific when the United States entered the war against Japan in 1941. Zamperini was anxious to see action for his country, but his plane went down over the vast ocean and he and a fellow crewman survived for forty-seven days with minimal food and water on a life raft in shark-infested waters that were patrolled and strafed by enemy fighter planes. Captured by the Japanese, he endured years of exceptional brutality in prisoner of war camps.

When eventually freed upon Japan's surrender, he found that war wounds had ended his dream of Olympic glory. Sinking into depression, violence, and alcoholism, he became consumed with hatred for the Japanese who had so mistreated him. Fantasies of revenge came to provide a focal reason for living, and he planned to go to Japan to find and murder his wartime tormentors. His marriage failing under the pressure, in 1949 he was persuaded by his wife and neighbors to attend (reluctantly) a Los Angeles tent campaign by the young evangelist Billy Graham. Zamperini responded to the preacher's invitation to turn from his sins and live for God following what he would later describe as "a confrontation with God." Returning home, he poured all his alcohol down the drain, and from that day on the daily nightmares of his wartime experiences stopped forever. His marriage renewed, he traveled to Japan to track down his former tormentors—now not to kill them, as previously planned, but to forgive them and to share the love of God with them. He spent the remainder of

23. Hauerwas and Wells, "Breaking Bread: Peace and War."
24. This remarkable example is drawn from Hillenbrand, *Unbroken*.

his life as a Christian speaker, telling his story all over America. At the age of eighty-four he returned to Japan as it staged the Winter Olympics, invited to carry the Olympic torch through the country where he had been tortured half a century earlier. Where once he had sought meaning and purpose through nationalism, either as an athlete or a soldier, he now found meaning, purpose, and glory in pursuit of the only trophy that will ever truly satisfy, the life lived in Christ.

The violent manifestation of nationalism is the scourge of our age. It has fueled titanic global wars, bloody revolutions and uprisings. It has stoked civil strife and led men and women made in the image of God to disdain and discriminate against others on the basis of their belonging to a different nation. So many parts of the world are crying out for a remedy. The Christian gospel is the greatest antidote to violent nationalism that the world has ever seen. In his commentary on the opening verses of the Letter to the Galatians, Tom Wright says that, for Paul, the gospel contains "the announcement that Jesus, the crucified Messiah, is exalted as Lord of the whole world," and that "he is calling into existence a single worldwide family." This worldwide family regards those of other nations as equally valuable in the eyes of God, loves them rather than disdains or fights them, knows that lasting glory is to be found not in achieving some transitory success on the battlefield or sports pitch but in serving the Prince of Peace, and finds its meaning and purpose in doing good to all and living a life of love for the Savior. Wright adds a challenge: "In the wider world, ethnic rivalry and hostility continue unabated. Isn't it time for the church to rediscover the apostolic gospel, and live by it?"[25]

Making Space for Peace

In the course of my work as a political geography lecturer (and in my holiday travel between times) I have been fortunate enough to visit many of the world's most unusual international boundaries. Although in theory it is easy to draw a boundary on a map, to agree where it actually lies is very difficult. Many of the world's boundaries are disputed. In 1978, Argentina and Chile were poised on the brink of war in an escalating maritime boundary dispute over the ownership of several small islands (with potentially lucrative oil and fishing rights) in the Beagle Channel. As both countries prepared for war, violence was averted at the eleventh

25. T. Wright, *Galations and Ephesians*, 6.

hour by the intervention of that most unlikely of boundary scholars, Pope John Paul II. Because the Catholic Church was an institution that was respected in both countries and regarded as possessing both neutrality and moral authority, the pope was able to act as an intermediary between the two nations.[26]

The Vatican's intervention to prevent war might have saved many lives. It is an example of an important way that the church as an institution can *make space for peace*. Christians are in the world, but not of the world (a paraphrase of John 17:14–15). Because we are "in the world"—neighborhoods, villages, cities, and countries—we have vital connections with those communities. At the same time, because we are not "of the world"—we are citizens of heaven, owing primary allegiance to the Prince of Peace and living according to the "gospel of peace"—we are able to stand outside those communities and create opportunities to bring them together. Followers of Jesus are thus uniquely positioned to be peacemakers.

The life of American Lutheran minister Frank Buchman (1878–1961) provides a different but compelling example of how the church can make space for peace. In the 1930s, Buchman (who was one of the inspirations behind the creation of Alcoholics Anonymous) founded the so-called Oxford Group. This movement encouraged group Bible study and reflection on how Christians could influence the moral and spiritual climates of their societies. The cross was central to the movement, and Buchman's recipe for reading the Bible was "read accurately, interpret honestly, apply drastically."[27] He also believed that "the political impact of a change of heart is hard to measure."[28]

It was out of Buchman's work that Moral Re-Armament (MRA) was launched in 1938, encouraging the church to mitigate the militarism of the age. Rooted in the evangelical tradition, it propagated a Christian message of repentance and reconciliation. Although it is claimed that Buchman's influence was evident in the active wartime resistance of Norwegian bishops and clergy who had been heavily involved with the Oxford work, it was after the Second World War that MRA made the most remarkable contributions to peace. In late 1945, soon after the Second World War ended, it began the process of Franco-German reconciliation

26. Matthews, *War Prevention Works*, 20–21.

27. Lean, *Frank Buchman*, 15.

28. Boobbyer, "Moral Re-armament in Africa," 231.

at a restored hotel in Caux, Switzerland. At a time of still great bitterness between the two nations, Buchman brought politicians, industrialists, academics, and other people who would be key members of the postwar elites of both countries together to quietly reflect for days or weeks at a time, along the lines of the 1930s Oxford groups. With Switzerland untouched by the carnage of the war, participants enjoyed the luxuries of hot water and unrationed food. No domestic staff were employed, so the emerging leaders of Europe cooked and cleaned together.

One French participant was Irène Laure, an MP and resistance leader, whose son had been tortured by the Gestapo. She despised Germans so much that she walked out of the room whenever a German spoke, and eventually packed her bags to leave. Buchman met her in the corridor and asked, "What kind of unity do you want for Europe?" The question plagued her, so she decided to stay. Eventually, she spoke up at a discussion where there was lots of argument about Austrian and German guilt. She said, "I have so hated Germany that I wanted to see her erased from the map of Europe. But I have seen here that my hatred is wrong. I wish to ask the forgiveness of all the Germans present." The effect was electric. One participant, Peter Petersen, a German who in turn hated the French, said, "I was dumbfounded. For several nights it was impossible for me to sleep. All my past rose up in revolt against the courage of the woman. But we knew, my friends and I, that she had shown us the only way open to Germany if we wanted to join in the reconstruction of Europe."[29]

Irène Laure later said that if Buchman had pitied her or sympathized with her in the corridor, she would have left—it was the quality of the challenge that arrested her. She subsequently became very active in Franco-German reconciliation. Other participants included François Mitterrand, who would later become French president, and Konrad Adenauer, the new German chancellor. Another participant was Robert Schuman, architect of the European Steel and Coal Community, the basis of what would later evolve into the European Union. This was founded in an to attempt to prevent future war in Europe by tying France and German closely together. They testified that MRA played a vital role in reconciliation and in rebuilding the continent along new, more cooperative lines.[30]

29. Lean, *Frank Buchman*, ch. 31.
30. Luttwak, "Franco-German Reconciliation."

By creating a Bible-based, prayer-soaked movement attentive to discerning how God might be leading his people to engage with the pressing issues of his time, Frank Buchman was able to fashion opportunities to bring other people together to make peace. It is reported that when European politicians told him that, with reference to his important work on Franco-German reconciliation, "you have achieved a lot," he replied, "No, I've done nothing, God did it—I just listened to Him and did what he told me."[31] What we can draw from Buchman is not a model to replicate today but the lesson that if we read the Bible carefully, pray honestly, understand what is going on in the world, and open ourselves in faith to how God wants to work in the conflicts of our age, then he can truly use us to "make spaces for peace." Followers of the Prince of Peace are uniquely positioned to create them, and they are a creative and original way to live out the church's calling to be a body that demonstrates what happens when the walls between enemies are broken down and they become one in Christ.

Repentance, Apology, and Forgiveness

On June 19, 2015, twenty-one-year-old Dylann Roof stood in a South Carolina courthouse, accused of the racially motivated mass killing of nine African American worshippers at their Emanuel AME Church in Charleston. After reading out the charges and the names of the slain, Chief Magistrate James B. Gosnell asked if any relatives present wanted to make a statement. In an act of grace that moved the nation and the world, every single relative who spoke offered forgiveness and prayers that God would have mercy on the man charged with murdering their loved ones.[32]

As we saw above, Christians can thus "make space for peace" and facilitate reconciliation between warring countries and neighbors. But non-Christians can do that, too. So what makes Christian peacemaking different? The answer is the cross. The cross speaks pardon to the worst of sinners and enables those most grievously offended to forgive their persecutors. That unforgettable moment in a South Carolina courthouse is evidence of that. But the cross is not simply a transaction long ago: it is a model of Christian behavior. Because of the unique role of the cross

31. Spoerri, *Dynamic Out of Silence.*
32. See Berman, "'I Forgive You.'"

in Christianity, the followers of Jesus can teach a violent world a great deal about forgiveness, repentance, and reconciliation in a way that few others can.

During the Cold War standoff between the Soviet Union and the capitalist West, Horace Dammers was a canon of Coventry Cathedral. The cathedral was gutted by German bombing during World War II, and after the war became a symbol of reconciliation and forgiveness. Dammers recalls giving students from the Soviet Union a tour, which ended by the preserved ruined altar behind which is incised in gold letters, "Father, forgive"—the words of Christ as they hung him on the cross. The students' leader, a young woman, made a short speech in which she said that forgiveness was not part of Marxism and it was hard to forgive the Germans who killed twenty million Soviets in the war. But, Dammers recounts, "they had come to realize that afternoon that mutual forgiveness, and reconciliation between people who had wronged each other, was essential if they were to live in peace with one another. Moreover, she was sure that when they returned home they would try to practise forgiveness in their personal lives."[33]

The Christian gospel provides a better ethic than any that atheism ever could. Although the Soviet Union has collapsed and its statues of Marx and Lenin have been torn down, the old rugged cross still towers above a world that seems unable to find a solution to war, just as it stands symbolically in the preserved ruins of Coventry Cathedral to this day.

Indeed, in recent years, Christians have led the world in repentance and forgiveness as strategies of peacemaking. And few activities have been as extraordinary in this regard as the Reconciliation Walk. On November 27, 1095, Pope Urban II preached a sermon in the French city of Clermont-Ferrand calling for Christian Europe to unite militarily and to defend itself against violent Seljuk Turkish attacks on Christian territory and pilgrims. On July 15, 1099, the soldiers inspired by this call to what history has termed "the First Crusade" finally reached Jerusalem, massacring its Jewish and Muslim inhabitants and defenders.

On November 27, 1995, a group of US-led, UK-based evangelical-charismatic Christians spent a day in prayer and repentance for the Crusades in Clermont-Ferrand. They began a pilgrimage of apology, called the Reconciliation Walk, that saw Christians from around the world follow original Crusader routes. It culminated, appropriately, in Jerusalem

33. Dammers, *Thank You, Holy Spirit*, 58.

on July 15, 1999, with ceremonies of apology to the city's Jewish, Muslim, and Christian populations. The following message was presented in local languages wherever the Reconciliation Walkers went:

> Nine hundred years ago, our forefathers carried the name of Jesus Christ in battle across the Middle East. Fueled by fear, greed and hatred, they betrayed the name of Christ by conducting themselves in a manner contrary to His wishes and character. The Crusaders lifted the banner of the Cross above your people. By this act, they corrupted its true meaning of reconciliation, forgiveness and selfless love.
>
> On the anniversary of the First Crusade, we also carry the name of Christ. We wish to retrace the footsteps of the Crusaders in apology for their deeds and in demonstration of the true meaning of the Cross. We deeply regret the atrocities committed in the name of Christ by our predecessors. We renounce greed, hatred and fear, and condemn all violence done in the name of Jesus Christ.
>
> Where they were motivated by hatred and prejudice, we offer love and brotherhood. Jesus the Messiah came to give life. Forgive us for allowing His name to be associated with death. Please accept again the true meaning of the Messiah's words: "The Spirit of the Lord is upon me, because He has anointed me to bring good news to the poor. He has sent me to proclaim release to the captives and recovery of sight to the blind, to let the oppressed go free, to proclaim the year of the Lord's favor."

Although this gesture apparently made a significant impact on many who received the apology,[34] it was greeted with ridicule and even anger in segments of the British press. "Their preference for a well-meaning over a well-informed gesture exposes them to well-deserved mockery," thundered an editorial in *The Times*. "Apology for its own sake is an empty gesture" the lead writer continued. "If they seek relevance rather than a selfishly enjoyable holiday in the sun, these latter-day crusaders should look for more practical missions."[35] Scholar Michel-Rolph Trouillot described the Reconciliation Walk as part of "an ongoing wave of collective apologies"[36] that marked the mid-late 1990s. For example, Pope John Paul

34. For more on the Reconciliation Walk, see Megoran, *War on Terror*, 56–57. For a scholarly analysis of it, see my "Towards a Geography of Peace."

35. "No Apology Needed: Crusading for Forgiveness Is a Pointless Exercise," editorial, *The Times*, January 7, 1999.

36. Trouillot, "Abortive Rituals," 172.

II apologized for more than one hundred historical injustices. In Britain, supposed past wrongs for which Prime Minister Tony Blair apologized included the nineteenth-century Irish famine, the 1972 "Bloody Sunday" shootings in Northern Ireland, and the execution of British soldiers for cowardice in World War I.

It is easy to find grounds to criticize such historical apologies. How can people today apologize for events for which they were not personally responsible? Don't these apologies mean taking sides with one particular view of history? Isn't there a danger of projecting today's values on the past? How do we decide what to apologize for and what not to? And isn't there a risk of such an apology becoming an empty gesture?

Apologies cannot expiate guilt—only the blood of Christ can do that. Certainly, apologies can be empty gestures. But when they are heartfelt confessions, when they recognize and sorrow over hurt done to another, and when they represent a genuine desire to repent and act differently, then they can be very powerful dimensions of peacemaking.

For the church, unfortunately, repentance and apology must often begin at home. In the colonial era, European and American churches often unwittingly adopted the racist attitudes of their host societies. To the extent that this created ruptures whose legacies endure today, confession and repentance expressed in formal apology may be called for. In 1995 the US Southern Baptist denomination apologized for supporting slavery, sending an important signal to members of the church and to African Americans outside it that a new standard of moral behavior had officially been adopted.[37] In 1986 the United Church of Canada issued an apology to native Canadians for the cultural imperialism of their missionary predecessors:

> We did not hear you when you shared your vision. In our zeal to tell you of the good news of Jesus Christ . . . we confused Western ways and culture with the depth and breadth and length and height of the gospel of Christ. We imposed our civilization as a condition for accepting the gospel. We tried to make you like us. . . . We ask you to forgive us and to walk together with us in the spirit of Christ so that our people may be blessed and God's creation healed.[38]

---

37. K. Gill, "Moral Functions of an Apology," 20.

38. Cited in Govier and Verwoerd, "The Promise and Pitfalls of Apology."

This step was important in improving relations with native Canadians and assisting their inclusion in the church. As Trudy Govier and Wilhelm Verwoerd argue, "A wholehearted apology, followed up with proper commitment to reform and practical amends, can provide a major initial step toward restoring injured relationships."[39]

Apologies for slavery and colonialism are nothing exceptional today—they are simply the church catching up with the times. But it is when Christians make countercultural apologies on behalf of larger groups—especially when those groups are in conflict—that the church has the power to startle and shock with the surpassing greatness of the reality of the gospel.

I took part in the Reconciliation Walk, and it was disarming to Muslims (who were used to thinking of Britain and America as hostile) to have Britons and Americans walk from Europe to the Middle East to apologize for a set of events that happened long ago but are still alive in historical memories. Such a gesture can chip away at negative stereotypes, breaking down bitter spiritual legacies that put the church in the way of people seeing Jesus. A more recent example comes from the Kyrgyzstani city of Osh. June 2010 saw the outbreak of days of deadly inter-ethnic violence between the Kyrgyz and the minority Uzbek population. Both sides suffered, but the Uzbeks bore the brunt of mass killings, looting, and seizure of property. The aftermath was in some ways worse. As order was restored, the Kyrgyz media blamed the Uzbeks, even accusing them of burning their own neighborhoods down to get foreign sympathy. Worse, the police joined criminals in arbitrarily kidnapping innocent Uzbeks, stealing their property, abusing them, and demanding massive sums of money in extortion.[40]

The response of one small group of Muslim-background Kyrgyz Christians was extraordinary. They visited family after family of Uzbeks in burned-down neighborhoods, apologizing on behalf of the Kyrgyz in general, giving emergency aid, and sharing the gospel of Jesus Christ. Below is an extract from a report by a foreigner who accompanied a certain Kyrgyz believer in the very dangerous enterprise of going into the heart of "the enemy's" territory and apologizing:

> The first thing she did was to apologize on behalf of the Kyrgyz people (and personally) for what happened to the Uzbeks. She

39. Ibid.

40. Amnesty International, "Still Waiting for Justice."

went to each lady and hugged them and apologized again. This is the difference Jesus makes. She also told the people she was a follower of Jesus and asked if they'd like a "Holy book" along with the other aid they were giving. Everyone said yes, and so they got a copy of the Psalms and New Testament in Uzbek. Muslims believe there are four books God has given us which include the Psalms and "Injil" (New Testament). We shared about Jesus with some of the people as we felt was right. One Uzbek lady had just been told by a Kyrgyz neighbor that the Uzbeks had burnt down their own houses.

The contrast between this and what the Kyrgyz believer was doing was such a picture of the difference Jesus makes. One of the places we visited was absolutely heart-rending. There was a lady there who had lost seven members of her family, including her mother, brother, and a one-year-old niece. We did not know what to say as we sat with her in her UNHCR tent in front of her burned-out house. She showed us pictures of her family and de-scribed how her brother, a lawyer, had kept reassuring her that everything was okay—she was at work on the other side of town. A neighbor described to us how the family were forced by a mob back into their burning house, where they died: "These Kyrgyz believers who are apologizing on behalf of their people are what is giving us hope. It is opening the hearts of Uzbeks to the gospel in a profound way. Please pray that there will be a multiplication of people like this. It is not an easy thing to do."

In 2011 I met one of the apology initiators: she was an ordinary, poor Kyrgyz woman. It took courage and faith to do this, not privilege or education. What she did was authentic gospel peacemaking: both creating better relations between groups in conflict and pointing them to the savior who is Prince of Peace. It is risky, difficult, creative, countercultural, and disarming. Very importantly, it clearly demonstrates through words and actions the reality of the gospel and the difference that believing in the Lord Jesus makes. Unsurprising, therefore, that communities that had hitherto been very resistant to the gospel were suddenly more open.

Christ overcame death and delivered us from it by loving his en-emies, as we are called to love ours in turn. As followers of Jesus, justified only by faith in his atoning sacrifice at Calvary, we realize that our peace with God is made possible because of confession and our reliance on the unmerited forgiveness of God. Christians are thus uniquely equipped to be peacemakers in the world through apology and forgiveness. When we do that we can both help improve relations between conflicting groups and show the world the Savior and his glorious gospel of peace.

Resisting War

I began the previous chapter with the example of antiwar activist Brian Haw, and his banner declaring "I think when Jesus said love your enemies he didn't mean kill them." He was right. But does that mean that the church's job is to emulate Mr. Haw and decamp outside parliament buildings shouting at politicians as they speed past in dark cars? If the church is antiwar, should it be a signed-up member of political movements opposing their countries' wars?

As we have seen in this book, early twentieth-century liberal Christian pacifism concluded that the church's job was to be a mass movement to persuade the world's countries to act towards each other along the lines of the Sermon on the Mount. But that is impossible. The New Testament describes a way of life for God's people to live by the power of the Holy Spirit: loving enemies in the way God loved us is impossible for people who have not themselves been transformed by God's love. Only the regenerate can be sanctified: everything else is just moral effort on our part. The New Testament tells us how to do discipleship, not public policy. It tells us how to follow Jesus, rather than telling the world how to run its business.[41] It does not give "policy answers" but shows us how to live Christianly, how to hope and to celebrate life, knowing that God has ultimately defeated death.[42] In God's providential ordering, the powers and authorities have the role of restraining evil and promoting virtue (for more on this, revisit the discussion above of Romans 12 and 13 starting on 69). Unlike Old Testament Israel they are not theocracies whom God has covenanted to protect from their enemies if they obey his laws.

The church's primary function—in wartime as much as peacetime—is to preach that war is a manifestation and a consequence of sin, and call a warring world back in repentance to obedience to its Maker's commandments. It is to be the window through which God's future of gospel peace can be seen, as his redeemed people live countercultural lives of holiness, love, faith, and peacemaking. This happens as Christians live the life of the Prince of Peace. If all Christians in the world consistently

41. Marshall, *Beyond Retribution*, 8.
42. Stringfellow, *Ethic for Christians*, 151.

refused to participate in or support in any way the armed forces or violent insurgencies in their countries, if they prayed and worshipped and acted in society in a way that was against war and demonstrated enemy love and forgiveness and reconciliation, how different would our world be? This position transformed the Roman world and was key to the early church's evangelism and rapid spread. Certainly the First and Second World Wars could not have been waged as they were. This is the church as an antiwar movement.

Bruce Winter suggests that Jeremiah's exhortation to the exiles in Babylon to "seek the peace and prosperity of the city" (Jer 29:7) was a model for the earliest churches in the Roman Empire.[43] Because God loves all creation and all are made in his image, the church's concern necessarily extends even to the good of those who reject its message. It can live out this concern by helping the societies in which it lives become more peaceful and just. We have seen throughout this book numerous examples of how authentic Christian discipleship leads to the church making positive contributions to peacemaking in the host neighborhoods, towns, and countries in which it resides: it really cannot help avoiding that, if it is authentically worshipping King Jesus as Lord and Prince of Peace. Sometimes, as we have seen, this will include opposing wars: John Colet's condemnation of Henry VIII's planned invasion of France (ch. 9, 242); mass Christian action against medieval Italy's warring city-states (ch. 5, 109); Erasmus' outspoken opposition to war with the Muslims (ch. 8, 193–94); Andre Trocmé's resistance to the collaboration of Vichy France with Nazi Germany (ch. 8, 222).

A more recent example is the opposition of American churches to their country's foreign policies in 1980s Central America. In the Cold War standoff between the United States and the Soviet Union, President Ronald Reagan's administration misread every local campaign for development and justice as the global march of Soviet communism. It therefore supported right-wing regimes and terrorist organizations in Central America, even training paramilitaries in its notorious School of the Americas, located at Fort Benning, near Columbus, Georgia. These allies included state torturers and nonstate death squads, such as the Nicaraguan "Contras," who murdered doctors, teachers, priests, and others seen as sympathetic to the poor, in an attempt to destabilize the left-wing Sandinista government. The low point of this episode was the Iran-Contra

---

43. Winter, *Seek the Welfare of the City.*

scandal, where the CIA broke an arms embargo to sell weapons to the fundamentalist Iranian regime, channeling off money to fund support of the Contras. Christians and others who fled from Central America to the United States were not granted asylum by the US government, as that would have been an admission that its Central American allies were not respecting human rights. So those refugees caught by the US authorities were deported, often to their deaths.

Many US Christians, like other American citizens, regarded this whole murky relationship as immoral and took action to change it. They set up an underground network to smuggle people into the country and conceal them and give them sanctuary. They modeled it on the famous nineteenth-century Underground Railroad established to help runaway slaves from the southern United States south escape to the North.[44] Some Christians visited Nicaragua to take part in "protective accompaniment."[45] This means they literally walked alongside potential targets of death squads to deter attacks on them, reckoning, generally quite accurately, that these squads would not want to risk killing citizens of the country that was funding them. These Christians often went out for only a week or two at a time during their holidays, but upon returning home began informing their churches of what was happening and lobbying politicians for change. They were influential in persuading Congress to prohibit further support of the Contras.

Another example from the Americas is the "street liturgies" of the Sebastián Acevedo Movement Against Torture in 1980s Chile, which resisted brutal dictator Augusto Pinochet's war of torture and murder against his own people. The movement was begun by church workers and ministers, but eventually lay believers became involved. A group would suddenly emerge from a crowd, holding banners and handing out literature. It would read a five-minute liturgy against torture that named victims, torturers, sites of torture, dates, and the officials at different levels who refused to act. The group would then melt away into the crowd before the police arrived, or sometimes get beaten up, gassed, and taken away if the police were quicker off the mark. William Cavanaugh argued that such actions turned nameless victims into martyrs and temporarily broke the spell of fear cast over the country by the regime. By stating that Jesus identifies with them because he was tortured by Roman justice,

44. Golden and McConnell, *Sanctuary*.
45. For more on protective accompaniment, see Brown, *Getting in the Way*.

they sought to harness the moral authority of the church against a regime that claimed to be Christian. By keeping alive the church's "subversive memory of Christ's past confrontation with, and triumph over, worldly power . . . the light of hope is thereby sustained in even the darkest hours of totalitarian power."[46]

Finally, a more recent example is that of church involvement in the global opposition to a US/UK war on Iraq in 2003. Christian churches around the world and their leaders, including the pope, the archbishop of Canterbury, and an executive of US President George W. Bush's own United Methodist Church (see ch. 1, 2), opposed the war, and Christians joined millions of people across the globe in public protests. These protests were not successful in stopping the war. But they nonetheless had unexpected effects. Mano Rumalshah, former bishop of Peshawar in Pakistan, told me that after the September 2001 attacks he gave interviews talking about his fears for Christians in Pakistan if the United States attacked Afghanistan. Sure enough, he said, after Friday prayers in the first week of the bombing, thousands of angry people ringed the Christian compound in Peshawar, shouting, "Death to the USA!" In the following weeks, many believers were murdered, and there were unprecedented large-scale attacks on churches around the country. Bishop Rumalshah contrasted the reaction to the attack on Afghanistan in 2001 with the reaction to the attack on Iraq in 2003. Although people in Pakistan were angry at the Iraq War, the condemnations by the pope and the archbishop of Canterbury had been widely reported in Pakistan, as was an antiwar march in London in February 2003 in which more than one million people participated. Even what Bishop Mano called Pakistan's "gutter press" were writing that Christians are with us on this issue. As a result, he claimed, there was not a single attack on Christians in his former jurisdiction when the war began.[47] The British church's opposition to the war did not stop it; but it probably saved the lives of many fellow believers elsewhere.

For the church, resisting war primarily does not mean merging itself with the "peace movement" or trying to become a policy expert on whichever part of the world our country is at war with. Rather, it means always explaining that war is a consequence and manifestation of sin, perpetually calling sinful humanity to repent and to worship Jesus as

46. Cavanaugh, *Torture and Eucharist,* 274–77.

47. Author interview, Mano Rumalshah, London 2003.

Lord, and living the lifestyles of peacemakers that are necessarily transformative of a violent world. It is belonging to an alternative community that worships Jesus as Prince of Peace and lives by higher laws and rules than the host states that Christians also happen to live in. It means refusing to take part in the violence of armies or the armed units of police forces, while recognizing that these powers and authorities might have legitimate roles to play under God in restraining evil and promoting good. It also means a refusal to take part in violent rebellions and insurgencies, while also acknowledging that these powers and authorities may represent authentic grievances and may sometimes pursue justice by restraining evil and promoting good where states fail to do so. However, the varied examples considered in this section show that sometimes churches *can* make tactical decisions to engage in organized opposition to war. These decisions will not always be easy. All of the above examples were controversial. Christians will disagree on appropriate tactics, and congregations must move forward together prayerfully and considerately—it could be disastrous for a pastor to suddenly hoist such an activity on a congregation. The church should no more become indistinguishable from an antiwar movement on the streets than it should from the prowar movement in parliaments and palaces. Indeed, in its opposition to all war and its fervent love of enemies, the church is very different from antiwar movements whose marchers may be animated by anti-Americanism or hatred of their own government. While a church may choose to support a certain campaign or issue for a season, it must be careful that it does not eventually become too closely identified with a particular "power and authority"—no matter how noble.[48] Although the church must always teach that war is sin, if a church carefully and prayerfully discerns that it is right to support a political campaign against a certain war, then that may be an authentic Christian response to violence.

48. On the relationship between theologies and politics of peace, see Eller, *Christian Anarchy*.

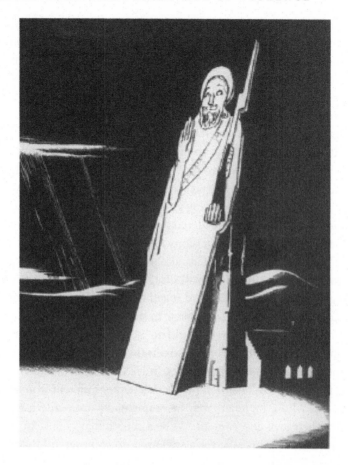

Conclusion: Peacemakers in an Age of Violence?

War is the scourge of our age. It deforms God's good creation and wreaks suffering and death on people made in his image. It is, as Martyn Lloyd-Jones puts it, a manifestation and a consequence of sin, an example of humanity's rebellion against the commandments of its Creator. War is the context in which much of the Bible was written. Allan Boesak points out that Matthew begins his gospel account with the violence of Herod against Jesus and the children of Bethlehem, and concludes it with the violence of Pilate against Jesus on the cross: "In all its forms," he summarizes, "violence is sin's most authentic expression."[49] If war is our age's scourge,

49. Boesak, "Loveless Power," 87.

then the gospel is its solution, as it is the diagnosis and remedy of all sin. The Bible does not, however, give us neatly packaged "policy answers" to questions posed by media commentators or politicians about how a certain government should respond to this or that particular conflict. Rather than instructing the world how to run its business, it calls humanity to repentance and instructs the church how to be disciples of Jesus. It equips us to be peacemakers in a world where violence is pervasive.

Unfortunately, however, the church's testimony in a violent world has so often been anything but that of peacemaker. It has made two main errors. First, by supporting "just wars," "humanitarian interventions," popular insurgencies, crusades, rebellions, and the like, churches might temporarily make themselves seem "relevant" and maybe even popular. Every such military adventure seems justifiable in its own terms for some doubtless noble end. But the cumulative effect of this departure from scripture has been disastrous. Disastrous for the world as the church has facilitated and promoted violence—World Wars I and II being the example we considered earlier. But it has also been disastrous for Christianity, earning it the reputation as a cause of war and dishonoring the name of the Prince of Peace. As Paul Dekar puts it, "In the past, the complicity of Christians in war-making and vacuous bleating by Christians about love or peace have discredited Christianity."[50] Thus for "New Atheist" thinkers like Sam Harris, violence is one of the "terrible consequences" that arises "logically and inevitably, out of Christian faith."[51] This charge needs answering, and the best way to answer it is to deprive these writers of evidence. We do that by acknowledging and repenting of the church's past mistakes in blessing violence, and also by displaying the type of peacemaking I have argued in these two concluding chapters is authentically Christian.

However, in reaction to the militarism of the past, the early twentieth-century liberal Protestant church made a second error. It saw Christianity as primarily a social movement building a liberal civilization that could abolish war through rational international organization or mass conscientious objection. This may make the church popular with left-wing politicians and movements at times of a surge in antiwar sentiment, but when its prescriptions or suggestions prove inadequate, it is left embarrassed. The rise and collapse of 1930s pacifism is a case in point.

50. Dekar, *Healing of the Nations*, 9.
51. S. Harris, *End of Faith*, 106.

Furthermore, in its wholly fallacious rejection of the biblical doctrine of the atonement (1 John 4:10) as somehow an incitement to violence, it missed the true power and potential of Bible-based gospel peacemaking.

Neither of these positions—just war theory or pacifism—takes sin seriously. Neither begins its analysis of the human condition with the Bible. Neither allows for the miraculous intervention of the power of the Holy Spirit. Neither understands history through the lens of the kingdom of God. Both turn the church into the servant of either the state or the citizenry. As a result, they make Christianity largely indistinguishable from other political or religious worldviews that exist today. Neither pathway is authentically Christian. The cross is ultimately the crux and the model of how we confront any sin, including violence. But while some sections of the church have found that it is easier to bomb our enemies than to bless them, others have found it easier to march angrily through the broad streets of London or Washington waving placards than to ascend the narrow pathway to Calvary.

Both of these courses of action are flawed, and these flaws emerge from their failure to reflect on war through the traditional Reformed/evangelical vision of creation, fall, and redemption. War was absent from *creation*: it is rebellion against God, an aberration from his good will for humanity, and not an inevitable part of the human condition. It is a manifestation and consequence of the *fall*: a demonstration of the sinfulness and depravity of individuals and of societies. We cannot ultimately deliver ourselves from sin by fighting wars to rid the world of evil. By the sin of war we have all become enemies of God and have no moral high ground to stand on to fight just wars against each other. Nor, equally, can we overcome war through progressive education, good government, and an active citizenry. These two alluring remedies are astoundingly arrogant in their claims to human mastery and divinity, and fail to take account of the sinfulness of humanity. And it is therefore through the *redemption* of humanity by the sinless Son of God, who died for our sins and was raised to life to put us right with God and each other, that humanity alone can have hope. Because of the death and resurrection of Jesus Christ we know that peace and justice, not war and violence, are the final words in history. We therefore do not put our hope in the powers and authorities for salvation from war—whether these be governments, the United Nations, science, philosophy, militaries fighting just wars or peace movements opposing them. Rather, we proclaim the eternal gospel, resist our enemies in love as God loved us, and live now as peacemakers trusting in the power of the Holy Spirit. We acknowledge that the church, God's new humanity and an alternative community to the warmaking powers and authorities, is our primary allegiance, and in obedience to the teachings of the Bible we reject war. The question of what we should do about this or that particular war is the wrong one if we have not asked, "How can my vision be transformed through the biblical worldview?"[52] This involves freeing ourselves from all the worldviews about peace and war that are unbiblical—from the redemptive violence of the Hollywood myth of World War II to the seductive hope of some happy, humanistic civilization that ends war on the wings of ever-increasing gross national product and ever-growing university enrollment numbers.

In response to war, rather, the church's function is simply, as Bishop George Bell put it, to be the church. That is, the universal body of Christ, a kingdom of peacemakers of every tribe and tongue and nation whose unity in Christ is the very evidence to the universe of God's triumph of the cross and resurrection, through which he is calling men and women to repentance, faith, and discipleship. This discipleship will transform the world around us. We have seen in this chapter and in the whole book numerous examples of what that "gospel peace" might look like. Bishops mediating disputes between nations. Pastors discipling their churches into cultures of life and peace in societies where violence is the norm. Believers using parliaments and mass campaigns to change the violent laws and practices of their countries. Congregations sheltering vulnerable minorities from the deathly grasp of their governments. Christian organizations mediating conflict between elites. The power of prayer meetings to challenge violence. Visiting and supporting peace and justice projects and campaigns by our brothers and sisters living in hard places. Helping our local communities and workplaces learn the skills of nonviolent conflict management. Recognizing past sins and joining organized trips to apologize for them. Preparing and discipling Christian communities in the ways of peace. Welcoming asylum seekers and others who may be victims of abuse in our communities. Pursuing fellowship with churches and believers in countries that our host states might be at war with. Finding creative ways to address the racial, gang-based or military violence afflicting our particular communities. Doing evangelism and apologetics, calling people from violence to the ways of gospel peace.

---

52. On this, see Walsh and Middleton, *Transforming Vision*.

But we can only do all this if we believe that the gospel of peace truly is the solution to humanity's greatest problems. We can only do it if we can point to the church as being genuinely an agent of peace, rather than an instrument of violence. For that to happen, we need to repent of our past failings and ensure that the church is known henceforth as a body of peacemakers instead of either cheerleaders for war or people unconcerned about the violence of our world. If all we can say is, "Peace is great in theory, so only kill under certain conditions and as kindly as possible," we really have little of value to say at all, and certainly nothing distinctively Christian. We need to ensure that we are known as part of the solution, rather than part of the problem. Worship and discipleship are crucial to this. The great task facing church leaders is to see to it that our preaching, teaching, Bible study, singing, praying, liturgies, fellow-shipping, sharing of communion, and church discipline train us to be authentic followers of the Prince of Peace. In the end it comes down to this: do we have enough faith to believe what Jesus said and to do it? We trust God to save us from our sins; can we also trust him to save us from our enemies?

The Christian church's historic and foundational witness to peace and against war was largely abandoned with the advent of "Christendom." This was the idea that a particular country could be officially "Christian," from which it followed that it was the duty of the church, under certain circumstances, to support that country and its wars. This sapped the church's radical commitment to holiness, as it traded spiritual dynamism and the integrity of scripture for social influence. The era of de-Christianization of public life offers the possibility of undoing that damage. We are increasingly able to be the church, not of England, or Russia, or China, or the United States, or anywhere else, but of Jesus Christ, the true King of the world at whose name every knee shall bow. We are at last able to be peacemakers and reconcilers, rather than propagandists or recruiters. That is why I do not believe all the doom and gloom about falling church membership or influence in the West. Since when was the gospel's influence indexed by the numbers of attendees at Sunday morning services? Since when was truth measured by the size of church coffers? Since when was the power of the Holy Spirit indicated by the existence of Christian prayers in parliaments, schools, coronations, inaugurations, military passing-out ceremonies, or university graduations? Rather, the demise of Christendom is a cause for celebration. It frees the church to be truly Christian. It allows us to ditch our addiction to war and become authentic followers of the Prince of Peace. I believe that we stand on the threshold of the most exciting period in church history since the time of Constantine.

Christianity is antiwar by definition. But this should be particularly the case for churches in the evangelical tradition because of the emphasis we place on a high view of scripture and the doctrines of grace: it is on these pillars that what the apostles call "the gospel of peace" is built. For much of the twentieth century the evangelical church was preoccupied with defending, against liberalism, the integrity of scripture and insisting on the need to preach repentance, conversion, and personal faith in Christ, whose atoning sacrifice on Calvary and resurrection is the only means of salvation. With those battles successfully fought, the evangelical and pentecostal/charismatic churches are recovering the truth that although the gospel is always personal, it is never private. The gospel speaks as much to the world situation as it does to individual lives. In recent years our churches have already been able to recover the historic Christian commitment to justice and apply it to a globalized age without compromising doctrinal truth. We are now well placed to do the same with peace. In so doing, we extend the Reformation quest of purging the church of unbiblical medieval practices and doctrines, like just war theory. We can become biblical peacemakers.

As Europe hurtled toward the catastrophe of the 1939–45 war, the illustrator Arthur Wragg drew an evocative black-and-white image depicting the monstrous deviation from the gospel that was represented by the militarism of the European churches of his time. A section of that picture can be seen above. A giant icon of a smiling Christ—one arm raised in blessing and the other supporting a rifle—leans against the steeple of a church, which it dwarfs. A grand mass of people bow in prayer before the icon. The real Christ, bowed under the weight of a cross, staggers away into the distance, unobserved by the masses. Underneath, Wragg simply reproduces one line of the 37th Article of Faith of the Church of England: "It is lawful for Christian men, at the commandment of the magistrate, to wear weapons and to serve in the wars."[53] Precisely the opposite is the case: it is unlawful for Christians to serve in wars. Even to entertain the thought that followers of the Prince of Peace have nothing better to offer the world than a blessing on killing their host nation's enemies is a desperately impoverished understanding of our faith. In the gospel we have

53. Wragg, *"Jesus Wept"*.

something so much better to offer a warring world, and yet we cannot do that if we are busy helping it fight its wars. For too much of its history, we have been warlike Christians in an age of violence. As a consequence, we have exacerbated rather than ameliorated the suffering of the world. We have placed unnecessary obstacles between men and women and the gospel. We have missed the blessing Christ promised to those who are peacemakers. The cost has been high, for the church and the world. It is time to change.

Bibliography

Ackerman, Peter, and Jack DuVall. *A Force More Powerful: A Century of Nonviolent Conflict.* New York: St. Martin's, 2000.

Adler, Jacques. "The French Churches and the Jewish Question: July 1940–March 1941." *Australian Journal of Politics and History* 46 (2000) 357–77.

Aldridge, Richard. *The Hidden Hand: Britain, America and Cold War Secret Intelligence.* London: John Murray, 2001.

Alexander, Denis. *Rebuilding the Matrix: Science and Faith in the 21st Century.* Oxford: Lion, 2001.

Amnesty International. *Still Waiting for Justice: One Year on from the Violence in Southern Kyrgyzstan.* London: Amnesty International, 2011. http://www.amnesty.org/en/documents/EUR58/001/2011/en/.

Anderson, Gary Clayton. *The Conquest of Texas: Ethnic Cleansing in the Promised Land, 1820–1875.* Norman: University of Oklahoma Press, 2005.

Andican, A. Ahat. *Turkestan Struggle Abroad: From Jadidism to Independence.* Haarlem: SOTA, 2007.

Anzaldúa, Gloria. *Borderlands, La Frontera.* 2nd ed. San Francisco: Aunt Lute, 1999.

Atkinson, David. *The Message of Genesis 1–11.* The Bible Speaks Today: Old Testament. Leicester: InterVarsity, 1990.

Aylward, Gladys. *The Little Woman.* Chicago: Moody, 1970.

Bainton, Roland. *Christian Attitudes toward War and Peace: A Historical Survey and Critical Re-evaluation.* London: Hodder and Stoughton, 1961.

Baranowski, Shelley. *The Confessing Church, Conservative Elites, and the Nazi State.* Lewiston, NY: E. Mellen, 1986.

Barclay, William. *The Gospel of Matthew.* Vol. 1, *Chapters 1 to 10.* Rev. ed. Edinburgh: Saint Andrew, 1975.

———. *The Letters to the Corinthians.* Rev. ed. Edinburgh: Saint Andrew, 1975.

Barkun, Michael. *Religion and the Racist Right: The Origins of the Christian Identity Movement.* Rev. ed. Chapel Hill: University of North Carolina Press, 1997.

Barnes, Kenneth. "Dietrich Bonhoeffer and Hitler's Persecution of the Jews." In *Betrayal: German Churches and the Holocaust,* edited by Robert P. Ericksen and Susannah Heschel, 110–28. Minneapolis: Fortress, 1999.

Barrett, Clive. *The Orthodoxy of Pacifism.* Oxford: Anglican Pacifist Fellowship, n.d.

———. *Subversive Peacemakers: War Resistance 1914–1918; an Anglican Perspective.* Cambridge: Lutterworth, 2014.

Baum, Gregory. "The Role of the Churches in Polish-German Reconciliation." In *The Reconciliation of the Peoples: Challenge to the Churches*, edited by Gregory Baum and Harold Wells, 129–43. Maryknoll, NY: Orbis, 1997.

Baxter, Richard. *The Reformed Pastor.* 1656. Reprint, Edinburgh: Banner of Truth, 1994.

Beeching, Jack. *The Chinese Opium Wars.* London: Hutchinson, 1975.

Behr, Hartmut. *A History of International Political Theory: Ontologies of the International.* Basingstoke, UK: Palgrave Macmillan, 2010.

Bell, G. K. A. "The Church's Function in War-Time." In *The Church and Humanity (1939–1946)*, 22–31. London: Longmans, Green, 1946.

———. "Obliteration Bombing." In *The Church and Humanity (1939–1946)*, 129–41. London: Longmans, Green, 1946.

Berman, Mark. "'I Forgive You': Relatives of Charleston Church Shooting Victims Address Dylann Roof." *Washington Post*, June 19, 2015. https://www. washingtonpost.com/news/post-nation/wp/2015/06/19/i-forgive-you-relatives-of-charleston-church-victims-address-dylann-roof/.

Bettelheim, Bruno. *The Informed Heart.* London: Paladin, 1970.

Blouet, Brian. *Halford Mackinder: A Biography.* College Station: Texas A&M University Press, 1987.

———. "The Imperial Vision of Halford Mackinder." *Geographical Journal* 170 (2004) 322–29.

Boesak, Allan. *Comfort and Protest: Reflections on the Apocalype of John of Patmos.* Edinburgh: St. Andrews, 1987.

———. "A Different Kind of War." In *The Fire Within: Sermons from the Edge of Exile*, 53–62. Glasgow: Wild Goose, 2004.

———. "Into the Fiery Furnace." In *Walking on Thorns: The Call to Christian Obedience*, 26–34. Geneva: World Council of Churches, 1983.

———. "Relevant Preaching in a Black Context." In *The Finger of God: Sermons on Faith and Responsibility*, 1–17. Maryknoll, NY: Orbis, 1987.

———. "When Loveless Power Meets the Power of Love." In *The Fire Within: Sermons from the Edge of Exile*, 85–96. Glasgow: Wild Goose, 2004.

———. "A Word to the Living." In *The Fire Within: Sermons from the Edge of Exile*, 41–50. Glasgow: Wild Goose, 2004.

Boettner, Loraine. *The Christian Attitude to War.* 3rd ed. Phillipsburg, NJ: Presbyterian and Reformed, 1985.

———. *The Millennium.* Philadelphia: Presbyterian and Reformed, 1957.

Boobbyer, Philip. "Moral Re-armament in Africa in the Era of Decolonization." In *Missions, Nationalism, and the End of Empire*, edited by Brian Stanley, 212–36. Grand Rapids: Eerdmans, 2003.

Boot, Max. *The Savage Wars of Peace: Small Wars and the Rise of American Power.* New York: Basic Books, 2002.

Bourke, Joanna. *An Intimate History of Killing: Face-to-Face Killing in Twentieth-Century Warfare.* London: Granta, 1999.

Brearley, Christopher. *Does God Approve of War?* Lancaster: Sovereign World, 2007.

Bredin, Mark. *Jesus, Revolutionary of Peace: A Nonviolent Christology in the Book of Revelation.* Paternoster Biblical and Theological Monographs. Carlisle: Paternoster, 2003.

Brittain, Vera. *Testament of Youth: An Autobiographical Study of the Years 1900–1925.* 1933. Reprint, London: Virago, 1979.

Brown, Tricia Gates, ed. *Getting in the Way: Stories from Christian Peacemaker Teams.* Scottdale, PA: Herald, 2005.

Browning, Christopher. *Ordinary Men: Reserve Police Battalion 101 and the Final Solution in Poland.* London: Penguin, 1992.

Bruggeman, Walter. *The Message of the Psalms: A Theological Commentary.* Minneapolis: Augsburg, 1984.

———. *The Prophetic* Imagination. 2nd ed. Minneapolis: Fortress, 2001.

Bush, George W. "Address to a Joint Session of Congress and the American People." September 20, 2001. https://georgewbush-whitehouse.archives.gov/news/releases /2001/09/20010920-8.html.

Cable, Mildred, and Francesca French. *Through Jade Gate and Central Asia: An Account of Journeys in Kansu, Turkestan and the Gobi Desert.* London: Hodder and Stoughton, 1927.

Cadoux, Cecil John. *The Early Christian Attitude to War.* Cheap ed. London: George Allen & Unwin, 1940.

Carlile, J. C. *C. H. Spurgeon: An Interpretative Biography.* London: Religious Tract Society, 1933.

Carroll R., M. Daniel. "Putting War on Trial: Lessons from the Case of Guatemala's Efraín Ríos Montt." *Christianity Today,* May 28, 2013. http://www.christianitytoday.com/ ct/2013/may-web-only/putting-war-on-trial.html.

Carson, D. A. *Love in Hard Places.* Wheaton, IL: Crossway, 2002.

Cavanaugh, William. *The Myth of Religious Violence: Secular Ideology and the Roots of Modern Conflicts.* Oxford: Oxford University Press, 2009.

———. *Torture and Eucharist: Theology, Politics, and the Body of Christ.* Oxford: Blackwell, 1998.

Chadwick, Owen. *Britain and the Vatican during the Second World War.* Cambridge: Cambridge University Press, 1986.

Chalke, Steve. *He Never Said . . . Discover the Real Message of Jesus.* London: Hodder and Stoughton, 2000.

Chambers, Oswald. *My Utmost for His Highest.* Special updated ed. Totnes, UK: Oswald Chambers Publications, 1995.

Chandler, Andrew. "The Church of England and Nazi Germany, 1933–1945." PhD diss., Cambridge University, 1990.

———. *Presences Felt: Encounters in a Lost Century.* London: Darton, Longman and Todd, 2005.

Chang, Iris. *The Rape of Nanking: The Forgotten Holocaust of World War II.* London: Penguin, 1997.

Chantry, Walter. *God's Righteous Kingdom: Focusing on the Law's Connection with the Gospel.* Edinburgh: Banner of Truth, 1980.

Chester, Tim. *Good News to the Poor: Sharing the Gospel through Social Involvement.* Nottingham, UK: InterVarsity, 2004.

Chomsky, Noam. *The New Military Humanism: Lessons from Kosovo.* London: Pluto, 1999.

Clark, Robert. *Does the Bible Teach Pacifism?* London: Marshalls, 1983.

Clarkson, Thomas. *An Essay on the Doctrines and Practice of the Early Christians as They Relate to War.* London: Society for the Promotion of Permanent and Universal Peace, 1818.

Coates, A. J. *The Ethics of War.* Manchester: Manchester University Press, 1997.

Cochrane, Arthur. *The Church's Confession under Hitler*. Philadelphia: Westminster, 1962.

Coker, Christopher. *Can War Be Eliminated?* Cambridge: Polity, 2014.

Conquest, Robert. *The Harvest of Sorrow: Soviet Collectivization and the Terror-Famine*. London: Hutchinson, 1986.

Cook, Hilary. *What Will the Neighbours Say?* Eastbourne, UK: Kingsway, 1986.

Cortright, David. *Peace: A History of Movements and Ideas*. Cambridge: Cambridge University Press, 2008.

Cox, Wade. "Christian Churches of God Working Paper 110: Theory of the Just War." 1999. Available at http://www.ccg.org. Downloaded June 2016.

Dalby, Simon. *Creating the Second Cold War: The Discourse of Politics*. London: Pinter, 1990.

———. "Peace and Critical Geopolitics." In *Geographies of Peace*, edited by Fiona McConnell et al., 29–46 London: I. B. Tauris, 2014.

Dallimore, Arnold. *Spurgeon: A New Biography*. Edinburgh: Banner of Truth Trust, 1985.

Dammers, Horace. *Thank You, Holy Spirit*. Stanhope, UK: The Memoir Club, 2004.

Davies, Mike. *Late Victorian Holocausts: El Niño Famines and the Making of the Third World*. London: Verso, 2001.

Davis, David Brion. "Should You Have Been an Abolitionist?" *New York Review of Books*, June 21, 2012, 56–58.

Dawkins, Richard. *The God Delusion*. London: Black Swan, 2007.

Day, Elizabeth. "The British Are Obsessed with Germany—and Not Always in a Funny Way." *The Telegraph*, May 8, 2005. http://www.telegraph.co.uk/news/uknews/1489581/The-British-are-obsessed-with-Germany-and-not-always-in-a-funny-way.html.

Dehqani-Tafti, Hassan. *Design of My World*. London: Lutterworth, 1959.

Dekar, Paul. *For the Healing of the Nations: Baptist Peacemakers*. Macon, GA: Smith and Helwys, 1993.

Diamond, Jared. *Collapse: How Societies Choose to Fail or Survive*. London: Penguin, 2005.

Dibaj, Mehdi. "The Written Defense of the Rev. Mehdi Dibaj Delivered to the Sari Court of Justice—Sari, Iran, December 3, 1993." http://www.farsinet.com/persecuted/dibaj.html.

Disney, Henry. *Lapsed Atheist and Other Poems*. Ware, UK: Rockingham, 1995.

Dolman, Everett. *Astropolitik: Classical Geopolitics in the Space Age*. London: Frank Cass, 2002.

Driver, John. *How Christians Made Peace with War: Early Christian Understandings of War*. Scottdale, PA: Herald, 1988.

Dyson, Freeman. Review of *Von Braun: Dreamer of Space, Engineer of War*, by Michael J. Neufeld. *New York Review of Books*, January 17, 2008, 8–12.

Egan, Eileen. *Peace Be with You: Justified Warfare or the Way of Nonviolence*. Maryknoll, NY: Orbis, 1999.

Eller, Vernard. *Christian Anarchy: Jesus' Primacy over the Powers*. Grand Rapids: Eerdmans, 1987.

Ellul, Jacques. *Anarchy and Christianity*. Translated by Geoffrey Bromiley. 1st English ed. Grand Rapids: Eerdmans, 1991.

Elshtain, Jean Bethke. *Just War against Terror: The Burden of American Power in a Violent World*. New York: Basic Books, 2003.

Ericksen, Robert P., and Susannah Heschel. "Introduction." In *Betrayal: German Churches and the Holocaust*, edited by Robert P. Ericksen and Susannah Heschel, 1–21. Minneapolis: Fortress, 1999.

Evans, Mark. "Moral Theory and the Idea of a Just War." In *Just War Theory: A Reappraisal*, edited by Mark Evans, 1–21. Edinburgh: Edinburgh University Press, 2005.

Evans, Richard. "How Willing Were They?" Review of *Life and Death in The Third Reich*, by Peter Fritzsche, and *Ghettostadt: Łódź and the Making of a Nazi City*, by Gordon Horwitz. *New York Review of Books*, June 26, 2008, 59–61.

———. *The Third Reich at War: How the Nazis Led Germany from Conquest to Disaster*. London: Penguin, 2009.

Ezard, John. "Poet Laureate Joins Doubters over Iraq." *The Guardian*, January 9, 2003. http://www.theguardian.com/uk/2003/jan/09/iraq.writersoniraq.

Falk, Aaron. "Mom Sells Face Space for Tattoo Advertisement." *Deseret Morning News*, June 30, 2005. http://www.deseretnews.com/article/600145187/Mom-sells-face-space-for-tattoo-advertisement.html.

Fletcher, Brian. "Anglicanism and Nationalism in Australia, 1901–1962." *Journal of Religious History* 23 (1999) 215–33.

Fleure, H. J. *The Treaty Settlement of Europe: Some Geographic and Ethnographic Aspects*. The World of Today. London: H. Milford, Oxford University Press, 1921.

Flint, Colin. *Introduction to Geopolitics*. London: Routledge, 2006.

Fox, George. *The Journal*. Edited by Nigel Smith. London: Penguin, 1998.

Frame, Tom. "Forgive Me, I Was Wrong on Iraq." *The Age*, June 18, 2004. http://www.theage.com.au/articles/2004/06/17/1087245036392.html?oneclick=true.

Fussell, Paul. *Wartime: Understanding and Behavior in the Second World War*. New York: Oxford University Press, 1989.

Gellner, Ernest. *Nations and Nationalism*. Oxford: Blackwell, 1983.

Gill, Jill K. "The Political Process of Prophetic Leadership: The National Council of Churches and the Vietnam War." *Peace & Change* 27 (2002) 271–300.

Gill, Kathleen. "The Moral Functions of an Apology." *The Philosophical Forum* 31 (2000) 11–27.

Golden, Renny, and Michael McConnell. *Sanctuary: The New Underground Railroad*. Maryknoll, NY: Orbis, 1986.

Goldhagen, Daniel John. *Hitler's Willing Executioners: Ordinary Germans and the Holocaust*. London: Abacus, 1996.

Goldingay, John. *Joshua, Judges and Ruth for Everyone*. London: SPCK, 2011.

Gottmann, Jean. *The Significance of Territory*. Charlottesville: University of Virginia Press, 1973.

Govier, Trudy, and Wilhelm Verwoerd. "The Promise and Pitfalls of Apology." *Journal of Social Philosophy* 33 (2002) 67–82.

Greenberg, David. "Fathers and Sons: George W. Bush and His Forebears." *The New Yorker*, July 12, 2004. http://www.newyorker.com/magazine/2004/07/12/fathers-and-sons-2.

Greenfeld, Liah. "Nationalism and the Mind." *Nations and Nationalism* 11 (2005) 325–41.

Griech-Polelle, Beth A. *Bishop von Galen: German Catholicism and National Socialism.* New Haven: Yale University Press, 2002.

Griffith, Lee. *The War on Terrorism and the Terror of God.* Grand Rapids: Eerdmans, 2002.

Gumbel, Nicky. "Why Did Jesus Die?" 2009. http://uk-england.alpha.org.

Hague, William. *William Wilberforce: The Life of the Great Anti-Slave Trade Campaigner.* London: Harper Perennial, 2008.

Hailsham, Lord. *The Door Wherein I Went.* London: Collins, 1975.

Hallie, Philip. *Lest Innocent Blood Be Shed.* London: Michael Joseph, 1979.

Halsell, Grace. *Prophecy and Politics: Militant Evangelists on the Road to Nuclear War.* Bullsbrook, Western Australia: Veritas, 1987.

Hamilton-Paterson, James. *America's Boy: The Marcoses and the Philippines.* London: Granta, 1998.

Hanebrink, Paul. *In Defense of Christian Hungary: Religion, Nationalism, and Antisemitism, 1890–1944.* Ithaca: Cornell University Press, 2006.

Harris, Richard. "Obituary: The Rt Rev Hassan Dehqani-Tafti." *The Guardian*, May 20, 2008. http://www.theguardian.com/world/2008/may/21/anglicanism.iran.

Harris, Sam. *The End of Faith: Religion, Terror, and the Future of Reason.* London: Simon & Schuster, 2006.

Harvey, A. E. *Demanding Peace: Christian Responses to War and Violence.* London: SCM, 1999.

Hastings, Adrian. *A History of English Christianity, 1920–2000.* 4th ed. London: SCM, 2001.

Hauerwas, Stanley. *The Peaceable Kingdom: A Primer in Christian Ethics.* Notre Dame: University of Notre Dame Press, 1983.

Hauerwas, Stanley, and Sam Wells. "Breaking Bread: Peace and War." In *The Blackwell Companion to Christian Ethics*, edited by Sam Wells and Stanley Hauerwas, 415–26. Oxford: Blackwell 2004.

Haushofer, Karl. "Why Geopolitik? (from *The World of General Haushofer*)." In *The Geopolitics Reader*, edited by Gearóid Ó Tuathail et al., 40–42. London: Routledge, 2006.

Hayden, Mark. "Security Beyond the State: Cosmopolitanism, Peace and the Role of Just War Theory." In *Just War Theory: A Reappraisal*, edited by Mark Evans, 157–76. Edinburgh: Edinburgh University Press, 2005.

Haynes, Stephen. "King and Bonhoeffer as Protestant Saints: The Use and Misuse of Contested Legacies." In *Bonhoeffer and King: Their Legacies and Import for Christian Social Thought*, edited by Willis Jenkins and Jennifer M. McBride, 21–31. Minneapolis: Fortress, 2010.

Hedges, Chris. *War Is a Force That Gives Us Meaning.* New York: Public Affairs, 2002.

Heffernan, Michael. *The Meaning of Europe: Geography and Geopolitics.* London: Arnold, 1998.

Hewitt, Kenneth. "Place Annihilation: Area Bombing and the Fate of Urban Places." *Annals of the Association of American Geographers* 73 (1983) 257–84.

Hillenbrand, Laura. *Unbroken: A World War II Story of Survival, Resilience, and Redemption.* New York: Random House, 2010.

Hitchens, Christopher. "Against Rationalization." *The Nation*, October 8, 2001. http://www.thenation.com/article/against-rationalization/.

———. *God Is Not Great: The Case against Religion.* London: Atlantic, 2007.

———. *Letters to a Young Contrarian*. Oxford: Perseus, 2001.

———. "A War to Be Proud Of." In *Christopher Hitchens and His Critics: Terror, Iraq, and the Left*, edited by Simon Cottee and Thomas Cushman, 152–60. New York: New York University Press, 2008.

Hobsbawm, E. J. *Nations and Nationalism since 1780: Programme, Myth, Reality*. 2nd ed. Cambridge: Cambridge University Press, 1990.

Hockenos, Matthew D. *A Church Divided: German Protestants Confront the Nazi Past*. Bloomington: Indiana University Press, 2004.

Hodge, Charles. *Systematic Theology*. Vol. 1. London: James Clarke, 1960.

Hoover, A. J. *God, Germany, and Britain in the Great War: A Study in Clerical Nationalism*. London: Praeger, 1989.

Horsley, Richard. *Jesus and Empire: The Kingdom of God and the New World Disorder*. Minneapolis: Fortress, 2003.

———. *Jesus and the Spiral of Violence: Popular Jewish Resistance in Roman Palestine*. San Francisco: Harper & Row, 1987.

Houweling, Henk, and Mehdi Amineh. "The Geopolitics of Power Projection in US Foreign Policy: From Colonization to Globalization." In *Central Eurasia in Global Politics*, edited by Mehdi Amineh and Henk Houweling, 25–75. Leiden: Brill, 2004.

Hunt, Nigel. "Health Consequences of War and Political Violence." In *Encyclopedia of Violence, Peace & Democracy*, edited by Lester Kurtz, 2:923–33. London: Academic, 2008.

Huxley, Aldous. "War and Nationalism." In *The Human Situation: Lectures at Santa Barbara, 1959*. Edited by Piero Ferrucci. London: Chatto and Windus, 1978.

Jackson, Thomas. *From Civil Rights to Human Rights: Martin Luther King, Jr. and the Struggle for Economic Justice*. Philadelphia: University of Pennsylvania Press, 2007.

Jenkins, Dominick. *The Final Frontier: America, Science, and Terror*. London: Verso, 2002.

Johnson, Daniel. "An Ice-Cold Embrace." Review of *Bishop von Galen: German Catholicism and National Socialism*, by Beth A. Griech-Polelle, and *The Holy Reich: Nazi Conceptions of Christianity, 1919–1945*, by Richard Steigmann-Gall. *Times Literary Supplement*, November 28, 2003, 10.

Johnson, James Turner. "Historical Roots and Sources of the Just War Tradition in Western Culture." In *Just War and Jihad: Historical and Theoretical Perspectives on War and Peace in Western and Islamic Traditions*, edited by John Kelsay and James Turner Johnson, 1–30. London: Greenwood, 1991.

Juergensmeyer, Mark. *Terror in the Mind of God: The Global Rise of Religious Violence*. Berkeley: University of California Press, 2001.

Kearns, Gerry. *Geopolitics and Empire: The Legacy of Halford Mackinder*. Oxford: Oxford University Press, 2009.

Keegan, John, ed. *The Times Atlas of the Second World War*. London: Times Books, 1989.

———. *War and Our World: The Reith Lectures, 1998*. London: Hutchinson, 1998.

Keller, Timothy. *Generous Justice: How God's Grace Makes Us Just*. London: Hodder & Stoughton, 2010.

Kierkegaard, Søren. "Kill the Commentators!" In *Provocations: Spiritual Writings of Kierkegaard*, compiled and edited by C. E. Moore. Farmington, PA: Plough, 1999.

King, Martin Luther, Jr. "Andidotes for Fear." No date. http://www.thekingcenter.org/archive/document/antidotes-fear#.

———. "A Knock at Midnight." In *A Knock at Midnight: Inspiration from the Great Sermons of Reverend Martin Luther King, Jr.*, edited by Clayborne Carson and Peter Holloran, 61–78. New York: Intellectual Properties Management in association with Warner Books, 1998.

———. *Strength to Love.* Philadelphia: Fortress, 1981.

Kirby, Dianne. "The Archbishop of York and Anglo-American Relations during the Second World War and Early Cold War, 1942–1955." *Journal of Religious History* 23 (1999) 327–45.

Kohls, Gary. "The Bombing of Nagasaki August 9, 1945: The Untold Story." August 9, 2007. http://www.informationclearinghouse.info/article18149.htm.

Kovacs, Judith, and Christopher Rowland. *Revelation: The Apocalypse of Jesus Christ.* Blackwell Bible Commentaries. Oxford: Blackwell, 2004.

Kovel, Joel. "Facing End-Time." *Capitalism Nature Socialism* 18 (2007) 1–6.

Kreider, Alan. *Journey towards Holiness: A Way of Living for God's Holy Nation.* Waterloo, ON: Herald, 1987.

———. *Worship and Evangelism in Pre-Christendom.* Alcuin/GROW Liturgical Study 32. Cambridge: Grove, 1995.

Kreider, Alan, and Eleanor Kreider. *Becoming a Peace Church.* London: New Ground, 2000.

Kreider, Alan, Eleanor Kreider, and Paulus Widjaja. *A Culture of Peace: God's Vision for the Church.* Intercourse, PA: Good Books, 2005.

Lane Fox, Robin. *Pagans and Christians in the Mediterranean World from the Second Century AD to the Conversion of Constantine.* London: Penguin, 1986.

Lansbury, George. *My England.* London: Selwyn & Blount, 1934.

Lean, Garth. *Frank Buchman: A Life.* London: Constable, 1985.

Legg, John. "John G. Paton." In *Five Pioneer Missionaries*, edited by S. M. Houghton, 303–45. Edinburgh: Banner of Truth, 1965.

Lewis, C. S. *The Christian Way: Readings for Reflection.* Edited by Walter Hooper. London: Fount, 1992.

———. "Learning in War-Time." In *Elephants and Fern Seeds: And Other Essays on Christianity*, edited by Walter Hooper, 26–38. Glasgow: William Collins, 1975.

Lindsey, Hal, and with C. C. Carlson. *The Late Great Planet Earth.* 9th ed. Grand Rapids: Zondervan, 1970.

Lloyd-Jones, Martyn. *Authentic Christianity: Sermons on the Acts of the Apostles.* Vol. 1, *Acts 1–3.* Edinburgh: Banner of Truth Trust, 1999.

———. *From Fear to Faith: Rejoicing in the Lord in Turbulent Times.* Leicester: InterVarsity, 2003.

———. *Why Does God Allow War?* Wheaton, IL: Crossway, 2003.

———. *Will the Hospital Replace the Church?* London: Christian Medical Fellowship, 1982.

Longley, Clifford. *Chosen People: The Big Idea That Shaped England and America.* London: Hodder & Stoughton, 2002.

Luttwak, Edward. "Franco-German Reconciliation: The Overlooked Role of the Moral Re-armament Movement." In *Religion: The Missing Dimension of Statecraft*, edited by Douglas Johnston and Cynthia Sampson, 37–63. Oxford: Oxford University Press, 1994.

Mackinder, Halford. *Democratic Ideals and Reality: A Study in the Politics of Reconstruction.* London: Constable, 1919.

————. "The Geographical Pivot of History." *The Geographical Journal* 23 (1904) 421–44.

Mann, Michael. *The Dark Side of Democracy: Explaining Ethnic Cleansing.* Cambridge: Cambridge University Press, 2005.

Marrin, Albert. *The Last Crusade: The Church of England in the First World War.* Durham: Duke University Press, 1974.

Marsden, George. *Fundamentalism and American Culture.* 2nd ed. Oxford: Oxford University Press, 2006.

Marshall, Christopher D. *Beyond Retribution: A New Testament Vision for Justice, Crime, and Punishment.* Studies in Peace and Scripture. Grand Rapids: Eerdmans, 2001.

Matheson, Peter, ed. *The Third Reich and the Christian Churches: A Documentary Account of Christian Resistance and Complicity during the Nazi Era.* Edinburgh: T. & T. Clark, 1981.

Matthews, Dylan. *War Prevention Works: 50 Stories of People Resolving Conflicts.* Oxford: Oxford Research Group, 2001.

McCabe, Herbert. "The Class Struggle and Christian Love (1980)." In *Radical Christian Writings: A Reader*, edited by Andrew Bradstock and Christopher Rowland, 273–76. Oxford: Blackwell, 2002.

McGrath, Alister. *Christian Theology: An Introduction.* 3rd ed. Blackwell: Oxford, 2001.

McTernan, Oliver. *Violence in God's Name: Religion in an Age of Conflict.* London: Darton, Longman and Todd, 2003.

Mead, Margaret. "Warfare Is Only an Invention—Not a Biological Necessity." In *War: Studies from Psychology, Sociology, Anthropology*, edited by Leon Bramson and George W. Goethals, 269–74. New York: Basic Books, 1964.

Megoran, Nick. "Henry Martyn: Iraq—Lessons in a Time of War." *Evangelical Times* 37 (2003) 36.

————. "Militarism, Realism, Just War, or Nonviolence? Critical Geopolitics and the Problem of Normativity." *Geopolitics* 13 (2008) 473–97.

————. "Radical Politics and the Apocalypse: Activist Readings of Revelation." *Area* 45 (2013) 141–47.

————. "Towards a Geography of Peace: Pacific Geopolitics and Evangelical Christian Crusade Apologies." *Transactions of the Institute of British Geographers* 35 (2010) 382–98.

————. "War and Peace? An Agenda for Peace Research and Practice in Geography." *Political Geography* 30 (2011) 178–89.

————. *The War on Terror: How Should Christians Respond?* Downers Grove, IL: InterVarsity, 2007.

Meredith, Albert. "The Social and Political Views of Charles Haddon Spurgeon, 1834–1892." PhD diss., Michigan State University, 1973.

Middlebrook, Martin. *The Battle of Hamburg: Allied Bomber Forces against a German City in 1943.* London: Cassell, 1980.

Moir, Guthrie, ed. *Why I Believe: Fifteen Lay Christians Speak in "Last Programmes" on Independent Television London 1964.* London: SCM, 1964.

Moltmann, Jürgen. *The Power of the Powerless.* Translated by Margaret Kohl. London: SCM, 1983.

Monsen, Marie. *A Present Help: Standing on the Promises of God.* Shoals, IN: Kingsley, 2011.

Morgan, G. Campbell. "The Church's Debt to the World." *The Westminster Pulpit*, 226–37, n.d.

Moses, John. *A Broad and Living Way: Church and State, a Continuing Establishment.* Norwich, UK: Canterbury, 1995.

Moxham, Roy. *The Great Hedge of India.* London: Constable, 2001.

Muggeridge, Malcolm. "But Not of Christ." In *Seeing through the Eye: Malcolm Muggeridge on Faith*, edited by Cecil Kunhe, 29–33. San Fransisco: Ignatius, 2005.

Murray, Iain. *The Forgotten Spurgeon.* Edinburgh: Banner of Truth Trust, 1966.

Murray, James. *Sermons to Asses, to Doctors of Divinity, to Lords Spiritual, and to Ministers of State.* London: William Hone, 1819.

Musto, Ronald G. *The Catholic Peace Tradition.* Maryknoll, NY: Orbis, 1986.

Nest, Michael. *Coltan.* Cambridge: Polity, 2011.

Nettles, Tom. *Living by Revealed Truth: The Life and Pastoral Theology of Charles Haddon Spurgeon.* Fearn, Scotland: Mentor, 2013.

Neufeld, Michael. *Von Braun: Dreamer of Space, Engineer of War.* New York: Knopf, 2008.

Nidditch, Susan. *War in the Hebrew Bible: A Study in the Ethics of Violence.* Oxford: Oxford University Press, 1993.

Niebuhr, Reinhold. *Moral Man and Immoral Society* New York: Scribner's, 1948.

———. *Why the Christian Church Is Not Pacifist.* London: Student Christian Movement Press, 1940.

Northcott, Michael. *An Angel Directs the Storm: Apocalyptic Religion and American Empire.* London: I. B. Tauris, 2004.

O'Donovan, Oliver. *Just War Revisited.* Cambridge: Cambridge University Press, 2003.

Olyott, Stuart. *The Gospel as It Really Is: Romans Simply Explained.* Welwyn, UK: Evangelical Press, 1979.

O'Neill, Patrick. "U.S. Firebombing of Tokyo in 1945 Killed 100,000." *The Militant*, March 28, 2005. http://www.themilitant.com/2005/6912/691255.html.

Osborn, Patrick. *Operation Pike: Britain versus the Soviet Union, 1939–1941.* Westport, CT: Greenwood, 2000.

Otterman, Sharon. "The Calculus of Civilian Casualties." *New York Times*, January 6, 2009. http://thelede.blogs.nytimes.com/2009/01/06/the-calculus-of-civilian-casualties.

Ó Tuathail, Gearóid. *Critical Geopolitics: The Politics of Writing Global Space.* London: Routledge, 1996.

———. "The Effacement of Place? US Foreign Policy and the Spatiality of the Gulf Crisis." *Antipode* 25 (1993) 4–31.

Ó Tuathail, Gearóid, and John Agnew. "Geopolitics and Discourse: Practical Geopolitical Reasoning in American Foreign Policy." *Political Geography* 11 (1992) 190–204.

Overstreet, Jeffrey. Review of *Sophie Scholl: The Final Days. Christianity Today*, February 17, 2006. http://www.christianitytoday.com/ct/2006/februaryweb-only/sophiescholl.html.

Paasi, Anssi. *Territories, Boundaries, and Consciousness: The Changing Geography of the Finnish-Russian Border.* Belhaven Studies in Political Geography. New York: J. Wiley, 1996.

Palmer-Fernandez, Gabriel, and Iaian Maclean, eds. *Encyclopedia of Religion and War.* New York: Routledge, 2004.

Pascal. *Pensées.* Translated by A. J. Krailsheimer. London: Penguin, 1966.

Pearce, Cyril, and Helen Durham. "Patterns of Dissent in Britain during the First World War." *War and Society* 34 (2015) 140–59.

Pearce, Joseph. *Literary Converts: Spiritual Inspiration in an Age of Unbelief.* London: HarperCollins, 2000.

Pearson, Harry. *Achtung Schweinehund! A Boy's Own Story of Imaginary Combat.* London: Little, Brown, 2007.

Peterson, Scott. "US Troops Prep for Fallujah Fight." *Christian Science* Monitor, November 1, 2004. http://www.csmonitor.com/2004/1101/p06s01-woiq.html.

Pinker, Stephen. *The Better Angels of Our Nature: The Decline of Violence in History and Its Causes.* London: Penguin, 2011.

Polelle, Mark. *Raising Cartographic Consciousness: The Social and Foreign Policy Vision of Geopolitics in the Twentieth Century.* Lanham, MD: Lexington, 1999.

Pollock, Susan, and Catherine Lutz. "Archaeology Deployed for the Gulf War." *Critique of Anthropology* 14 (1994) 263–84.

Pontius the Deacon. "The Life and Passion of Cyprian, Bishop and Martyr." In *Readings in Church History*, edited by Jonathan Marshall. Hiram, ME: Hubbard Hill, 2009.

Putz, Erna. *Against the Stream: Franz Jägerstätter—the Man Who Refused to Fight for Hitler.* Translated by Michael Duggan. Milton Keynes: Anglican Pacfist Fellowship, 1996.

Ratzel, Friedrich. "The Laws of the Spatial Growth of States." Translated by Ronald L. Bolin. In *The Structure of Political Geography*, edited by Roger E. Kasperson and Julian V. Minghi, 17–28. London: University of London Press, 1969.

Rauschenbusch, Walter. *A Theology for the Social Gospel.* New York: Macmillan, 1918.

Reed, Charles. *Just War?* London: SPCK, 2004.

Reuber, Paul. "The Tale of the Just War—a Post-Structuralist Objection." *The Arab World Geographer* 6 (2003) 44–46.

Robertson, Geoffrey. *Crimes against Humanity: The Struggle for Global Justice.* 2nd ed. London: Penguin, 2002.

Ryle, J. C. *Expository Thoughts on Luke.* Edinburgh: Banner of Truth Trust, 1986.

———. *Expository Thoughts on Matthew.* Edinburgh: Banner of Truth Trust, 1986.

Sack, Robert David. *Human Territoriality: Its Theory and History.* Cambridge: Cambridge University Press, 1986.

Sangster, W. E. *They Met at Calvary.* London: Hodder and Stoughton, 1956.

Schaeffer, Francis A. *The Great Evangelical Disaster.* Westchester, IL: Crossway, 1984.

Schivelbusch, Wolfgang. *Three New Deals: Reflections on Roosevelt's America, Mussolini's Italy, and Hitler's Germany, 1933–1939.* Translated by Jefferson Chase. New York: Henry Holt, 2006.

Searle, Joshua. *The Scarlet Woman and the Red Hand: Evangelical Apocalyptic Belief in the Northern Ireland Troubles.* Eugene, OR: Pickwick, 2014.

Seiple, Chris. "Guns, Government, & God: How Then Shall We Think?" Washington, DC: Institute for Global Engagement, 2002.

———. "Wars and Rumors of (Preemptive) Wars." *Brandywine Review of Faith & International Affairs* 1 (2003) 41–44.

Sempangi, Kefa. *From the Dust.* Cambridge: Lutterworth, 2009.

———. *Reign of Terror, Regin of Love: A Firsthand Account of Life and Death in Amin's Uganda.* Tring, UK: Lion, 1979.

Shapiro, Michael. *Violent Cartographies: Mapping Cultures of War.* Minneapolis: University of Minnesota Press, 1997.

Sharp, Gene. *The Methods of Nonviolent Action*. Part 2 of *The Politics of Nonviolent Action*. Boston: P. Sargent, 1973.

———. *The Politics of Nonviolent Action*. Boston: P. Sargent, 1973.

———. *Power and Struggle*. Part 1 of *The Politics of Nonviolent Action*. Boston: P. Sargent, 1973.

Sheppard, H. R. L. *We Say "No": The Plain Man's Guide to Pacifism*. London: John Murray, 1935.

Siberry, Elizabeth. "Missionaries and Crusaders, 1095–1274: Opponents or Allies?" In *The Church and War: Papers Read at the Twenty-Second Summer Meeting and the Twenty-Second Winter Meeting of the Ecclesiastical History Society*, edited by W. Sheils, 103–10. Studies in Church History. Oxford: Blackwell, 1983.

Sider, Ronald J. "The Scandal of the Evangelical Conscience: Why Don't Christians Live What They Preach?" *Books & Culture*, January-February 2005. http://www.christianitytoday.com/bc/2005/001/3.8.html.

———. *Rich Christians in an Age of Hunger: A Biblical Study*. London: Hodder and Stoughton, 1977.

Sider, Ronald J., and Richard K. Taylor. *Nuclear Holocuast and Christian Hope*. London: Hodder and Stoughton, 1982.

Simons, Menno. "Foundation of Christian Doctrine (1539)." In *The Complete Writings of Menno Simons c. 1496–1561*, edited by J. C. Wenger, 105–226. Scottdale, PA: Herald, 1984.

Sizer, Stephen. *Christian Zionism: Road-Map to Armageddon?* Leicester: InterVarsity, 2004.

Skinner, Tom. *Black and Free*. Paternoster Pocket Books 12. Exeter, UK: Paternoster, 1968.

Smith, Anthony D. *National Identity*. London: Penguin, 1991.

Smith, Gipsy. *Gipsy Smith: His Life and Work*. London: National Council of the Evangelical Free Churches, 1906.

———. *A Mission of Peace: Evangelistic Triumphs in South Africa*. London: National Council of Evangelical Free Churches, 1904.

Smith, Graham. "Post-colonialism and Borderland Identities." In *Nation-Building in the Post-Soviet Borderlands: The Politics of National Identities*, edited by Graham Smith et al., 1–20. Cambridge: Cambridge University Press, 1998.

Sorrell, Mark. *The Peculiar People*. Exeter, UK: Paternoster, 1979.

Spoerri, Theophil. *Dynamic Out of Silence: Frank Buchman's Relevance Today*. Translated by John Morrison and Peter Thwaites. London: Grosvenor, 1976.

Spurgeon, C. H. *C. H. Spurgeon Autobiography*. Vol. 2, *The Full Harvest, 1860–1892*. Originally compiled by Susannah Spurgeon and Joseph Harrald. Rev. ed. Edinburgh: Banner of Truth Trust, 1962 (1897–1900).

———. "John Ploughman's Letter on the War: To Napoleon, Emperor of the French, and William, King of Prussia." *The Sword and the Trowel: A Record of Combat with Sin and of Labour for the Lord*, August 1, 1870, 352–54.

———. "Periodical War Madness." *The Sword and the Trowel: A Record of Combat with Sin and of Labour for the Lord*, April 1878, 145–49.

———. *The Treasury of David: An Original Exposition of the Book of Psalms*. Vol. 3, *Psalm 53–78*. London: Marshall Brothers, n.d.

Stanley, Brian. "Christianity and the End of Empire." In *Missions, Nationalism, and the End of Empire*, edited by Brian Stanley, 1–11. Studies in the History of Christian Missions. Grand Rapids: Eerdmans, 2003.

Stargardt, Nicholas. "The Wages of Destruction." Review of *The Wages of Destruction: The Making and Breaking of the Nazi Economy*, by Adam Tooze. *History Today* 56.12 (December 2006). http://www.historytoday.com/nicholas-stargardt/wages-destruction.

Stassen, Glen. *Just Peacemaking: Transforming Initiatives for Justice and Peace*. Louisville: Westimnister John Knox, 1992.

Steigmann-Gall, Richard. "Apostasy or Religiosity? The Cultural Meanings of the Protestant Vote for Hitler." *Social History* 25 (2000) 267–84.

Stein, Robert H. *The Method and Message of Jesus' Teachings*. Rev. ed. Louisville: Westminster John Knox, 1994.

Stoltzfus, Nathan. *Resistance of the Heart: Intermarriage and the Rosenstrasse Protest in Nazi Germany*. New York: Norton, 1996.

Stone, Dan. "Beyond the Auschwitz Syndrome." *History Today* 60.7 (2010) 27–33.

Storey, Dave. *Territory: The Claiming of Space*. Insights in Human Geography. London: Prentice Hall, 2001.

Stott, John. *The Message of 1 Timothy and Titus*. The Bible Speaks Today. Leicester: InterVarsity, 1996.

———. *The Message of Romans*. Leicester: InterVarsity, 1994.

Stringfellow, William. *An Ethic for Christians and Other Aliens in a Strange Land*. Waco, TX: Word, 1973.

Swartley, Willard. *Covenant of Peace: The Missing Peace in New Testament Theology and Ethics*. Grand Rapids: Eerdmans, 2006.

Taylor, Charles. *Sources of the Self: The Making of the Modern Identity*. Cambridge: Cambridge University Press, 1989.

Thomas, Aquinas. *Summa Theologica*. Translated by Fathers of the English Dominican Province. 1st American ed. New York: Benziger Bros., 1947.

Thomas, Scott. "Faith, History and Martin Wight: The Role of Religion in the Historical Sociology of the English School of International Relations." *International Affairs* 77 (2001) 905–29.

Tiplady, Richard. *World of Difference: Global Missions at the Pic 'n Mix Counter*. Carlisle, UK: Paternoster, 2003.

Tolstoy, Leo. *The Kingdom of God Is within You; Christianity and Patriotism*. London: J. M. Dent, 1905.

Tooze, Adam. *The Wages of Destruction: The Making and Breaking of the Nazi Economy*. London: Penguin, 2006.

Trouillot, Michel-Rolph. "Abortive Rituals: Historical Apologies in the Global Era." *Interventions* 2 (2000) 171–86.

Volf, Miroslav. *Exclusion and Embrace: A Theological Exploration of Identity, Otherness, and Reconciliation*. Nashville: Abingdon, 1996.

Walsh, Brian, and Richard Middleton. *Transforming Vision: Shaping a Christian Worldview*. Downers Grove, IL: InterVarsity, 1984.

Walzer, Michael. *Just and Unjust Wars: A Moral Argument with Historical Illustrations*. 3rd ed. New York: Basic Books, 2000.

Webb, Robert. *John the Baptizer and Prophet*. Journal for the Study of the New Testament Supplement Series 62. Sheffield: JSOT Press, 1991.

Weinland, Ronald. *2008: God's Final Witness*. Cincinnati: The-end.com, 2006.

Werth, Alexander. *Moscow '41*. London: Hamish Hamilton, 1942.

Weyeneth, Robert. "The Power of Apology and the Process of Historical Reconciliation." *Public Historian* 23 (2001) 9–38.

Whittal, Daniel. "Colonial Fascism." *History Today* 60.10 (2010) 44–48.

Wilkinson, Paul. "Why Modern Terrorism? Differentiating Types and Distinguishing Ideological Motivations." In *The New Global Terrorism: Characteristics, Causes, Controls*, edited by Charles W. Kegley Jr., 106–38. Upper Saddle River, NJ: Prentice Hall, 2003.

Williams, Rhondda. *How I Found My Faith: A Religious Pilgrimage*. London: Cassell, 1938.

Williams, Rowan. *The Truce of God: Peacemaking in Troubled Times*. Norwich, UK: Canterbury, 2005.

Wink, Walter. *Engaging the Powers: Discernment and Resistance in a World of Domination*. Philadelphia: Fortress, 1992.

Winter, Bruce W. *Seek the Welfare of the City: Christians as Benefactors and Citizens*. First-Century Christians in the Graeco-Roman World. Carlisle, UK: Paternoster, 1994.

Witherington, Ben. *Revelation*. The New Cambridge Bible Commentary. Cambridge: Cambridge University Press, 2003.

Wolffe, John. *God and Greater Britain: Religion and National Life in Britain and Ireland, 1843–1945*. London: Routledge, 1994.

Woolman, John. *The Journal of John Woolman, and a Plea for the Poor*. The John Greenleaf Whittier Edition Text. Secaucus, NJ: Citadel, 1961 [1774].

Wragg, Arthur. *"Jesus Wept": A Commentary in Black-and-White on Ourselves and the World to-Day*. London: Selwyn and Blount, 1935.

Wright, Evan. "Dead-Check in Falluja: Embedded with the Marines in Iraq." *Village Voice*, November 16, 2004. http://www.villagevoice.com/news/dead-check-in-falluja-6399178.

———. *Generation Kill: Living Dangerously on the Road to Baghdad with the Ultraviolent Marines of Bravo Company*. London: Bantam, 2004.

Wright, Tom. *Luke for Everyone*. London: SPCK, 2004.

———. *Matthew for Everyone, Part I: Chapters 1–15*. London: SPCK, 2004.

———. *Matthew for Everyone, Part II: Chapters 16–28*. London: SPCK, 2004.

———. *Paul for Everyone: Galatians and Thessalonians*. London: SPCK, 2002.

———. *Revelation for Everyone*. London: SPCK, 2012.

Wrobel, Johannes. "Jehovah's Witnesses in National Socialist Concentration Camps, 1933–45." *Religion, State and Society* 34 (2006) 89–125.

Wurmbrand, Richard. *Tortured for Christ: Today's Martyr Church*. London: Hayfield, 1967.

Wyman, David. *The Abandonment of the Jews: America and the Holocaust, 1941–1945*. New York: Pantheon, 1984.

Yoder, John Howard. *The Christian Witness to the State*. 2nd ed. Scottdale, PA: Herald, 2002.

———. *The Politics of Jesus: Vicit Agnus Noster*. 2nd ed. Carlisle: Paternoster, 1994.

Yoder, Perry. *Shalom: The Bible's Word for Salvation, Justice, and Peace*. Sevenoaks, UK: Hodder and Stoughton, 1987.

Zabelka, George. "'I Was Told It Was Necessary': *Sojourners*' 1980 Interview with U. S. Chaplain Who Served the Hiroshima and Nagasaki Bomb Squadrons." By Charles C. McCarthy. *Sojourners*, August 3, 2015, https://sojo.net/articles/i-was-told-it-was-necessary.

Zhenying, Liu, with Paul Hattaway. *The Heavenly Man: The Remarkable True Story of Chinese Christian Brother Yun*. Oxford: Monarch, 2002.

Scripture Index

General Index